REVIEW OF RESEARCH IN EDUCATION, 26

REVIEW
OF
RESEARCH

CONTRIBUTORS

ARNETHA F. BALL
DANIELLE A. CROSBY
JACQUELYNNE S. ECCLES
R. MATTHEW GLADDEN
OKHEE LEE
MICHELE S. MOSES
MARIKA N. RIPKE
JANICE TEMPLETON

IN EDUCATION
26
2002

WALTER G. SECADA
Editor
University of Wisconsin–Madison

PUBLISHED BY THE
AMERICAN EDUCATIONAL RESEARCH ASSOCIATION
1230 Seventeenth Street, NW
Washington, DC 20036-3078

Contents

Complex Problems in Education

WALTER G. SECADA

University of Wisconsin–Madison

Like a pair of abhorrent bookends, violence involving students has marked both ends of my tenure as editor of this AERA publication. Like many other participants at the annual meeting that was held Toronto, I sat in stupefied horror as events at Columbine High School unfolded. I scanned the annual meeting program, asking myself what AERA might contribute to the larger society's understandings of this event. Though, as Matthew Gladden points out in *Reducing School Violence: Strengthening Student Programs and Addressing the Role of School Organizations,* the actual rate of violence within schools has been dropping over the past few years, the impacts of those events has escalated, in large part due to the availability of increasingly sophisticated weaponry. Gladden goes beyond the well-worn irony of noting that programs to "combat violence" and "zero tolerance" policies have mixed results to argue that schools, as social organizations whose adults express and act upon the shared values of respect and academic work, create the kinds of relationships where violence becomes less likely.

Although Columbine was the first of many such high-profile incidents—as I write, another young man who killed his fellow students and some adults in his school is being sentenced—there is another no less disturbing phenomenon in the emergence of the school-aged person as an instrument of violence within the larger society. The child soldier was evident during the civil wars and wars of independence in Southeast Asia and sub–Saharan Africa over the past 40 years. Yet now, we read about Palestinian students who, in an act of suicide, kill others of their age—an act that many adults in their society term "martyrdom" but that many others term "murder." It is too facile to note that for both forms of violence—in and out of schools—some students are merely learning what adults have taught them. And although there seems to be broad consensus that violence within a society's schools is abhorrent, such consensus seems absent when societies are in conflict.

Just as education and violence intersect in complex ways, so do education and welfare—both social interventions intended to support children's growth and development. The 1990s brought with them the "end of welfare as we know it" in the United States through welfare reform. As I began my tenure as editor, I was struck by how few articles in mainstream educational journals dispassionately yet critically examined the assumptions underlying how education would support welfare reform and how education, in its own turn, would be affected by this reform. In *The Effects of Welfare Reform on the Educational Outcomes of Parents and Their Children,* Marika N. Ripke and Danielle A. Crosby explore the complex relationship between education and welfare. As is the case with most policy innovations, the trade-offs in this arena have resulted in a mixed set of outcomes.

Not only are schools asked to focus on educating an increasingly diverse population of young people, they provide sites where other social interventions are implemented. In *Extracurricular and Other After-School Activities for Youth,* Jacquelynne S. Eccles and Janice Templeton explore the impacts of such interventions on supporting the prosocial development of youth. Their chapter supports the observation that, insofar as healthy youth development is predicated on experiences that support outcomes similar to the goals of schooling, there should be cooperation between high-quality programs and schools. Their comments on how mixed research methods can help develop more compelling understandings of complex phenomena should help move educational researchers beyond the "either/or" stance of the old quantitative–qualitative or positivist–critical–postpositivist debates.

Okhee Lee, in *Promoting Scientific Inquiry With Elementary Students From Diverse Cultures and Languages,* and Arnetha F. Ball, in *Three Decades of Research on Classroom Life: Illuminating the Classroom Communicative Lives of America's At-Risk Students,* help us to revisit issues on the processes of schooling. To Lee, the question of whether minority-language students—even those whose mastery of English is challenging to their schools and teachers—can participate in classes that promote scientific reasoning has been answered affirmatively. More importantly, however, her review gives insights as to the characteristics of the practices that promote such participation. Ball's review of students' lives in their classrooms, with the lens set at two levels of analysis, reminds us of the complexity of students' lives.

Michele S. Moses, in *The Heart of the Matter: Philosophy and Educational Research,* provides a reminder as to the very important contributions that philosophers make through their insistence on clarity when researchers frame a problem in one or another. Moreover, her compelling distinction between philosophy of education and philosophy in education echoes Ball's two levels of analysis involving classroom processes.

Many themes echo across these chapters. For example, Ball, by looking at macro- and micro-level classroom processes; Gladden, by considering individual programs and schools as organizations; and Moses, by drawing a distinction between philosophy in and of education, make important distinctions without falling into the trap of "either/or."

Yet as a group, they remind me—very forcefully—that education extends beyond what happens within schools. I end my tenure as editor wondering if educational researchers, through our focus on framing problems in ways that we understand among ourselves, are not mirroring how schools try to use their walls to keep out the violence, uncomfortable social forces that impact on students' lives, and programs (that if properly implemented might be beneficial to students). Education intersects with larger social phenomena in many different ways. We need to better understand these intersections not just as educational phenomena but also as legal, social, psychological, and political acts. To engage in these large and complex problems, the next generation of educational research may need to mount work that crosses disciplinary boundaries and draws on the talents on research scholars representing those disciplines in the ways that echo the reviews by Gladden, Ripke and Crosby, and Eccles and Templeton. But it should not forget the nuance found in the more focused reviews of Lee, Ball, and Moses.

Chapter 1

The Heart of the Matter: Philosophy and Educational Research

MICHELE S. MOSES
Arizona State University

Philosophy has long played a significant role in educational scholarship, from the thought of Plato to Jean-Jacques Rousseau to John Dewey to Nel Noddings. In this chapter, I demonstrate how philosophy continues to be a vital part of careful education scholarship. Because the primary audience is the broader educational research community, I as far as possible avoid the intricacies of philosophers' internecine contentions in order to concentrate on characterizing the general positions taken, though I do take up this issue toward the end.

I divide the discussion into examples of philosophy *in* educational research and philosophy *as* educational research. Philosophy *in* educational research refers to the kind of philosophical analysis that takes the practice of empirical educational research as its point of departure. It involves critical discussions of research methodology and how empirical educational research is framed.

Philosophy *as* educational research is relatively more autonomous and more long standing, and it construes "educational research" more broadly. Philosophy *as* educational research refers to the kind of analysis that has been, traditionally, associated with the philosophy *of* education, which is, in its own turn, a subarea of philosophy that draws on the parent discipline to determine how to frame and analyze philosophical problems peculiar to education.

The distinction is a matter of emphasis; the two categories obviously overlap significantly. One point that I wish to emphasize with my use of philosophy *as* educational research is that philosophical analysis is a genre of educational research in its own right. Because empirical work is dominant and central to educational research, especially within graduate schools of education, philosophical research is often not considered to be real research or, to qualify, is forced into a framework that it does not fit. Because philosophical work is not the same as empirical work, it is often taken to be *divorced* from it (e.g., National Research Council, 2002). But this is a misconception. Philosophers routinely use the findings of empirical research in developing and testing the adequacy of their theories; at the same time, empirical work makes commitments to positions on issues that are, at their core, philosophical. In this vein, I highlight a major contribution that philosophy has made to scholarship on the problem of inequality as an exemplar of the role that philosophical analysis plays within educational research.

PHILOSOPHY *IN* EDUCATIONAL RESEARCH

Questions of scientific research and methodology have long been a central part of the discipline of philosophy. Epistemology and the philosophy of science are the philosophical subfields that lay claim to the specific examination of these questions. Philosophers of education have long engaged in methodological inquiries as well. Harry Broudy, Bob Ennis, and Leonard Krimerman's (1973) edited volume focused on questions such as the following: How scientific should educational research be? And, more specifically, "Will the methods that have worked so brilliantly in the physical sciences be equally fruitful in the social and behavioral domains?" (p. vi).

These methodological discussions are key for fostering an understanding of the landscape of social and educational research, from positivistic to critical research (e.g., House & Howe, 1999; Howe, 1985, in press; Phillips, 1987; Phillips & Burbules, 2000; Schrag, 1989). Philosophical investigation comes into play when a particular methodological issue is best analyzed through the lenses of, say, epistemology or philosophy of science. Indeed, regardless of who engages in it, much of the conversation about educational research methodology is carried out in terms of concepts whose original home is philosophy. "Positivism," "epistemology," "paradigm," and "postmodernism" are just a few examples.

The exemplars of philosophical analysis that follow fall into two loose categories: analyses of deep methodological issues and critiques of current empirical work and educational reform and policy ideas. Although different in focus, these two kinds of philosophical analysis share an interest in illuminating the terrain of educational research, from clarifying methodological discussions to evaluating research findings and policy prescriptions.

Overarching Discussions of Research Methodology

In a series of articles published in the *Educational Researcher,* philosophers of education joined the contentious debate about educational research methodology prompted by the advent of qualitative methods (Garrison, 1986; Howe, 1985, 1988, 1998; Howe & Eisenhart, 1990; Phillips, 1983). Drawing on developments in the philosophy of science in the second half of the 20th century, they show how and why positivism is philosophically moribund, and they characterize several viable successors, such as postpositivism and pragmatism. One of their central themes is that the educational research community should not set up positivism as one epistemology to which others ought to negatively define themselves, since positivism is not a philosophically viable alternative.

An important corollary point is that quantitative and qualitative research methods ought not (and cannot) be distinguished and set in opposition to one another on the grounds that quantitative methods are inherently and exclusively positivistic and suited only for *confirmation,* whereas qualitative methods are inherently and exclusively interpretative and suited only for *understanding.* These philosophers of education have not tried to end controversies about educational research methodology—

inherently philosophical controversies—but to spur the educational research community to engage in them in a more philosophically defensible way.

Several philosophers of education have recently developed book-length examinations of educational research methodology that grow out of the ongoing controversies. One example is D. C. Phillips and Nicholas Burbules's *Postpositivism and Educational Research* (2000). They offer a historically grounded account of positivism, postpositivism, and the issues these paradigmatic approaches raise for social and educational researchers. Phillips and Burbules tackle many controversial issues within epistemology and philosophy of science. They defend postpositivism as the best available approach for sound social and educational research. In so doing, they endeavor to cull what is good and useful from positivism and to debunk myths about postpositivism surrounding the experimental method, value neutrality, and quantitative analysis. Even though they concede that many logical positivist tenets are mistaken, Phillips and Burbules maintain that the positivist emphases "on clarity and the grounding of our beliefs on observations still stand as ideals we ought not to dismiss too lightly" (p. 11).

In addition, they attempt to explain why foundationalism is rightly no longer a dominant epistemology. Among the reasons they cite are that one person's rational faculties need not match another's; perceptions are theory laden; evidence underdetermines theory; evidence is problematic as it relates to people's network of beliefs; induction is uncertain; and research is often a social/communal activity, which means that researchers influence each other. Accordingly, they characterize postpositivism as "a *nonfoundationalist* approach to human knowledge that rejects the view that knowledge is erected on absolutely secure foundations—for there are no such things; postpositivists accept *fallibilism* as an unavoidable fact of life" (p. 29).

Finally, Phillips and Burbules argue that educational inquiry should be scientific, and that the best inquiry is. They argue for a vision of research that transcends beliefs and feelings. As a result, they argue that researchers "need to aspire to something a little stronger, seeking beliefs that (1) have been generated through rigorous inquiry and (2) are likely to be true; in short, they need to seek *knowledge*" (p. 3). These tenets form what they, following Karl Popper, call a regulative ideal that should guide inquiry. Through philosophical inquiry, Phillips and Burbules help educators, educational researchers, and others navigate the terrain of disciplined inquiry in education from a postpositivistic perspective.

Kenneth Howe's *Closing Methodological Divides: Toward Democratic Educational Research* (in press) provides a second example of an extended philosophical examination of methodological issues in educational research. Locating the issues within the purview of philosophy, Howe states:

Qualitative versus quantitative methods, facts versus values, science versus politics, subjectivity versus objectivity, postmodernism versus pragmatism, to name a few—are at the core of a lively, sometimes divisive, conversation that has been unfolding in the theory of educational research for some time. These issues fall squarely within the province of philosophy, and thus philosophical investigation has an especially useful contribution to make.

Howe is careful, however, to point out that while these issues are of great philosophical interest, scholars based in other disciplines have contributed to the conversation as well. An educational foundation in philosophy of science and in epistemology provides philosophers of education with a particular vantage point, one that is unique among scholars of education, with which to examine these methodological controversies.

Howe examines the landscape of educational inquiry from a pragmatic perspective and focuses on resolving some of the most controversial issues. He aims to render untenable what he calls the "two dogmas of educational research"—the fact-value bifurcation and the quantitative-qualitative split. Howe argues that these dogmas have been responsible for counterproductive debates about the assumptions and methodology of educational research and for unnecessarily dividing the educational research community into factions.

Howe concludes that educational research is inherently laden with values and politics but need not lack the capacity to support methodologically sound, unbiased conclusions for that reason. He maintains that educational research ought to be rooted in and guided by the values associated with a genuine form of democratic politics.

Critique of Research and Policy

Another way that philosophy is present *in* educational research is through its contribution to critiquing and framing empirical educational research. By participating in educational research in this way, philosophers engage the empirical research world and help make needed theoretical connections to education policy and practice.

In the teaching and learning arena, philosophers of education have provided a major voice in the conversation about the problems and prospects of "constructivism." Kenneth Strike (1992) and Nel Noddings (Davis, Maher, & Noddings, 1990) joined the discussion early on, which has come to include the contributions of James Garrison (1995), D. C. Phillips (1995, 2000), and Michael Matthews (1997, 2000). Additional philosophers of education joined in philosophical analyses of constructivism in the 2000 yearbook of the National Society for the Study of Education (NSSE) (e.g., Eric Bredo, Nicholas Burbules, Kenneth Howe, Jason Berv, and Luise McCarty). Among the issues analyzed were how constructivism itself may be characterized, the difference between and problems with social constructivism and psychological constructivism, what bodies of knowledge are socially constructed and how strongly, how constructivism affects science and math education, and the impact of constructivist ideas on educational research.

In the political policy arena, school choice has provided fertile ground for philosophy *in* educational research. Amy Gutmann (1987) and Mary Ann Raywid (1983, 1987) entered the conversation early on, when little if any empirical research was available. Gutmann questioned the use of market ideas to reform public schools that were supposed to educate students for democratic participation. Raywid put forth a more moderate approach to school choice while still arguing against voucher schemes.

Howe (1997) used the scant empirical evidence available even in the 1990s to point to developing difficulties in whether the theory behind choice was playing out in the way choice advocates predicted, including the theory of democracy outlined in John Chubb and Terry Moe's *Politics, Markets and America's Schools* (1990).

More recently, Stacy Smith (1999) has provided a philosophically astute investigation of charter schools in light of current developments in the political theory of democracy. Smith argues that charter schools ought to be in concurrence with the ideals of deliberative democratic theory if they are to be able to balance their private aims with public educational interests. While she affirms the hopeful possibilities for choice and autonomy offered by charter schools, she cautions that "charter schools are in need of normative standards that can be employed to balance their particularistic aims against public interests in things like fair representation, democratic governance, and civic education" (p. 131). Her analysis provides researchers of charter schools with a redefinition of the charter school questions, which has significant implications for further empirical study. In a similar vein, Harry Brighouse (2000) provides an extended philosophical analysis of school choice that takes into account empirical research findings to help determine what is *feasible*, constraining the policy recommendations he proffers at the end.

Next on the horizon for philosophy *in* educational research is likely to be the standards movement and its marriage to high-stakes testing and accountability. Several philosophers of education have already joined this conversation (e.g., Howe, 1994, 1995; Noddings, 1992; Raywid, 2002).[1]

PHILOSOPHY *AS* EDUCATIONAL RESEARCH

Like philosophy *in* educational research, philosophy *as* educational research also deals with controversial educational issues. It is characterized in part by the more traditional types of philosophy of education, including analyses of the deeper purposes of education. In addition, it is characterized by the development of clear conceptual frameworks that aid in the examination of educational policy and practice. In the sections that follow, I provide several illustrations of how philosophy functions as educational research. Philosophical contributions to the study of the problem of inequality in education, which are concerned with both educational aims and conceptual frameworks for education policy, will serve as a final, extended example.

Educational Aims

Philosophical scholarship that clarifies the broad aims and meanings of education in general (e.g., Callan, 1988; Dewey, 1916, 1938; Fullinwider, 1996; Gutmann, 1987; Locke, 1892; Martin, 1992; Plato, 1990; Reich, 2002) is most often what people think of when they think about philosophy of education. This more traditional philosophical work addresses questions such as the following: What is knowledge? What is education? and What ought education to be in a liberal democratic society?

Dewey's work provides the most well-known example of philosophy of education concerned with the aims and meanings of education itself. In one of his later books, *Experience and Education* (1938), Dewey responded to those who did not really understand his theories of education or who took his ideas to the extreme, such as those who set up schools where children were allowed to do as they pleased. He pointed out that many so-called progressives built their new education as a negative reaction to the traditional basic education with which they did not agree. Dewey, on the other hand, built his new vision of education on a theory of experience, with growth as the primary aim of education. He defined growth as the constant enriching and expanding of our knowledge, akin to the critical thinking and problem solving focused on today. Thus, Dewey tried to make explicit his own brand of progressivism and to correct the excesses of many of his followers. As such, he argued against the either/or mentality wherein education was seen either as traditional (content based) or as progressive (skills based). His arguments are well worth dusting off in the current policy climate.

Gutmann's (1987) theory of democratic education is another example of philosophical scholarship on the purposes of education. A philosopher and political theorist, Gutmann puts forth a normative democratic theory of what the main educational aims ought to be in a liberal democratic society such as that of the United States. Within Gutmann's notion of a "democratic state of education," the authority and governance of public education are shared among educators, parents, and the public, and the core aim of education is to consciously reproduce the democratic way of life. In arguing for her conception of democratic education, Gutmann defends two main purposes of primary education that she claims are essential in a healthy, functioning democracy. First is fostering deliberation so that students learn to behave and think critically and, thus, learn both respect for authority and skepticism of it. The second purpose is the development of democratic character, so that students are educated in character and moral reasoning. The idea is that these aims, when met, will foster students' ability to participate fully in a democracy as citizens.

Similarly, in more recent work in political philosophy, Rob Reich (2002) aims to demonstrate the paramount importance of the principle of autonomy as an educational aim in a liberal democracy. He examines autonomy within the philosophical literature in order, first, to make sense of the concept and put forth his own conception, which he terms minimal autonomy, and, second, to outline what minimal autonomy means for education. Reich advocates for an education that emphasizes students' development of critical and reflective abilities so as to foster their capacity for autonomy. His vision is that such an education will allow schools to both foster democratic citizenship and honor multiculturalism.

Albeit in different ways, Dewey (1916, 1938), Gutmann (1987), and Reich (2002) all serve as exemplars of how philosophy *as* educational research provides educators and researchers alike with a foundational understanding of the fundamental aims and meanings of education. Such theoretical work both adds to and informs issues within the larger study of education, such as teaching, learning, and policy.

Conceptualizing Frameworks for Education Policy and Practice

Another way that philosophy functions *as* educational research is by conceptualizing alternative frameworks for the analysis of educational policy and practice. And to reinforce my earlier remark, this is where philosophy *as* educational research routinely *uses* empirical research.

In *Embracing Race: Why We Need Race-Conscious Education Policy* (Moses, 2002), I address the question of what the educational system must do to promote social justice for students of color and poor students. I examine what is required to help these students develop self-determination and argue that race-conscious education policies are defensible because they play a central role in the development of self-determination of students who otherwise are left with a deficient education. To support my contention, I analyze four race-conscious education policies: bilingual education, multicultural curricula, affirmative action, and remedial education. In doing so, I briefly trace the histories of each policy, identify underlying principles and assumptions, and examine relevant empirical research. I then measure these against a contemporary liberal framework.

Consider affirmative action policy. Analyzed simply, affirmative action may be either supported or opposed as a matter of fairness: It is fair to remedy past discrimination with affirmative action programs, or, alternatively, it is unfair to prefer some persons at the expense of others. However, examined philosophically, those on both sides of the debate can come to understand that affirmative action is not simply fair or unfair but is a necessary education policy that promotes the self-determination of students of color whose self-determination has historically not been considered important (Moses, 2001). As this example illustrates, the philosophical and practical issues within policy debates are actually inseparable. The general argument in *Embracing Race* hinges on the premise that self-determination is required for justice. In a time of political backlash against most race-conscious education policies, it is critical for philosophers to contribute to reasonable and well-considered policy decisions by providing educators and policymakers with a principled and nuanced foundation—a foundation that is clearly and thoughtfully articulated, not taken for granted.

Noddings's (1992) work is a fine example of scholarship that is excellent philosophy and extremely valuable as educational research on curricular and school reform. In *The Challenge to Care in Schools: An Alternative Approach to Education*, Noddings brings the ethical framework from her previous work on caring to bear on the nature of public schooling in the United States. In so doing, she criticizes several prominent characteristics of contemporary public schooling: the emphasis on competition and testing, the disciplinary knowledge that defines a liberal education, the idea of the same education for all in the name of equal opportunity, and the evaluation of school activities mainly in terms of how well they contribute to learning the given curricula. These characteristics are indicative of what Noddings calls a male-oriented ethic of principles, which she advocates moving to the background in favor of the ethics of care. By taking the ethics of care seriously, the educational system could come to be defined in terms of relationship rather than principles. In order to take the ethics of care seriously, Noddings calls for a fundamental revision of the curriculum, instruction, and structure of public schooling in the United States.

This last type of contribution made by philosophers to educational research may be viewed as at the heart of philosophy of education, especially when taking into account what the larger educational research community finds valuable in philosophy of education. Philosophy, then, may be placed at the heart of educational research, both by providing conceptual and theoretical grounding for important empirical work and, perhaps even more important, by providing alternative theoretical perspectives that can be normatively applied to the most significant educational issues and debates of the day.

Inequality

The problem of inequality—in schools, of education—is arguably the most vexing issue facing educational researchers of every stripe. Philosophy's single largest contribution, in my estimation, has been its analysis of inequality. It has been a frequent subtheme throughout but deserves more explicit examination. I thus provide a relatively extended discussion of it as a final example.

The unequal treatment of persons is a social problem that has disturbingly permeated the educational system in the United States from its inception. It has thus been the source of much philosophical study, from questions about what equality is to whether it ought to be the highest priority of a liberal democratic society and how to conceptualize equal educational opportunity. Philosophers in general and philosophers of education in particular have worked to shed light on this thorny problem. Of course, philosophy is not the only foundational discipline concerned with the problem of inequality in education—not by a long shot. However, philosophy of education has the singular ability to cross between the discipline of philosophy and its writings to education and important educational debates. In studying equality of education, for example, insightful theories of equality put forth by philosophers (e.g., Dworkin, 2000; Sen, 1992) may be brought to bear on educational questions surrounding equality of educational opportunity and other issues of social justice in a democratic society.

The philosophical literature is home to many analyses concerning the problem of inequality (e.g., Ackerman, 1980; Dworkin, 2000; Frankfurt, 1987; O'Neill, 2000; Rawls, 1971; Sen, 1992; Taylor, 1994; Young, 1990). Ronald Dworkin (2000) has put forth one recent and influential examination of the principle of equality and its place in a liberal democratic society. In his recent book, *Sovereign Virtue: The Theory and Practice of Equality,* he offers a comprehensive theory of justice centering on equality. For Dworkin, equality is and ought to be *the* fundamental value within liberal political theory. He acknowledges and grapples with the tension between liberty and equality as sovereign virtues, and he acknowledges that the two ideals work together; "they are mutually reflecting aspects of a single humanist ideal" (p. 134).

"Can it really be more important," he asks, "that the liberty of some people be protected, to improve the lives those people lead, than that other people, who are already worse off, have the various resources and other opportunities that *they* need to lead decent lives?" (p. 121). His major concern is that while equality may be a political ideal, it is not striven for in practice.

Consequently, Dworkin (2000) develops a conception of equality that he hopes can serve to justify government's redistribution of resources. He argues for the idea of "equality of resources," which emphasizes people's resources and opportunities, rather than equality of welfare, or persons' well-being throughout life. He defines equality of resources as a fair distribution of "whatever resources are owned privately by individuals" (p. 65). A person's resources would include wealth together with personal resources such as health, strength, and talent, and these together with "legal and other opportunities" (p. 286). I should note that it is not unproblematic for Dworkin to emphasize the importance of distributional equality. Iris Marion Young (1990), for one, criticizes theories that involve what she considers to be too heavy an emphasis on distributional justice. She prefers instead a relational conception of equality and justice. In her view, the liberal political emphasis on distribution of material possessions puts too much of an emphasis on *having* rather than *doing* and on the relations entailed therein.

According to Young, in order to have a just society, we ought to see justice as the elimination of institutional oppression and domination. In addition, the logic of distribution abstracts individuals from their social and institutional contexts. Relevant here from Young's critique is her emphasis on societal structures and on nondistributional issues such as decision making and division of labor. A focus on decision making leads to questions such as who has/had the power to decide on rules and procedures. In exploring the division of labor, we examine not only who has what job or position, but exactly what kinds of work those jobs entail. The issues that Young brings up are important to the discussion of educational opportunities.

Yet, Dworkin notes that his notion of equality of resources is fundamentally different from equality of opportunity. His major objection to theories of equality that focus on opportunity or capabilities, such as that of Amartya Sen (1992), is that they collapse into the notion of equality of welfare. Unlike equalizing opportunity, equalizing resources is an issue of distribution. While this is true, an issue of distribution may also be an issue of opportunity. For instance, if school A is well funded and can afford to pay a high price for curriculum materials, it is more difficult for school B, a poorly funded school, to buy those same materials. While such an example is indeed indicative of an inequality of resources, it is also indicative of an inequality of opportunity for students in school B. It seems that Dworkin's strict separation of equality of resources and equality of opportunity is misguided, or at least it fails to recognize how inextricably linked the two are. Equality of opportunity and equality of resources seem to be part and parcel of each other when analyzed in terms of education.

This is the basic thrust of Howe's (1997) *Understanding Equal Educational Opportunity: Social Justice, Democracy, and Schooling*, in which he examines three different interpretations of the ideal of equality of educational opportunity: formalist, compensatory, and participatory. He does this in an attempt to advance a meaningful interpretation (participatory) built on defensible philosophical principles within the sea of misunderstanding surrounding this ideal.

Under the formalist interpretation, equal educational opportunity merely entails that there be no formal, or legal, barriers. As long as there is no physical barrier (like, for example, the separate but equal doctrine) stopping someone from the opportunity, then it may be considered an equal one. This conception is simplistic in that it ignores the relationship between students and the educational institution. Consider the monolingual Chinese-speaking students in the *Lau v. Nichols* (1974) case. Since they were allowed to attend school, formalists would argue that they had the same opportunity as other students to go to school and learn. Yet, with no bilingual education measures in place, that opportunity was an empty one because they could not understand the language of instruction and thus could not learn.

Under the compensatory interpretation, equal educational opportunity is fulfilled when students' disadvantages are remedied. The idea is that once individual student deficiencies are corrected, students can better adapt to the dominant system and achieve equal educational opportunity. The problem is that the compensatory interpretation advocates compensating students who, because they have not been a part of forming the educational system, are considered to be at a deficit. They thus have to sacrifice themselves by having to make unreasonable changes in order to fit in to the dominant structures, when it is those structures that ought to adapt to the needs of diverse students.

In response to the formalist and compensatory notions, which Howe sees as creating opportunities that are not "worth wanting," he fashions the participatory ideal (Howe, 1997, p. 3). The participatory ideal transcends both the formalist and the compensatory interpretations by focusing on the structural and institutional facets of education that cause oppression. In addition, it places inclusion and democratic deliberation at center stage and involves a renegotiation of the goals and procedures of education so that diverse perspectives can be included. This way, people who have been historically and are currently excluded from the educational conversation can have a voice and take part in the negotiation of educational opportunities that are actually worth having.

One compelling facet of Howe's work is that he examines various pressing educational problems through the lens of equality of educational opportunity. He uses his conception of equality of educational opportunity to stake out positions on hotly debated issues such as multicultural education, tracking, gender and schooling, vouchers, and testing.

Philosophers of education working in this egalitarian vein advance educational research on issues of inequality within education by attending not only to the theoretical analyses of the concepts of equality and justice but also to the issues of educational policy and practice that are intimately affected by these concepts (e.g., Gutmann, 1987; Moses, 2002; Reich, 2002). These exemplars show that philosophy provides a unique perspective on issues of inequality in education that other disciplines do not.[2] This has to do with the tools, techniques, and analytical insights provided by those who are both disposed to and trained in philosophical inquiry. They provide examples of good, solid philosophical scholarship, but more important for my purposes here, they show that philosophical work can do more than merely contribute to theoretical conversation. Indeed, it can (and should) contribute philosophical perspectives on important normative questions of educational policy and practice, such as the problem of inequality within schools and colleges.

PHILOSOPHERS' CONTENTIONS

Philosophers of education are a diverse group, and there is much more disagreement about the place of philosophy within educational research than preceding sections of this chapter might suggest (e.g., Broudy et al., 1973; Burbules, 1990; Phillips, 1992; Soltis, 1981; Thomas, 1972). I will not undertake a thorough review of the contentions made by philosophers of education regarding the issues here.[3] However, some mapping of the terrain and locating the place my position occupies within in it will help better round out the chapter.

The two ways of doing philosophy described earlier—philosophy *in* educational research and philosophy *as* educational research—are artifacts of a deeper argument within philosophy of education. This argument centers on whether or not it is appropriate for philosophers to get involved in the messiness of contemporary educational issues.

Historically, philosophers of education have brought the analytical tools of the discipline of philosophy to bear on fundamental questions of education such as "What should education look like in a given society?" (Dewey, 1916; Gutmann, 1987; Peters, 1967; Plato, 1990; Reich, 2002). More recently, they have engaged in critical analyses of research methodology and empirical research (Garrison & Macmillan, 1994; House & Howe, 1999; Howe, 1997, in press; Phillips, 1987; Phillips & Burbules, 2000). They have also contributed to conceptualizing frameworks that may be used to ground and advance research, policy, and practice (Fletcher, 2000; Howe, 1997; Moses, 2002; Noddings, 1992; Reich, 2002). These philosophers are part of the legacy of Dewey, who brought to prominence the idea that educational practice needed to be based on solid philosophical footing. Although this seems like a reasonable enough claim to many, it was (and is) not without some controversy. As Burbules (2000a) sums up the matter, philosophy of education has a generally "contested status" (p. 3).

In the 1950s, philosophers of education debated whether or not normative claims about educational practice could rightly be derived from the general theories upon which philosophers love to expound (Broudy, 1981). Soon thereafter, during the arguably more socially conscious 1960s and 1970s, it became more accepted for philosophers of education to focus their scholarship on issues of schooling and its role in a changing society (Greene, 2000). In 1972, NSSE issued its third volume with philosophy of education as a theme; it was titled *Philosophical Redirection of Educational Research,* and it actively linked philosophy with educational research (Thomas, 1972). The volume's central claim, as stated in the introduction, was that philosophers of education were now focused on "developing new models and paradigms to guide educational practice, including the important practice of educational research" (Dunkel, Gowin, & Thomas, 1972, p. 1). When philosophers of education engage in such work, the field has a closer relationship with the real world of schools and universities.

But philosophers of education involved in their main professional organization in the United States, the Philosophy of Education Society, have come under criticism from within their own ranks for neglecting important education policy issues surrounding school reform and other political trends (Tozer, 1991). From the point of view of such critics, philosophers of education should not only use philosophy *in* educational research, that is, clarify issues of educational importance as an intellectual endeavor; they should use philosophy *as* educational research, that is, apply their philosophical training and knowledge to questions of educational policy and practice so as to foster educational justice and progressive social change.

Some philosophers of education have gone further in this direction, believing that philosophy of education is *necessarily* based on examinations of educational policy and practice. Giarelli (1991), for one, argues that "philosophy is rooted in an analysis of educational practices" (p. 36). He further claims that philosophy does not just deliver a "grounding to education, but . . . educational practice . . . delivers to philosophy a point and a purpose for its existence and identity" (p. 36). With this set of claims, Giarelli makes the case for a conception of the interrelationships among the discipline of philosophy, philosophy of education, and educational practice, in which the paramount focus is on issues of practice. This, he maintains, is a "hopeful" position for philosophy of education (p. 37).

In a similar vein, Chris Higgins (2001) takes issue with the idea championed by Harvey Siegel (1981a, 1981b, 2001) that there should be no distinction between "pure" philosophy and philosophy of education (Higgins, 2001, p. 274). Higgins (2001) points out that many philosophers of education pursued the field of inquiry "precisely in the hope of doing something more 'real' philosophically than what passes for philosophy in most philosophy departments" (p. 274). His criticism of philosophy departments notwithstanding, Higgins makes a good point. A central aim and emphasis of scholarship for philosophers of *education* should be making a greater social contribution. Higgins's focus is teacher education, but his arguments may be broadened to include the philosophical movement within educational research advocating a focus on issues of social policy debates over social problems within education (see, e.g., Duarte, 1998; Fullinwider, 1991; Howe, 1997; Moses, 2002). I am not suggesting that there is no room for other kinds of philosophical scholarship under the rubric of philosophy of education. I am suggesting, however, that such work should not be seen as the heart of philosophical work in education.

The Problem of Relevance

Jonas Soltis (1981) distinguished between two senses of philosophy of education. One is a public sense, which has to do with *having* a philosophy of education, something important to many educational scholars and practitioners. This sense has led to studying philosophy of education through an "-isms" approach, or a philosophical positions approach, focusing on specific schools of thought within philosophy such as existentialism or progressivism (Broudy, 1981; Nelson, 1942, 1955). That approach has become less popular because it is perceived as being somewhat superficial and too rigidly compartmentalized.

The other sense Soltis discusses is a professional sense, in which trained philosophers of education use a technical philosophical perspective within discussions of issues of educational theory, policy, and practice. Soltis claims that in the latter half of the 20th century, the field of philosophy of education leaned more toward fostering the professional sense. He describes the philosopher of education as one who tries to "stimulate thought, elucidate meaning, provide critical appraisals, force careful judgment, and create conceptual frameworks for understanding the many philosophical dimensions of the complex business of education" (p. xi).

A decade after Soltis, Burbules (1990) pushed the discussion forward in terms of the so-called "dilemma of relevance" being faced by philosophers of education at the end of the 20th century (p. 187). He described an unfolding debate over the relevance of philosophy to education between two groups from within the ranks of philosophers of education. One group of scholars was more concerned with having philosophers of education engage in and produce sound work in the analytical philosophical tradition. Another group was more concerned with having them apply philosophy of education concepts and analytical techniques to educational issues and problems. This second group wanted to make sure that philosophy was relevant to educational research overall; indeed, some within this group argued that it was their responsibility to do so.

Burbules (1990) is among those who claim a middle ground for philosophy of education and maintain that there is room enough for diverse paths ranging from esoteric philosophical pursuits, critical analyses of empirical work, and examinations of traditional problems to philosophical analyses of contemporary educational issues. Burbules attempts to sidestep the horns of dilemma by claiming that "there isn't *any* one thing that all philosophers of education ought to do, except to be intellectually honest and as perceptive as possible" (p. 189).

Burbules is correct in that there is a place for many flavors of philosophy of education. But one may question whether philosophers of education can avoid the dilemma of relevance by merely being as honest and perceptive as possible. A given philosophical discussion may be perceptive, and even accessible, and yet, somehow, it may remain pedantic and of little use. Insofar as philosophy of education is stereotyped and dismissed as just so much scholasticism or polemic, the issue of relevance (to educational research) becomes important indeed.

While philosophical attention to more esoteric problems can be interesting and intellectually stimulating (and honest and perceptive), philosophy of education ought to give considerable attention to issues important to the field of education as a whole. A significant emphasis on this kind of work by philosophers of education will help to resolve—perhaps dissolve—the dilemma of relevance once and for all.

The Shifting Role of Philosophy of Education and Its Subject Matter

Philosophy of education serves to clarify the many, complex concepts put forth and positions taken by educational scholars, especially on controversial policy topics (Broudy, 1981). Indeed, as Francis Schrag (1994) points out, philosophers of education play an important role "in alerting educators to the hollowness and lack of substance found in some of the fads and movements that invade the educational stage" (p. 369). Examples of contemporary movements include cultural literacy/core knowledge, vouchers, and school report cards (see, e.g., Howe, 1997; Moses, 2000; Noddings, 1992; Raywid, 1987, 2002).

Philosophers of education may also alert educators to the value and rightheadedness of some movements, and thus to the need for changes in policy and practice. Consider Reich's (2002) work on liberalism and multiculturalism in education. He situates contemporary school reform movements within the deeper aims of education in a politically liberal society. His philosophical work helps show that multiculturalism should not be thought of as a fad invading the educational stage, but as a complex issue that needs to be taken seriously by educators interested in fostering democratic citizenship.

As early as 1981, Tom Green observed the growing connections among foundations of education in general, philosophy of education in particular, and education policy studies.[4] As Green (1981) points out, philosophers are

disposed to feed on the problems of public policy. That is where the action is. Where once they aspired to speak to leadership on problems of teaching, they now seek to give direction by attending to politics and policy. (p. 84)

It is not, perhaps, such an either/or proposition; philosophers of education still comment on problems of teaching (e.g., Stengel, 2002; Zigler, 2002). Nevertheless, Green's point that philosophers shifted their attention to matters of politics and policy is an important one.

Although Green (1981) highlights the relationship between philosophy of education and policy studies, he goes on to argue that philosophers may have little that will add to or enhance policy development and action. Instead, engaging in policy debates can greatly enhance philosophy.

Questions of educational policy do not come clearly labeled "philosophical." They are not theoretical questions. Neither are they speculative. Nor is it at all clear that if policy makers—whoever they are— were philosophically more astute, they would therefore make better decisions. (Green, 1981, p. 84)

This is where Green's view may be challenged. Policy questions incorporate theoretical commitments, even if only implicitly, and the best policymakers and policy decisions recognize this. Consider affirmative action policy, a controversial policy that often draws fire along the lines of political ideology (Edley, 1996; Moses, 2001). As I mentioned earlier, by providing nuanced and reasoned justifications for affirmative action policy, philosophical work may actually contribute to policy development and revision. While interests and political ideology are certainly at play within policy issues, they need not eclipse philosophical contributions to policy discussions (Moses & Gair, in press). The relationship between philosophy and education policy, then, is more reciprocal than Green (1981) allows.

It is not enough for philosophers of education to contribute to the abstract clarification of the complexities of the educational system. A deeper understanding of the world and of social structures such as the educational system really cannot ever be held separate from action. So, are philosophers of education obliged to go out and picket or stage sit-ins or takeovers of university administrations? Perhaps, when those actions are warranted and when the right philosopher of education is involved. But the point here is that scholarship by philosophers of education is most meaningful and yes, relevant, when it delves into the important issues of the day. This means that a philosophical examination of the value and drawbacks of charter schools, for instance (e.g., Knight Abowitz, 2001; Smith, 1999), better exemplifies what philosophers of education should be doing and should be known for doing than, say, an examination of why the use of the term *teaching* is or is not better than the term *instructing*.

Burbules (1990) provides another perspective on the shift in philosophy of education toward a greater emphasis on policy. He contends that it is not obligatory for the work of philosophers of education to be relevant to educational policy and practice; there may be good reasons for it to be relevant, but being relevant is not the duty of philosophers of education. He claims that when philosophers of education do make their work relevant, it tends to be out of self-interest rather than altruism or righteousness. Burbules is right that it is in the field's best interest to be relevant to education practice. However, self-interest can also be (maybe even ought to be) nothing more than a by-product of doing work that is concerned with educational improvement and justice. At the heart of the philosophical enterprise is Socrates's legacy that philosophers should join in contentious debates on the pressing social problems of the day.

A third perspective on the shift to an emphasis on policy is provided by D. C. Phillips. In his presidential address to the Philosophy of Education Society, Phillips (1992) examined whether "philosophizing should be related to social action" (p. 3) or limited to "an intellectual endeavor aimed at fostering deeper understanding" (p. 8). He maintained that, overall, philosophizing should best be aimed at fostering understanding and clarifying ideas. Its relation to social action may be real but should nonetheless be in the background, behind the analyses that philosophers are better at conducting. As such, Phillips claimed that "on the whole, when philosophers of education become policy people, or dabble in empirical issues, on average they do a rather poor job because they do not have the training or the relevant background knowledge" (p. 7).

Therefore, philosophers should not be in the scholarly business of offering up solutions for social and educational problems, though philosophical work may be used to inspire the betterment of educational policy and practice. Phillips supports social action by philosophers of education as people, but not as philosophers and scholars. He writes that "as a concerned and educated person I do what I can to help combat" pressing social and educational problems, "but, as a philosopher, or as a philosopher of education, I don't have very much to say about them—the means of combating poverty is not a philosophical question" (p. 16).

Phillips's (1992) point of view is shared by others (Pratte, 1981; Siegel, 1981a; Siegel, 2001). Indeed, there is room within the field to pursue work in a more esoteric philosophical tradition, as mentioned earlier. However, to say that philosophers in general and philosophers of education in particular need not or should not engage in work that has direct application to educational policy and practice seems overly restrictive and unimaginative.

In direct response to one of Phillips's examples, the means of combating poverty can most definitely be a philosophical question. Consider Martha Nussbaum's (1999) excellent work in *Sex and Social Justice*. A philosopher of note, Nussbaum argues that there are universal obligations to protect human functioning; human beings *qua* human beings deserve certain things, foremost of which is the capability to perform and function in certain ways. She applies this argument to poor women in developing countries and maintains that women in any society have a variety of basic rights, including the right to develop their own capabilities, especially the capability to provide themselves with fundamental necessities such as food, nutrition, and literacy. In the course of her complex and multifaceted analysis, Nussbaum makes prescriptive policy recommendations that concern the *means* of combating persistent poverty.

One can find numerous examples of recommendations specifically regarding how to resolve various problems within education in the work of philosophers of education as well (e.g., Brighouse, 2000; Feinberg, 1998; Howe, 1997; Jessamin, 2002; Knight Abowitz, 2001; Moses, 2002; Noddings, 1992; Smith, 1999). Phillips and company might rejoin that these people are not *really* doing philosophy, or that they are, but they are also mixing in other intellectual pursuits with it. But these kinds of rejoinders just beg the question.

CONCLUSION

What tends to come to mind when "philosophy" is mentioned in the context of educational research? All too often nonphilosophers are confused, intimidated, or skeptical about philosophy of education. They are confused about what philosophy really is and how it can be rightfully included in research discussions—research that is, after all, empirical, whereas philosophical inquiry generally is not. They wonder: Where are the data? What is the research design? They are intimidated by stereotypical philosophical analyses that are abstract, dense, and removed from the practical. This may be especially true for practitioner/researchers, who may feel that philosophical issues are too erudite or difficult and ultimately not worth understanding. They are skeptical about a type of inquiry that, although it may be interesting, does not seem to be an integral part of the business of educational research.

Theoretical discussions may be thought to have little bearing on education policy and practice. Yet, policy, methods, and practice in education presuppose philosophy and theory, though they often remain hidden (Gutmann, 1987). If only implicitly, a certain philosophical position underpins any education policy that may be advanced.

In this chapter, I have made the case that examination of education policy issues and debates is central to the field of philosophy of education. This, in turn, places philosophy of education scholarship at the heart of educational research. The various philosophical examinations of inequality in schools and universities highlight the importance of such work. In a time when schools and colleges of education are facing increased public criticism and questioning of the core endeavors of teacher education, it seems crucial to underscore the philosophical heart of an educational research establishment that is committed to educational improvement and social justice.

NOTES

[1] And at its 2000 annual meeting, the Philosophy of Education Society passed a motion to call on its members to "bring to the public serious philosophical consideration of standardized testing in the public schools" (Stengel, 2000, Section 8).

[2] Other disciplinary specialists have, of course, made major contributions to the study of inequality (e.g., Coleman, 1968); my point here is only that they are qualitatively different from philosophers' contributions.

[3] For a thorough survey of the history of philosophy of education as a field of study, see Burbules (2000a).

[4] Indeed, many academic programs in educational foundations are housed within the larger area of education policy studies. This makes good sense, particularly when we take into account the strong connection between the discipline of philosophy (especially social and political philosophy) and political science and political theory.

REFERENCES

Ackerman, B. A. (1980). *Social justice in the liberal state*. New Haven, CT: Yale University Press.

Bredo, E. (2000). Reconsidering social constructivism: The relevance of George Herbert Mead's interactionism. In D. C. Phillips (Ed.), *Constructivism in education: Opinions and second opinions on controversial issues: Ninety-ninth yearbook of the National Society for the Study of Education, Part 1* (pp. 127–157). Chicago: National Society for the Study of Education.

Brighouse, H. (2000). *School choice and social justice*. New York: Oxford University Press.

Broudy, H. S. (1981). Philosophy of education between yearbooks. In J. F. Soltis (Ed.), *Philosophy of education since mid-century* (pp. 2–16). New York: Teachers College Press.

Broudy, H. S., Ennis, R. H., & Krimerman, L. I. (1973). Preface. In H. S. Broudy, R. H. Ennis, & L. I. Krimerman (Eds.), *Philosophy of educational research* (pp. v–ix). New York: Wiley.

Burbules, N. C. (1990). The dilemma of "relevance" in the philosophy of education. In R. Page (Ed.), *Philosophy of education 1989* (pp. 187–196). Normal, IL: Philosophy of Education Society.

Burbules, N. C. (2000a). Philosophy of education. In B. Moon, M. Ben-Peretz, & S. Brown (Eds.), *Routledge international companion to education* (pp. 3–18). New York: Routledge.

Burbules, N. C. (2000b). Moving beyond the impasse. In D. C. Phillips (Ed.), *Constructivism in education: Opinions and second opinions on controversial issues: Ninety-ninth yearbook of the National Society for the Study of Education, Part 1* (pp. 308–330). Chicago: National Society for the Study of Education.

Callan, E. (1988). *Autonomy and schooling*. Montreal: McGill-Queen's University Press.

Chubb, J. E., & Moe, T. M. (1990). *Politics, markets, and America's schools*. Washington, DC: Brookings Institution.

Coleman, J. (1968). The concept of equality of educational opportunity. *Harvard Educational Review, 38*, 7–22.

Davis, R. B., Maher, C. A., & Noddings, N. (Eds.). (1990). *Constructivist views on the teaching and learning of mathematics*. Reston, VA: National Council of Teachers of Mathematics.

Dewey, J. (1916). *Democracy and education*. New York: Macmillan.

Dewey, J. (1938). *Experience and education*. New York: Collier.

Duarte, E. M. (1998). Expanding the borders of liberal democracy: Multicultural education and the struggle for cultural identity. *Educational Foundations, 12*(2), 5–30.

Dunkel, H. B., Gowin, D. B., & Thomas, L. G. (1972). Introduction. In L. G. Thomas (Ed.), *Philosophical redirection of educational research: The Seventy-first Yearbook of the National Society for the Study of Education* (pp. 1–5). Chicago: National Society for the Study of Education.

Dworkin, R. (2000). *Sovereign virtue: The theory and practice of equality*. Cambridge, MA: Harvard University Press.

Edley, C. J. (1996). *Not all black and white: Affirmative action, race, and American values*. New York: Hill & Wang.

Feinberg, W. (1998). *On higher ground: Education and the case for affirmative action*. New York: Teachers College Press.

Fletcher, S. (2000). *Education and emancipation: Theory and practice in a new constellation*. New York: Teachers College Press.

Frankfurt, H. (1987). Equality as a moral ideal. *Ethics, 98*, 21–43.

Fullinwider, R. K. (1991). Multicultural education. *Report from the Institute for Philosophy and Public Policy, 11*(3), 12–14.

Fullinwider, R. K. (Ed.). (1996). *Public education in a multicultural society*. New York: Cambridge University Press.

Garrison, J. W. (1986). Some principles of positivistic philosophy of science. *Educational Researcher, 15*(9), 12–18.

Garrison, J. W. (1995). Deweyan pragmatism and the epistemology of contemporary social constructivism. *American Educational Research Journal, 32*, 716–740.

Garrison, J. W., & Macmillan, C. J. B. (1994). Process-product research on teaching: Ten years later. *Educational Theory, 44*, 385–397.

Giarelli, J. (1991). Philosophy, education and public practice. In D. P. Ericson (Ed.), *Philosophy of education 1990* (pp. 34–44). Normal, IL: Philosophy of Education Society.

Green, T. F. (1981). Philosophy and policy studies: Personal reflections. In J. F. Soltis (Ed.), *Philosophy of education since mid-century* (pp. 83–96). New York: Teachers College Press.

Greene, M. (2000). The sixties: The calm against the storm, or, levels of concern. *Educational Theory, 50*, 307–320.

Gutmann, A. (1987). *Democratic education*. Princeton, NJ: Princeton University Press.

Higgins, C. (2001). Educational philosophy as liberal teacher education: Charting a course beyond the dilemma of relevance. In L. Stone (Ed.), *Philosophy of education 2000* (pp. 271–282). Urbana, IL: Philosophy of Education Society.

House, E. R., & Howe, K. R. (1999). *Values in evaluation and social research.* Thousand Oaks, CA: Sage.

Howe, K. R. (1985). Two dogmas of educational research. *Educational Researcher, 14*(8), 10–18.

Howe, K. R. (1988). Against the quantitative-qualitative incompatibility thesis (or dogmas die hard). *Educational Researcher, 17*(8), 10–16.

Howe, K. R. (1994). Standards, assessment, and equality of educational opportunity. *Educational Researcher, 23*(8), 27–33.

Howe, K. R. (1995). Setting standards for standards: Wrong solution, wrong problem. *Educational Leadership, 52*(6), 22–23.

Howe, K. R. (1997). *Understanding equal educational opportunity: Social justice, democracy, and schooling.* New York: Teachers College Press.

Howe, K. R. (1998). What (epistemic) benefit inclusion? In S. Laird (Ed.), *Philosophy of education 1997* (pp. 89–96). Normal, IL: Philosophy of Education Society.

Howe, K. R. (in press). *Closing methodological divides: Toward democratic educational research.* New York: Kluwer.

Howe, K. R., & Berv, J. (2000). Constructing constructivism, epistemological and pedagogical. In D. C. Phillips (Ed.), *Constructivism in education: Opinions and second opinions on controversial issues: Ninety-ninth yearbook of the National Society for the Study of Education, Part 1* (pp. 19–40). Chicago: National Society for the Study of Education.

Howe, K. R., & Eisenhart, M. (1990). Standards for qualitative (and quantitative) research: A prologomenon. *Educational Researcher, 19*(4), 2–9.

Jessamin, M. (2002). Philosophers at the policy table: A theory of schooling confronts real school reform. In S. Rice (Ed.), *Philosophy of education 2001* (pp. 241–251). Urbana, IL: Philosophy of Education Society.

Knight Abowitz, K. (2001). Charter schooling and social justice. *Educational Theory, 51,* 151–170.

Locke, J. (1892). *Some thoughts concerning education.* Cambridge, England: Cambridge University Press.

Martin, J. R. (1992). *The schoolhome: Rethinking schools for changing families.* Cambridge, MA: Harvard University Press.

Matthews, M. (1997). Introductory comments on philosophy and constructivism in science education. *Science and Education, 6,* 5–14.

Matthews, M. R. (2000). Appraising constructivism in science and mathematics education. In D. C. Phillips (Ed.), *Constructivism in education: Opinions and second opinions on controversial issues: Ninety-ninth yearbook of the National Society for the Study of Education, Part 1* (pp. 161–192). Chicago: National Society for the Study of Education.

McCarty, L. P., & Schwandt, T. A. (2000). Seductive illusions: Von Glasersfeld and Gergen on epistemology and education. In D. C. Phillips (Ed.), *Constructivism in education: Opinions and second opinions on controversial issues: Ninety-ninth yearbook of the National Society for the Study of Education, Part 1* (pp. 41–85). Chicago: National Society for the Study of Education.

Moses, M. S. (2000). The Arizona education tax credit and hidden considerations of justice. Available: http://epaa.asu.edu/epaa/v8n37.html

Moses, M. S. (2001). Affirmative action and the creation of more favorable contexts of choice. *American Educational Research Journal, 38,* 3–36.

Moses, M. S. (2002). *Embracing race: Why we need race-conscious education policy.* New York: Teachers College Press.

Moses, M. S., & Gair, M. (in press). Ideology in educational research and policy making in the United States: The possibility and importance of transcendence. In M. B. Ginsburg &

J. M. Gorostiaga (Eds.), *Limitations and possibilities of dialogue among researchers, policy makers, and practitioners: International perspectives on the field of education.* New York: RoutledgeFalmer.

National Research Council. (2002). *Scientific research in education.* Washington, DC: National Academy Press.

Nelson, H. B. (Ed.). (1942). *Philosophies of education: Forty-first yearbook of the National Society for the Study of Education, Part 1.* Chicago: National Society for the Study of Education.

Nelson, H. B. (Ed.). (1955). *Modern philosophies of education: Fifty-forth yearbook of the National Society for the Study of Education, Part 1.* Chicago: National Society for the Study of Education.

Noddings, N. (1992). *The challenge to care in schools: An alternative approach to education.* New York: Teachers College Press.

Nussbaum, M. C. (1999). *Sex and social justice.* Oxford, England: Oxford University Press.

O'Neill, O. (2000). *Bounds of justice.* Cambridge, England: Cambridge University Press.

Peters, R. S. (1967). *Ethics and education.* Atlanta, GA: Scott, Foresman.

Phillips, D. C. (1983). Postpositivistic educational thought. *Educational Researcher, 12*(5), 4–12.

Phillips, D. C. (1987). *Philosophy, science, and social inquiry: Contemporary methodological controversies in social science.* Oxford, England: Pergamon Press.

Phillips, D. C. (1992). Philosophy of education on cloud nine. In H. A. Alexander (Ed.), *Philosophy of education 1991* (pp. 2–17). Normal, IL: Philosophy of Education Society.

Phillips, D. C. (1995). The good, the bad, and the ugly: The many faces of constructivism. *Educational Researcher, 24*(7), 5–12.

Phillips, D. C. (Ed.). (2000). *Constructivism in education: Opinions and second opinions on controversial issues: Ninety-ninth yearbook of the National Society for the Study of Education, Part 1.* Chicago: National Society for the Study of Education.

Phillips, D. C., & Burbules, N. C. (2000). *Postpositivism and educational research.* Lanham, MD: Rowman & Littlefield.

Plato. (1990). *The republic* (F. M. Cornford, Trans.). London: Oxford University Press.

Pratte, R. (1981). Analytic philosophy of education: A historical perspective. In J. F. Soltis (Ed.), *Philosophy of education since mid-century* (pp. 17–37). New York: Teachers College Press.

Rawls, J. (1971). *A theory of justice.* Cambridge, MA: Harvard University Press.

Raywid, M. A. (1983). Schools of choice: Their current nature and prospects. *Phi Delta Kappan, 64,* 684–688.

Raywid, M. A. (1987). Public choice, yes; vouchers, no! *Phi Delta Kappan, 68,* 762–769.

Raywid, M. A. (2002). Accountability: What's worth measuring? *Phi Delta Kappan, 83,* 433–436.

Reich, R. (2002). *Bridging liberalism and multiculturalism in American education.* Chicago: University of Chicago Press.

Schrag, F. (1989). Values in educational inquiry. *American Journal of Education, 97,* 171–183.

Schrag, F. (1994). A view of our enterprise. *Educational Theory, 44,* 361–369.

Sen, A. (1992). *Inequality reexamined.* New York: Russell Sage Foundation.

Siegel, H. (1981a). The future and purpose of philosophy and education. *Educational Theory, 31,* 11–15.

Siegel, H. (1981b). How "practical" should philosophy of education be? *Education Studies, 12,* 125–134.

Siegel, H. (2001). Relevance, pluralism, and philosophy of education. In L. Stone (Ed.), *Philosophy of education 2000* (pp. 280–282). Urbana, IL: Philosophy of Education Society.

Smith, S. (1999). Charter schools: Voluntary associations of political communities? In S. Tozer (Ed.), *Philosophy of education 1998* (pp. 131–139). Urbana, IL: Philosophy of Education Society.

Soltis, J. F. (1981). Philosophy of education for educators: The eightieth NSSE yearbook. In J. F. Soltis (Ed.), *Philosophy of education since mid-century* (pp. 97–120). New York: Teachers College Press.

Stengel, B. S. (2000). General business meeting minutes: Philosophy of Education Society. Available: http://cuip.uchicago.edu/pes/2001BusMtgMinutes.htm

Stengel, B. S. (2002). Teaching as response. In S. Rice (Ed.), *Philosophy of education 2001* (pp. 349–357). Urbana, IL: Philosophy of Education Society.

Strike, K., with Posner, G. J. (1992). A revisionist theory of conceptual change. In R. A. Duschl, K. Strike, & R. J. Hamilton (Eds.), *Cognitive psychology and educational theory and practice* (pp. 147–176). Albany: State University of New York Press.

Taylor, C. (1994). The politics of recognition. In A. Gutmann (Ed.), *Multiculturalism: Examining the politics of recognition.* Princeton, NJ: Princeton University Press.

Thomas, L. G. (Ed.). (1972). *Philosophical redirection of educational research: The seventy-first yearbook of the National Society for the Study of Education, Part 1.* Chicago: National Society for the Study of Education.

Tozer, S. (1991). PES and school reform. *Educational Theory, 41,* 301–310.

Young, I. M. (1990). *Justice and the politics of difference.* Princeton, NJ: Princeton University Press.

Zigler, R. L. (2002). John Dewey, eros, ideals and collateral learning: Toward a descriptive model of the exemplary teacher. In S. Rice (Ed.), *Philosophy of education 2001* (pp. 276–284). Urbana, IL: Philosophy of Education Society.

Chapter 2

Promoting Scientific Inquiry With Elementary Students From Diverse Cultures and Languages

OKHEE LEE
University of Miami

Although current education reform in the United States emphasizes high academic achievement for all students across subject areas, including science, the knowledge base to achieve this ambitious goal is limited. The increasing diversity of the school-aged population, coupled with differential science performance among student demographic groups, makes the goal of "science for all" a national challenge. Achieving this goal requires an understanding of the nature of science as well as consideration of the cultural and linguistic experiences that students bring to science learning.

In science education, "scientific inquiry is at the heart of science and science learning" (National Research Council [NRC], 1996, p. 15), and "inquiry into authentic questions generated from student experiences is the central strategy for teaching science" (p. 31). Despite such emphasis, scientific inquiry is not clearly defined, and little is known about instructional approaches to promote scientific inquiry for elementary students, especially those from diverse cultures and languages. Children's ability to engage in scientific inquiry has been under debate in the cognitive development literature (e.g., the exchange between Kuhn, 1997, and Metz, 1995, 1997). The goal of "science for all" extends the debate to consider students' cultural and linguistic experiences in science teaching and learning.

I would like to acknowledge the valuable feedback on earlier versions of the chapter from Peggy Cuevas, Juliet Hart, Aurolyn Luykx, and Jane Sinagub. Special thanks to Walter Secada, the general editor of this volume, and Sandra Fradd, Beth Warren, and Ann Rosebery. The writing of this chapter was supported by the National Science Foundation (Grants ESI-9255830, REC-9552556, REC-9725525, and REC-0089231); the National Institute for Science Education (Grant NSF-RED-9452971); the Center for Research on Education, Diversity and Excellence (Grant OERI-R306A60001); and the National Center for Improving Student Learning and Achievement in Mathematics and Science (Grant OERI-R305A60007). Any opinions, findings, conclusions, or recommendations expressed are those of the author and do not necessarily reflect the position, policy, or endorsement of the funding agencies.

This chapter addresses scientific inquiry with elementary students from diverse cultures and languages. It examines relationships among student backgrounds, science disciplines, and school science in the context of diverse languages and cultures. Particularly, it focuses on the role of school science in linking science disciplines with students' languages and cultures. The discussion is largely based on the cognitive development literature examining children's abilities in conducting scientific inquiry and on the multicultural education literature addressing diversity and equity.

The first section provides backgrounds and contexts for the discussion in this chapter. It provides brief descriptions of demographic trend data indicating dramatic shifts in the U.S. student population in the direction of increasing cultural and linguistic diversity. It then offers the rationale for focusing on scientific inquiry at elementary grade levels. It also describes how the chapter differs from, yet builds on and complements, existing reviews in the cognitive development literature and the multicultural education literature.

The second section addresses scientific inquiry in the context of science education reform. It examines views of scientific inquiry in science standards documents, including the *National Science Education Standards* (NSES) (NRC, 1996, 2000) and Project 2061 (American Association for the Advancement of Science [AAAS], 1989, 1993). Science achievements among diverse student groups over the years in large-scale assessments, including the National Assessment of Educational Progress (NAEP) and the Third International Mathematics and Science Study (TIMSS), are also described. Then critiques of standards documents and large-scale assessments in the cognitive development literature and the multicultural education literature are offered.

The third section presents the literature on scientific inquiry with culturally and linguistically diverse students. It examines the discussion about whether these students' ways of knowing and talking are compatible or incompatible with the ways of knowing and talking characteristic of scientists in scientific communities. The "incompatibility" perspective is based on the multicultural education literature, whereas the "compatibility" perspective is framed by the cognitive development literature. These two perspectives involve different conceptions of science, scientific inquiry, and culture as well as different approaches to instructional practices.

To illustrate key issues in the literature on scientific inquiry with diverse students, the fourth section describes two representative research programs: the "Chèche Konnen" project of Rosebery and Warren and the "Science for All" project of O. Lee and Fradd. In the case of each program, the description focuses on views of science and scientific inquiry, language and culture, instructional approaches, and student learning and achievement.

Finally, a research agenda and directions for future scholarship are offered. Seemingly conflicting theoretical perspectives and different areas of literature may be merged into a theoretically coherent and sound body of knowledge in promoting the learning of all students, including those from diverse cultures and languages.

BACKGROUNDS AND CONTEXTS

Demographic trends show the increasing number of culturally and linguistically diverse students in the nation, underscoring the urgency of addressing the educational needs of these students. As this chapter focuses on scientific inquiry of elementary students of diverse backgrounds, it builds on and expands existing reviews of children's scientific inquiry in the cognitive development literature, on the one hand, and reviews of diversity and equity in the multicultural education literature, on the other.

A caution should be kept in mind in interpreting general patterns with diverse student groups: Overemphasizing differences between groups tends to mask variations within a group or among individuals. For example, although White students on average are in higher socioeconomic situations than Black and Hispanic students, there are many White students living in poverty, as there are many Black and Hispanic students living in affluence. Although White students, on average, perform higher than Black and Hispanic students in large-scale science assessments, there are many White students who perform lower than many Black and Hispanic students individually. Group differences should not be reduced to a measure of central tendency or be construed as implying homogeneity among group members.

Indeed, intragroup or individual variation is a complex issue with culturally and linguistically diverse students, considering the vast range of proficiency levels in the home language and English, socioeconomic status (SES), immigration history, acculturation within mainstream society, and family orientations toward education. This tension regarding differences among groups, subgroups, and individuals presents a challenge. Although knowledge about group patterns offers important insights about what is typical, there is a danger in reinforcing stereotypes based on group membership (Eisenhart, 2001). Knowledge of group patterns serves as a guideline, not as a prescription, and it needs to be adjusted in response to individuals within or outside the boundaries of general patterns.

Student Demographics

Demographic trend data enumerating the past, present, and future indicate astonishing shifts in the U.S. student population in the direction of increasing cultural and linguistic diversity. On the basis of reports published by the College Board and the Western Interstate Commission for Higher Education (1991), García (1999) summarized the increasing student diversity in U.S. schools. Non-White and Hispanic student enrollment will grow from 10 million in 1976 to nearly 50 million in 2026. As a subset of the student population, the number of students who are learning English as a new language in U.S. schools is increasing dramatically (García, 1999). In 1986, 3 million non-White and Hispanic students were identified as residing in homes in which English was not the primary language. By the year 2026, the number will reach a conservative estimate of 15 million.

Culturally and linguistically diverse students tend to live in environments that are not always conducive to a stable learning experience. On the basis of a U.S. Bureau of the Census report (cited by the National Center for Children in Poverty, 1995),

García (1999) presented a bleak picture of educational opportunities for these students. In 1986, about 14 million U.S. children less than 18 years of age were living in poverty. This represented approximately 20% of the total population of this age group and an increase of 2 million since 1975. Of these children, 6.5 million, or 45%, were non-White and Hispanic. In comparison with 1986, the number of children in poverty will double to 28 million by the year 2026. More than half of these children (about 15 million) will be non-White and Hispanic. Students living in poverty are three times more likely to drop out of school than are students with economic advantages (NRC, 1993). Poverty at home is further exacerbated by insufficient and declining educational funding, scarce resources, and limited learning opportunities in the schools many of these students attend (García, 1999; Kozol, 1991).

Rationale for Focusing on Scientific Inquiry at Elementary Grade Levels

This chapter focuses on particular student groups and a particular area of science education with implications for larger student populations and other school subjects. Students in the process of acquiring the U.S. mainstream culture, language, and discourse are from diverse ethnic backgrounds (African American, Asian American, Hispanic, Native American), and they are often speakers of a home language other than English and from low-income families. The terms *culturally and linguistically diverse students, diverse students,* and *students from diverse backgrounds* are used interchangeably here.

This chapter focuses on scientific inquiry as central to scientific practices and current science education reform (AAAS, 1989, 1993; NRC, 1996, 2000). To conduct scientific inquiry, students also need to develop scientific understanding, discourse, and habits of mind (O. Lee & Fradd, 1998; O. Lee & Paik, 2000). The discussion about science is applicable to other subject areas inasmuch as they emphasize student inquiry, problem solving, discourse, and dispositions or habits of mind.

Science achievement scores of U.S. students deteriorate drastically from fourth through eighth grade (National Center for Education Statistics, 1996; U.S. National Research Center for TIMSS, 1996), while achievement gaps between mainstream and diverse students persist at the fourth- and eighth-grade levels (Campbell, Hombo, & Mazzeo, 2000). Closing the gap between White and other ethnic/racial groups, including Black, Hispanic, and Native American, is a major concern in multicultural education. In the cognitive development literature, on the other hand, the debate on scientific inquiry centers on whether elementary students are capable of conducting inquiry (e.g., Kuhn, 1997; Metz, 1995, 1997). This debate has grown out of the historical context of Piaget's stage theory proposing the transition from concrete to abstract thinking during elementary age spans. The discussion is applicable to adjacent age or grade levels, including early adolescence.

Relation of This Chapter to Relevant Areas of Literature

This chapter is related to existing areas of research, including the multicultural education literature addressing diversity and equity and the cognitive development literature examining children's abilities in conducting inquiry. Consideration of both cognitive and cultural views of students' scientific inquiry can offer a broader and more complete understanding of science and scientific inquiry for students of diverse backgrounds.

Multicultural Education

In response to the persistent science achievement gaps between mainstream and other student groups, coupled with the overall poor science achievement of U.S. students in international comparisons (discussed subsequently; see also S. Lynch, 2000; Rodríguez, 1998a), research has focused on a range of issues related to diversity and equity in science education. Such issues include the debate between universalism based on Western modern science and multicultural science on defining the nature of science and the school science curriculum (Loving, 1997; Siegel, in press; Stanley & Brickhouse, 1994; see Cobern, 2001); reconceptualization of the teaching and learning process to provide "equitable opportunities for *all* students to learn *quality* science" (Atwater, 1996, p. 822; Loving, 1998; Rodríguez, 1998b); culturally appropriate science assessments with diverse students (Solano-Flores & Nelson-Barber, 2001); technology-rich environments offering multiple ways of engaging in academic tasks in urban school districts (Krajcik et al., 1998; Marx, Blumenfeld, Krajcik, & Soloway, 1997); community-based youth programs or parental participation programs to enhance science learning and foster connections between school and community in urban settings (Barton, 1998a, 1998b; Hammond, 2001); and development of an equity metric to assess whether systemic reform is moving toward equity (Hewson, Kahle, Scantlebury, & Davis, 2001; Kahle, 1998).

Building on and extending the existing body of literature, this chapter reviews issues of culture and language in science classrooms, particularly when students of diverse backgrounds are engaged in scientific inquiry. It can contribute to the literature, considering that scientific inquiry is at the heart of science teaching and learning and that students' language and culture play a crucial role in the science teaching and learning process.

Cognitive Development

This literature examines developmental issues regarding children's capabilities in conducting scientific inquiry. Researchers and research programs differ in their views as to the role of maturation versus learning in cognitive development, the key aspects of science or scientific inquiry, children's capabilities in conducting scientific inquiry, and educational implications or instructional approaches (see the exchange between Kuhn, 1997, and Metz, 1995, 1997). Fundamentally, the core of the discussion involves what counts as scientific inquiry and what capability children have (or need) in order to engage in inquiry (Leona Schauble, personal communication, October 2001).

While the researchers in the cognitive development tradition consider development as maturation, researchers do not agree on what counts as scientific inquiry and how children's capabilities develop across age spans. Some researchers think of scientific inquiry as domain-general reasoning or heuristics (e.g., Chen & Klahr, 1999; Klahr & Dunbar, 1988; Klahr, Fay, & Dunbar, 1993; Kuhn, 1989; Kuhn, Garcia-Mila, Zohar, & Andersen, 1995; Kuhn, Schauble, & Garcia-Mila, 1992). Their work centers on two key questions: (a) Can children control variables in controlled experiments? and (b) Can children differentiate between theory and evidence? Other researchers think of scientific inquiry as conceptual structures and theories about the natural world (e.g., Carey, 1985; Carey & Smith, 1993; Smith, Carey, & Wiser, 1985). This research highlights how knowledge is restructured in the course of its acquisition and the role of domain-specific knowledge in scientific thinking and inquiry.

Recently, design research has taken a different approach from the traditional cognitive development literature. Instead of regarding development as maturation, design research considers learning environments as essential "engines" of development and teachers as using "design tools" to foster inquiry. However, design researchers and research programs differ in terms of what counts as scientific inquiry and how they, in collaboration with teachers, design learning environments. For example, Brown and Campione focus on activity structures in a collaborative learning community (Brown, 1992, 1994; Brown et al., 1993; Brown & Campione, 1996). Their work emphasizes socially distributed expertise among groups and individuals using a variety of design features, including reciprocal teaching groups, the jigsaw method, individual children "majoring" in particular areas of their choice and serving as experts, and the support of technological tools and science specialists in addition to the teacher.

Metz (2000) thinks of science as method or research designs. Her work proposes fostering children's independent scientific inquiry by scaffolding those spheres of knowledge most fundamental to inquiry: (a) domain-specific knowledge; (b) knowledge of the enterprise of empirical inquiry, including theory-evidence differentiation, controlled experiments, and scientific argumentation; (c) domain-specific methodologies or problem-solving strategies; (d) data representation and analysis; and (e) relevant tools.

Lehrer and Schauble think of science as a modeling enterprise grounded in an epistemological understanding of science (Lehrer, Carpenter, Schauble, & Putz, 2000; Lehrer & Schauble, in press). As scientists' work involves constructing and revising models of natural phenomena, children develop model-based reasoning through experimentation (Lehrer, Schauble, & Petrosino, in press) or design (Lehrer & Schauble, 1998). Lehrer and Schauble propose a developmental taxonomy of modeling ranging from a model based on resemblance toward a hypothetical-deductive model. Rather than providing children with prescribed forms of description and data display, teachers rely on children's progressive inventions for inscribing data in writing, drawing, or some other form of symbolizing over the course of inquiry.

This chapter can contribute to the cognitive development literature, which has paid little attention to student diversity (Mosham, 1998; O'Loughlin, 1992).

Students' intellectual capabilities are constructed in their cultural and linguistic environments and are revealed (or obscured) in contexts that are culturally, linguistically, and cognitively meaningful and relevant to them. Design tools for fostering inquiry need to consider cultural and linguistic as well as cognitive aspects of learning environments.

SCIENTIFIC INQUIRY AND SCIENCE ACHIEVEMENT

To understand scientific inquiry with students from diverse cultures and languages, it is necessary to examine what scientific inquiry is. It is also necessary to examine how students from diverse backgrounds perform in science and scientific inquiry. To situate this discussion in the context of current science reform, it is helpful to examine the definitions of scientific inquiry in standards documents (AAAS, 1989, 1993; NRC, 1996, 2000) and student achievement data from large-scale assessments, including NAEP and TIMSS. The standards indicate what all students should know, understand, and be able to do in science, while the assessments indicate the extent to which students have achieved these standards. Critiques of standards and large-scale assessments are also presented.

Definitions of Scientific Inquiry in Science Standards Documents

Major reform documents, including the NSES (NRC, 1996, 2000) and Project 2061 (AAAS, 1989, 1993), provide general definitions of scientific inquiry before offering specific guidelines for certain age spans. Considering the overall agreement between these two sets of documents (O. Lee & Paik, 2000; Raizen, 1998), the present discussion focuses on the NSES documents. However, specific differences between the two sets are pointed out.

General Definitions

Both NSES (NRC, 1996, 2000) and Project 2061 (AAAS, 1989, 1993) define scientific inquiry in a broad sense. NSES provides a definition of scientific inquiry modeled after the work of scientists:

> Scientific inquiry refers to the diverse ways in which scientists study the natural world and propose explanations based on the evidence derived from their work. Inquiry also refers to the activities of students in which they develop knowledge and understanding of scientific ideas, as well as an understanding of how scientists study the natural world. (p. 23)

On the basis of this definition, NSES describes what scientific inquiry involves:

> Inquiry is a multifaceted activity that involves making observations; posing questions; examining books and other sources of information to see what is already known; planning investigations; reviewing what is already known in light of experimental evidence; using tools to gather, analyze, and interpret data; proposing answers, explanations, and predictions; and communicating results. Inquiry requires identification of assumptions, use of critical and logical thinking, and consideration of alternative explanations. (p. 23)

Within this broad view, NSES highlights scientific inquiry in terms of (a) abilities necessary to do scientific inquiry and (b) understandings about scientific inquiry (NRC, 1996, 2000). Abilities refer to conducting scientific experiments or investigations, whereas understandings involve the nature or epistemology of scientific inquiry.

Developmental Differences

Although K–12 general standards are the same, the fundamental abilities and understandings about inquiry increase in complexity across age spans, "reflecting the cognitive development of students" (NRC, 2000, p. 18). Both NSES (NRC, 1996, 2000) and Project 2061 (AAAS, 1989, 1993) provide specific guidelines to promote scientific inquiry with students at different grade levels. Highlighting two aspects of scientific inquiry (i.e., controlled experiments and theory-evidence differentiation), NSES describes students' limitations in controlling multiple variables in experiments and in differentiating theories or explanations from evidence and logic:

Grades K–4. In elementary grades, students begin to develop the physical and intellectual abilities of scientific inquiry. They can design investigations to try things to see what happens—they tend to focus on concrete results of tests and will entertain the idea of a "fair" test (a test in which only one variable at a time is changed). However, children in K–4 have difficulty with experimentation as a process of testing ideas and the logic of using evidence to formulate explanations. (p. 122)

Grades 5–8. With an appropriate curriculum and adequate instruction, middle-school students can develop the skills of investigation and the understanding that scientific inquiry is guided by knowledge, observations, ideas, and questions. Middle-school students might have trouble identifying variables and controlling more than one variable in an experiment. . . . Students tend to center on evidence that confirms their current beliefs and concepts (i.e., personal explanations), and ignore or fail to perceive evidence that does not agree with their current concepts. (pp. 143–144)

Grades 9–12. Students should develop sophistication in their abilities and understanding of scientific inquiry. Students can understand that experiments are guided by concepts and are performed to test ideas. Some students still have trouble with variables and controlled experiments. Further, students often have trouble dealing with data that seem anomalous and in proposing explanations based on evidence and logic rather than on their prior beliefs about the natural world. (p. 173)

Although Project 2061 is generally in agreement with the NSES guidelines, it differs in a critical way in that it speculates on the potential of students' capabilities given appropriate instruction. According to Project 2061 (AAAS, 1993), in describing the limitations of Grades 3–5 students with controlled experiments and theory-evidence differentiation, "the studies say more about what students at this level do not learn in today's schools than about what they might possibly learn if instruction were more effective" (pp. 11–12). In this sense, Project 2061 reflects the goal of design research to examine students' capabilities given effective instruction (Metz, 1995, 1997).

Science Achievement

Differential science performance or achievement gaps among diverse student groups are highlighted in large-scale assessments in national and international studies. In the 1995 TIMSS, U.S. students were far from reaching the goal of being first in mathematics and science in the world (National Center for Education Statistics, 1996; U.S. National Research Center for TIMSS, 1996). While U.S. 4th-grade students performed within the cluster of top-performing nations, 8th-grade students' performance deteriorated to slightly above the international average score, and 12th-grade students' performance further deteriorated to a dismal ranking. In the 1999 TIMSS Repeat (TIMSS-R), U.S. 8th-grade students performed slightly above the international average score (Martin et al., 2001). Of the 14 school districts participating in the TIMSS-R, 4 urban districts performed significantly below the international average score. In addition, TIMSS examined the performance of different student groups in the United States. There was little change in the performance of African American, Hispanic, or White students in science from 1995 to 1999. White students continued to score higher than African American or Hispanic students (Martin et al., 2001).

Science achievement, as measured by the NAEP trends, has slightly increased at every age level since the 1970s (Campbell, Hombo, & Mazzeo, 2000). Science proficiency means by age and ethnicity from 1977 to 1999 are presented in Table 1. For 9-year-old students, the average score rose from 220 in 1977 to 229 in 1999; for 13-year-old students, the average rose from 247 in 1977 to 256 in 1999; and for 17-year-old students, the average rose from 290 in 1977 to 295 in 1999. In addition, science achievement has slightly increased for students of every ethnicity since the 1970s. Science scores of Black and Hispanic students are slowly but steadily improving, and the gap with White students is gradually narrowing. Despite the modest closing of the gap since the 1970s, science achievement of Black and Hispanic students remains well below that of White students.

Critiques of Standards Documents and Large-Scale Assessments

Critics have raised concerns about the definitions of scientific inquiry in standards documents and student achievement in large-scale assessments. From the multicultural education perspective, critics question whether the views of science and scientific inquiry in these documents and assessments are inclusive of alternative ways of knowing and expressing knowledge in diverse cultures and languages. From the cognitive development perspective based on models of the science disciplines, critics question whether the definitions of scientific inquiry in these documents and the abilities and understandings of scientific inquiry measured by these assessments are accurate representations of scientific practices.

Multicultural Education Perspective

Critics raise epistemological and pedagogical concerns about the nature of science, learning, and teaching as traditionally defined in scientific communities and school science (Barton, 1998a, 1998b; Eisenhart, Finkel, & Marion, 1996; O. Lee, 1999a; Rodríguez, 1997). From an epistemological stance, critics argue that the views of science and scientific inquiry in standards documents and large-scale assessments represent the norms and practices of Western modern science. The documents and

TABLE 1 Average Science Proficiency by Age and Ethnicity of Students: 1977 to 1999

Race/ethnicity	1977	1982	1986	1990	1992	1994	1996	1999
9-year-olds								
Total	220 (1.2)	221 (1.8)	224 (1.2)	229 (0.8)	231 (1.0)	231 (1.2)	230 (1.2)	229 (0.9)
White, non-Hispanic	230 (0.9)	229 (1.9)	232 (1.2)	238 (0.8)	239 (1.0)	240 (1.3)	239 (1.4)	240 (0.9)
Black, non-Hispanic	175 (1.8)	187 (3.0)	196 (1.9)	196 (2.0)	200 (2.7)	201 (1.7)	202 (3.0)	199 (2.5)
Hispanic	192 (2.7)	189 (4.2)	199 (3.1)	206 (2.2)	205 (2.8)	201 (2.7)	207 (2.8)	206 (2.2)
13-year-olds								
Total	247 (1.1)	250 (1.3)	251 (1.4)	255 (0.9)	258 (0.8)	257 (1.0)	256 (1.0)	256 (0.7)
White, non-Hispanic	256 (0.8)	257 (1.1)	259 (1.4)	264 (0.9)	267 (1.0)	267 (1.0)	266 (1.1)	266 (0.8)
Black, non-Hispanic	208 (2.4)	217 (1.3)	222 (2.5)	226 (3.1)	224 (2.7)	224 (4.2)	226 (2.1)	227 (2.4)
Hispanic	213 (1.9)	226 (3.9)	226 (3.1)	232 (2.6)	238 (2.6)	232 (2.4)	232 (2.5)	227 (1.9)
17-year-olds								
Total	290 (1.0)	283 (1.2)	289 (1.4)	290 (1.1)	294 (1.3)	294 (1.6)	296 (1.2)	295 (1.3)
White, non-Hispanic	298 (0.7)	293 (1.0)	298 (1.7)	301 (1.1)	304 (1.3)	306 (1.5)	307 (1.2)	306 (1.3)
Black, non-Hispanic	240 (1.5)	235 (1.7)	253 (4.5)	253 (4.5)	256 (3.2)	257 (3.1)	260 (2.4)	254 (2.9)
Hispanic	262 (2.2)	249 (2.3)	259 (3.8)	262 (4.4)	270 (5.6)	262 (6.7)	269 (3.3)	276 (4.2)

Note. Standard deviations are in parentheses.

assessments stress a worldview based on Western science, a way of knowing that distinguishes itself from other ways of knowing or other bodies of knowledge (AAAS, 1989, pp. 3–5; NRC, 1996, p. 201). According to Stanley and Brickhouse (1994), "science education has remained immune to the multiculturalist critique by appealing to a universalist epistemology . . . the culture, gender, race, ethnicity, or sexual orientation of the knower is irrelevant to scientific knowledge" (p. 388). Critics ask questions such as what counts as science, what should be taught in school science, and whether there are alternative ways of knowing or alternative worldviews in addition to the scientific way of knowing (Aikenhead, 1996; Cobern & Aikenhead, 1998; O. Lee, 1999a).

From a pedagogical stance, critics argue that by narrowly defining Western science as the proper domain of science, the documents assume that all students will learn science when provided with opportunities. They caution that this "one-size-fits-all" approach is particularly problematic with students from diverse backgrounds (Barton, 1998a, 1998b; Eisenhart et al., 1996; O. Lee & Fradd, 1998; Rodríguez, 1997, 1998a). Rodríguez (1997) argues that despite an emphasis on equity as the key principle, equity issues are almost invisible in the NSES (NRC, 1996): "The invisibility discourse dangerously compromises the well-intended goals of the NRC by not directly addressing the ethnic, socioeconomic, gender, and theoretical issues which influence the teaching and learning of science in today's schools" (p. 19). Eisenhart et al. (1996) also point out that although the vision of science for all is commendable, NSES and Project 2061 documents do not address obstacles and barriers in implementation:

> We applaud this vision of scientifically literate citizenry. . . . However, we are concerned that the means being used to promote this vision are too narrowly focused. . . . These limitations of the current implementation plans will, we think, make achievement of "science for all Americans" difficult. (p. 266)

Cognitive Development Perspective

Scientific inquiry has multiple interpretations, ranging from the sociology of science's focus on political and human endeavor to mechanistic and reductionistic notions (Cunningham & Helms, 1998; Kelly, Carlsen, & Cunningham, 1993). Some critics, referring to recent research on the sociology of science, argue that the views of science and scientific inquiry in standards documents do not reflect the practices of scientific communities (Latour & Woolgar, 1986; M. Lynch, 1985; Ochs, Jacoby, & Gonzales, 1996). They contend that the view of scientific inquiry in the standards documents, particularly the overemphasis on control of variables in experiments, is narrow, distorted, or truncated. Others, referring to cognitive science research on promoting meaningful learning of science, point out that the views in standards documents fail to represent the deep and thoughtful reasoning that children are capable of in science (Brown, 1992, 1994; Driver, Asoko, Leach, Mortimer, & Scott, 1994; Lehrer, Carpenter, Schauble, & Putz, 2000; Lehrer & Schauble, in press; Metz, 1995, 1998, 2000; Rosebery, Warren, & Conant, 1992; Warren & Rosebery, 1996).

Critics also question whether large-scale assessments accurately measure students' abilities to do scientific inquiry and whether achievement scores accurately represent such abilities (Baxtor & Glaser, 1998; Glaser & Linn, 1997; Ruiz-Primo & Shavelson, 1996; Solano-Flores & Shavelson, 1997; Solano-Flores, Jovanovic, Shavelson, & Bachman, 1999). Attempts to address inquiry in large-scale assessments have not been successful, because most tend to measure facts and concepts. Performance assessments, on the other hand, have not overcome reliability problems. In addition, large-scale assessments attempting to measure students' inquiry abilities tend to treat inquiry as a set of context- and content-free skills rather than a set of practices anchored in science content and history in specific learning environments. Thus, there is an unresolved gap between students' inquiry abilities and achievement scores.

As the present discussion indicates, recent studies in redefining science and scientific inquiry remain separate and isolated from science standards. Also, achievement scores in large-scale assessments may not reflect what students are really capable of in science or scientific inquiry. Despite such concerns and problems, these standards and assessments are used as indicators of what students should know and be able to do and how students perform. In addition, assessment information has served as a cause and catalyst to inform the public and the education community about the urgency of closing achievement gaps among diverse student groups and as a tool for testing any progress in closing or narrowing the gaps over the years. Science educators are faced with a dilemma in reconciling these two sets of expectations: views of science and scientific inquiry implicit in standards and large-scale assessments, on the one hand, and those in recent studies in sociology of science and cognitive science promoting meaningful learning of science based on how it is practiced in scientific communities, on the other.

SCIENTIFIC INQUIRY WITH DIVERSE STUDENTS

All students have formed ways of looking at the world based on personal experiences and environments (Driver et al., 1994). Students from diverse cultures and languages have acquired everyday knowledge and primary discourse in their homes, while they also learn science disciplines and the secondary discourse of science in school. To enable these students to learn science, a pedagogy merging subject-specific and diversity-oriented approaches is needed, although these approaches have traditionally remained distinct and separate from each other.

In effective learning environments, it is essential that the teacher and students understand how to interact and communicate with each other, as well as how to relate academic disciplines to students' previous knowledge and experience. The present discussion focuses on three major dimensions of promoting scientific inquiry with culturally and linguistically diverse students: (a) discourse processes in classroom communication and interaction, (b) cultural values and practices related to scientific inquiry, and (c) children's cognition based on their cultural knowledge of scientific inquiry. Discourse patterns among diverse cultures and languages differ from discourse patterns in school, resulting in miscommunications and misunderstandings. In addition, accepted ways of knowing in some cultures may be incompatible with the nature of science disciplines as defined in the Western science tradition. Yet, diverse students capitalize on their cultural and linguistic resources that are compatible with the nature of science disciplines. Research programs examining compatibility or incompatibility between students' everyday experience and knowledge and the nature of science are in their early stages of testing these emerging hypotheses.

Discourse Patterns and Cultural Congruence

All children acquire discourse patterns initially in their homes and communities. Extensive literature has described the discourse patterns of diverse cultural groups, including African Americans (Heath, 1983; C. Lee, 2001), Hawaiians (Au, 1980; Au & Jordan, 1981), Native Americans (Deyhle & Swisher, 1997; Erickson & Mohatt, 1982; Philips, 1972, 1983), Haitian Americans (Ballenger, 1992; O. Lee & Fradd, 1996a), Mexican Americans (Losey, 1995), and Puerto Ricans (McCollum, 1989). For example, multiparty, overlapping talk and simultaneous turn taking are typical in some cultures, whereas long pauses in turn taking are expected in other cultures.

This literature has also documented conflicts between the home cultures of diverse students and mainstream values and practices. In culturally congruent contexts, however, children from diverse backgrounds have demonstrated improved performance that is not observed in incongruent settings. For example, in a classic study conducted by Labov (1972), results showed that an 8-year-old African American boy who produced limited verbal responses to a White or an African American adult in a formal setting generated extensive verbal production with a friend in an informal setting. Philips (1972) found that Native American children who showed limited verbal responses in teacher-directed situations actively engaged in peer-learning situations.

Research on *cultural congruence* generally focuses on two related hypotheses (Au & Kawakami, 1994):

The overall hypothesis in research on cultural congruence is that students of diverse backgrounds often do poorly in school because of a mismatch between the culture of the school and the culture of the home. Students have less opportunity to learn when school lessons and other activities are conducted, or socially organized, in a manner inconsistent with the values and norms of their home culture. A related hypothesis is that students of diverse backgrounds will have better learning opportunities if classroom instruction is conducted in a manner congruent with the culture of the home. (pp. 5–6)

Because classroom communication and interactions occur largely through language, oral and written, understanding discourse patterns of students from diverse cultures and languages is "a necessary tool in a teacher's pedagogical toolkit" (C. Lee, 2001, p. 131). In addition, teachers need to understand a variety of cultural experiences, in that students of diverse backgrounds socialize according to shared norms and practices in their home and community environments (Ballenger, 1992; Deyhle & Swisher, 1997; Losey, 1995; Valdés, 1996). Pedagogies addressing cultural and linguistic diversity have various designations, including "culturally relevant," "culturally appropriate," "culturally responsive," "culturally compatible," and "culturally congruent" (for summaries, see Ladson-Billings, 1995, and Osborne, 1996).

Much of this research has centered on literacy instruction or general instructional practices. While earlier research focused on cultural congruence with teachers who share the same language and culture as their students, recent research indicates that teachers who come from backgrounds different from their students can also provide effective instruction when they have an understanding of students' language and culture (Ballenger, 1992; Brenner, 1998; Foster, 1993; Reyes & Pazey, 1999). For example, KEEP (Kamehameha Early Education Program) adopted the native Hawaiian discourse pattern, "talk story," to promote reading comprehension (Au & Carroll, 1997; Au & Jordan, 1981; Tharp, 1982). Ladson-Billings (1994, 1995) examined, in the case of African American students, exemplary teaching practices among White as well as African American teachers. She identified three key components of culturally relevant pedagogy: (a) enhancement of students' academic achievement, (b) acceptance and affirmation of their cultural identity, and (c) development of critical perspectives that challenge inequities perpetuated by schools and other institutions.

The literature also emphasizes the importance of using children's home language resources in the teaching and learning process. For example, Moll, Diaz, Estrada, and Lopes (1992) observed that, with a Spanish-English bilingual teacher in a Spanish-English dual-language program, Spanish-speaking elementary students successfully applied reading comprehension strategies they had acquired in Spanish to reading in English, even though they were not fully fluent in English. In contrast, a monolingual English-speaking teacher underestimated the students' competence and provided them with instruction at a much lower level in English than the instruction they were receiving in Spanish. Guthrie and Pung Guthrie (1989) examined a Chinese teacher in a Chinese-English bilingual program who responded to the learning needs of beginning and low-achieving Chinese students by promoting interactions bilingually and encouraging group work with more advanced peers. In contrast, a monolingual English-speaking teacher foreclosed learning opportunities for struggling students by insisting that all communication occur individually and only in English (Guthrie & Pung Guthrie, 1989).

In summary, students from diverse backgrounds acquire discourse patterns in their homes and communities that are sometimes incongruent with discourse patterns in school. When provided with culturally congruent instruction, students demonstrate improved verbal and academic performance. This literature has traditionally focused on classroom interactions, communication, and literacy development. Studies considering the nature of academic disciplines in relation to the cultural practices of different groups are emerging in the areas of literature (e.g., C. Lee, 2001), mathematics (e.g., Adler, 1995; Brenner, 1998), social studies (e.g., McCarty, Lynch, Wallace, & Benally, 1991), and science (discussed next).

Cultural Practices and Children's Cognition in Scientific Inquiry

The literature focuses on whether the ways of knowing, values, and practices of science are compatible or incompatible with ways of knowing, values, and practices in diverse cultures and languages. The "incompatibility" perspective is reflected in the multicultural education literature, whereas the "compatibility" perspective is framed by the cognitive development literature. The two perspectives differ in terms of their assumptions about science and scientific inquiry, culture, and their relationships.

Incompatibility

A substantial body of literature in multicultural science education indicates that students from diverse backgrounds display ways of knowing about the natural world that are sometimes incompatible with the nature of science and scientific inquiry as defined in Western modern science. The literature presents cultural and linguistic patterns from diverse student groups that sometimes conflict with scientific inquiry (Barba, 1993; Barba & Reynolds, 1998; Brickhouse, 1994, 1998; Gallard, 1993; Garaway, 1994; George, 1992; Howes, 1998; Matthews & Smith, 1994; Nelson-Barber & Estrin, 1995; Rakow & Bermudez, 1993). The examples described subsequently illustrate such differences in terms of scientific inquiry, discourse, and habits of mind.

Research in science education in the United States and other countries indicates that some cultures do not encourage students to engage in the practice of scientific inquiry by asking questions, designing and implementing investigations, and finding answers on their own (Arellano et al., 2001; Hodson, 1993; Jegede & Okebukola, 1992; Losey, 1995; McKinley, Waiti, & Bell, 1992; Ninnes, 1994, 1995; Prophet, 1990; Prophet & Rowell, 1993; Solano-Flores & Nelson-Barber, 2001; Swift, 1992). Certain cultural values and practices may dispose students to unquestioningly accept teachers' authority rather than questioning, exploring, or seeking alternative solutions. Validity of knowledge is often based on the validity of its source rather than the validity of knowledge claims. To the degree that teachers are respected as authorities and sources of knowledge, students may be reluctant to raise questions if their culture considers this to be a sign of disrespect. Students may be discouraged from asking questions or querying the knowledge claims and reasoning of teachers. The authority of parents, adults, and elders carries a similar status in the students' home and community. As a result, some students may not practice questioning and inquiry at home or at school.

Discourse patterns among diverse groups sometimes differ from the modes of discourse that require evidence and logic to support one's assertions, theories, or arguments. Some groups freely incorporate emotion to frame an argument with academic tasks (Estrin, 1993; Kochman, 1989; Nelson-Barber & Estrin, 1995). The separation of affect and emotion from cognition is incongruent for some cultural groups (Anderson, 1988; Atwater, 1994; Deyhle & Swisher, 1997). Thus, for some groups, shared social and emotional networks play as important a role in knowledge claims as do empirical validation and reasoning. In addition, some cultures do not have the discourse patterns of science, even when students have scientific understandings. Michaels and O'Connor (1990) described a situation in which a Haitian girl understood the concept of balance but did not give an explanation of her mental calculation until after much probing, because she did not understand that the discourse pattern of "why-because" was expected in classroom interactions. Students from some cultures that do not encourage extended and detailed responses may give brief responses and, as a consequence, may be erroneously perceived as lacking complete and comprehensive knowledge (O. Lee & Fradd, 1996a; Solano-Flores & Nelson-Barber, 2001). In some languages that tend to be circular, students may be perceived as lacking a sequential mode of constructing ideas.

Western science requires certain dispositions or habits of mind. Although some scientific values and attitudes are found in most cultures (e.g., curiosity, wonder, interest, diligence, persistence, imagination), others are characteristic of Western science. For example, Western science promotes a "critical and questioning stance" (Williams, 1994, p. 517) that calls for being skeptical, making logical arguments, critiquing others' viewpoints, and thinking independently (AAAS, 1989, 1993; NRC, 1996). These values and attitudes may be incongruent with the norms of cultures that favor cooperation, consensus building, social and emotional support, and acceptance of the authority of teachers and elders (Ballenger, 1992; O. Lee & Fradd, 1996a; McKinley et al., 1992; Ninnes, 1994, 1995).

Worldview theory has gained attention as an important part of the epistemology of science (see Cobern, 1991, for a comprehensive framework on worldviews). Students from diverse backgrounds tend to express alternative worldviews more strongly than their mainstream counterparts, and these alternative views are sometimes incompatible with scientific worldviews or ways of knowing. For example, one study showed that after personally experiencing a major natural disaster, African American and Hispanic elementary students attributed the cause of the disaster to societal problems (e.g., race, crime, violence) and spiritual and supernatural forces (e.g., God, the devil, or evil spirits) more frequently than mainstream White students, who tended to give explanations in terms of natural phenomena (O. Lee, 1999b). Shared and public acceptance of supernatural, spiritual, or animistic accounts of nature is documented in the case of members of various U.S. cultures, including Native Americans (e.g., Allen & Crawley, 1998; Kawagley, Norris-Tull, & Norris-Tull, 1998; Pomeroy, 1994; Robbins, 1983), African Americans and Hispanics (Atwater, 1994; O. Lee, 1999b), and Haitians (Ballenger, 1992). Similar results have been reported in international studies (e.g., Hewson, 1988; Jegede & Okebukola, 1991a, 1991b, 1992; Lawrenz & Gray, 1995; Lowe, 1995; Snively & Corsiglia, 2001).

Compatibility

An emerging body of literature argues that ways of knowing and talking of children from diverse cultures and languages are generally compatible with ways of knowing and talking in science disciplines. This literature is based on three areas of research. First, on the basis of detailed analyses of the everyday practice and talk of scientists, recent work on sociology of science defines science and scientific inquiry more broadly than the traditional emphasis on experimentation and theory building (Latour & Woolgar, 1986; M. Lynch, 1985; Ochs et al., 1996). This expanded view considers scientific practices within personal, social, and historical contexts of scientific communities. Some of these practices include the role of imagination, conjecture, cultivation of the unexpected, beliefs and desires of individual scientists, and construction of variables during the process of investigation rather than control of predetermined variables.

Second, the literature considers students' everyday language and experience as intellectual resources for enhancing their understanding of science. Instead of looking at students' everyday conceptions as erroneous—as does the research on misconceptions and conceptual change—this literature considers these conceptions as resources to build robust understanding (Clement, Brown, & Zeitsman, 1989; diSessa, Hammer, Sherin, & Kolpakowski, 1991; Lehrer & Schauble, in press; Minstrell, 1989). For example, Lehrer and Schauble (in press) propose a developmental taxonomy of models for examining children's understanding of the correspondence between the models and the world. They hypothesize that a model based on physical resemblance of the world may be the easiest entry point toward a functional model (essential functions of a system) and, eventually, toward a hypothetical-deductive model.

Finally, recent research conducted within the Chèche Konnen project documents the various ways in which poor and minority children's ideas and ways of knowing and talking are related to those characteristic of scientific communities (Ballenger, 1997, 2000; Conant, Rosebery, Warren, & Hudicourt-Barnes, 2001; Warren et al., 2001; Warren & Rosebery, 1996). Students as young as first grade use accounts of everyday experience not merely as a context for understanding scientific phenomena but as a perspective through which to infer previously unnoticed aspects of a given phenomenon and to create possibilities for interpreting the phenomenon differently. The Chèche Konnen research is described in more detail in the next section.

On the basis of this expanded view of science and a more flexible and fluid view of children's everyday sense making, the compatibility perspective considers the complex, interactive, and complementary relationships between scientific practices and the everyday sense making of children from diverse cultures and languages. This perspective indicates that the ways of knowing and talking used by these students are compatible with the ways of knowing and talking found in scientific communities (Ballenger, 1997; Warren & Rosebery, 1996; Warren et al., 2001). On the basis of case studies of Haitian and Latino elementary students demonstrating intellectual resources of their everyday knowledge in scientific inquiry, Warren et al. (2001) concluded:

We are arguing for the need to analyze carefully, on one hand, the ways of knowing and talking that comprise everyday life within linguistic and ethnic minority communities and, on the other hand, the ways of talking and knowing characteristic of scientific disciplines. . . . What children from low income, linguistic, and ethnic minority communities do as they make sense of the world—while perhaps different in some respects from what European American children are socialized to do—is in fact intellectually rigorous and generatively connected with academic disciplinary knowledge and practice. (p. 546)

Instructional Approaches to Promote Children's Scientific Inquiry

Students come to school with already constructed knowledge from their home and community environments, including their home languages and cultural values (García, 1999; Tharp & Gallimore, 1988). Learning is enhanced when it occurs in contexts that are culturally, linguistically, and cognitively meaningful and relevant to the students. It is through their home languages and cultures that students create frameworks for new understandings. Instruction that does not consider these home languages and cultures ignores or even negates the tools the students have used to construct basic cognitive frameworks, tools that can serve as meaningful contexts for construction of new frameworks (García, 1999; Tharp & Gallimore, 1988). Thus, effective science instruction considers students' cultures and languages in relation to the nature of science disciplines. How this is done, however, may differ depending on whether scientific practices are compatible or incompatible with children's cultures and languages.

Making Incompatibility Explicit

According to the incompatibility perspective, children from diverse backgrounds need to learn to relate two distinct sets of knowledge, values, and practices, that is, acculturating to science practices in the Western science tradition while simultaneously integrating cultural ways of knowing and talking in their homes and communities. Cultural transitions are critically important in learning, and the notion of *border crossing* is used to describe this process (Giroux, 1992). Students cross borders from their home and community environments into school and school science. School success depends largely on how well students learn to negotiate the boundaries separating multiple cultural worlds (Aikenhead, 1996; Aikenhead & Jegede, 1999; Cobern & Aikenhead, 1998; Costa, 1995; Maddock, 1981; O'Loughlin, 1992; Phelan, Davidson, & Cao, 1991; Pomeroy, 1994).

Science teaching should enable students to make smooth transitions between their home cultures and the culture of science. According to the multicultural education literature, school knowledge represents the "culture of power" of the dominant society (Au, 1998; Banks, 1993a, 1993b; Cochran-Smith, 1995; Delpit, 1988, 1995; Ladson-Billings, 1994, 1995; Nelson-Barber & Estrin, 1995; Reyes, 1992). The rules of discourse students are supposed to follow are largely implicit and tacit, thus making it difficult for students who have not learned the rules at home (Gee, 1994, 1997, in press; Heath, 1983; Moje, Collazo, Carillo, & Marx, 2001). In the case of students who are not from the culture of power, teachers need to provide explicit instruction about that culture's rules and norms rather than expecting students to figure out these rules on their own. Without explicit instruction, the students lack opportunities to acquire the rules. Such learning opportunities are essential because students are ultimately held accountable for knowing the rules, whether they have been taught or not. Explicit instruction within the context of authentic and meaningful tasks and activities has been advocated for students from diverse languages and cultures in literacy instruction (Au, 1998; Delpit, 1986, 1988, 1995; Jiménez & Gersten, 1999; Reyes, 1991, 1992), literature instruction (C. Lee, 2001), science instruction (Fradd & Lee, 1999), and classroom discourse, including science talk (Gee, 1994, 1997, in press).

Explicit instruction seems to imply at least two notions (Delpit, 1988; Fradd & Lee, 1999; C. Lee, 2001; Ninnes, 1994, 1995). First, it requires instructional scaffolding to make the transition from one set of values and practices to another explicit and visible. Teachers need to make visible students' everyday knowledge, the relationship between students' knowledge and academic tasks, and the transition from one domain to the other. For example, Delpit (1988) provides an example in which a Native Alaskan teacher helped Native Indian students distinguish between "village English" (or "our heritage language") and "standard English" (or "formal English") in both social and academic settings. In the Cultural Modeling Project, designed to promote literature among underachieving African American high school students, C. Lee (2001) found that "the rules of the literacy game will not be learned by immersion," and "it is highly unlikely that they will learn the rules of the literacy game without being explicitly taught" (p. 130). Thus, "one of the pivotal goals [of the project] . . . is to make explicit forms of knowledge that students use tacitly in their routine everyday practices as well as to make explicit the links between these new explicitly articulated strategies and the academic tasks at hand" (p. 119). This explicit knowledge is a starting point and can become a metacognitive toolkit for students' further learning. For example, questioning and argumentation with teachers and peers are explicitly encouraged in the science classroom, even though these behaviors may not be acceptable with parents and adults at home.

Second, explicit instruction implies teacher-directed instruction in which teachers tell students what to do or provide extensive guidance. For students who have limited experience with Western science or school science, teachers may need to provide direct instruction to build necessary concepts and skills within the context of meaningful and authentic tasks. For example, C. Lee (2001) describes how a teacher of underachieving African American high school students provides direct instruction to help students build strategies for comprehending the kinds of texts taught in the high school literature curricula that might be unfamiliar to them initially.

In promoting students' scientific inquiry, there needs to be a balance between teacher direction and student initiation or exploration. Effective instructional scaffolding takes into account the cultural and linguistic backgrounds as well as the science experience of students who come from backgrounds in which questioning and inquiry are not encouraged and students with limited experience in Western science. The aim is to encourage students to question and inquire without devaluing the norms and practices of their homes and communities (Cobern & Aikenhead, 1998; Deyhle & Swisher, 1997; O. Lee & Fradd, 1996a; McKinley et al., 1992; Prophet & Rowell, 1993; Swift, 1992). Students may take the initiative and engage in exploration more frequently as they gain knowledge and metacognitive awareness of the role of questioning and argumentation in inquiry.

Building on Compatibility

The compatibility perspective views the relationship between scientific practices and students' sense making in a complex and reflexive way (i.e., as similar, different, interactive, and generative) (diSessa et al., 1991; Lehrer & Schauble, in press; Warren et al., 2001). The entry point for effective teaching and learning is to examine the everyday experience and informal language practices that individual students bring to the learning process. Students have acquired forms of argumentation and reasoning in their everyday lives that can serve as intellectual resources in academic learning. A major problem in teaching is that teachers fail to recognize the diverse ways in which these intellectual resources manifest themselves. This problem can occur more often with students from diverse languages and cultures than with their mainstream counterparts because of differences between cultural practices and classroom expectations. The results can also be more detrimental in that these students may withdraw from learning and have fewer and fewer opportunities.

Once individual students' everyday experience and informal language are identified, including their cultural and linguistic resources relevant to science tasks, the intersections between students' everyday knowledge and scientific practices can be examined (Ballenger, 1997, 2000; Warren & Rosebery, 1995, 1996; Warren et al., 2001). Teachers need to relate, enlarge, and elaborate on these intersections or areas of contact between what students know and know how to do in science, on the one hand, and scientific practices and ways of knowing, on the other. Teachers need to learn to identify and harness these intersections or areas of contact.

To promote scientific inquiry, teachers provide students with opportunities to participate in a science learning community (Brown, 1992, 1994; Lehrer & Schauble, 1998, in press; Metz, 1995, 1997; Rosebery et al., 1992; Warren et al., 2001). On the basis of a model of what scientists do in the real world, students engage in scientific inquiry as they learn to use language, to think, and to act as members of a science learning community. Although science disciplines are used as a model for instructional approaches, students may not engage in scientific inquiry as scientists do in professional communities, because there is a fundamental difference between what scientists do and what children are capable of (Metz, 1995; Lehrer & Schauble, in press). Thus, science instruction occurs in a simplified form that children can participate in, comprehend, and communicate.

Learning is shaped by social interactions with others in a community, such as a shared activity and dialogue between teacher and students in a classroom (Cole, 1996; Rogoff, 1994, 1996). In learning science, children participate in a community of scientific practices that offers experiences and tools to explore and construct knowledge. The emphasis is on meanings that students generate and construct, rather than the forms of thinking and talking through which the meanings are communicated. Teachers encourage student-generated questions and inquiry while offering guidance and assistance as needed (Brown, 1992, 1994). Since the emphasis is on students' initiation and exploration, teacher-directed instruction is minimized or avoided.

When students' cultural and linguistic experiences are used as intellectual resources, those students with limited science experience or those of diverse backgrounds are able to conduct scientific inquiry and to appropriate scientific discourse as members of a science learning community (Rosebery et al., 1992; Warren et al., 2001). Studies in other subjects report similar results. For example, in designing and implementing a bilingual-bicultural curriculum in social studies, McCarty and colleagues (1991) incorporated the ways of knowledge construction in the Navaho and other Native American cultures as well as children's learning resources rooted in their cultures. K–9 children showed positive responses in regard to questioning, inductive and analytical reasoning, and speaking up in class, in contrast to other situations in which the same children refused to respond to questioning. C. Lee (2001) also indicates that cultural funds of knowledge of underachieving African American high school students, such as the use of "signifying" in African American English vernacular, offer a fertile bridge for the students to engage in cultural practices in literature instruction.

Summary

The two perspectives described—compatibility and incompatibility—reflect different views of science, diverse cultures and languages, and the relationship between them. The incompatibility perspective considers science and school science in the Western modern science tradition. This view of science is sometimes incompatible with the ways of knowing, values, and practices present in diverse cultures and languages. When students are not from the "culture of power" of the dominant society (e.g., Western modern science), teachers need to make that culture's rules and norms explicit and visible so that students learn to cross cultural borders. In the case of students who come from backgrounds in which questioning and inquiry are not encouraged or students with limited science experience, teachers move progressively along the teacher-explicit to student-exploratory continuum, while students learn to take the initiative and assume responsibility on their own.

The compatibility perspective takes an expanded view of science that reflects the everyday practices of scientists, as well as a fluid view of children's everyday experience and language. By examining interactive and reflexive relationships between the two, this perspective finds intersections at which children's everyday sense making provides intellectual resources to promote scientific inquiry. Teachers need to understand complex dynamics between scientific practices and students' everyday knowledge. As teachers capture students' cultural and linguistic experiences that can serve as intellectual resources, they provide opportunities for students to learn to use language, to think, and to act as members of a science learning community.

REPRESENTATIVE RESEARCH PROGRAMS

To illustrate how the compatibility and incompatibility perspectives are manifested in instructional interventions, two research programs promoting scientific inquiry with culturally and linguistically diverse students are described: *Science for All* and *Chèche Konnen*. Within the context of the evolution of each program over the years, the description focuses on key issues relevant to the purpose of this chapter, including views of science and scientific inquiry, language and culture, instructional approaches, and student learning and achievement.

Science for All Project

Since the early 1990s, this research program has promoted science learning and literacy development among elementary students from three language groups: bilingual Haitian Creole speakers, bilingual Spanish speakers, and English speakers of African American and Caucasian descent. The research has focused on the following questions: (a) What is effective instructional scaffolding that considers students' cultural and linguistic experiences and the nature of science along the teacher-explicit to student-exploratory continuum? (b) What are the trajectories of science learning and achievement—particularly scientific inquiry—and literacy development among culturally and linguistically diverse elementary students? and (c) How do state and district policies influence science instruction? Although the intervention promotes English language development along with science, the description here focuses on the science component.

Research Context

As the research program has expanded in size and scope over the years, the conceptual framework has evolved based on participating teachers' insights and perspectives as well as emerging research and literature on science instruction for culturally and linguistically diverse students. The research program began with a small-scale exploratory study examining the interrelationships of language development, science knowledge, and cognitive strategies as students engaged in three science tasks requiring them to describe, explain, and predict the natural phenomena of a tornado, lever, and sinking and floating. Conducted in controlled settings outside the classroom, the study involved dyads of fourth-grade students from the three ethnolinguistic groups. Bilingual teachers were matched with student dyads of the same language and gender (e.g., a Hispanic female teacher with two Hispanic girls).

The results indicated notable differences in students' previous experiences in literacy, science, and cognitive strategies (Fradd & Lee, 1995; O. Lee & Fradd, 1996b; O. Lee, Fradd, & Sutman, 1995). Analysis of interactions between teachers and student dyads revealed patterns of discourse and engagement in science tasks that were unique to each group (O. Lee & Fradd, 1996a). Some of these patterns were inconsistent with mainstream expectations for discourse and task engagement in science. The results highlighted the importance of *cultural congruence,* when teachers and students of similar ethnolinguistic backgrounds communicated in ways that promoted student performance.

On the basis of the exploratory results, a subsequent study addressed cultural congruence in science instruction with linguistically diverse students in elementary classroom settings in a large urban school district. The study examined how fourth-grade elementary teachers who shared elements of the language and culture with their students made science meaningful and relevant based on their shared understandings. The study initially involved volunteer teachers, including six Hispanic teachers at two predominantly Hispanic schools, two Haitian teachers at two predominantly

Haitian schools, and one African American and two Caucasian teachers at two predominantly monolingual English-speaking schools. All of the Hispanic and Haitian teachers were immigrants to the United States and were fluent in English and Spanish or Haitian Creole.

As a continuation of this research, the following study involved all fourth-grade teachers from the six schools (about 30 teachers each year) representing the three language groups. Many of the Hispanic and Haitian students were newly arrived or first-generation immigrants with various levels of English language proficiency. Most of the Hispanic and Haitian students were from low-SES homes, whereas most of the monolingual English-speaking students were from middle-SES homes. Thus, the students' cultures and languages were confounded with SES, because the participating schools were located within economically stratified ethnic enclaves.

Views of Science, Language, and Culture

As part of standards-based reform aimed at high achievement and equity, the research is based on the definition of science in standards documents as an approximation of scientific practices and as guidelines for school science (AAAS, 1989, 1993; NRC, 1996; for a summary, see O. Lee & Paik, 2000, and Raizen, 1998). Major components of science include the following: (a) science concepts and big ideas in terms of patterns of change, systems, models, and relationships ("knowing"); (b) science inquiry as students ask appropriate questions, design and carry out investigations, and draw valid conclusions ("doing"); (c) science discourse and multiple representations using various written and oral communication forms ("talking"); and (d) scientific habits of mind in terms of the values, attitudes, and worldviews of science.

The research emphasized teachers' perspectives as essential in building a theoretical as well as practical knowledge base for teaching. While learning to teach science according to the standards, teachers were asked to provide insights about how to relate science to students' languages and cultures. Cultural congruence occurs when teachers engage in culturally appropriate discourse patterns in communication and interaction with students, consider students' cultural values and beliefs related to science, and use students' cultural artifacts, examples, analogies, and community resources (Au & Kawakimi, 1994; O. Lee & Fradd, 1996a; Trueba & Wright, 1992; Villegas & Lucas, in press). In addition to facilitating social interactions to promote students' participation and engagement, cultural congruence relates academic subjects, such as science, to students' previous knowledge and experience in their cultural contexts.

Curriculum Materials

Early on in the research program, instruction focused on two science topics, matter and weather, from the district fourth-grade science curriculum. The initial intent of the research was to use existing instructional materials. In the absence of effective materials that address science education standards for culturally and linguistically diverse students, the research team designed two instructional units on matter and weather (for detailed descriptions, see Fradd, Lee, Sutman, & Saxton, 2002). In the current research, as the project expands into Grades 3–5 for schoolwide implementation, the research team has developed a total of six units on measurement and matter (Grade 3), the water cycle and weather (Grade 4), and the ecosystem and the solar system (Grade 5). These topics follow the sequence of instruction from basic skills and concepts (measurement and matter) to variable, global systems (the water cycle and weather) and, finally, increasingly large-scale systems (the ecosystem and solar system). Teachers have participated in the development, revision, and refinement of the units based on their insights and perspectives from classroom implementation. Development of the instructional units is guided by the frameworks of instructional congruence and the teacher-explicit to student-exploratory continuum (Fradd et al., 2002), described next.

Instructional Approaches

As the teachers learned science as defined in science standards documents and taught science to their students in culturally congruent ways, they merged the two areas in ways that were meaningful and relevant to their students (Fradd et al., 1997, 2002; O. Lee, in press; O. Lee & Fradd, 1998, 2000, 2001). For example, a Hispanic teacher described how she used students' cultural funds of knowledge in science instruction:

One example is taking temperature. I know now that I have to talk about the different measurements that you can get with the thermometer. Many students know that 38° means a fever, but some of them know it as around 100°. They don't use terms like Celsius or Fahrenheit. They bring in these different experiences that we need to recognize. Another example is all of the foods we cook at home. Cooking is important in feeding a family, and they relate to that well. Hispanics do a lot of cooking in our homes. All the foods we cook at home require a lot of boiling, and they see the evaporation. So when they have lessons that involve boiling and evaporating, they have something to build on to learn science. When we do the activity on boiling, we talk about boiling *frijoles* (beans) and *arroz* (rice), things they relate to. When we measure the temperature of boiling water, we do it in both Celsius and Fahrenheit. Then they realize there are two systems of measuring the temperature. It is like speaking two languages, like bilingual.

While relating science to students' cultures and languages was a challenge to the teachers, it presented additional challenges when the two areas were potentially incompatible. This finding is consistent with the multicultural science education literature indicating that cultural and linguistic patterns among diverse student groups are sometimes in conflict with scientific inquiry (Arellano et al., 2001; Hodson, 1993; Jegede & Okebukola, 1992; Losey, 1995; McKinley et al., 1992; Ninnes, 1994, 1995; Prophet, 1990; Prophet & Rowell, 1993; Solano-Flores & Nelson-Barber, 2001; Swift, 1992). For example, bilingual Hispanic teachers noted that many students came from home environments where questioning and inquiry might not be promoted. According to one teacher:

I think students' culture has a lot to do with learning science. If you are brought up in a culture where you don't ask questions, then it could be a difficulty. Many of our kids don't ask "why" questions because questioning is not an appropriate behavior at home. . . . It comes back to us, the teachers. If we encourage questioning, we can get kids asking why. Eventually, they learn to ask and answer their own questions.

Extending the literature on cultural congruence (Au & Kawakimi, 1994; Trueba & Wright, 1992) and culturally relevant pedagogy (see the summary in Osborne, 1996; Ladson-Billings, 1994, 1995), the research proposed the notion of *instructional congruence* as a process of mediating the nature of academic disciplines, such as science, with students' language and cultural experiences to make the academic content accessible, meaningful, and relevant for all students (O. Lee, in press; O. Lee & Fradd, 1996a, 1998, 2001; Westby, Dezale, Fradd, & Lee, 1999). The goal is to enable students to learn the nature of academic disciplines while recognizing and valuing the norms and practices of their homes and communities. While culturally relevant pedagogies focus primarily on cultural and linguistic aspects of teaching, instructional congruence refers to the relationship between students' languages and cultures and the nature of academic disciplines. Establishing instructional congruence is particularly demanding when the nature of science is incompatible with students' cultural and linguistic experiences.

The aspect of science instruction that presented the greatest challenge was scientific inquiry (Fradd & Lee, 1999; O. Lee & Fradd, 2001), which has become the focus of the research in recent years. Based on standards documents and relevant literature (Krajcik et al., 1998; Marx et al., 1997), the research defined scientific inquiry that involves (a) generating questions, (b) designing investigations and planning procedures, (c) carrying out the investigations, (d) analyzing and drawing conclusions, and (e) reporting findings. Inquiry is not a linear or discrete process; rather, aspects of inquiry interact in complex ways.

The teachers initially indicated that they were not comfortable with science in general and scientific inquiry in particular (Fradd & Lee, 1995; Fradd et al., 1997, in press). They also indicated that the students came from home environments where questioning and inquiry were not promoted. In addition, they observed that many students had not received formal science instruction in earlier grades. They pointed out three main reasons why science instruction was often ignored in elementary schools, particularly for English language learners: (a) a heavy emphasis on reading, writing, and mathematics; (b) elementary teachers' lack of preparation for teaching science; and (c) lack of science supplies.

On both cultural and academic grounds, the teachers suggested that the students needed more explicit instruction in order to gradually learn to conduct inquiry on their own. This finding is supported by the multicultural education literature suggesting that students from diverse languages and cultures can benefit from explicit instruction within the context of authentic and meaningful tasks and activities in various subject areas (Au, 1998; Delpit, 1986, 1988, 1995; Gee, 1994, 1997, in press; Jiménez & Gersten, 1999; C. Lee, 2001; Reyes, 1991, 1992). Student-centered inquiry, in which students ask questions and find answers on their own, may be the instructional goal. The issue is where to start and what to do to reach this goal for students from diverse backgrounds and levels of science experience. The research proposed the *teacher-explicit to student-exploratory continuum,* taking into account students' cultural backgrounds as well as previous science experiences (Fradd & Lee, 1999; Fradd et al., in press). In progressing along the teacher-explicit to student-exploratory continuum, teachers gradually reduce assistance and encourage students to take initiative and assume responsibility for their own learning.

Initially, bilingual Hispanic teachers provided instruction in ways that they perceived as culturally congruent (O. Lee & Fradd, 2000, 2001). Major patterns included teacher-explicit instruction, whole-group participation, and teacher authority and control. In guiding students through explicit instruction, the teachers orchestrated the class as a whole. Even when students worked in small groups, the teachers organized the groups as part of the entire class and encouraged collaboration and teamwork. This teacher-explicit, whole-group participation seemed effective initially in ensuring that all students engaged in the tasks. Later, through reflection and sharing of ideas, the teachers became aware that this instructional practice limited students' opportunities to take initiative, gain autonomy, and perform independently. As instruction progressed, they encouraged students to take initiative, exercise a greater degree of autonomy, and perform individually and independently as well as work collaboratively in groups.

The following example illustrates how a Hispanic teacher helped students progress from teacher-explicit instruction to student-exploratory inquiry. At the beginning of the year, realizing that most students were unfamiliar with using basic measurement instruments or doing investigations, the teacher gave explicit guidance about how to use equipment, do measurement, represent data in multiple formats, recognize patterns, and draw conclusions. In testing changes in the weight and volume of water during freezing, the teacher orchestrated small-group activities as part of whole-class instruction while students completed the tasks in step-by-step unison. With limited equipment, such as scales, the teacher ensured that every student had access to the equipment, used it correctly, and learned to record accurate measurements. The teacher guided the class to construct graphs based on the class data, identify patterns, and draw accurate conclusions.

As students gained experience in basic skills and concepts, the teacher moved toward more exploratory types of inquiry. In measuring temperature differences at different levels in the classroom, students recognized a pattern: Temperatures were highest near the ceiling, lower at desk level, and lowest near floor level. Based on their data from several small groups, they developed a theory that hot air rises and cool air falls. However, they observed that in one location of the classroom, the temperature at desk level was lower than the temperature at floor level. Discovering that frozen water bottles on the desks had changed the temperature of the air around the desks, students discussed exceptions due to sources of heating or cooling. Applying the theory of hot air rising and cool air falling, students discussed why they would lie on the floor during fire drills and where they would place a heater or an air conditioner in a room.

As instruction progressed, the teacher encouraged students to take the initiative in doing inquiry. In discussing temperature patterns around the world, the teacher asked the class to make some generalizations about temperatures near the equator and the poles. Students talked about temperatures around the equator being warmer than at the poles. One student stated that temperatures on the equator were warmer than anywhere else. Another disagreed by sharing his experience from his home country, Ecuador, which is actually cool. The teacher led the class to consider that elevation as well as latitude is an important factor influencing weather conditions.

As illustrated in this example, bilingual Hispanic students learned to take the initiative in asking questions, designing investigations, developing theories through investigations, identifying exceptions to general patterns, and engaging in debate by confirming or refuting findings based on evidence (Fradd & Lee, 1999; Fradd et al., in press). They also related the inquiry tasks and the topics of class discussion to their home language or their experiences at home and in their country of origin (O. Lee & Fradd, 2000, 2001).

Current Research

Current research examines the process and impact of instructional intervention designed to promote science learning and literacy development among diverse student groups, particularly focusing on scientific inquiry. The instructional intervention has been designed through the frameworks of instructional congruence and the teacher-explicit to student-exploratory continuum. As scale-up implementation, the research is conducted at 12 schools in two urban school districts with high proportions of culturally and linguistically diverse students, one in the Southeast and one on the West Coast. To examine developmental trajectories of student learning and achievement in science and literacy, the research involves elementary students from Grades 3 through 5. The impact of the instructional intervention on student learning and achievement in a longitudinal research design is addressed within the context of state and district policies on science and literacy instruction and assessment (e.g., high-stakes assessment and accountability as well as English for speakers of other languages/bilingual instruction). While the research involves a rather large number of teachers, it emphasizes case studies with a smaller number of highly effective teachers and randomly selected students in these classrooms.

Student Learning and Achievement

By means of qualitative methods, major themes and patterns of students' languages and cultures in science learning from classroom observations and student elicitations are reported (e.g., Fradd & Lee, 2000; O. Lee & Fradd, 2001; Westby et al., 1999). Paper-and-pencil tests were the primary source of group achievement information (Fradd et al., in press; O. Lee & Fradd, 2001). Pretest and posttest scores on project-developed unit tests are used to report statistical results in terms of total scores as well as subset scores for science concepts and inquiry among bilingual Haitian Creole, bilingual Spanish, and monolingual English-speaking students.

In the current research, data on student learning and achievement come from multiple sources simultaneously. First, pretests and posttests on instructional units are administered to all students. The tests measure (a) key science concepts and ideas and (b) science inquiry using more structured inquiry tasks (similar to NAEP performance tasks) and more open-ended inquiry tasks in which students generate questions and design investigations. Second, pretest/posttest elicitations are conducted with randomly selected students. The elicitation protocol is developed for in-depth assessment of students' understanding of science concepts and ability to conduct science inquiry in oral and written performance. Students participate in the inquiry tasks as they generate questions, design investigations, and discuss ways to report findings. Third, public-release items from the NAEP and TIMSS related to the instructional units are administered to all students for pretests and posttests. Fourth, scores on standardized statewide assessments in reading, writing, and mathematics (and science as of the 2002–2003 school year) are collected. Finally, during classroom visits, observers use rating scales as well as keep running records of students' engagement in classroom tasks in three categories: (a) science, (b) home language and culture, and (c) English language and literacy.

Chèche Konnen Project

"Chèche Konnen" means "search for knowledge" in Haitian Creole. Since the late 1980s, this research program has fostered scientific sense making among culturally, linguistically, and socioeconomically diverse students by engaging them in scientific inquiry and argumentation. The research has focused on three strands of questions: (a) How do students of diverse backgrounds make sense of science as they use their cultural and linguistic experiences as intellectual resources? (b) How do teachers create classroom communities of scientific sense making by integrating children's intellectual resources with science as it is practiced in the scientific community? and (c) How do teachers learn to promote students' scientific sense making as they participate in the practice of teacher research?

Research Context

The research was pilot tested in two contexts of bilingual education in an urban public school system. One was a self-contained, combined classroom of 7th- and 8th-grade Haitian students, and the other was a basic skills program within the general bilingual program for Haitian and other language groups in a high school (Rosebery et al., 1992; Warren, Rosebery, & Conant, 1989). Over the years, the research has involved groups of K–12 teachers (e.g., 8 teachers in Warren & Rosebery, 1995, and 12 teachers in Warren & Rosebery, 2001) of diverse language, ethnic, and disciplinary backgrounds who work in urban schools. Student groups have differed widely in terms of socioeconomic level, first language, and ethnicity, including Haitian Creole and Spanish speakers as well as English speakers of African American and Caucasian descent in bilingual and heterogeneous classrooms. While most of the research has been conducted in one school district with a multiethnic and multilingual community, the program has been implemented in a dozen school districts across the nation. The intervention involves volunteer teachers across school districts.

Views of Science, Language, and Culture

The research initially addressed how students learned to appropriate scientific ways of knowing, talking, and reasoning as a result of their participation in collaborative scientific inquiry. Based on how science is practiced by scientists, the research aimed at getting students to "do science" in ways similar to those of practicing scientists (Rosebery et al., 1992; Warren & Rosebery, 1995, 1996; Warren et al., 1989). Science is organized around students' own questions and inquiries. In "communities of scientific practice," students design studies to explore their questions; collect, analyze, and interpret data; establish criteria for evaluating evidence; negotiate knowledge claims; build, critique, and revise theories; and, when appropriate, take action based on their results.

As the research has evolved, it has expanded its view of scientific sense making to encompass a varied complex of resources, including practices of argumentation and embedded imagining, the generative power of everyday experience, and the role of informal language in meaning making (Ballenger, 1997; Warren et al., 2001; Warren & Rosebery, 2001). This view is supported by recent work in sociology of science suggesting that within the scientific profession itself, personal contents (e.g., the interests and values of the scientist) are present in various stages of a scientist's practical work and theorizing but are generally absent or at least not made explicit in the public product (Latour & Woolgar, 1986; M. Lynch, 1985; Ochs et al., 1996). This literature indicates the intricate intertwining of conceptual, imaginative, material, discursive, and experiential resources in scientists' work.

The Chèche Konnen research has also evolved toward a view of children's experimental reasoning that differs from the cognitive development tradition (Warren et al., 2001). Most studies in the cognitive development tradition have used constrained experimental tasks to assess how well children's reasoning conforms to a canonical view of experimentation as a method for identifying and controlling variables or as a syntax of rules and strategies for making valid inferences (Klahr et al., 1983; Kuhn et al., 1992, 1995; Schauble, 1996). The tasks used in these studies privilege logical inference or hypothetical deductive reasoning as the ideal of scientific reasoning. These studies approach experimentation as a process of logical inference through which children identify variables and uncover relationships already designed into the experimental setup. The studies examine the extent to which children's experimental reasoning approximates a logic of inference presumed to characterize the thinking of scientists.

In contrast, the Chèche Konnen research uses fairly open-ended tasks in which experimentation is approached as an exploratory process of constructing meanings for emerging variables (Warren et al., 2001). From an ethnographic stance, the research addresses questions such as the following: What do children do as they engage in experimental tasks? What resources—linguistic, conceptual, material, and imaginative—do they draw on as they develop and evaluate experimental tasks? How does children's scientific reasoning correspond to the nature of experimentation as practiced by scientists?

In its initial stage, the Chèche Konnen research focused primarily on scientific inquiry and argumentation; it has evolved to consider the role of students' language in scientific sense making. The research considers students' first language in two senses (Ballenger, 1997, 2000; Warren et al., 2001). First, there is a student's national language, such as Haitian Creole or Spanish. The use of students' first language provides an easier way for them to communicate and is a resource for their learning. Students' deep knowledge of their first language and their facility with its syntax and vocabulary allow them to refine distinctions and to express subtle nuances of meaning. The second meaning is in reference to what Heath (1983) termed "ways with words," indicating patterns of language socialization and use. Individuals may speak the same national language, and yet linguistic and social practices, such as storytelling and argumentation, may occur in different contexts in their lives, occur to different extents, and assume different forms. Thus, students come to school with varying levels of familiarity with the ways in which words are used there (e.g., the kinds of stories that are appropriate and when, the kinds of arguments that are allowed, significance of various shifts in vocabulary that are typical of talk in science).

The research also considers students' everyday experiences and ways of knowing and talking. Students' everyday knowledge includes cultural practices from their home and community. For example, argumentative discussion is a major feature of social interaction among Haitian adults and can be seen in the way people in Haiti *bay odyans* ("give talk"). This adult mode of discourse can be a resource for students as they practice argumentation in science. Haitian students are typically quiet and respectful in the classroom (Ballenger, 1992, 1997); in a culturally familiar environment, however, they can participate in animated arguments about scientific phenomena in a way that is integral with Haitian culture and congruent with scientific practice (Ballenger, 1997, 2000; Conant et al., 2001; Hudicourt-Barnes, 2001; Warren & Rosebery, 1996; Warren et al., 2001).

Curriculum Materials

Working with volunteer teachers across grade levels, the research program does not select particular science topics or instructional units. Individual teachers choose science topics of their interest for classroom instruction, or teachers as a group decide on the same topics according to the school district's guidelines. They select and adapt available materials, including the school district's approved curriculum, or develop their own materials.

Over the years, students' scientific activities have encompassed different phenomena and taken various forms. Students from kindergarten through high school have investigated the ecology of a local pond, the water quality of fountains on a school ground, the acoustics of a traditional Haitian drum, local weather, the relationship between salt intake and physical fitness, reproductive cycles of snails, formation of molds, the behavioral ecology of ants, metamorphosis, force and motion, and plant growth and development.

Instructional Approaches

Earlier work emphasized how students learned to engage in scientific inquiry and to appropriate scientific argumentation in a collaborative learning community (Rosebery et al., 1992; Warren & Rosebery, 1995, 1996; Warren et al., 1989). Based on the model of the way science is practiced by scientists, the research promoted collaborative scientific inquiry as students learned to use language, to think, and to act as members of a science learning community. The premise is that there is much to be learned about what science in schools can be by examining science as it is practiced in professional communities. Although scientific practice in schools may not, and even should not, exactly mirror scientific practice in the world, understanding the relationship will help clarify what it means to teach and learn science (Warren & Rosebery, 1995).

The course of students' inquiry is not predetermined; rather, it grows directly out of students' beliefs and questions. Investigation of one question motivates additional explorations, initially unforeseen. Because science instruction is organized around students' own questions and inquiries, much of the science that goes on (i.e., the "curriculum") emerges from the questions the students pose, the experiments they design, the arguments they engage in, and the theories they articulate. The use of students' own questions as curriculum grounds the curriculum in "their voices and lives" (Ballenger, 2000, p. 97). Teachers' role is to facilitate and guide students' investigations of their own questions.

The results indicate that students with limited English proficiency or limited science experience were capable of conducting scientific inquiry. For example, Rosebery et al. (1992; also reported in Warren & Rosebery, 1995) examined the effects of "doing science" on language minority students' appropriation of scientific ways of knowing and reasoning. The study involved bilingual students from a variety of linguistic and cultural backgrounds in a middle school and a high school. In September, students showed almost no evidence that they understood what it means to reason scientifically and, specifically, to put forward hypotheses having deductive consequences that can be evaluated through experimentation. Students used personal experience as evidence for a particular belief rather than using the discourse of conjecture and experimentation that calls for critical, analytic evaluation of given information or evidence. Throughout the school year, the students engaged in scientific inquiry, such as testing the water quality of fountains on a school ground or the ecology of a local pond. By June, the students were able to go beyond the information given to put forward hypotheses that were explanatory and testable. They were aware that hypotheses drive scientific inquiry and that experimentation is a means for developing evidence.

Over the years, the research has expanded its view of science, as described earlier. At the same time, the research has considered the everyday knowledge and informal knowledge that students of diverse backgrounds bring to the learning process. Based on the expanded view of science and a more flexible and fluid view of children's everyday sense making, the research proposes that children's everyday experience and ways of knowing and talking are consistent with those of science. Warren et al. (2001) stated this position as follows:

Traditionally, those who have thought about the relationship between particular cultural groups and the culture of science have identified tensions between what they describe as the knowledge, values, and practices of science and the knowledge, values, and practices of children from particular racial, ethnic, and linguistic minority communities. We would argue that the perspective we have put forward in this article can effectively reframe these tensions by opening up for examination what is meant by science on the one hand and diversity in cultural and linguistic practices on the other. By examining both in an integrated and reflexive way, we can begin to envision pedagogical possibilities that build on diversity as an intellectual resource rather than a problem or tension in science learning. (p. 548)

The results indicate that students of diverse backgrounds use their first language (in the sense of both national language and ways with words) in sense-making practices. Ballenger (2000; also reported in Warren et al., 2001) describes how a fifth-grade Haitian boy, who was learning English as a new language and was considered a special education student, used his first language, Haitian Creole, and then English to understand metamorphosis as a particular kind of change in biology. Speaking in Haitian Creole and using Haitian Creole syntax, the student differentiated the meanings of the two terms *grow* (referring to continuous change) and *develop* (referring to reliably patterned transformation from one discrete stage to the next). Then the student switched to English and used the terms to further enhance his understanding of these two aspects of change.

The results also indicate that students use their cultural practices in scientific reasoning and argumentation (Ballenger, 1997, 2000; Conant et al., 2001; Hudicourt-Barnes, 2001; Warren & Rosebery, 1996; Warren et al., 2001). When a sixth-grade Haitian student asserted that "the bathrooms in Haiti have mold, the bathrooms here don't get moldy," a classmate challenged this claim, and an animated discussion ensued in which students offered arguments and counterarguments and had to defend their positions (Ballenger, 1997).

Overall, the results suggest that children from diverse languages and cultures deploy sense-making practices—deep questions, vigorous argumentation, situated guesswork, embedded imagining, multiple perspectives, and innovative uses of everyday words to construct new meanings—that serve as intellectual resources in science learning and teaching. Thus, the ideas and everyday knowledge that children of diverse backgrounds bring to science learning should be taken seriously. Attention needs to be paid to potential continuities between children's ways of knowing and talking and scientific practices. Such analysis may offer pedagogical possibilities, especially for typically marginalized children.

The research has considered the notion of explicit instruction with students of diverse backgrounds (Ballenger, 1997; Warren & Rosebery, 1995, 2001). Recognizing that children who are socialized into ways of talking and knowing different from those of the school—typically low-income ethnic and linguistic minority students—are presumably unfamiliar with how language and knowledge are organized in school, Ballenger (1997) addressed the following question: Do they successfully engage in inquiry tasks if they are able to bring more of their everyday language and ways of making sense to the tasks, or do they simply remain where they are, comfortable in a nonacademic discourse and unlikely to explore science as a different way of thinking and talking? Warren and Rosebery (2001) also point out the need to address the notion of explicit instruction as students construct meanings through inquiry.

Current Research

Current research examines two main questions: (a) What is the nature of the relationships between everyday and scientific meanings and ways of representing those meanings, and how can they be built upon pedagogically in science? and (b) Would all children benefit academically from close attention to these relationships? The research has two main goals. The first is to develop a pedagogical approach that integrates emphases on the centrality of students' ideas and questions in inquiry-based learning with concerns regarding the importance of explicit instruction in the forms and functions of language and symbol use in sense making in science. This pedagogical synthesis harnesses the diversity in children's ideas and ways of knowing and talking as an intellectual resource. The second goal is to study what children learn as a result of their participation in inquiry practices. The research addresses how children learn to see the relationships between everyday and scientific accounts of the natural world. The work is undertaken in close collaboration with a small number of practitioner-researchers in heterogeneous and bilingual first- through fourth-grade classrooms. The research focuses on motion and force in physics and growth and development of organisms in biology.

Student Learning and Achievement

The research has produced case studies of classroom practices or individual students. These case studies are grounded in ethnographic and discourse analytic methods using videotape documentation of talk and work in the classroom. A limited corpus of achievement data is collected through project-developed tests (Rosebery et al., 1992) or selected items from TIMSS, NAEP, and state achievement tests (Rosebery & Warren, 2000).

In the current research, data about student learning and achievement come from multiple sources. First, during classroom visits, lessons are videotaped, field notes are taken, and copies of students' written work are collected. Second, to assess student understanding of science concepts, all students complete a set of problems fashioned after the models of benchmark and model-eliciting problems. To assess student competence in comparative inquiry, all students complete a small set of problems focused on interpreting, critiquing, and transforming everyday and scientific accounts. Third, selected students in each classroom complete these two forms of assessment in extensive interview sessions. The purpose is to develop in-depth interpretations of how students take up practices of comparative inquiry. Finally, all students complete selected items from TIMSS, NAEP, and state achievement tests.

Summary

The two research programs described here pursue the common goal of promoting science learning, particularly scientific inquiry, among students from culturally, linguistically, and socioeconomically diverse backgrounds. As design research, both programs craft and implement the design of learning environments and then conduct research on student learning that results from the intervention (Brown, 1992; Collins, 1999). Both programs agree that (a) teachers need to incorporate cultural and linguistic funds of knowledge that students of diverse backgrounds bring to science, (b) teachers need to examine how students' everyday knowledge and language intersect with scientific practices, and (c) students of diverse backgrounds are capable of learning science and engaging in scientific inquiry. Both programs also recognize that science educators usually have little understanding of the intellectual resources that these students bring to science. The two programs differ with regard to views of science, language, and culture as well as instructional approaches.

Views of Science, Language, and Culture

Based on the notion of cultural congruence, Science for All started with the question of how teachers who shared the language and culture of their students related science to the students' backgrounds. The hypothesis was that these teachers would have insights in relating science to students' experiences, although these insights might be tacit and need to be examined in light of student learning. As part of standards-based reform aimed at high achievement and equity, the research employs science standards documents as guidelines for school science. While shifting its focus on scientific inquiry over the years, the research also considers other areas of science, including scientific understanding, discourse, and habits of mind. By considering students' cultural values and practices as compared with the values and practices of Western modern science, the research indicates areas of incompatibility as well as compatibility between these two sets of values and practices.

Grounded in sociology of science and cognitive science research, Chèche Konnen initially focused on how students of diverse backgrounds, particularly Haitian bilingual students, learned to talk, think, and act like scientists in collaborative learning communities. The research conceives science in a broad sense beyond the narrow definitions in standards documents. Emphasizing scientific inquiry as the core of scientific practices and using the model of everyday practices of scientists, the research promotes children's sense making in science. As the research has evolved, it has expanded its view of scientific sense making to encompass a varied complex of resources and to consider the role of students' first language and cultural practices in scientific sense making. The results indicate that students' everyday experience and ways of knowing and talking are compatible with those of science.

Instructional Approaches

Based on different views of science, language, and culture, the two programs employ different design principles for student learning. From a cross-cultural or cultural anthropological perspective based on the multicultural education literature, Science for All considers learning as a process of border crossing or cultural transitions between the home culture and the culture of science. While relating science to students' cultural and linguistic experiences, teachers make it explicit or visible when the two areas are sometimes incompatible. Teachers initially provide extensive guidance, including direct instruction, and gradually withdraw assistance as students learn to take initiative and conduct inquiry on their own.

In Chèche Konnen, based on the model of the way science is practiced in scientific communities, teachers provide learning environments in which students explore their ideas and investigate questions. The course of students' inquiry emerges from students' questions rather than being predetermined by the curriculum or teachers. As students engage in scientific inquiry and argumentation, teachers identify intersections between students' everyday knowledge and scientific practices and use these intersections as the basis for instructional practices.

RESEARCH AGENDA

Differential science achievement among diverse cultural and linguistic groups has raised calls for action. As science education reform documents emphasize scientific inquiry as central to science instruction, efforts have focused on promoting scientific inquiry as both science content and a way to teach and learn science (NRC, 2000). The debate has centered on elementary grades in part because of the historical influence of the cognitive development literature on science curriculum and instruction. With increasingly diverse student populations in the nation's schools, there is an urgent need to consider cultural and linguistic as well as cognitive issues if effective instruction is to be provided for all students (García, 1999).

Various theoretical perspectives propose different relationships among science disciplines, students, and school science. The cognitive development literature frames the debate in terms of whether or not students are capable of conducting scientific inquiry—"children as scientists" or "children as nonscientists" (Kuhn, 1997, 1999; Metz, 1995, 1997, 1998). If students are capable, the role of school science is to design learning environments that promote students' scientific inquiry. If students are not capable at certain age levels, school science may withhold specific types of instructional activities until students are developmentally ready to engage in scientific inquiry. The multicultural education literature frames the debate in terms of whether or not the everyday knowledge or ways of knowing of students from diverse backgrounds are compatible with scientific knowledge or ways of knowing in science disciplines (e.g., O. Lee, 1999a, in press; O. Lee & Fradd, 1998; Warren et al., 2001). A fundamental issue, however, is that these perspectives offer different conceptions of what counts as science and scientific inquiry.

The existing areas of literature offer an interesting and important array of questions for further research in promoting scientific inquiry with elementary students from diverse cultures and languages. The research agenda involves teasing out complex relationships among students, science disciplines, and school science in the contexts of home/community and school.

First, the conception of scientific inquiry needs to be reexamined. Based on the traditional cognitive development literature, science standards documents emphasize scientific inquiry primarily in terms of controlled experiments and theory-evidence differentiation (AAAS, 1989, 1993; NRC, 1996, 2000). The sociology of science (Latour & Woolgar, 1986; M. Lynch, 1985; Ochs et al., 1996) and cognitive science (Brown, 1992; Lehrer & Schauble, in press; Metz, 1998, 2000) literatures criticize this conception as too narrow and argue for a broader conception that represents the practices of scientists and scientific communities. The multicultural education literature, on the other hand, criticizes the conception for failing to consider alternative views of science from diverse cultures and languages (Eisenhart et al., 1996; O. Lee, 1999a; Rodríguez, 1997).

This debate involves not only a conceptual issue but also a practical concern for classroom instruction. If scientific inquiry is defined too narrowly, instruction may fail to represent scientific practices and become instead a strictly defined method or a set of procedures. If it is defined too broadly, instruction may be incomprehensible to all but the most dedicated teachers and the most capable and motivated students. If alternative views of science and scientific inquiry are not considered as part of science disciplines, cultural identities of diverse students may be ignored. If alternative views are given equal prominence with the traditional view in science disciplines, the enterprise of science may become relativistic without shared values and beliefs. Because (re)conceptualization of scientific inquiry is linked to science curriculum, this debate has political implications with regard to defining the nation's educational goals; moreover, it influences the research agenda with regard to examining curricular approaches and students' learning outcomes.

Second, a key point of contention among different research traditions involves how each considers the relationship between science disciplines and students' cultural backgrounds. Potential explanations may be offered for seemingly conflicting perspectives on compatibility or incompatibility. First, based on a cross-cultural or cultural anthropological view, the incompatibility perspective identifies patterns of cultural beliefs and practices that shape students' scientific inquiry. Based on a cognitive science view, the compatibility perspective examines students' sense making as they engage in scientific inquiry in specific situations. Second, while one perspective addresses potential incompatibilities between science disciplines and students' cultural experiences, the other focuses on potential compatibilities. The debate may turn on different interpretations of degree of compatibility or incompatibility rather than an "all-or-nothing" dichotomy. Promising lines of research may reside in the middle ground between the two perspectives, such as the interplay of sense-making practices and underlying cultural beliefs and practices, the degree of compatibility or incompatibility with regard to different aspects of science and scientific inquiry, and the process of transfer across different contexts (e.g., interactions with teachers or peers in the classroom, playground, street corner, barbershop, etc.).

Third, once the relationship between science disciplines and students' cultural backgrounds is defined, the next question involves the role of school science. As suggested, seemingly competing perspectives on compatibility or incompatibility may really be differences in degree rather than in fundamental premises. Students of all backgrounds should be provided with learning opportunities to explore and construct meanings based on their linguistic and cultural resources. At the same time, some may need more explicit guidance to recognize how their linguistic and cultural experiences might be compatible or incompatible with scientific practices. The teacher-explicit to student-exploratory continuum may be a function of the degree of compatibility or incompatibility between science disciplines and students' backgrounds, the extent of students' experience with science and scientific inquiry, and the level of cognitive demands or difficulty of inquiry tasks. Further research could examine students' scientific sense making in relation to their cultural expectations, their previous science experiences, and types of inquiry tasks. It could also examine what explicit instruction means, when and how to be explicit, and how to determine the appropriate extent of support along the teacher-explicit to student-exploratory continuum in instructional practices.

Finally, the role of teachers in providing effective instructional scaffolding is critically important. In design research, teachers create learning environments that capitalize on students' potential cognitive abilities and provide assistance as needed (Brown, 1992, 1994; Lehrer & Schauble, in press; Metz, 1995, 1998). To be effective with all students, instructional scaffolding also needs to consider their linguistic and cultural experiences. Students bring rich experiences and resources from their home languages and cultures that may not be easily recognized in science classrooms. This presents a major challenge to teachers who may not have the cultural knowledge necessary to identify students' learning resources (O. Lee, in press; O. Lee & Fradd, 1998; Moje et al., 2001; Warren et al., 2001). The challenge becomes greater when teachers are unsure of how to relate students' experiences to science disciplines, particularly when the two areas are potentially incompatible. Research could examine changes in teachers' knowledge, beliefs, and practices as they learn to integrate students' cultural and linguistic experiences with science disciplines (O. Lee & Fradd, 2000).

CONCLUSION

This chapter has addressed the role of school science in providing students from diverse languages and cultures with meaningful access to science disciplines. The discussion indicates that the integration of different perspectives is not a straightforward solution. Tensions and potential contradictions abound in theoretical assumptions and instructional approaches. With students from diverse languages and cultures, divergent perspectives and related areas of literature need to be considered simultaneously. The current knowledge base highlights critically important and fertile areas of research that require consideration of seemingly conflicting theoretical perspectives. These perspectives and areas of literature may be merged into a theoretically coherent and sound body of knowledge. Research results will offer insights in identifying effective instructional scaffolding to enable students to conduct scientific inquiry as practiced in scientific communities while helping them recognize and value the ways of knowing and talking in their own cultures. Ideally, the students will eventually become bilingual and bicultural, bridging their own cultures with the culture of science and behaving competently in a variety of contexts.

REFERENCES

Adler, J. (1995). Dilemmas and a paradox—Secondary mathematics teachers' knowledge of their teaching in multicultural classrooms. *Teaching and Teacher Education, 11*, 263–274.

Aikenhead, G. S. (1996). Science education: Border crossing into the subculture of science. *Studies in Science Education, 26*, 1–52.

Aikenhead, G. S., & Jegede, O. J. (1999). Cross-cultural science education: A cognitive explanation of a cultural phenomenon. *Journal of Research in Science Teaching, 36*, 269–287.

Allen, N. J., & Crawley, F. E. (1998). Voices from the bridge: Worldview conflicts of Kickapoo students of science. *Journal of Research in Science Teaching, 35*, 111–132.

American Association for the Advancement of Science. (1989). *Science for all Americans.* New York: Oxford University Press.

American Association for the Advancement of Science. (1993). *Benchmarks for science literacy.* New York: Oxford University Press.

Anderson, J. A. (1988). Cognitive styles and multicultural populations. *Journal of Teacher Education, 39*, 2–9.

Arellano, E. L., Barcenal, T., Bilbao, P. P., Castellano, M. A., Nichols, S., & Tippins, D. J. (2001). Case-based pedagogy as a context for collaborative inquiry in the Philippines. *Journal of Research in Science Teaching, 38*, 502–528.

Atwater, M. M. (1994). Research on cultural diversity in the classroom. In D. L. Gabel (Ed.), *Handbook of research on science teaching and learning* (pp. 558–576). New York: Macmillan.

Atwater, M. M. (1996). Social constructivism: Infusion into the multicultural science education research agenda. *Journal of Research in Science Teaching, 33*, 821–837.

Au, K. H. (1980). Participation structures in a reading lesson with Hawaiian children: Analysis of a culturally appropriate instructional event. *Anthropology and Education Quarterly, 11*, 91–115.

Au, K. H. (1998). Social constructivism and the school literacy learning of students of diverse backgrounds. *Journal of Literacy Research, 30*, 297–319.

Au, K. H., & Carroll, J. H. (1997). Improving literacy achievement through a constructivist approach: The *KEEP* Demonstration Classroom Project. *Elementary School Journal, 97*, 203–221.

Au, K. H., & Jordan, C. (1981). Teaching reading to Hawaiian children: Finding a culturally appropriate solution. In H. T. Trueba, G. P. Guthrie, & K. H. Au (Eds.), *Culture in the bilingual classroom: Studies in classroom ethnography* (pp. 139–152). Rowley, MA: Newbury House.

Au, K. H., & Kawakami, A. J. (1994). Cultural congruence in instruction. In E. R. Hollins, J. E. King, & W. C. Hayman (Eds.), *Teaching diverse populations: Formulating a knowledge base* (pp. 5–24). Albany: State University of New York Press.

Ballenger, C. (1992). Because you like us: The language of control. *Harvard Educational Review, 62,* 199–208.

Ballenger, C. (1997). Social identities, moral narratives, scientific argumentation: Science talk in a bilingual classroom. *Language and Education, 11,* 1–14.

Ballenger, C. (2000). Bilingual in two senses. In Z. Beykont (Ed.), *Lifting every voice: Pedagogy and the politics of bilingualism* (pp. 95–112). Cambridge, MA: Harvard Education.

Banks, J. (1993a). Canon debate, knowledge construction, and multicultural education. *Educational Researcher, 22*(5), 4–14.

Banks, J. (1993b). Multicultural education: Historical development, dimensions, and practice. In L. Darling-Hammond (Ed.), *Review of research in education* (Vol. 19, pp. 3–49). Washington, DC: American Educational Research Association.

Barba, R. H. (1993). A study of culturally syntonic variables in the bilingual/bicultural science classroom. *Journal of Research in Science Teaching, 30,* 1053–1071.

Barba, R. H., & Reynolds, K. E. (1998). Toward an equitable learning environment in science for Hispanic students. In B. Fraser & K. Tobin (Eds.), *International handbook of science education: Part 2* (pp. 925–940). Dordrecht, the Netherlands: Kluwer Academic.

Barton, A. C. (1998a). Reframing "science for all" through the politics of poverty. *Educational Policy, 12,* 525–541.

Barton, A. C. (1998b). Teaching science with homeless children: Pedagogy, representation, and identity. *Journal of Research in Science Teaching, 35,* 379–394.

Baxtor, G. P., & Glaser, R. (1998). Investigating the cognitive complexity of science assessments. *Educational Measurement: Issues and Practice, 17*(3), 37–45.

Brenner, M. E. (1998). Adding cognition to the formula for culturally relevant instruction in mathematics. *Anthropology and Education Quarterly, 29,* 213–244.

Brickhouse, N. (1994). Bringing in the outsiders: Reshaping the sciences of the future. *Curriculum Studies, 26,* 401–416.

Brickhouse, N. (1998). Feminism(s) in science education. In B. Fraser & K. Tobin (Eds.), *International handbook of science education: Part 2* (pp. 1067–1082). Dordrecht, the Netherlands: Kluwer Academic.

Brown, A. L. (1992). Design experiments: Theoretical and methodological challenges in creating complex interventions in classroom settings. *Journal of the Learning Sciences, 2,* 141–178.

Brown, A. L. (1994). The advancement of learning. *Educational Researcher, 23*(8), 4–12.

Brown, A. L., Ash, D., Rutherford, M., Nakagawa, K., Gordon, A., & Campione, J. (1993). Distributed expertise in the classroom. In G. Salomon (Ed.), *Distributed cognitions: Psychological and educational considerations* (pp. 188–228). New York: Cambridge University Press.

Brown, A. L., & Campione, J. C. (1996). Psychological theory and the design of innovative learning environments: On procedures, principles, and systems. In L. Schauble & R. Glaser (Eds.), *Innovations in learning new environments for education* (pp. 289–325). Mahwah, NJ: Erlbaum.

Campbell, J. R., Hombo, C. M., & Mazzeo, J. (2000). *NAEP 1999 trends in academic progress: Three decades of student performance.* Washington, DC: U.S. Department of Education, National Center for Education Statistics.

Carey, S. (1985). Are children fundamentally different kinds of thinkers than adults? In S. F. Chipman, J. W. Segal, & R. Glaser (Eds.), *Thinking and learning skills, Vol. 2* (pp. 485–517). Hillsdale, NJ: Erlbaum.

Carey, S., & Smith, C. (1993). On understanding the nature of scientific knowledge. *Educational Psychologist, 28,* 235–251.

Chen, Z., & Klahr, D. (1999). All other things being equal: Acquisition and transfer of the control of variables strategy. *Child Development, 70,* 1098–1120.

Clement, J., Brown, D., & Zeitsman, A. (1989). Not all preconceptions are misconceptions: Finding "anchoring conceptions" for grounding instruction on students' intuitions. *International Journal of Science Education, 11,* 555–565.

Cobern, W. W. (1991). *World view theory and science education research* (NARST Monograph No. 3). Manhattan, KS: National Association for Research in Science Teaching.

Cobern, W. W. (2001). Science teacher education section paper set [Special issue]. *Science Education, 85,* 1–88.

Cobern, W. W., & Aikenhead, G. S. (1998). Cultural aspects of learning science. In B. Fraser & K. Tobin (Eds.), *International handbook of science education: Part 1* (pp. 39–52). Dordrecht, the Netherlands: Kluwer Academic.

Cochran-Smith, M. (1995). Color blindness and basket making are not the answers: Confronting the dilemmas of race, culture, and language diversity in teacher education. *American Educational Research Journal, 32,* 493–522.

Cole, M. (1996). *Cultural psychology: A once and future discipline.* Cambridge, MA: Belknap Press of Harvard University Press.

College Board and Western Interstate Commission for Higher Education. (1991). *The road to college: Educational progress by race and ethnicity.* New York: College Board.

Collins, A. (1999). The changing infrastructure of education research. In E. C. Lagemann & L. S. Shulman (Eds.), *Issues in education research* (pp. 289–298). San Francisco: Jossey-Bass.

Conant, F., Rosebery, A., Warren, B., & Hudicourt-Barnes, J. (2001). The sound of drums. In E. McIntyre, A. Rosebery, & N. Gonzalez (Eds.), *Building bridges: Linking home and school* (pp. 51–60). Portsmouth, NH: Heinemann.

Costa, V. B. (1995). When science is another world': Relationships between worlds of family, friends, school, and science. *Science Education, 79,* 313–333.

Cunningham, C. M., & Helms, J. V. (1998). Sociology of science as a means to a more authentic, inclusive science education. *Journal of Research in Science Teaching, 35,* 483–499.

Delpit, L. (1986). Skills and other dilemmas of a progressive Black educator. *Harvard Educational Review, 56,* 379–385.

Delpit, L. (1988). The silenced dialogue: Power and pedagogy in educating other people's children. *Harvard Educational Review, 58,* 280–298.

Delpit, L. (1995). *Other people's children: Cultural conflict in the classroom.* New York: Norton.

Deyhle, D., & Swisher, K. (1997). Research in American Indian and Alaska Native education: From assimilation to self-determination. In M. W. Apple (Ed.), *Review of research in education* (Vol. 22, pp. 113–194). Washington, DC: American Educational Research Association.

diSessa, A., Hammer, D., Sherin, B., & Kolpakowski, T. (1991). Inventing graphing: Metarepresentational expertise in children. *Journal of Mathematical Behavior, 10,* 117–160.

Driver, R., Asoko, H., Leach, J., Mortimer, E., & Scott, P. (1994). Constructing scientific knowledge in the classroom. *Educational Researcher, 23*(7), 5–12.

Eisenhart, M. (2001). Educational ethnography past, present, and future: Ideas to think with. *Educational Researcher, 30*(8), 16–27.

Eisenhart, M., Finkel, E., & Marion, S. F. (1996). Creating the conditions for scientific literacy: A re-examination. *American Educational Research Journal, 33,* 261–295.

Erickson, F., & Mohatt, G. (1982). Participant structures in two communities. In G. Spindler (Ed.), *Doing the ethnography of schooling* (pp. 132–174). New York: Holt, Rinehart & Winston.

Estrin, E. T. (1993). *Alternative assessment: Issues in language, culture, and equity*. San Francisco: Far West Laboratory.

Foster, M. (1993). Educating for competence in community and culture. *Urban Education, 27*, 370–394.

Fradd, S. H., & Lee, O. (1995). Science for all: A promise or a pipe dream? *Bilingual Research Journal, 19*, 261–278.

Fradd, S. H., & Lee, O. (1999). Teachers' roles in promoting science inquiry with students from diverse language backgrounds. *Educational Researcher, 28*(6), 4–20, 42.

Fradd, S. H., & Lee, O. (2000). Needed: A framework for integrating standardized and informal assessment for students developing academic language proficiency in English. In J. V. Tenajero & S. Hurley (Eds.), *Literacy assessment of bilingual learners* (pp. 130–148). Boston: Allyn & Bacon.

Fradd, S. H., Lee, O., Cabrera, P., del Rio, V., Leth, A., Morin, R., Ceballos, M., Santalla, M., Cross, L., & Mathieu, T. (1997). School-university partnership to promote science with students learning English. *TESOL Journal, 7*, 35–40.

Fradd, S. H., Lee, O., Sutman, F. X., & Saxton, M. K. (2002). Materials development promoting science inquiry with English language learners: A case study. *Bilingual Research Journal, 25*, 479–501.

Gallard, A. J. (1993). Learning science in multicultural environments. In K. Tobin (Ed.), *The practice of constructivism in science education*. Washington, DC: American Association for the Advancement of Science.

Garaway, G. B. (1994). Language, culture, and attitude in mathematics and science learning: A review of the literature. *Journal of Research and Development in Education, 27*, 102–111.

García, E. (1999). *Student cultural diversity: Understanding and meeting the challenge* (2nd ed.). Boston: Houghton Mifflin.

Gee, J. P. (1994, April). *Science talk: How do you start to do what you don't know how to do?* Paper presented at the annual meeting of the American Educational Research Association, New Orleans, LA.

Gee, J. P. (1997, April). *Science talk: Language and knowledge in classroom discussion*. Paper presented at the annual meeting of the National Association for Research in Science Teaching, Oak Brook, IL.

Gee, J. P. (in press). Progressivism, critique, and socially situated minds. In C. Edelsky & C. Dudley-Marling (Eds.), *Progressive education: History and critique*. Urbana, IL: National Council for the Teaching of English.

George, J. M. (1992). Science teachers as innovators using indigenous resources. *International Journal of Science Education, 14*, 95–109.

Giroux, H. (1992). *Border crossings: Cultural workers and the politics of education*. New York: Routledge.

Glaser, R., & Linn, R. (1997). *Assessment in transition: Monitoring the nation's educational progress*. Stanford, CA: Stanford University, National Academy of Education.

Guthrie, L. F., & Pung Guthrie, G. (1989). Teacher language use in a Chinese bilingual classroom. In S. R. Goldman & H. T. Trueba (Eds.), *Becoming literate in English as a second language* (pp. 205–234). Norwood, NJ: Ablex.

Hammond, L. (2001). An anthropological approach to urban science education for language minority families. *Journal of Research in Science Teaching, 38*, 983–999.

Heath, S. B. (1983). *Ways with words: Language, life, and work in communities and classrooms*. New York: Cambridge University Press.

Hewson, M. G. (1988). The ecological context of knowledge: Implications for learning science in developing countries. *Journal of Curriculum Studies, 20*, 317–326.

Hewson, P. W., Kahle, J. B., Scantlebury, K., & Davis, D. (2001). Equitable science education in urban middle schools: Do reform efforts make a difference? *Journal of Research in Science Teaching, 38*, 1130–1144.

Hodson, D. (1993). In search of a rationale for multicultural science education. *Science Education, 77,* 685–711.

Howes, E. V. (1998). Connecting girls and science: A feminist teacher research study of a high school prenatal testing unit. *Journal of Research in Science Teaching, 35,* 877–896.

Hudicourt-Barnes, J. (2001). Argumentation in Haitian Creole classrooms. *Hands On, 24*(2), 7–9.

Jegede, O. J., & Okebukola, P. A. (1991a). The effect of instruction on socio-cultural beliefs hindering the learning of science. *Journal of Research in Science Teaching, 28,* 275–285.

Jegede, O. J., & Okebukola, P. A. (1991b). The relationship between African traditional cosmology and students' acquisition of a science process skill. *International Journal of Science Education, 13,* 37–47.

Jegede, O. J., & Okebukola, P. A. (1992). Differences in sociocultural environment perceptions associated with gender in science classrooms. *Journal of Research in Science Teaching, 29,* 637–647.

Jiménez, R. T., & Gersten, R. (1999). Lessons and dilemmas derived from the literacy instruction of two Latina/o teachers. *American Educational Research Journal, 36,* 265–301.

Kahle, J. B. (1998). Equitable systemic reform in science and mathematics: Assessing progress. *Journal of Women and Minorities in Science and Engineering, 4,* 91–112.

Kawagley, A. O., Norris-Tull, D., & Norris-Tull, R. A. (1998). The indigenous worldview of Yupiaq culture: Its scientific nature and relevance to the practice and teaching of science. *Journal of Research in Science Teaching, 35,* 133–144.

Kelly, G. J., Carlsen, W. S., & Cunningham, C. M. (1993). Science education in sociocultural context: Perspectives from the sociology of science. *Science Education, 77,* 207–220.

Klahr, D., & Dunbar, K. (1988). Dual space search during scientific reasoning. *Cognitive Science, 12,* 1–48.

Klahr, D., Fay, A. L., & Dunbar, K. (1993). Heuristics for scientific experimentation: A developmental study. *Cognitive Psychology, 25,* 111–146.

Kochman, T. (1989). Black and White cultural styles in pluralistic perspective. In B. Gifford (Ed.), *Test policy and test performance: Education, language, and culture.* Boston: Kluwer Academic.

Kozol, J. (1991). *Savage inequalities: Children in America's schools.* New York: Crown.

Krajcik, J., Blumenfeld, P. C., Marx, R. W., Bass, K. M., Fredricks, J., & Soloway, E. (1998). Inquiry in project-based science classrooms: Initial attempts by middle school students. *Journal of Learning Sciences, 7,* 313–350.

Kuhn, D. (1989). Children and adults as intuitive scientists. *Psychological Review, 96,* 674–689.

Kuhn, D. (1997). Constraints or guideposts? Developmental psychology and science education. *Review of Educational Research, 67,* 141–150.

Kuhn, D., Garcia-Mila, M., Zohar, A., & Andersen, C. (1995). Strategies of knowledge acquisition. *Monographs of the Society for Research in Child Development, 60*(4, Serial No. 245).

Kuhn, D., Schauble, L., & Garcia-Mila, M. (1992). Cross-domain development of scientific reasoning. *Cognition and Instruction, 9,* 285–327.

Labov, W. (1972). *Language in the inner city: Studies in the Black English vernacular.* Philadelphia: University of Pennsylvania Press.

Ladson-Billings, G. (1994). *The dreammakers: Successful teachers of African American children.* San Francisco: Jossey-Bass.

Ladson-Billings, G. (1995). Toward a theory of culturally relevant pedagogy. *American Educational Research Journal, 32,* 465–491.

Latour, B., & Woolgar, S. (1986). *Laboratory life: The social construction of scientific facts.* Princeton, NJ: Princeton University Press.

Lawrenz, F., & Gray, B. (1995). Investigation of worldview theory in a South African context. *Journal of Research in Science Teaching, 32,* 555–568.

Lee, C. D. (2001). Is October Brown Chinese? A cultural modeling activity system for underachieving students. *American Educational Research Journal, 38,* 97–141.

Lee, O. (1999a). Equity implications based on the conceptions of science achievement in major reform documents. *Review of Educational Research, 69,* 83–115.

Lee, O. (1999b). Science knowledge, world views, and information sources in social and cultural contexts: Making sense after a natural disaster. *American Educational Research Journal, 36,* 187–219.

Lee, O. (in press). Equity for culturally and linguistically diverse students in science education. *Teachers College Record.*

Lee, O., & Fradd, S. H. (1996a). Interactional patterns of linguistically diverse students and teachers: Insights for promoting science learning. *Linguistics and Education: An International Research Journal, 8,*269–297.

Lee, O., & Fradd, S. H. (1996b). Literacy skills in science performance among culturally and linguistically diverse students. *Science Education, 80,* 651–671.

Lee, O., & Fradd, S. H. (1998). Science for all, including students from non-English language backgrounds. *Educational Researcher, 27*(3), 12–21.

Lee, O., & Fradd, S. H. (2000, April). *Teacher learning and change in science and literacy instruction for linguistically diverse students.* Paper presented at the annual meeting of the American Educational Research Association, New Orleans, LA.

Lee, O., & Fradd, S. H. (2001). Instructional congruence to promote science learning and literacy development for linguistically diverse students. In D. R. Lavoie & M.-W. Roth (Eds.), *Models for science teacher preparation: Bridging the gap between research and practice* (pp. 109–126). Dordrecht, the Netherlands: Kluwer Academic.

Lee, O., Fradd, S. H., & Sutman, F. X. (1995). Science knowledge and cognitive strategy use among culturally and linguistically diverse students. *Journal of Research in Science Teaching, 32,* 797–816.

Lee, O., & Paik, S. (2000). Conceptions of science achievement in major reform documents. *School Science and Mathematics, 100,* 16–26.

Lehrer, R., Carpenter, S., Schauble, L., & Putz, A. (2000). Designing classrooms that support inquiry. In J. Minstrell & E. van Zee (Eds.), *Teaching science in the inquiry-based classroom* (pp. 80–99). Washington, DC: American Association for the Advancement of Science.

Lehrer, R., & Schauble, L. (1998). Reasoning about structure and function: Children's conceptions of gears. *Journal of Research in Science Teaching, 35,* 3–25.

Lehrer, R., & Schauble, L. (in press). Modeling in mathematics and science. In R. Glaser (Ed.), *Advances in instructional psychology, Vol. 5.* Mahwah, NJ: Erlbaum.

Lehrer, R., Schauble, L., & Petrosino, A. (in press). Reconsidering the role of experiment in science education. In K. Crowley, C. Schunn, & T. Okada (Eds.), *Designing for instruction: Implications for everyday, classroom, and professional settings.* Mahwah, NJ: Erlbaum.

Losey, K. M. (1995). Mexican American students and classroom interaction: An overview and critique. *Review of Educational Research, 65,* 283–318.

Loving, C. C. (1997). From the summit of truth to its slippery slopes: Science education's journey through positivist-postmodern territory. *American Educational Research Journal, 34,* 421–452.

Loving, C. C. (1998). Cortes' multicultural empowerment model and generative teaching and learning in science. *Science and Education, 7,* 533–552.

Lowe, J. A. (1995). The impact of school science on the world-view of Solomon Islands students. *Prospects, 25,* 653–667.

Lynch, M. (1985). *Art and artifact in laboratory science: A study of shop work and shop talk in a research laboratory.* Boston: Routledge & Kegan Paul.

Lynch, S. (2000). *Equity and science education reform.* Mahwah, NJ: Erlbaum.

Maddock, M. N. (1981). Science education: An anthropological viewpoint. *Studies in Science Education, 8,* 1–26.

Martin, M. O., Mullis, I. V. S., Gonzalez, E. J., O'Connor, K. M., Chrostowski, S. J., Gregory, K. D., Smith, T. A., & Garden, R. A. (2001). *Science benchmarking report TIMSS 1999–eighth grade: Achievement for U.S. states and districts in an international context.* Chestnut Hill, MA: Boston College, International Study Center.

Marx, R. W., Blumenfeld, P. C., Krajcik, J. S., & Soloway, E. (1997). Enacting project-based science: Challenges for practice and policy. *Elementary School Journal, 97,* 341–358.

Matthews, C. E., & Smith, W. S. (1994). Native American related materials in elementary science instruction. *Journal of Research in Science Teaching, 31,* 363–380.

McCarty, T. L., Lynch, R. H., Wallace, S., & Benally, A. (1991). Classroom inquiry and Navajo learning styles: A call for reassessment. *Anthropology and Education Quarterly, 22,* 42–59.

McCollum, P. (1989). Turn-allocation in lessons with North American and Puerto Rican students: A comparative study. *Anthropology and Education Quarterly, 20,* 133–156.

McKinley, E., Waiti, P. M., & Bell, B. (1992). Language, culture and science education. *International Journal of Science Education, 14,* 579–595.

Metz, K. E. (1995). Reassessment of developmental constraints on children's science instruction. *Review of Educational Research, 65,* 93–127.

Metz, K. E. (1997). On the complex relation between cognitive developmental research and children's science curricula. *Review of Educational Research, 67,* 151–163.

Metz, K. E. (1998). *Scientific inquiry within reach of young children.* In B. Fraser & K. Tobin (Eds.), *International handbook of science education: Part 1* (pp. 81–96). Dordrecht, the Netherlands: Kluwer Academic.

Metz, K. E. (2000). Young children's inquiry in biology: Building the knowledge bases to empower independent inquiry. In J. Minstrell & E. H. van Zee (Eds.), *Inquiring into inquiry learning and teaching in science* (pp. 371–404). Washington, DC: American Association for the Advancement of Science.

Michaels, S., & O'Connor, M. C. (1990). *Literacy as reasoning within multiple discourses: Implications for policy and educational reform.* Paper presented at the Council of Chief State School Officers Summer Institute on "Restructuring Learning," Newton, MA.

Minstrell, J. (1989). Teaching science for understanding. In L. Resnick & L. Klopfer (Eds.), *Toward the thinking curriculum: Current cognitive research* (pp. 131–149). Alexandria, VA: Association for Supervision and Curriculum Development.

Moje, E., Collazo, T., Carillo, R., & Marx, R. W. (2001). "Maestro, what is quality?": Examining competing discourses in project-based science. *Journal of Research in Science Teaching, 38,* 469–495.

Moll, L. C., Diaz, S., Estrada, E., & Lopes, L. M. (1992). Making contexts: The social construction of lessons in two languages. In M. Saravia-Shore & S. F. Arvizu (Eds.), *Cross-cultural literacy: Ethnographies of communication in multicultural classrooms.* New York: Garland Press.

Mosham, D. (1998). Cognitive development beyond childhood: Constraints on cognitive development and learning. In W. Damon (Series Ed.), D. Kuhn & R. Siegler (Vol. Eds.), *Handbook of child psychology: Vol. 2. Cognition, language, and perception* (5th ed., pp. 947–978). New York: Wiley.

National Center for Children in Poverty. (1995). *Five million children: A statistical profile of our poorest young citizens.* New York: Columbia University.

National Center for Education Statistics. (1996). *Pursuing excellence: A study of U.S. eighth-grade mathematics and science teaching, learning, curriculum, and achievement in international context.* Washington, DC: U.S. Department of Education, Office of Educational Research and Improvement.

National Research Council. (1993). *Losing generations: Adolescents in high-risk settings.* Washington, DC: National Academy Press.

National Research Council. (1996). *National science education standards*. Washington, DC: National Academy Press.

National Research Council. (2000). *Inquiry and the national science education standards: A guide for teaching and learning*. Washington, DC: National Academy Press.

Nelson-Barber, S., & Estrin, E. T. (1995). Bringing Native American perspectives to mathematics and science teaching. *Theory into Practice, 34,* 174–185.

Ninnes, P. (1994). Toward a functional learning system for Solomon Island secondary science classrooms. *International Journal of Science Education, 16,* 677–688.

Ninnes, P. (1995). Informal learning contexts in Solomon Islands and their implications for the cross-cultural classroom. *International Journal of Educational Development, 15,* 15–26.

Ochs, E., Jacoby, S., & Gonzales, P. (1996). "When I come down I'm in the domain state": Grammar and graphic representation in the interpretive activity of physicists. In E. Ochs, E. A. Schegloff, & S. A. Thompson (Eds.), *Interaction and grammar* (pp. 328–369). New York: Cambridge University Press.

O'Loughlin, M. (1992). Rethinking science education: Beyond Piagetian constructivism toward a sociocultural model of teaching and learning. *Journal of Research in Science Teaching, 29,* 791–820.

Osborne, A. B. (1996). Practice into theory into practice: Culturally relevant pedagogy for students we have marginalized and normalized. *Anthropology and Education Quarterly, 27,* 285–314.

Phelan, P., Davidson, A., & Cao, H. (1991). Students' multiple worlds: Negotiating the boundaries of family, peer, and school cultures. *Anthropology and Education Quarterly, 22,* 224–250.

Philips, S. (1972). Participant structures and communicative competence: Warm Springs children in community and classroom. In C. Cazden, D. Hymes, & V. John (Eds.), *Functions of language in the classroom* (pp. 370–394). New York: Teachers College Press.

Philips, S. (1983). *The invisible culture: Communication in classroom and community on the Warm Springs Indian Reservation*. New York: Longman.

Pomeroy, D. (1994). Science education and cultural diversity: Mapping the field. *Studies in Science Education, 24,* 49–73.

Prophet, R. B. (1990). Rhetoric and reality in science curriculum development in Botswana. *International Journal of Science Education, 12,* 13–23.

Prophet, R. B., & Rowell, P. M. (1993). Coping and control: Science teaching strategies in Botswana. *Qualitative Studies in Education, 6,* 197–209.

Raizen, S. (1998). Standards for science education. *Teachers College Record, 100,* 66–121.

Rakow, S. J., & Bermudez, A. B. (1993). Science is "Cicencia": Meeting the needs of Hispanic American students. *Science Education, 77,* 547–560.

Reyes, M. (1991). A process approach to literacy using dialogue journals and literature logs with second language learners. *Research in the Teaching of English, 25,* 291–313.

Reyes, M. (1992). Challenging venerable assumptions: Literacy instruction for linguistically diverse students. *Harvard Educational Review, 62,* 427–446.

Reyes, P., & Pazey, B. (1999). Creating student-centered classroom environments: The case of mathematics. In P. Reyes, J. D. Scribner, & A. P. Scribner (Eds.), *Lessons from high-performing Hispanic schools* (pp. 94–130). New York: Teachers College Press.

Robbins, R. (1983). John Dewey's philosophy and American Indians: A brief discussion of how it could work. *Journal of American Indian Education, 22,* 1–9.

Rodríguez, A. (1997). The dangerous discourse of invisibility: A critique of the NRC's National Science Education Standards. *Journal of Research in Science Teaching, 34,* 19–37.

Rodríguez, A. (1998a). Busting open the meritocracy myth: Rethinking equity and student achievement in science education. *Journal of Women and Minorities in Science and Engineering, 4,* 195–216.

Rodríguez, A. (1998b). Strategies for counter-resistance: Toward sociotransformative constructivism and learning to teach science for diversity and for understanding. *Journal of Research in Science Teaching, 35,* 589–622.

Rogoff, B. (1994). Developing understanding of the idea of communities of learners. *Mind, Culture, and Activity, 1,* 209–229.

Rogoff, B. (1996). Models of teaching and learning: Participation in a community of learners. In *Handbook of education and human development* (pp. 388–414). Oxford, England: Blackwell.

Rosebery, A. S., & Warren, B. (2000). *Professional development and children's understanding of force and motion: Assessment results.* Cambridge, MA: TERC, Chèche Konnen Center.

Rosebery, A. S., Warren, B., & Conant, F. R. (1992). Appropriating scientific discourse: Findings from language minority classrooms. *Journal of the Learning Sciences, 21,* 61–94.

Ruiz-Primo, M. A., & Shavelson, R. J. (1996). Rhetoric and reality in science performance assessments: An update. *Journal of Research in Science Teaching, 33,* 1045–1063.

Schauble, L. (1996). The development of scientific reasoning in knowledge-rich contexts. *Developmental Psychology, 32,* 102–119.

Siegel, H. (in press). Multiculturalism, universalism, and science education: In search of common ground. *Science Education.*

Smith, C., Carey, S., & Wiser, M. (1985). On differentiation: A case study of the development of concepts of size, weight, and density. *Cognition, 21,* 177–233.

Snively, G., & Corsiglia, J. (2001). Discovering indigenous science: Implications for science education. *Science Education, 85,* 6–34.

Solano-Flores, G., Jovanovic, J., Shavelson, R. J., & Bachman, M. (1999). On the development and evaluation of a shell for generating science performance assessments. *International Journal of Science Education, 21,* 293–315.

Solano-Flores, G., & Nelson-Barber, S. (2001). On the cultural validity of science assessments. *Journal of Research in Science Teaching, 38,* 553–573.

Solano-Flores, G., & Shavelson, R. J. (1997). Development of performance assessments in science: Conceptual, practical, and logistical issues. *Educational Measurement: Issues and Practice, 16*(3), 16–25.

Stanley, W. B., & Brickhouse, N. (1994). Multiculturalism, universalism, and science education. *Science Education, 78,* 387–398.

Swift, D. (1992). Indigenous knowledge in the service of science and technology in developing countries. *Studies in Science Education, 20,* 1–28.

Tharp, R. (1982). The effective instruction of comprehension: Results and description of the Kamehameha Early Education Program. *Reading Research Quarterly, 17,* 503–527.

Tharp, R., & Gallimore, R. (1988). *Rousing minds to life: Teaching, learning, and schooling in social context.* Cambridge, England: Cambridge University Press.

Trueba, H. T., & Wright, P. G. (1992). On ethnographic studies and multicultural education. In M. Saravia-Shore & S. Arvizu (Eds.), *Cross-cultural literacy: Ethnographies of communication in multiethnic classrooms* (pp. 299–338). New York: Garland Press.

U.S. National Research Center for TIMSS. (1996). *A splintered vision: An investigation of U.S. science and mathematics education.* Dordrecht, the Netherlands: Kluwer.

Valdés, G. (1996). *Con respeto: Bridging the distances between culturally diverse families and schools.* New York: Teachers College Press.

Villegas, A. M., & Lucas, T. (in press). *Educating culturally responsive teachers: A coherent approach.* Albany: State University of New York Press.

Warren, B., Ballenger, C., Ogonowski, M., Rosebery, A., & Hudicourt-Barnes, J. (2001). Rethinking diversity in learning science: The logic of everyday language. *Journal of Research in Science Teaching, 38,* 529–552.

Warren, B., & Rosebery, A. S. (1995). Equity in the future tense: Redefining relationships among teachers, students, and science in linguistic minority classrooms. In W. G. Secada,

E. Fennema, & L. B. Adajian (Eds.), *New directions for equity in mathematics education* (pp. 298–328). New York: Cambridge University Press.

Warren, B., & Rosebery, A. S. (1996). "This question is just too, too easy!" Students' perspectives on accountability in science. In L. Schauble & R. Glaser (Eds.), *Innovations in learning new environments for education* (pp. 97–125). Mahwah, NJ: Erlbaum.

Warren, B., & Rosebery, A. S. (2001). *Teaching science to at-risk students: Teacher research communities as a context for professional development and school reform* (Final Report, Project 4.1). Cambridge, MA: TERC.

Warren, B., Rosebery, A. S., & Conant, F. R. (1989). *Chèche Konnen: Science and literacy in language minority classrooms* (Tech. Rep. No. 7305). Cambridge, MA: Bolt, Beranek & Newman.

Westby, C., Dezale, J., Fradd, S. H., & Lee, O. (1999). Learning to do science: Influences of language and culture. *Communication Disorders Quarterly, 21,* 50–64.

Williams, H. (1994). A critique of Hodson's "In search of a rationale for multicultural science education." *Science Education, 78,* 515–519.

Chapter 3

Three Decades of Research on Classroom Life: Illuminating the Classroom Communicative Lives of America's At-Risk Students

ARNETHA F. BALL
Stanford University

This exploration of research on classroom life has two goals. First is the goal of revisiting some of the research that has emerged over the past three decades to illuminate classroom life at a broad, overarching level. This has been accomplished by looking at classroom research that focuses on four topics: teachers, students, curriculum, and other internal or external structures that influence classroom life. Trends in the research examining classroom life at a broad or macro level are extracted and summarized through brief snapshots of the research in these four areas over the past three decades. These snapshots provide an overview of this research as a contextual background for the chapter. This review of the research shows how studies conducted within changing social and political contexts reflect the complexities of classroom life and the changes in our perceptions concerning the diverse challenges that have faced education. Over the decades, this macro-level research has revealed the interconnectedness among variables that affect classroom life as a context for learning within a larger sociopolitical setting.

In order to gain a better understanding of the nature of this interconnectedness, my goal in the second part of the chapter is to provide a review of the literature on one key area that permeates and links all aspects of classroom life: research on classroom communication. This section shows how research on classroom discourse has illuminated the communicative lives of America's diverse and at-risk student populations at a micro level. It also considers the notion that macro-level classroom research helped to cultivate a climate that was ripe for the emerging research on this topic at the micro level as well.

I would like to thank the consulting editors, Gloria Ladson-Billings and Carol D. Lee, for their insightful comments on an earlier version of this chapter; Walter G. Secada for his editorial leadership; and Jennifer Tackman for her assistance during the completion of the manuscript. I would also like to thank David T. Hansen and Anika Anthony for their critique and suggestions on various drafts. Support for this work was provided by the Spencer Foundation. That support is gratefully acknowledged.

Some of the passion that underlies the development of this exploration was inspired by a quote that I have taken from Philip Jackson's book *Life in Classrooms*. In the years since it first appeared in 1968, this book has attained the status of a classic, marking a milestone in the close study of classrooms at the most fundamental level. The book was reprinted in 1990, and the author speaks in his new introduction of researchers who seek "to relieve the deeper source of an early uneasiness which sprang from something like a sense of guilt over [their] unwillingness to devote [themselves] to one or more of the pressing educational problems of the day" (p. xviii). In an effort to relieve that earlier sense of guilt—and perhaps to expedite the completion of some unfinished business—many researches have chosen to focus their research on the pressing issues of the day. In reference to this kind of research, Jackson makes the following statement, which I have interpreted as a challenge to the educational community:

In bluntest terms, the question to be addressed is this: If an interpretation of what goes on in classrooms does not point directly to how teaching [and learning] might be improved or how classrooms might be better managed, why bother with it? (Jackson 1990, p. xviii)[1]

Inspired by this quote, I provide in this chapter a summary of important research on classroom life at both the macro and micro levels, arguing that, perhaps, if an interpretation of this research does not point to how teaching and learning might be improved or how classrooms might become better, why bother with it? The first part of the review provides an overview of this research that helps us understand the sociopolitical context of the times. The second part provides a review of the research that emerged within these sociopolitical contexts to investigate classroom life at a micro level through lenses focusing on the oral and written discourses that occur in classrooms. Questions posed include the following: What was the purpose of this research? and What have these researchers been able to accomplish? The final section builds on the existing strands of research that I have identified and uses them as a means for contemplating needed directions for future research. Questions addressed here include: What are the areas of research that need to be addressed concerning classrooms and classroom life? and What is the probability that these areas will be adequately addressed given the current sociopolitical climate?

While some studies have looked at the mundane and seemingly trivial events that fill the bulk of the more than 7,000 accumulated hours of classroom life that occur in the 6 or 7 hours of a student's life each school day over a 12-year period, other studies have turned their attention to the more difficult and substantive issues that help to determine academic success or failure in the lives of students from varied and diverse backgrounds. I choose to focus on these more difficult and substantive studies as we consider the needs of our 21st-century schools.

RESEARCH ON CLASSROOM LIFE AT THE MACRO LEVEL

Our initial understandings of classroom life are first-hand; we were students. Our first understandings of classroom life emerge from our experiences as students. We grew up in schools, spending 6 or more hours a day there, 5 days a week and 9 months a year, interacting with peers and adults while learning a wide range of academic and social lessons. Most of us can recall our first day of school vividly. We entered classrooms as wide-eyed observers, eager to learn, immigrants to a foreign homeland that was unique in its culture and setting, with its own norms, values, procedures, routines, and populations. Aside from the novelty of that very "first day of school," we rarely reflect upon the complexity of the day-to-day experiences within those classroom walls. School was simply a way of life, a routine; it was what we "did" each day, with an ultimate goal of receiving a diploma at graduation. This is an expected milestone in our society, a symbol of collective spirit and shared experience.

Having spent much of our lives in schools, we have a tendency to view ourselves as "experts" on what occurs in classrooms. Intuitively, we know that classrooms are different from what they were like 30, 40, or 50 years ago. But if asked to describe those differences beyond acknowledging an increased presence of technology in many classrooms, most would find themselves at a loss for words. The complexity of the components that come together to compose what we casually refer to as "classroom life" must be consciously deconstructed and brought to a metacognitive level if we are to critically consider important changes over the past 30 years. In the face of recurring calls for school reform, there is much to consider under the umbrella term "classroom life." Reflecting on where the research has been, what we have learned from it, and where we want to go in light of changing variables can help us address these issues more comprehensively.

As we look at the research on classrooms over the past three decades, we realize that researchers have spoken increasingly to the complexity of the life that occurs within them and have demonstrated that capturing an understanding of such complexities is not a simple matter. Lortie (1975) noted that public schools shape our young and influence their life chances. They are among our major social, economic, and political institutions. Yet, despite their pivotal role in our society, up until the 1960s, researchers had conducted relatively little detailed systematic study of the life that goes on within them (Lortie, 1975). The 1960s, however, were a time of social, political, and economic change in this country; it was a time when the themes of social reform, child-centered pedagogy, curriculum change, and self-liberation that had marked the progressive movement decades earlier reappeared, and it was a time when research revealed the unequal attainments of students from different social, cultural, and economic backgrounds. Important events took place to redirect national attention, including the passage of the Economic Opportunity Act of 1964 and Martin Luther King Jr.'s march on Washington, D.C., on August 28, 1963.

The Economic Opportunity Act aided and augmented the community control movement. The law mandated that programs be developed, conducted, and administered with the maximum feasible participation of the residents of the areas and members of the groups served. It called for community action programs to mobilize resources that could be used in a direct attack on the roots of poverty. The act funded community school programs that would bring about a significant shift in the sources of power affecting the control and support of schools and opened a revolution in the politics of educational policy-making (Wayson, 1966, pp. 333–339).

Along with the school and district administration, community groups and minority parents would share in the process of determining how schools would be run. Significant policy-making power was extended to citizens in order to influence schools' personnel, curriculum, and budget levels. The purpose of community control was to increase community participation in the making of school policy, especially for the poor and those not previously involved (Schugurensky, 2002).

The concept of community control over classroom life emerged from attempts to end racism and discrimination in schools. Many disenfranchised groups across the country spoke out against what they perceived to be racism in classrooms because the communities served by the schools had little power over how school funds would be spent, who would be hired or fired as their children's teachers, and the organization of the classrooms. The overriding rationale for community control was its promise for improving the educational process for children. Through the involvement of parents, in a meaningful manner, in the policy making and operations of the school, it was argued that their children would develop a positive orientation towards the school and the educational process. Some of the benefits to the school and the educational process were seen as a lessening of discipline problems and vandalism, and higher academic achievement. (Osborne, 1977)

At about the same time, the subject of open classrooms and open education gained increased recognition from both theorists and researchers (Klein & Eshel, 1980; McPartland & Epstein, 1977; Silberman, 1973; Weber, 1971), reflecting a general consensus that open classrooms shared a common set of characteristics distinguishing them from what are generally called conventional school settings. Some assumptions underlying this movement included the following: (a) Children are innately curious; (b) children will explore their environment if it is not threatening; (c) children have the competence and the right to make significant decisions concerning their own learning; and (d) children who learn something of importance to them wish to share it with others.

The proponents of open classrooms and open education concluded that children would learn best if provided with a variety of readily accessible materials and regular opportunities to freely select the materials that most interested them (Halsted, Bober, & Streit, 1977). Gulley and Norwood (1976) described the open classroom and open education movements as having flexibility in the available space; the role of the teacher as instructor, diagnostician, and evaluator was to ensure the progress of all students and create a humane classroom environment. Cuban compared the patterns of classroom life and instruction that emerged from the data he collected in North Dakota, New York City, Washington, D.C., and elsewhere. He reported:

Like the progressive approaches of a generation earlier, certain teaching practices that can be labeled informal were evident in a considerable number of elementary classrooms, especially in the primary grades. Artifacts of open classrooms include learning centers, tables clustered so that students could speak and work together, increased use of small groups of instruction, and students' relative freedom to move about without securing the teacher's permission. (Cuban, 1993, p. 202)

These open classrooms were designed as large open spaces to accommodate open and flexible forms of classroom life and organization.

This movement, however, which is generally considered to have begun in the mid-1960s, was beginning to fade by the mid-1970s. By that time, concern for basic skills, test scores, and traditional classrooms replaced open classrooms on the agenda of many school boards, superintendents, principals, and teachers. According to Cuban:

> Seldom did more than a fourth of a given district's staff adopt these new approaches. Even fewer teachers employed other informal approaches such as allowing students to decide what to study and how much time to spend on particular topics, or using learning centers as the primary means of instruction. . . . The picture of high school teaching that emerges from these accounts is unmistakably teacher-centered and remarkably akin to what had existed three to four decades earlier. (Cuban, 1993, pp. 202–203)

According to Murphy and Beck (1995), traditional supporters of the civil rights movement, for example, Jewish liberals, began to feel alienated when the movement's leaders changed their focus from integration to community control. And when the community control movement began to call for the dismissal of teachers for racist attitudes, the teachers' unions, which had once supported the movement, withdrew their support. These and other similar issues had a rippling effect across the country on the community control movement. By the end of the 1970s, the movement was losing its popularity. In addition, open classroom spaces were being divided into traditional classroom settings. Larry Cuban (1993) searched to locate some of the reasons for the demise of open classrooms and argued that student-centered instruction had failed to have a major effect on schools because of the conservative nature of teacher culture, the structure of schools, and the fact that schools were primarily interested in the social control and sorting of students.

Lawrence A. Cremin has observed that progressive education declined in part because reform leaders lost touch with community citizens who were not educators. They concentrated on convincing their professional peers to join the reforms and failed to cultivate broader support for educational and social change. It was difficult to retain the resources and enthusiasm needed for sustained change as public opinion became more conservative. In addition, burnout among educational reformers added to the decline of progressive reform in education. Although the community control and open classroom movements were short lived, the seeds that were planted during this period laid a foundation for socially relevant research on the communicative lives of diverse student populations to emerge and to occur along with other research agendas at a micro level for several decades to come.

Following the community control and open classroom movements, the late 1970s was a time when conservatism again dominated the life and structure of most classrooms and schools witnessed the emergence of the accountability movement. In an effort to restore power to professional educators, the accountability movement emphasized testing and instructional practices that were in accordance with specific behavioral objectives that fit the pattern of traditional approaches to classroom instruction. Beginning in the early 1980s and extending to the present, a parallel movement is under way that greatly influences classroom life. Many refer to this movement as the "standards movement." Federal and state commissions, foundations and corporations, and state laws have inundated the nation's schools and classrooms with a wave of policies requiring testing and the raising of academic standards. Preparations for taking local, state, and national exams have overtaken today's classroom life. The creation of standardized achievement tests was also a central feature of national educational policy in the early 1990s. In 1991, federal plans were unveiled for achieving a set of national educational goals by the year 2000. The four main features of that plan were the creation of national standards, national achievement tests, model schools, and incentives for parental choice. These national policies have not changed substantially in the past decade; however, they have had a large impact on the classroom lives of most students.

During each of the movements described, important studies have emerged to provide insightful details concerning classroom life. Among these studies is the work of John Goodlad and his team of researchers. They collected classroom information throughout the 1970s in what was initially called "A Study of Schooling" (Goodlad, 1984). In 1981, Kenneth Sirotnik published a technical report of observations from this study involving more than 1,000 elementary and secondary classrooms in 38 schools across the nation. These schools represented different regions, sizes, and student racial, socioeconomic, and ethnic backgrounds. Classroom data were collected by trained observers who used an instrument to count the number of classroom events that occurred within a 5-minute period, doing so 4 times daily during high school classes and 16 times daily in elementary classrooms. These periodic observations offered continuous pictures of classroom life through snapshots of classroom exchanges.

These brief descriptions were collected in each classroom to locate the activity that was going on, who directed the activity, and the form of grouping used. Several interesting findings concerning classroom life emerged from this research: About two thirds of all classes spent their time on five teacher-centered activities, including preparation or clean-up of assignments, lecturing, explaining or read-alouds, discussion, written assignments, and taking tests or quizzes; approximately half of class time was devoted to teacher talk; and the majority of students at all schooling levels (nearly two thirds in elementary and three fourths in secondary) worked as a total class. Also, the model classroom configuration of interactions included the teacher explaining or lecturing to the entire class or a single student, the teacher asking direct questions or observing students, and the students listening to the teacher or responding to teacher-initiated questions. These observations were generally consistent with National Science Foundation survey data and with "class activities" findings for regular high schools (Cuban, 1993, pp. 225–226).

While Goodlad's and Sirotnik's research during the 1970s and 1980s provided valuable information on classrooms, the qualitative investigations conducted by researchers such as Spindler (1982), Page (1991), and Beane and Brodhagen (2001) provided insights on classroom life that could not be captured through quantitative studies. James Beane and Barbara Brodhagen (2001) discussed research on teaching in middle school classrooms, while Reba Page's (1991) ethnographic study examined classroom interactions in two high schools. Page found that the classroom climate in the regular-track courses she observed was orderly but formal, purposive and academically demanding, exploratory yet spontaneous. The students in these classrooms were described as able, affluent, and college bound. Page (1991) also found that, although the teacher directed the recitation much of the time, students in these courses were encouraged "to inquire, to investigate, to develop their own points of view using skills of critical thinking and analysis" (p. 84). In these regular-track classrooms, there was an air of respect and expectancy regarding what discoveries the day's lesson would produce.

In contrast to these regular-track classrooms, Page found that the climate in the lower-track classrooms she observed could be described either as disorderly, competitive, and chaotic or as no-nonsense, disciplined, and regimented environments where the emphasis on worksheets and practical exercises limited spontaneous engagement with dynamic teaching and learning experiences. Life in these lower-track classrooms consisted of an environment dominated by exchanges of jokes, insults, and anecdotes and an atmosphere in which genuine educational encounters rarely occurred. Students' attendance in these teacher-centered environments was erratic, and these classrooms were perceived as troubling challenges to the prevailing conceptions of classrooms populated by college-bound students. While some innovative programs have emerged over the years to provide creative models of alternative classroom lifestyles, the classrooms so vividly depicted in the studies of Goodlad (1984), Sirotnik (1981), Spindler (1982), Page (1991), and Beane and Brodhagen (2001) can still be observed as the predominant model of classroom life in schools located across the country today.

Research in Four Important Areas Over the Past 30 Years

In studies of classrooms conducted over the past 30 years, innumerable perspectives have been magnified to disclose specific aspects of classroom life and the quality of experiences for students and teachers. Within the many perspectives, four topics have been used most often to categorize studies of classroom life: teachers, students, curriculum, and internal or external structures that subtly or abruptly impact the overall quality of classroom life. The development of research in each of these areas has been affected by the social and political climate of the times, and taken together they reveal major trends that have emerged in the research on classroom life at the macro level.

Research on these four topics has grown steadily over the past three decades. For example, one library search conducted on the topic of "educational research on students in classroom environments" produced 51 sources from 1970 to 1979. When the search was conducted on this same topic for the period 1980 to 1989, 331 references emerged, owing in part to the expanded presence of research focusing on issues such as women and gender, microcomputers in classrooms, and diversity as they relate to educational research and life within classroom environments. When the same topic was searched for the years 1990 to 2001, the number of references increased to 569, in part as a result of the emergence of research focusing on mass testing, assessment, and national standards, particularly in inner-city and underachieving schools, and on reform issues, technology and its potential for restructuring learning, and authentic instruction as it relates to life within classroom environments.

Research on Teachers

The teacher plays an obvious and central role in creating the classroom environment. Therefore, a large amount of research on classroom life over the last three decades has focused on teachers and/or teaching. One point of considerable consensus in this research is that improvements in classroom teaching and learning can occur only through the direct involvement of teachers. According to Cuban (1993), efforts to reform education that ignore the expertise of the practicing teacher are doomed to fail, as they have in the past.

Research that emerged during the late 1960s and early 1970s focused on social and political reform, child-centered education, and open classrooms, while much of the research that emerged in the late 1970s focused on classroom control. By the late 1970s, Lortie's (1975) research confirmed that classrooms were complex spaces in which the teacher generally worked to maintain control and a sense of order in addition to arousing and sustaining students' interest. Lortie further noted that most teaching behavior was addressed to groups of children (1975, pp. 184, 186). As we approached the 1980s, Grannis (1979) noted that although classrooms varied in design and populations, there were certain features common to virtually all classrooms, including crowding of pupils, compulsory school attendance, and the expectation that teachers would foster learning. The manner in which these features are dealt with in a classroom constitutes the core problem of control in schooling.

The most common solution applied to the problem of control is implementation of the model of the "standard classroom," that is, a teacher-centered classroom in which students sit in rows and the dominant focus next to learning is control. Alternative classroom settings that appear to be associated with differences in classroom life can best be understood as variations on the standard classroom model. In some of these alternative classrooms, higher support conditions and the positive cast of classroom activities seem to reduce the disorder and alienation found in some of the more standard classrooms, particularly with regard to disadvantaged and ethnically diverse children. However, as a number of studies suggest, differences stemming from students' and teachers' styles within a classroom are more prominent than differences stemming from the structure of standard versus alternative educational settings.

In the 1990s, Goodson (1994) and Gale (1996) provided updated discussions of teachers' life and work and their voices of authority in the modern classroom. Other studies focused on classroom teachers as researchers and teachers' involvement in action research. These studies argued that classroom research helps teachers explore their classrooms in a focused and systematic way to discover what works with their students, to discover whether problems can be solved by changes in the classroom environment, and to position themselves as agents of their own learning and change (Bissex, 1994; Cochran-Smith & Lytle, 1992; Rose, 1989).

Michael Tanner's (1992) book, *Classroom Research by Classroom Teachers,* celebrates teachers as lifelong learners of the art of teaching and shares the classroom research of 21 teachers. Ball and Cohen (1999) focused on the importance of learning in and from the practice of teaching. They argued that teachers must become insightful in listening to and interpreting students' ideas about academic subjects if we are to realize current visions of school reform in which schools are transformed into places where all students learn with understanding and are able to accomplish intellectually rigorous work. In addition, if we are to realize these visions of school reform, they argued that teachers must come to see their students as capable of thinking and reasoning, and they must expand the interpretive frames they bring to their observations of students so that they can see more possibilities in what students do (Ball & Cohen, 1999).

Over the past three decades, there has been a growing demand for teachers to meet the needs of students from diverse backgrounds and a call for teacher professional development in this area. As issues of diversity emerged as a central area of focus in schools, these issues also began to show up in the research literature. One study by Christine Bennett (1979) investigated the nature of a classroom's "climate of acceptance" in desegregated schools. In this study, verbal initiations and student friendships across race and gender were examined in 41 seventh- and eighth-grade classrooms. Teachers were interviewed and attitudinal questionnaires completed. The study revealed clear patterns of interracial friendships, verbal interaction patterns, and four distinct classroom climate types that ranged from low to high levels of acceptance across race and gender groups; all of these elements were affected by teacher attitude.

In comparing teachers in urban schools with those in suburban schools, Orfield and Reardon (1993) found profound differences in quality of educational opportunity and quality of teaching staff, with urban schools functioning at a grossly inferior level. With the realization that teacher quality is the best predictor of students' academic success, preparation of teachers to teach diverse populations stands out as a critical area for improvement in teacher education. Orfield and Reardon's (1993) description of the current teaching force in urban schools draws attention to the need to prepare more excellent teachers who are committed to improving education for all students and the education of urban students in particular. Research that focuses on the preparation of excellent teachers to teach diverse student populations has been prominent in the literature in recent decades and continues to be an issue of central concern in the early part of the 21st century (see Grant & Secada, 1990, and Ladson-Billings, 1995, for excellent reviews of this research; see also Darling-Hammond, 1986, 1990, 1992, 1995, 1996, 1997, and Ball, 2000a, 2000b, 2000c, for recent research on the continued challenges of reform in teacher preparation programs).

Research on Students

A second critical component shaping the development of research on classroom life is the student. The work of Rosenthal and Jacobson (1968) revealed that within a given classroom, if the teacher expected greater intellectual growth from students, those children showed much greater growth, even after control for differences in initial academic achievement. In this research, teachers were told that a group of students were gifted, even if this was not the case. And these children performed better if the teacher had higher expectations for them. This phenomenon was referred to as "Pygmalion in the classroom."

In the 1970s, the underlying conceptions of students, student self-identities, and perceptions of what students know occupied an important dimension of the research on classroom life. Much of this research focused on student achievement and how that achievement is influenced by perceptions of the resources that students bring to the classroom environment. Looking at the lives of students in classrooms during the 1970s, Rand and Rand (1978) found that students performed better on tests when they were in a relaxed atmosphere versus a stressful classroom environment. Nielsen and Moos (1978) found that high school students have different exploration preferences within classrooms that differ in terms of social exploration climates. They noted that, in high exploration classrooms, students high in exploration preference were more satisfied and better adjusted. Tjosvold and Santamaria (1978) found that students are more confident and more likely to become involved in classroom decision making in elementary science classrooms where teachers support their students' competence to make classroom decisions. Numerous studies document successful classrooms that encourage students to engage in purposeful and constructive classroom activities (Reid, 1999).

In the late 1970s, Sara Lawrence Lightfoot (1978) noted that the predominance of classroom research focused on teachers, neglecting the power and presence of children in classroom life. Lightfoot proposed that this bias in the research provided a partial vision and unrealistic picture of classroom life and supported the irresponsible, dependent, and powerless roles assigned to children in our culture, particularly in the case of students of color. Indictments such as these challenged researchers to conduct more student-centered investigations, and studies on issues related to student diversity and gender also emerged. In the 1980s, Rosser (1989) found that the presence of sexist classroom behaviors and the absence of information about the achievements, roles, and experiences of women from the curriculum left female students alienated from what they were learning.

According to Applebee (1991), research on the education of "at-risk" students received more attention in the late 1980s as a result of the increased focus on their continuing patterns of unacceptably low achievement scores on standardized tests. With a growing recognition that students who were once considered minority populations were now becoming the majority populations in many schools, it became acceptable to focus attention on the gap in achievement scores between historically at-risk students, who were predominantly students of color, and students who have historically fared well in schools, who generally come from middle- and upper-class European American backgrounds.

Gross imbalances in the quality of teachers, school resources, and rates of achievement have drawn the attention of researchers to this area of investigation. Wauters et al. (1989) found that, among 200 Alaskan high school seniors completing the Productivity Environmental Preference Survey (PEPS), natives and nonnatives differed significantly from each other and from the PEPS norm group on selected aspects of learning styles. As a result, he offered pedagogical recommendations for Alaskan students.

Santamaria's (1978) work looked at the effects of cooperation and teacher support on student attitudes toward decision making in the elementary science classroom. Ellison, Boykin, Towns, and Stokes (1990) conducted a study designed to gain descriptive insights into the routines, practices, perceptions, and interactions that make up the everyday ecology of classrooms serving African American children from low-income backgrounds. These researchers looked at five dimensions of the students' classroom lives: their social/psychological relations, technical core instruction, classroom physical structure and organizational routines, discipline and classroom management, and their teachers' attitudes, perceptions, and expectations. Results of this study indicated that students had positive attitudes toward schooling despite the fact that the prevalent cultural themes presented in their classrooms were associated with mainstream rather than African American culture. They also indicated the importance of a teacher's personality and early morning demeanor in setting the students' tone toward instruction for the day. Other research on the classroom lives of students included Ruberg's (1996) work on student interaction and participation within a computer-mediated communication environment that encouraged experimentation, sharing of early ideas, increased and more distributed participation, and collaborative thinking and Mael's (1998) report of mixed findings on the impact of single-sex versus coeducational schooling.

Research on Curriculum

The curriculum is a third major component that contributes to research on classroom life. According to Cuban (1993):

After Sputnik, reformers in the 1950s and 1960s generated math, science, and social studies texts and materials in which students handled Cuisenaire rods and light bulbs, simulated situations, and in general behaved like scientists. While many of the enthusiastic proponents of and participants in the change effort ended up disappointed in what actually materialized in classrooms across the country, the focus upon children's interests and motivation and the tying of content to contemporary concerns echoed the work of earlier generations. The themes of social reform, child-centered pedagogy, curriculum change, and self-liberation that had marked the progressive movement decades earlier reappeared in the late 1960s. (p. 152)

Research on curriculum over the past three decades has focused on issues of content knowledge, development of higher order thinking skills, problem-solving and problem-based learning, relating curriculum to the background of learners, and the need to link curriculum to assessment. When Sinclair and Ward (1979) examined curricula that considered learning environments, a set of premises to assist in curriculum planning and curricular priorities emerged. Sinclair and Ward (1979) found that although the principal is a key leader for initiating curriculum change, the teacher must ultimately decide how curriculum improvements are put into practice. In 1999, Reid and Golub offered discussions about classroom practices and curriculum that encouraged students to learn purposefully and constructively by reflecting on their own learning processes and by making connections between what they read and the lives they lead. Extending from middle and high school through college, the essays in Reid and Golub's book provide practical and innovative ideas to establish a climate that supports reflection, to help students make connections via multiple discursive processes, and to help both students and teachers engage in effective self-assessment.

In recent years, Labbo and Reinking (1999) have examined the multiple realities of technology in literacy instruction, Ruddell (2000) has looked at literacy curricula in upper elementary grades, and Singer, Marx, Krajick, and Chambers (2000), as curriculum developers who realize that standards can transform the nature of students' experiences within a classroom, have considered the impact of standards on their designs. Also, in 2000, the National Council of Teachers of English published the book *Trends and Issues in Secondary English*, which provides an up-to-date discussion of curricular issues that affect classroom life, including technology and diversifying the curriculum in multicultural classrooms.

Internal and External Structures

Working from the outside in, structures play a crucial role in affecting the quality of classroom life long before teachers and students walk through the door. In addition to the presence of highly motivated and well-prepared teachers, each of the following can have a major impact on the life of classrooms: size and condition of the classroom; presence of permanent structures such as sinks and counter or floor space crucial in art, science, and other activities; availability and arrangement of desks and tables; floor coverings; peripheral devices such as chalk/white boards, overhead projectors, and various technologies (e.g., telephones, TVs, VCRs, and computers); presence and condition of textbooks, tradebooks, science equipment, and math manipulatives; and last, but certainly not least, access to and abundance of supplies such as paper, pencils, and art materials. Students who have supplies and equipment at their disposal can design and build an assortment of potentially innovative and imaginative creations. The same creations can be constructed without an abundance of choices, but the time and maintenance required in makeshift spaces can alter the overall experience to varying extents.

Less obvious structures, such as those set in place by teachers, administrators, and/or policymakers, can also affect what happens in classrooms. For example, scheduling and use of time are primary driving factors. Some middle and secondary schools break subjects into 50-minute, isolated classes in which students are "randomly" placed into tracks based on academic program, special needs, elective preferences, and availability of seats per class (see the tracking studies of Oakes, 1985). In contrast, other schools may try to implement block scheduling in which "schools within schools" house students in teams with teachers who collaborate in order to implement interdisciplinary studies in longer blocks of science/math or language arts/humanities. Both structures have advantages and disadvantages, have different obstacles to success (see Oakes, 1985), and are closely connected to educational philosophy and issues of power and social class (Anyon, 1981).

At all grade levels and in all classrooms, teachers and students use procedures and routines and methods of organization and classroom management to structure and manage the daily events of classroom life (see Goodlad, 1984; Jackson, 1990; Lortie, 1975). Visions of how schools should be constructed can affect overall structures and, in turn, affect students' classroom life. Large, comprehensive high schools with large student populations can provide a very different educational life than that of small schools in rural areas. While the larger urban high school might provide more course offerings and extracurricular opportunities, personal connections among students and between students and faculty might be sacrificed—strongly affecting classroom life.

Perhaps one of the most influential factors affecting classroom life is a school's location. As in real estate, location can be a telling factor of what students will experience within particular classrooms at a specific school. School funding varies drastically from state to state, county to county, and sometimes even school to school within a district. Disparities can be astounding. Not only can the age, square footage, and condition of buildings be contrasted; provision of resources for capital and consumable budgets can ultimately lead to vast dissimilarities in allocation of funds. These stark inequities are not difficult to notice. While some schools are forced to cut programs in sports and the arts, other schools are buying state-of-the art equipment and sending students on overseas enrichment tours.

These disparities result in very different classroom life experiences. Aside from the obvious sources of funding, there are other means of attaining funds from external sources. While parents in one community can reach into deep pockets for donations, families in other communities may look to school and government subsidies to help provide their students with basic needs, as seen in the free and reduced breakfast and lunch programs at some schools. These contrasting conditions are not new; nor is obvious discrimination that crosses socioeconomic lines. Arguments in Supreme Court cases such as *Plessy v. Ferguson* and *Brown v. Board of Education* illustrated these disparities on the basis of obvious racial discrimination.

In recent times, other studies indicate that the same disparities continue to haunt our nation's schools. From 1988 to 1990, Jonathan Kozol documented the extremes in power, wealth, and poverty present in America's public schools. *Savage Inequalities*, published in 1992, provided a searing portrait of the education system and a call to action by the public. Schauble and Glaser (1996) and Schauble and Beane (1996) focused on innovations in learning environments outside schools. Schauble and Glaser's (1996) collection of 13 articles described informal learning environments that occur outside traditional school settings, covered research-supported strategies for helping both students and teachers engage with and master concepts in school subject matter, and reviewed school reform and current knowledge about practices and principles most likely to lead to successful school changes that may result in improved classroom life.

RESEARCH ON CLASSROOM LIFE AT THE MICRO LEVEL

As stated earlier in this chapter, research has spoken increasingly to the complexity of life that goes on in classrooms. It has also been noted that capturing an understanding of these complexities is not a simple matter, particularly if we seek to gain an understanding of them in heuristic ways. If we want to accomplish these goals, we not only need to know that teachers play a central role in fostering learning in the classroom; we also need to explore, describe, and understand how particularly meaningful teaching and learning practices are constructed over time in the day-to-day discourse of a newly constructed group culture such as a classroom or a collaborative study group. We not only need to know that students' achievement is influenced by teachers' perceptions and expectations; we also need to understand how these perceptions and expectations are made evident to students through normative discourse patterns in the classroom, through discourse rules and participation rights, and through teacher and student script patterns that develop in the classroom.

Also, we need to understand how teacher-centered classrooms differ from student-centered classrooms in terms of the interactional dynamics that dictate who talks, when, and for what purposes. We not only need to know that curriculum development now emphasizes higher order thinking skills, problem solving, and problem-based learning; we also need to understand the cognitive and linguistic demands of the instructional materials. In addition, we not only need to know that internal and external structures play a central role in creating the life of the classroom; we also need to understand contextual factors that accompany the language in use. These contextual factors include the material setting, policy mandates that influence classroom practices, and cultural, historical, and institutional factors. Over the past three decades, study of classroom discourse has become an important theoretical and methodological perspective for investigating these areas in order to gain a deeper, more textured understanding of classroom life and the academic success or failure of our nation's diverse student populations.

Language is the medium and the vehicle through which teaching and learning take place, whether it is through oral or written language, visual literacies, multiple literacies, or verbal and nonverbal symbolic systems. While the literature review just provided gives us insights into the overarching complex interconnections that come together to shape classroom life, we also need an understanding of the research examining how language influences classroom life at a micro level. Researchers who focus on classroom discourse use methodological approaches that are particularly well suited to addressing these types of questions. According to Gee and Green (1998), the research on classroom discourse has provided understandings of the ways in which opportunities for learning are constructed across time, groups, and events; how knowledge constructed in classrooms shapes, and is shaped by, discursive activity and social practices; how patterns of practice simultaneously support and constrain access to the academic content of the "official" curriculum; and how opportunities for learning are influenced by the actions of actors beyond the classroom setting. Therefore, in addition to describing research that investigates classroom life at a macro level through lenses that focus on teachers, students, curriculum, and structures, the sections that follow provide a review of research that investigates classroom life at a micro level through lenses that focus on the oral and written discourses occurring in classrooms.

Approaches to discourse analysis have emerged to examine participant structures and how knowledge is constructed and shaped in educational settings. These approaches have emerged from the theoretical and methodological traditions developed in several disciplines, including linguistics, sociolinguistics, applied linguistics, sociology, psychology, anthropology, literary studies, law, medicine, and business. According to Luke (1995), two major demographic and socioeconomic changes since World War II have placed issues of language, discourse, and difference on the educational agenda: expanded recognition of the educational entitlements of migrants, people of color, indigenous peoples, and women and the shifting labor demands toward service and information. Luke (1995) further noted that

the emergence of postcolonial perspectives on cultural and linguistic differences (McCarthy, 1993; Williams, 1994) is hardly a figment of political liberalism or so-called political correctness. It is in part an attempt by those who have been and, in some cases, remain colonized and colonizers to reconnoiter and deconstruct imperialist histories and institutions (Applebee, 1991; Dirlik, 1994; Puar, 1994). And it is in part the product of migration and language change, multiculturalism, and multilingualism in countries that previously conceived of themselves in monocultural and assimilationist terms. This situation has put the matter of languages squarely on the table for educators, whether in the ameliorative terms of second-language instruction, multilingual curriculum, and broader agendas for workplace literacy and productive diversity or through more conservative responses of state monolingualism, exclusionary "cultural literacy" agendas, and legislative and legal moves to exclude alien residents from schools and other public services. (p. 4)

Thus, over the past 30 years, there has been a shift toward research that focuses on cultures, languages, and discourses in classroom life and research that demonstrates the increasing promise and validity of sociohistorical and sociocultural psychology (Moll, 1990; Wertsch, 1991). With a growing recognition of the right to learn for all students (Darling-Hammond, 1997), research has emerged on meeting the needs of culturally and linguistically diverse students and women in classrooms. The classical questions concerning who succeeds in schools, who fails, and why have become more relevant than ever. Discourse analysis has emerged as a tool for addressing such questions. It is in this context that analyses of language, text, and discourse have emerged to address issues of educational access to intellectual, cultural, political, and economic resources. As I review the research that has developed in these areas, I ask the following questions: "What was the purpose of this research?" "What have these researchers accomplished?" and "Where do we need to go from here?"

Purpose of the Research

With increasing demands to meet the needs of culturally and linguistically diverse students and women in the classroom, research examining the role of discourse in classroom life began to focus on questions of who succeeds and who fails in schools and the role of oral and written discourse in the success and/or failure of these students. It is in this historical and demographic context that the role of language, discourse, and text in classroom life has become a focal educational issue. Within this context, reform efforts seek to ensure that educational access and equity will include not only opportunities to acquire skills but also opportunities to have rich classroom life experiences as students learn to question and to challenge prevailing cultural, gender, and social class perspectives (Luke, 1995; Moll, 1990).

According to Luke (1995), until the 1980s, few education researchers used discourse-analytic theories and methods. Those that existed relied heavily on the application of interactional sociolinguistics, ethnography of communication, and ethnomethodology to the study of classroom talk (e.g., Cazden, John, & Hymes, 1972; Mehan, 1979; Sinclair & Coulthard, 1975). Much of this work focused on the consequences of language, literacy, and cultural variation for students from migrant, indigenous, poor, and minority groups and on the educational implications of differential patterns of classroom talk within the context of classroom life (for reviews, see Bloome & Green, 1984; Cazden, 1988).

Cazden (1986b) discussed several approaches to discourse analysis that emerged during the 1970s and 1980s to examine classroom events and participation structures, features of teacher talk and cultural differences in the classroom, interactions among peers, and classroom discourse and student learning. The emerging goal of educational research at that time was to help us understand how language unites the social and the cognitive and to help us gain insight into the social events of classroom life. Discussions emerged concerning the work by Vygotsky on speaking and thinking and Leont'ev on the role of culturally organized experience in the development of mind. While much of the prior research had focused on recitation lessons in which the teacher controlled both development of topic and turn taking in the classroom, seminal work emerged such as Sinclair and Coulthard's (1975) classroom discourse analysis based on speech act theory and Mehan's (1979) applied conversational analysis of classrooms. Also, Cazden's (2001) book *Classroom Discourse* investigated discourse within the framework of applied linguistics and discussed research drawn from elementary, secondary, and postsecondary classrooms, and Lemke (1990) presented a discourse analysis of a science lesson.

Early research also focused on second-language pedagogy and child development and the growing body of literature on social construction in classroom and curriculum. These remain significant studies providing valuable pedagogical tools; however, as pointed out by Luke (1995), many of these early approaches focused principally on the study of language development and use per se rather than on the relationship between discourse and larger social formation. These earlier approaches tended to analyze language as a way of explaining the psychological intents, motivations, skills, and competencies of individuals rather than explaining how discourse systematically constructs versions of the social and natural worlds and positions subjects in relations of power (Abdullah, Kamberelis, & McGinley, 1992; Williams, 1992). Although the perspective that he articulates has been challenged, Luke (1995) proposes the use of critical discourse analysis, an orientation derived from poststructuralist, neo-Marxian, and feminist theory and from critical linguistics, to address those issues.

Pinnell (1991) reminds us that a great deal of daily classroom life is conducted in spoken language. She discusses the critical role of negotiation, discussion, and debate and the need for effective oral communication if classroom life is to be successful for all students. Pinnell's work reviews the research on how children learn to be effective speakers and listeners. She also discusses the implications of this research as it relates to teaching and the current interests in developing school curricula to help all students become effective oral language users. Deborah Hicks (1995) provides a review of recent theoretical perspectives on the relationships between discourse and the processes of teaching and learning. Viewing discourse as communication that is socially situated and that sustains social positioning in face-to-face interaction and between authors and readers in written texts, Hicks discusses discourse in classroom life as a mediator of students' learning and considers academic discourse in the classroom, intertextuality and sociolinguistic diversity, and classroom discourse and educational reform. Her review is informative and, when viewed in conjunction with the reviews provided by Wertsch (1991) and Luke (1995), sheds light on the development of recent research on discourse in classroom life.

In the 1990s, concepts of voice and subjectivity emerged as a central focus of many studies on the education of women and girls (e.g., Davies, 1989; Fine, 1992; Gilbert & Taylor, 1991; Lewis, 1993) and students of color (e.g., McElroy-Johnson, 1993; Nieto, 1992). During this same period, discourse analysis was used as a tool for investigating teacher and student positioning in teacher education (e.g., Britzman, 1991; McGuire & Weiner, 1994; Popkewitz, 1993) and the construction of particular areas of school knowledge and curriculum in textbooks and in face-to-face classroom interaction (e.g., Baker & Freebody, 1989; Lee, 1995; Luke, 1988; Singh, 1993). Ethnographic and case study research has also been used to enrich investigations of language use and social interactions in classrooms (e.g., J. L. Green & Dixon, 1993; Michaels, 1981; Michaels & Collins, 1984) as well as narrative analyses of written and spoken texts (Barone, 1992; Rogers, 1993). According to Luke (1995), much of this work has attempted to move beyond descriptive research and use discourse analysis to critique and challenge dominant institutional practices.

In a similar vein, Gutierrez, Baquedano-Lopez, and Tejeda (1999) used discourse analysis to focus on the organization of learning in a largely Latino, working poor, and immigrant-populated classroom. Using examples from an ethnographic study of the literacy practices of one dual-immersion elementary school classroom, these researchers illustrated classroom literacy practices within a culture of collaboration in order to investigate how hybrid activities, roles, and practices can lead to productive contexts for development.

Research on Classroom Writing Over the Past 30 Years

Over the past three decades, the study of writing in classrooms has revealed much about the lives of students and teachers in these contexts. It is therefore important that, as we explore the development of research on classroom life over the past 30 years, we consider the emergence of studies on classroom writing and seminal studies that have emerged in this area. Much of the educational research on writing in traditional and nontraditional classrooms is designed to help us understand how written language unites the social and the cognitive and to help us gain insights into the events of classrooms that support student achievement and acquisition of effective communication systems.

Beginning in the late 1970s and continuing today, anthropologists, linguists, and psychologists have tried to specify writing's varied functions and forms and its usefulness in a range of situations. Some researchers have looked at oral and written language embedded within ways of living and how it is influenced by different social and economic resources and opportunities, religious beliefs, values, and motivations (Heath, 1983; Philips, 1974; Scollon & Scollon, 1979; Scribner & Cole, 1981a).

With the focus on how writing develops over time, stages (sequences of described behaviors) were explored in the 1970s as ways to describe how children develop written language abilities (Graves, 1983). Researchers referred to specific "strands" of language growth, that is, how children come to understand the orthographic encoding system (Ferreiro & Teberosky, 1982; Read, 1975), the intricacies of graphic segmentation and punctuation (Sulzby, 1986), and the evolution from early forms to more conventional writing (Sulzby, 1986). Ethnographic and sociolinguistic research has illustrated how writing activities are socially organized within the ongoing life of particular groups (Basso, 1974; Diaz, Moll, & Mehan, 1986; Heath, 1983; Philips, 1974; Schieffelin & Cochran-Smith, 1984).

A substantial body of sociolinguistic research developed to document some of the linguistic characteristics of nonmainstream, low-prestige varieties of American English (Labov, 1972b; Wolfram & Fasold, 1974), including African American vernacular English (AAVE) (Ball, 1992; Baugh, 1990, 1992; Edwards, 1992; Fasold, 1972; Kochman, 1972; Labov, 1972a; Poplack, Shana, & Tagliamonte, 1994; Wolfram, 1969), Puerto Rican English (Wolfram, 1974; Zentella, 1981), Appalachian English (Wolfram & Christian, 1976), varieties of American Indian English (Leap, 1993; Wolfram, Christian, Potter, & Leap, 1979), Vietnamese English (Wolfram & Hatfield, 1984), and others (Amastae & Elias-Olivares, 1982; Ferguson & Heath, 1981; Labov, 1980). The primary findings of this work were that nonmainstream varieties of English—in fact, all language varieties—are as complex and as regularly patterned as are mainstream varieties. These researchers confirmed that although speakers of these nonmainstream varieties often have different linguistic rules that govern their grammars or use of lexical items, they do not, contrary to conventional "wisdom" among mainstreamers, have linguistic deficits.

Other sociolinguistic research focused on culturally embedded aspects of language use (both oral and written) rather than on grammatical characteristics of nonstandard dialects. Much of this work has been carried out within the conceptual framework developed by Hymes (1972, 1974), what he termed "the ethnography of communication" (Saville-Troike, 1982). These studies have taken place both within classrooms

(Ball, 1995a; Bloome, 1987; Cazden et al., 1972; Charrow, 1981; Cook-Gumperz, 1986; Gilmore & Glatthorn, 1982; Green & Wallat, 1981; Saravia-Shore & Arvizu, 1992) and within home and community contexts (Ball, 1995b; Cintron, 1997; Delgado-Gaitan, 1990, 1996; Delgado-Gaitan & Trueba, 1991; Farr, 1993, 1994a, 1994b, 1994c, 2000; Farr & Guerra, 1995; Gumperz, 1982a, 1982b; Heath, 1983; Kochman, 1981; Mahiri, 1994; Moss, 1994; Scollon & Scollon, 1981, 1995; Tannen, 1982, 1984; Valdés, 1992, 1996; Zentella, 1981). These researchers have confirmed that ways of using language can vary extensively from one cultural group to another and that such difference can cause miscommunication through written as well as through oral exchanges.

Classrooms are particularly significant arenas for such cross-cultural communication, and the learning of writing, in particular, is often a context in which communicative systems not only differ but conflict. That is, when learning to write, many students from nonmainstream groups are faced with a conflict between their own cultural and linguistic systems (and their own sense of identity) and those of the standard academic written language. The difficulties inherent in resolving such conflicts enhance our understanding of the classroom lives of these students and provide one explanation for low literacy levels among diverse populations.

A few other studies have focused on the writing of culturally and linguistically diverse students—shedding light on the classroom life experiences of these students (Balester, 1993; Ball, 1992, 1995c, 1997; Farr Whiteman, 1981; Reed, 1981; Smitherman, 1994; Valdés, 1992, 1996; Valdez, 1981). Studies also have focused on written literacies in homes and other nonschool community settings among culturally and linguistically diverse students (Ball, 1995b; Heath, 1983; Mahiri, 1994; Scribner & Cole, 1981b; Street, 1984, 1993; Taylor & Dorsey Gaines, 1988). Other researchers have contributed to our understanding of the language and literacy resources that diverse student populations bring to their classroom experience (Delpit, 1996; Gutierrez, 1992; Lee, 1992; Means, 1991; Moll, 1987; Redd, 1992).

Staton, Shuy, Kreeft Payton, and Reed (1988) studied the use of dialogue journals in a sixth-grade classroom in a multicultural section of Los Angeles. Even those students who had minimal literacy skills in English were asked to write at least three sentences per day. The teacher did not evaluate this writing but, instead, responded to it as a natural form of communication between two people. Over the course of a year, the researchers found substantial growth in writing quantity, elaboration of student-initiated topics, fluency, and control of English syntax (Kreeft & Shuy, 1985; Staton et al., 1988). Moreover, these students experienced, some for the first time, writing and reading for a purpose of their own within the context of classroom life.

Heath and Branscombe (1985) also showed that structuring activities that combine functional and interactive communication enhances students' classroom life experiences and helps them learn how to write and read in mainstream academic ways. In this study, 9th-grade remedial-track English students (primarily nonmainstream African Americans and a few nonmainstream Whites in a southern city) being taught by Branscombe wrote and read letters to and from the researchers, their families, and Branscombe's regular 11th-grade students. As in the journals of the Staton et al. study, these letters emphasized "real" communication, and, over the course of the year, the students learned much about school literacy in the process. As students wrote back to the teacher, they began to model standard academic literacy, expository prose, and mainstream reasoning processes.

The research on language variation and writing has identified particular linguistic features characteristic of the "home language" of various groups that speak nonmainstream varieties of English that occur in the writing of children, adolescents, and adults from these groups (Ball, 1998). Research in this area has identified similar characteristics in the writing of AAVE speakers, Latino and Indian bilinguals, and deaf users of American sign language. A particular challenge to researchers is investigation of assessment of the writing of students from diverse linguistic backgrounds within the classroom setting. Ball (1999) discusses issues of assessment with culturally and linguistically diverse students and provides examples of instances in which characteristic features of students' home language appear in their written text at the phonological, syntactic, semantic, and discourse levels. Ball (1997) discusses how including the voices of teachers from diverse backgrounds can help improve the classroom writing lives of students and broaden debates about the reform of writing instruction.

Other studies have provided an understanding of principles underlying effective writing instruction (for a more detailed review of sociolinguistic research and its relevance to the writing lives of students in classrooms, see Farr, 1986). These reviews synthesize research on culturally and linguistically diverse groups and provide specific examples, drawn from the research, of particular conflicts between mainstream and nonmainstream communicative systems. Farr (1986) provided examples of conflicts at the phonological, syntactic, semantic, pragmatic, and discourse levels of language, as well as the broader cultural level of language use. Smitherman (1994) published a chapter titled " 'The Blacker the Berry, the Sweeter the Juice': African American Student Writers and the National Assessment of Educational Progress" (NAEP). In her study, she analyzed the degree to which African American verbal traditions survive in the classroom writing lives of African American students across a generational time span. A total of 867 essays from the 1984 and 1988/1989 NAEP were subjected to primary trait and holistic scoring analysis and were ranked in terms of degree of African American discourse. These scores were compared with the scores given by NAEP raters and with scores from the 1969 and 1979 NAEP.

Results indicated that (a) no correlation existed between a discernibly African American discourse style and the production of Black English vernacular (BEV) syntax, supporting results of earlier studies of the 1969 and 1979 NAEP essays; (b) the more discernibly African American the discourse, the higher the primary trait and holistic scores, and the less discernibly African American the discourse, the lower the primary trait and holistic scores, contrary to earlier studies; and (c) "imaginative/narrative" essays continued to be Black students' strong suit. The findings suggested that students who used a Black expressive discourse style in their classroom writing had higher NAEP scores than those who did not. Smitherman's conclusions included recommendations to writing instructors that are sure to affect the classroom lives of African American students in positive ways. These recommendations encourage writing instructors to capitalize on the strengths of African American cultural discourse; encourage students toward the field dependency style, which would enable them to produce more powerful, meaningful, and highly rated essays; and deemphasize concerns about BEV grammar (Smitherman, 1994).

As the research on writing in classrooms has emerged over the past 30 years, some studies have focused on how interpretations of what goes on in classrooms can point to how teaching and learning might be improved and how classroom life might become better. In *Writing Matters*, Freedman and Hechinger (1992) discuss recent research designed to create a better understanding of how writing is best learned, taught, and used for learning in school and life. Research conducted by Dyson (1989) indicates that many low-income African American children may bring resources to school that are often overlooked. Matthew Downey (1992) moves from Dyson and Stack's findings about how children first learn to write to examine how writing can help spark the interest of third graders in history. Valdés and Sanders (1999) discuss the development of writing in nonnative, ESL-background students.

In *Untapped Resources: "Styling" in Black Students' Writing for Black Audiences*, Teresa Redd (1992) discusses two studies that compared the impact of Black and White audiences on Black students' writing style. Results of the studies revealed that significant occurrences of "styling" in the students' writing could be elicited by varying the audiences to which students write. Findings suggested that assignments for a Black audience can elicit "styling" that may be absent or rare in writing for a White audience and that teachers of Black students should be aware of the African American tradition so that they can help students become aware of the resources they bring to the classroom (Redd, 1992). In "Probing the Structure of Mathematical Writing," David Clarke (1993) examined the use of student journal writing as a mode of mathematical communication in the classroom. The study demonstrates a link between language and mathematics and suggests a relationship between students' mathematical writings and their perceptions of mathematics.

In "Analyzing the Role of the Vernacular in Student Writing: A Social Literacies Approach," Blackburn and Stern (2000) use a social literacies perspective to analyze a rap written by a high school student. The researchers examine the student's uses of AAVE and "standard" English and conclude that teachers and researchers must engage students' literacy practices in order to enrich classroom life and to conduct meaningful and socially just research. The study reinforces the need to continue the scholarly debate about the wisdom and efficacy of trying to impose "standard" English on all speakers and writers and argues that new ways to validate alternative literacies should be found that can be used as a means of helping students become proficient users of dominant literacies (Blackburn & Stern, 2000). Much of the research reported here on writing in classrooms deals with the researchers' desire to explore ways to improve educational practice and classroom life and points to new strategies aimed at reducing educational failure.

What Have Researchers Accomplished Through This Work?

The early psycholinguistic research had several significant educational consequences, beginning with language-based studies that established a strong foundation for continued classroom studies based on language learning and development and on studies of English as a second language that eventually had an impact on curriculum and instruction. Subsequent work by sociolinguists and ethnographers of communication stressed the social character of language use (Gumperz & Hymes, 1972; cf. Hymes, 1995). This research systematically connected language development with socialization, language use with norms and roles, and situated schools and classrooms as discourse communities with their own conventions of appropriateness. According to Luke (1995), sociolinguistic research tended to explain texts by reference to rule-governed, learned social interaction and performance (e.g., Ochs & Schieffelin, 1983; Schieffelin & Ochs, 1986). Much of this research was initiated to help us better understand how to improve teaching and learning in classrooms.

In 1988, Cazden explicitly stated that she came to language acquisition research in the early 1960s out of interest in two questions: What kinds of individual or cultural differences in children's language influence educational success? and How can educational contexts provide environmental assistance to language development? In the same text, she noted that in a historical essay on 50 years of publications by the *Harvard Educational Review*, Schudson (1981) recalled why language became a central concern of this journal in the 1970s:

> As educators have grown disheartened with the power of schools to affect students or change society, they have turned to a faith in the natural abilities of children to achieve for themselves. This emphasis is most evident in research on the child's capacity for learning language. . . .
> That study of language touched on universal themes, revealed common human elements, and illuminated the biological nature of learners and, perhaps, their divine spark as well, as symbolized in Brown and Bellugi's decision to provide the two children they studied with the names Adam and Eve. . . .
> An understanding of language, then, seemed to offer a way through social policy debacles and intellectual despair. A focus on language and the ability of the preschool child to show the most remarkable capacity for rule-governed behavior and the learning of exquisitely complex grammatical systems—regardless of genes, family background, or the quality of schooling—offered hope for the liberal position that the educational community had long tried to sustain. There was almost a new theology of education arising out of the study of language. (p. 282)

In a chapter on classroom discourse appearing in the *Handbook of Research on Teaching*, Cazden (1986a) begins and ends by emphasizing the notion that "the study of linguistic phenomena in school settings should seek to answer educational questions. We are interested in linguistic forms only insofar as through them we can gain insight into the social events of the classroom and thereby into the understandings which students achieve" (pp. 432, 458).

A recent turn toward critical discourse studies has been based on Foucault's (1972, 1977, 1979, 1980) poststructuralist analysis of social history and contemporary culture. Foucault described the constructing character of discourse, that is, how both in broader social formations and in local sites discourse defines, constructs, and positions human subjects. According to Luke (1995), a central task of this contemporary approach to discourse analysis is to theorize and study the micropolitics of discourse, to examine actual patterns of language use with some degree of detail and explicitness but in ways that reconnect instances of local discourse with salient political, economic, and cultural formations (McHoul & Luke, 1989).

According to this interpretation, the task of a critical sociological discourse analysis is to see how broader formations of discourse and power are manifest in everyday aspects of texts in use. As Luke points out, this task fits well with the imperatives of a critical sociology of education, such as documenting how larger patterns of social reproduction and cultural representation occur in everyday classroom life. One of the main purposes of critical language studies is to denaturalize everyday language and to make sensible and available for analysis everyday patterns of talk, writing, and symbolic exchange that are often invisible to participants. This is particularly pertinent to studies of classroom life.

The goal of the work of Melisa Cahnmann (2000) in "Rhythm and Resource: Repetition as a Linguistic Style in an Urban Elementary Classroom" is to understand the role of culturally specific styles of discourse in the classroom. This research uses and expands on three categories of classroom language use (control, curriculum, and critique) to present data on how a Puerto Rican American teacher uses repetition and discourse styles that have African and African American origins to perform a variety of classroom functions: controlling classroom behavior and talk, better teaching and highlighting elements of the curriculum, and critiquing the use of standard English in an elementary classroom context. It is concluded that the teacher's use of culturally specific forms of repetition enhanced the way the teacher controlled classroom talk and behavior and increased students' participation and learning of the curriculum.

The studies on writing conducted by Ball, Dyson, Farr, Freedman, Redd, Smitherman, Taylor and Dorsey Gaines, Valdés, and others were all motivated by a desire to improve teaching and learning for all students and the classroom lives of culturally and linguistically diverse students in particular. When we look at the work of these and other researchers who have focused on classroom writing, it becomes apparent that much of the research mentioned in this chapter has been motivated by important trends. Prior to the 1970s, the research on writing focused primarily on the outcome of writing, that is, the product. At that time, there was not sufficient research on how writing ability developed, and thus most work focused on evaluation of the end product, with some addressing the effectiveness of a variety of ad hoc instructional methods (see Dyson & Freedman, 1995; Freedman et al., 1995).

In the 1970s, several factors contributed to a shift in the direction of writing research. Before that time, good writing was difficult to define; most researchers looked at individual cognitive processes and at individualized singular pieces of writing, and most viewed writing as independent in its own right (Goody & Watt, 1963; Olson, 1977). In the 1980s, the focus of writing research shifted toward the context of writing and examined multiple environments as "critical social contexts" in which people learned to write and experience writing. Research here indicated that language use differed among subcultures and between genres and nonacademic purposes and depended widely on the function and purposes of the writing.

In addition, studies emerged to show how writing knowledge and function developed in homes and communities before schooling began (e.g., lists, messages, stories, greetings). By this time, researchers realized that in order for us to understand the teaching and learning of writing, we needed to also consider the intricacy of communication within the natural environments in which the processes emerged and developed over time. In the 1980s, changes in education and in the sociopolitical climate called attention to writing by placing importance on the need for understanding the changing conventions of writing needed for changing times, especially in light of technological advances in communication and increased diversity in most classrooms. Freedman et al. (1987) argued that two unproductive schisms had arisen, (a) separating studies of language process from studies of language product and (b) separating studies of classroom contexts from studies of cognitive processes (p. 2). As a result, these researchers proposed a social-cognitive theory of writing that would focus attention on the "richly tangled web" connecting cognition, context, and language.

In the 1990s, Dyson and Freedman (1995) encouraged writing researchers to move beyond the generalities of current writing theory and pedagogy to develop theories, research agendas, and principles of assessment and instruction that were built on a thorough understanding of the diversity of the population and of literacy itself. Also in the 1990s, Ball (1997) encouraged inclusion of the voices of teachers from diverse backgrounds in discussions or research on writing, because the inclusion of such voices can inform the reshaping of current practices, research priorities, and policy debates that focus on finding solutions to problems of assessment when teaching diverse student populations.

Writing holds a special place in research on classroom life. Beginning in the late 1970s and continuing today, anthropologists, linguists, and psychologists have tried to specify writing's varied functions and forms and its usefulness in a range of classroom situations. Researchers have looked at how writing develops, how written language is embedded within ways of living, and how it is influenced by different social and economic resources and opportunities, religious beliefs, values, and motivations. Farr and Daniels (1986) presented 15 principles of effective writing instruction for culturally and linguistically diverse students; Langer and Applebee (1986) described 5 components of effective literacy instruction for all students; and Ball (1999) described 5 key principles that underlie the creation of successful writing and assessment contexts for all students and important points that should be kept in mind when facilitating, supporting, and evaluating the writing of diverse students.

Two important principles have emerged from this research that contribute to improving classroom life experiences. One principle involves the need to structure writing activities that comprise functional and interactive communication and that allow students to feel "ownership" of their own writing. That is, writing that is intended as actual communication is much more effective in engaging students in literacy learning. Staton et al. (1988) provide an example of this. The second principle involves the need for students to have a wide range of classroom experiences with written academic and nonacademic texts. This principle is demonstrated in the work of Staton et al., Heath and Branscombe, and others.

These studies illustrate the need for abundant experience with written academic texts. Such texts are replete with the linguistic resources of Western "essayist" literacy (Farr, 1993; Scollon & Scollon, 1981) such as standard grammar, explicit connectives (e.g., therefore, consequently, although), Latinate vocabulary, a clear sequencing of "points," allusions to other written texts, and so on. The more encounters students have with such texts as a part of their classroom experiences, the more easily they will acquire the particular linguistic devices and cultural orientations they contain. This means that extensive reading and writing of extended discourse is necessary, not the reading and writing of multiple-choice or fill-in-the-blank forms. Unfortunately, the latter now prevail in most U.S. schools, particularly schools serving culturally and linguistically diverse populations (Goodlad, 1984).

It is important to stress that in these and many other studies, the emphasis in classroom activities was on actual communication through reading and writing rather than the linguistic forms of mainstream literacy. That is, these activities did not involve rote drills and exercises in which students practiced academic literate forms. In contrast, the students, while actually writing and reading with another real writer/reader, were exposed to a variety of literate forms. These students had multiple and redundant opportunities to become familiar with literate academic language resources and to value their nonacademic resources as they engaged in dialogue with teachers and others and through personal narratives, journals, letters, and books.

Where Do We Go From Here?

Since Jackson wrote his seminal book on classroom life, many changes have taken place. The United States has been a place of increasing cultural and linguistic diversity. Recognition of the nature and extent of that diversity is increasing as Americans are forced to acknowledge our role as a member of a global society. This recognition comes none too soon, as individuals who have historically been considered "minorities" in this country are now becoming the majority population in many of the nation's largest cities (Banks, 1991). According to Garcia (1993), this trend toward ethnic and linguistic diversity is most apparent in the classroom lives of our nation's young and school-aged children.

By 1991, for example, 52% of the students in California came from what had previously been considered "minority" populations, and this figure is expected to increase to 70% by the year 2005 (Garcia, 1993). Recent census figures reveal that 31.9% of the nation's population consists of persons of color, and in California a majority of the residents come from what had previously been considered "minority" populations. Nationwide, White, non-Hispanic student enrollments decreased by 13% between 1976 and 1986 and by an additional 5.6% between 1986 and 1995, while "minority" enrollment as a proportion of total enrollment in elementary schools rose by 6%

between 1976 and 1986 and by an additional 5.4% between 1986 and 1995. Garcia (1993) and others have predicted that by the year 2030, White, non-Hispanic students will be a minority in every category of public education as we now know it, while culturally and linguistically diverse students will continue to be the nation's "emerging majority."

As this emerging majority enters classroom life, they bring with them the rich linguistic resources that are generally used in their home and community settings. In earlier decades, the varieties of language spoken and written by "minorities" were considered inappropriate for use in formal, institutional settings such as schools. Although linguists agree that the many varieties of English spoken by diverse groups in our society are cohesive, logical, highly structured linguistic systems in their own right, negative values have often been associated with many varieties of English used by diverse members of our society at large. In most cases, nonacademic varieties of English are seen as inferior to their mainstream academic English counterparts. Clearly, with the demographic changes that are occurring in our country, Americans will need to realign their attitudes concerning oral and written language use in classrooms with the realities of our changing population.

Researchers who are interested in investigating ways to improve teaching and learning for all students are concerned about the fact that the "emerging majority" of culturally and linguistically diverse students in our country are continuing to be placed at risk for educational failure. This reality is highlighted by statistics that show dropout rates of 7.3% among White, non-Hispanic students in 1996 but 13% among African American students and 29.4% among Hispanic students. These figures illustrate the need for an intensified research agenda over the next 30 years that focuses on the educational plight of the "emerging majority."

The first part of this chapter presented information that clearly revealed the late 1960s and early 1970s as a time in our history when the sociopolitical climate supported the conduct of research focusing on America's diverse student populations and on issues of equality, access, and social justice for all students. The research described illustrates how local and federal support was provided to fund community school programs that would bring about a significant shift in the sources of power affecting the control and support of schools. In the 1960s and early 1970s, when we knew less about the importance of discourse in students' classroom lives, the sociopolitical climate was ripe for new ideas, and new and innovative models were sought for implementing practices that would enhance the classroom lives and learning experiences of all students.

It is ironic that today, when we know so much more about language diversity and the relationship between the communicative lives of students in classrooms and academic success, we find ourselves in a sociopolitical climate that is less supportive of the conduct of this kind of research and its implementation in America's classrooms. Today's sociopolitical climate demands a focus on issues of standards, testing, and accountability, which has an inhibiting and constraining effect on classroom teachers' ability to act upon the knowledge that is available to them concerning the use of students' home language as a resource to enhance their classroom lives. Instead, today's teachers are given mandates that they occupy their time teaching students to pass accountability tests, which have little relevance to their personal lives.

Given the social, political, and demographic changes that have taken place in our society over the past three decades and the realities of today's diverse classrooms, perhaps we need to revisit and rewrite Jackson's 1990 quote so that it reads as follows:

> In bluntest terms, the question to be addressed is this: If an interpretation of what goes on in classrooms does not point in some way to how teaching and learning might be improved for diverse student populations or how teachers can be better prepared and highly motivated to teach diverse students more effectively, why bother with it?

The research that I have reviewed in this chapter and my own research (Ball, 2000a, 2000b, 2000c) lead me to conclude that, as we concentrate on the critical need to improve teaching and learning for diverse students and the preparation of their teachers, we are working to improve classroom life and teaching and learning for all students. Just as "looking at the research on classroom life" is no easy matter, conducting research that points to the improvement of teaching and learning for diverse students and the preparation of their teachers is no easy matter. However, one way to accomplish this goal is through research that focuses on improving the writing[2] of diverse students and the development of teachers who are able to build on the oral and written literacy resources that underachieving students bring to the classroom.

As we develop paradigms of research to accomplish this goal, we must resist mandates that dictate the types of methodologies that can be used. Rather, researchers should employ methodologies that are most appropriate for addressing important research questions. The findings from such research can be applied to improving teaching and learning for all students. This research would demonstrate how to use students' home and community language and literacies as bridges to developing academic literacies. This 21st-century research agenda should (a) build on cultural historical activity theory to construct a framework for improving teaching and teacher preparation, in that it provides a theoretical framework that is capable of addressing complex social, political, and cognitive variables; (b) contribute to research on the development of teachers who are prepared and motivated to use literacies in strategic ways to improve classroom life; and (c) contribute to research on how to use the nonacademic writing of underachieving students as a scaffold for developing their academic literacy skills.

Numerous studies have focused on the failure and underachievement of students of color who are placed at risk for academic failure. However, few studies are currently being funded to provide innovative models that address the development of writing and literacy skills for these students, particularly at the secondary level, or the development of models and resources for the preparation of excellent teachers who are prepared and motivated to accomplish these tasks or to teach diverse students effectively. The research agenda that I propose for the 21st century builds on three research traditions: ethnographic and discourse studies of local uses of oral and written language, research that introduces improved instruction congruent with students' local ways of using language, and development of research-based approaches to preparing teachers for diversity.

In the past, ethnographic studies of local uses of the oral and written language of diverse students were used to improve instruction in two ways: by modifying instruction to be congruent with what research has shown to be local ways of using language and by involving students themselves in doing and writing up the results of ethnographic research in their own communities. Heath (1983) provided a model for both uses. Her ethnographic research on language acquisition in one African American and one White southern, rural, working-class community was used in the local school to modify instruction to students from these communities. Moreover, in a science classroom, students were involved in ethnographic research in their communities on such topics as ways of growing foodstuffs, and they compared these local methods with scientific approaches in an effort to determine whether or not science could explain why the local folk methods either worked or did not work (Heath, 1983, p. 317).

Researchers in Hawaii and in San Diego, California, also have applied the results of ethnographic research to instruction. Au (1980) and Au and Jordan (1981) reported on the successful results obtained by modifying reading instruction to be more congruent with the Hawaiian "talk story," a local speech event identified and described by ethnographers (Watson, 1975; Watson-Gegeo & Boggs, 1977). Diaz, Moll, and Mehan (1986) and Moll and Diaz (1987) reported on another use of ethnographic research results in the classroom. In this project, social content—"the substance of . . . discourse, parents' educational values, life history, and [the] condition of . . . sample families" (Diaz et al., 1986, p. 223)—was used to reorganize instruction in ways that increased student participation and, consequently, improved student performance and classroom life.

Other researchers who have introduced improved instruction congruent with students' local ways of using language include Lee (1992, 1995) and Ball and Cooks (1998). Lee's (1992) work builds on the practice of cultural scaffolding and demonstrates how African American students are capable of using the verbal art form of signifying as a scaffold in interpreting and elaborating on different literary texts. Lee offers this study as an example of the value of using an African American discourse genre as a scaffold for academic success and explains how the act of signifying—a social discourse practice primarily used and rooted in the AAVE speaking community—can have a positive influence on students' classroom life and yield positive cognitive consequences in the form of support for the development of critical strategies for interpreting literature. More recently, Lee (2000, 2001) described the notion of cultural modeling.

Building on Ball's (1992) earlier work that revealed African American adolescents' preferred ways of organizing oral and written expository texts in formal and informal settings, Ball and Cooks (1998) report on research designed to implement a literacy training program that uses interactive technology to link at-risk high school students and preservice teachers together to teach expository writing skills by building bridges between the students' home and community-based communicative skills and the academic literacy skills needed in today's schools. Drawing upon such models, educators can help students to see similarities between their preferred home-based language patterns and academic tasks, thus aiding the students in developing competencies in new and diverse areas of literacy. Using these models, teachers draw on what students already know from their own home and community practices in order to teach them how to master various aspects of classroom culture.

A third area of research that is critical for improving teaching and learning among culturally and linguistically diverse students is teacher preparation. Although the term *multicultural education* began to appear in the literature in the early 1970s, only a few reviews have looked at multicultural teacher education (Baptiste & Baptiste, 1980; Commission on Multicultural Education, 1978; Grant & Secada, 1990). Ladson-Billings (1995) provides a summary of these reviews as well as a discussion of the nature of other studies that have been generated on multicultural teacher education since the Grant and Secada (1990) review. Ladson-Billings concludes that of the 39 ERIC research entries located between 1988 and 1992, 18 were position or opinion papers, 11 were descriptive studies, 2 were evaluative studies, and only 4 were empirical studies.

Ladson-Billings (1995) further notes that "one of the 'cutting-edge' trends in multicultural teacher education . . . is the examination of classroom practice of successful teachers in diverse classrooms" (p. 747). While most of this literature has focused on effective practice with African American students, a parallel literature exists in uncovering the effective practices of teachers of linguistically diverse students (see Bountress, 1994; Garcia, 1991; Hornberger, 1990; Moll, 1988). In addition, Sleeter (2001) provides a review of the epistemological diversity in research on preservice teacher preparation for historically underserved children.

Lucas and Borders's (1994) review of the information made available to developing teachers in the teacher education materials of the late 1980s and early 1990s revealed that these texts pay varying amounts of attention to the issue of linguistic diversity in schools. While many of the materials show an awareness of the issue, some provide more details than others on the nature of the linguistic diversity that teachers can expect to encounter in their future classrooms. According to Lucas and Borders (1994), two things seem to be lacking in these materials: (a) information on exactly when and how dialect features are used in the classroom (which their research addresses) and (b) discussions of the overall role of language in education. They conclude that a great deal more information is needed to help teachers understand what it means to have cultural and linguistically diverse students in the classroom.

In response to that need, Ball (1999, 2000b, 2000c) provides specific information geared toward raising teachers' levels of linguistic sensitivity, increasing their knowledge base concerning the nature of the linguistic characteristics students bring to the classroom, and changing their perspectives on students' literacy practices. Ball, Williams, and Cooks (1997) provide specific applications of the research to the classroom setting. Clearly, more research is needed focusing on teacher preparation programs that enable teachers to work effectively with students who are culturally and linguistically diverse (Carnegie Council on Adolescent Development, 1989; Darling-Hammond, 1986; Quality Education for Minority Project, 1990).

In particular, video case-based studies are needed that better conceptualize and illustrate the processes by which preservice and in-service teachers develop the reflection and commitment necessary to transform the theory they encounter in teacher education programs into practical curriculum and pedagogy that better serve the educational needs of diverse students (Ball, 2000b, 2000c). As Grant and Secada (1990) point out, empirical research is needed to give direction and focus to current debates on classroom practice, curriculum development, and policy and to find solutions to problems of teaching and learning with culturally and linguistically diverse students (Darling-Hammond, 1994). A research agenda for the 21st century should focus on accomplishing these goals.

CONCLUSION

Earlier in this chapter, it was noted that culturally and linguistically diverse groups, taken together, are becoming the "emerging majority" in many of our nation's largest cities. In California, persons of color are now the majority population, and within 40 years these groups will outnumber non-Hispanic European-origin Whites in many contexts. This reality must be addressed within our educational system, or that system will be doomed to repeat its current failures with culturally and linguistically diverse populations.

In addition to changing the attitudes and values of mainstream America toward the literacy resources of nonmainstream populations, other improvements in the current educational system must be made. Luke (1995) proposes that what is needed is a systematic attempt to build on "minority" discourses in schools, classrooms, and other public institutions (Fairclough, 1992a, 1992b; Gutierrez et al., 1995). From this perspective, we can begin reframing issues of educational access and equity to ask what kinds of textual positions and practices are constructed in official knowledge and who has access to them. Rose (1989) proposes that if schools are to play a significant role in improving writing and literacy skills in our nation for all students, "we'll need a guiding set of principles that do not encourage us to retreat from, but . . . move us closer to, an understanding of the rich mix of speech and ritual story that is America" (p. 238). This implies the need for the following:

- a broader theory of literacy and learning that includes an understanding of cultures and cultural resources that all students bring to the learning environment
- an expanded agenda for research that asks how learners adapt the language and literacy resources they already control to a range of writing practices (e.g., shaping narrative, doing analytical and expository writing, composing a multimedia electronic document, explaining scientific concepts, arguing persuasively, and inquiring effectively)

- an expanded image of—rather than a simple tolerance for—literacy education and teacher professional development that recognizes the multiple purposes and practices of literacy and the diverse patchwork of learners who now inhabit our schools
- an expanded agenda for supporting research designed to accomplish these goals

While a predominance of the research conducted over the past 30 years has focused on improving the classroom lives of students from the dominant culture, far less has focused on improving the classroom lives of culturally and linguistically diverse students in classrooms. Support for this type of important work will make it possible for researchers to explore theoretical and methodological approaches that enhance the classroom lives of all students. Such work can provide improved conceptualizations that will enable teachers, students, curriculum developers, teacher educators, administrators, and policymakers to better understand and support not only the classroom lives of our nation's poor, marginalized, and underachieving populations but the classroom lives of all students.

In addition, by better understanding how teachers' commitment to diversity can be facilitated, we can gain greater insight into the development of pedagogical approaches that will help teacher educators design more effective professional development programs and help teachers understand how they can grow to become agents of change within current reform efforts to improve our nation's schools. The long-term goal should be to provide both basic, decision-oriented research that seeks to explore the unknown and to reveal sources of imaginative new points of view and applied, decision-oriented research that provides students, teachers, and policymakers with evidence of linguistic resources used by diverse populations outside of the classroom that can be used to create more successful learning environments. In doing so, we can provide the necessary empirical foundation for establishing effective yet imaginative theory and practice that can serve to accelerate educational parity across racial and social boundaries.

It is my hope that, through the work described here, the legacy of academic failure that plagues so many students can be overcome through an expanded understanding of and sensitivity to our similarities and dissimilarities. Returning once more to the earlier quotation—"if an interpretation of what goes on in classrooms does not point in some way to how teaching, learning, and classrooms can be improved, why bother with it?"—the agenda described here involves the kind of research that we should be bothered with and, in fact, totally embrace.

NOTES

[1] In the question that Jackson poses here, many readers have sensed that he was being intentionally ironic. Because of the earlier position that Jackson had articulated on this topic (e.g., in his 1990 American Educational Research Association presidential address), they conclude that he makes this statement in hopes of jarring the research community to think about debates concerning applied or decision-oriented research that focuses on "the pressing issues

of the day" versus basic or conclusion-oriented research that seeks to explore the unknown. Like Jackson, I urge the research community to make spaces for both forms of research—both serve a purpose, and both are necessary. However, with recent attention to the nation's changing demographics and the critical need to provide both excellent and equitable education for all students, the move toward applied research has received increased attention and will most likely continue to be a prominent direction for some time to come.

² It is important to note that writing has emerged as a primary gatekeeper that prevents students of color from being admitted to institutions of higher education and is regularly used as a criterion for placing students in "remedial" courses.

REFERENCES

Abdullah, S., Kamberelis, G., & McGinley, W. (1992). Literacy, identity, and resistance within the African-American slave community and some reflections for new forms of literacy pedagogy. In *Literacy, research, theory, and practice: Views from many perspectives*. Chicago: National Reading Conference.

Amastae, J., & Elias-Olivares, L. (Eds.). (1982). *Spanish in the United States: Sociolinguistic aspects*. Cambridge, England: Cambridge University Press.

Anyon, J. (1981). Social class and school knowledge. *Curriculum Inquiry, 11,* 1–42.

Applebee, A. N. (1991). Environments for language teaching and learning: Contemporary issues and future directions. In J. M. J. J. Flood, D. Lapp, & J. R. Squire (Eds.), *Handbook of research on teaching of English language arts*. New York: Macmillan.

Baker, C. D., & Freebody, P. (1989). *Children's first schoolbooks*. Oxford, England: Basil Blackwell.

Balester, V. M. (1993). *Cultural divide: A study of African-American college-level writers*. Portsmouth, NH: Boynton/Cook.

Ball, A. F. (1992). Cultural preference and the expository writing of African-American adolescents. *Written Communication, 9,* 501–532.

Ball, A. F. (1995a). Investigating language, learning, and linguistic competence of African-American children: Torrey revisited. *Linguistics and Education, 7,* 23–46.

Ball, A. F. (1995b). Community-based learning in urban settings as a model for educational reform. *Applied Behavioral Science Review, 3,* 127–146.

Ball, A. F. (1995c). Text design patterns in the writing of urban African-American students: Teaching to the strengths of students in multicultural settings. *Urban Education, 30,* 253–289.

Ball, A. F. (1997). Expanding the dialogue on culture as a critical component when assessing writing. *Assessing Writing, 4,* 169–202.

Ball, A. F. (1999). Evaluating the writing of culturally and linguistically diverse students: The case of the African American English speaker. In C. R. Cooper & L. Odell (Eds.), *Evaluating writing* (2nd ed., pp. 225–230). Urbana, IL: National Council of Teachers of English.

Ball, A. F. (2000a). Empowering pedagogies that enhance the learning of multicultural students. *Teachers College Record, 102,* 1006–1034.

Ball, A. F. (2000b). Preparing teachers for diversity: Lessons learned from the U.S. and South Africa. *Teaching and Teacher Education,* 491–509.

Ball, A. F. (2000c). Preservice teachers' perspectives on literacy and its use in urban schools: A Vygotskian perspective on internal activity and teacher change. In C. L. P. Smagorinsky (Ed.), *Worlds of meaning: Vygotskian perspectives on literacy research* (pp. 314–359). Cambridge, England: Cambridge University Press.

Ball, A. F., & Cooks, J. (1998, February). *Literacies unleashed through technology: Expanding community-based discourse practices and instilling a passion to write in urban at-risk youth and their teachers.* Paper presented at the meeting of the National Council of Teachers of English, Los Angeles, CA.

Ball, A. F., Williams, J., & Cooks, J. (1997). An ebonics-based curriculum: The educational value. *Thought & Action: The NEA Higher Education Journal, 13*(2), 39–50.

Ball, D., & Cohen, D. (1999). Developing practice, developing practitioners: Toward a practice-based theory of professional education. In L. Darling-Hammond & D. Sykes (Eds.), *Teaching as the learning profession: Handbook of policy and practice.* San Francisco: Jossey-Bass.

Banks, J. A. (1991). Multicultural literacy and curriculum reform. *Educational Horizons, 69,* 135–140.

Baptiste, H. P., & Baptiste, M. (1980). Competencies toward multiculturalism. In H. P. Baptiste, M. Baptiste, & D. Gollnick (Eds.), *Multicultural teacher education: Preparing educators to provide educational equity* (Vol. 1, pp. 44–72). Washington, DC: American Association of Colleges for Teacher Education.

Barone, T. (1992). Beyond theory and method: A case for critical storytelling. *Theory into Practice, 31,* 142–146.

Basso, K. (1974). The ethnography of writing. In R. Bauman & J. Sherzer (Eds.), *Explorations in the ethnography of speaking* (pp. 425–432). Cambridge, England: Cambridge University Press.

Baugh, J. (1990). A survey of the suffix /-s/ analyses in Black English. In J. A. Edmondson, C. Feagin, & P. Muhlhausler (Eds.), *Development and diversity: Language variation across time and space.* Arlington: University of Texas and Summer Institute of Linguistics.

Baugh, J. (1992). Hypercorrection: Mistakes in production of vernacular African American English as a second dialect. *Language and Education, 6,* 47–61.

Beane, J., & Brodhagen, B. (2001). Teaching in middle schools. In V. Richardson (Ed.), *Handbook of research on teaching* (pp. 1157–1174). Washington, DC: American Educational Research Association.

Bennett, C. (1979, April). *Identifying classroom climates of acceptance in desegregated schools.* Paper presented at the annual meeting of the American Educational Research Association, San Francisco, CA.

Bissex, G. L. (1994). Teacher research: Seeing what we are doing. In T. Shanahan (Ed.), *Teachers thinking, teachers knowing: Reflections on literacy and language education* (pp. 88–104). Urbana, IL: National Council of Research on English.

Blackburn, M., & Stern, D. (2000). Analyzing the role of the vernacular in student writing: A social literacies approach. *Working Papers in Educational Linguistics, 61,* 53–69.

Bloome, D. (Ed.). (1987). *Literacy, language and schooling.* Norwood, NJ: Ablex.

Bloome, D., & Green, J. (1984). Directions in sociolinguistic study of reading. In P. D. Pearson (Ed.), *Handbook of reading research* (pp. 395–421). New York: Longman.

Bountress, N. G. (1994). The classroom teacher and the language-different student: Why, when, and how of intervention. *Preventing School Failure, 38,* 10–15.

Britzman, D. (1991). Decentering discourse in teacher education: Or, the unleashing of unpopular things. *Journal of Education, 173,* 60–80.

Cahnmann, M. (2000). Rhythm and resource: Repetition as a linguistic style in an urban elementary classroom. *Working Papers in Educational Linguistics, 16,* 39–52.

Carnegie Council on Adolescent Development. (1989). *Turning point: Preparing American youth for the 21st century.* New York: Carnegie Corporation.

Cazden, C. B. (1986a). Classroom discourse. In M. C. Wittrock (Ed.), *Handbook of research on teaching* (pp. 432–463). New York: Macmillan.

Cazden, C. B. (1986b). Language in the classroom. In R. B. Kaplan (Ed.), *Annual review of applied linguistics* (Vol. 7, pp. 18–33). Cambridge, England: Cambridge University Press.

Cazden, C. (1988). Environmental assistance revisited: Variation and functional equivalence. In F. S. Kessel (Ed.), *The development of language and language researchers: Essays in honor of Roger Brown* (pp. 281–297). Hillsdale, NJ: Erlbaum.

Cazden, C. (2001). *Classroom discourse: The language of teaching and learning.* Portsmouth, NJ: Heineman.

Cazden, C., John, V., & Hymes, D. (Eds.). (1972). *Functions of language in the classroom.* New York: Teachers College Press.

Charrow, V. (1981). The written English of deaf adolescents. In M. Farr Whiteman (Ed.), *Variation in writing: Functional and linguistic-cultural differences.* Hillsdale, NJ: Erlbaum.

Cintron, R. (1997). *Angels town: Chero ways, gang life, and rhetorics of the everyday.* Boston: Beacon Press.

Clarke, D. J. (1993). Probing the structure of mathematical writing. *Educational Studies in Mathematics, 25,* 235–250.

Cochran-Smith, M., & Lytle, S. (1992). Teacher research as a way of knowing. *Harvard Educational Review, 62,* 447–474.

Cook-Gumperz, J. (Ed.). (1986). *The social construction of literacy.* Cambridge, England: Cambridge University Press.

Cuban, L. (1993). *How teachers taught: Constancy and change in American classrooms 1890–1990.* New York: Teachers College Press.

Darling-Hammond, L. (1986). A proposal for evaluation in the teaching profession. *Elementary School Journal, 86,* 531–551.

Darling-Hammond, L. (1990). Teacher quality and equality. In J. Goodlad, & P. Keating (Eds.), *Access the knowledge: An agenda for our nation's schools* (pp. 237–258). New York: College Entrance Examination Board.

Darling-Hammond, L. (1992). Teaching and knowledge: Policy issues posed by alternate certification for teachers. *Peabody Journal of Education, 67,* 123–154.

Darling-Hammond, L. (1995). Inequality and access to knowledge. In J. Banks & C. Banks (Eds.), *Handbook of research on multicultural education.* New York: Macmillan.

Darling-Hammond, L. (1996). The right to learn and the advancement of teaching: Research, policy, and practice for democratic education. *Educational Researcher, 25*(6), 5–17.

Darling-Hammond, L. (1997). *The right to learn: A blueprint for creating schools that work.* San Francisco: Jossey-Bass.

Davies, B. (1989). The discursive production of the male/female dualism in school settings. *Oxford Review of Education, 15,* 229–241.

Delgado-Gaitan, C. (1990). *Literacy for empowerment: The role of parents in children's education.* New York: Falmer.

Delgado-Gaitan, C. (1996). *Protean literacy: Extending the discourse on empowerment.* New York: Falmer.

Delgado-Gaitan, C., & Trueba, H. (1991). *Crossing cultural borders: Education for immigrant families in America.* New York: Falmer.

Delpit, L. (1996). Skills and other dilemmas of a progressive Black educator. *American Educator, 20*(3), 9–11.

Diaz, S., Moll, L., & Mehan, H. (1986). Sociocultural resources in instruction: A context-specific approach. In *Beyond language: Social and cultural factors in schooling language minority students.* Los Angeles: Evaluation, Dissemination and Assessment Center, California State University.

Dirlik, A. (1994). The postcolonial aura: Third world criticism in the age of global capitalism. *Critical Inquiry, 20,* 328–356.

Dyson, A. H. (1989). *Multiple worlds of child writers: Friends learning to write.* New York: Teachers College Press.

Dyson, A. H., & Freedman, S. W. (1995). *Critical challenges for research on writing and literacy: 1990–1995.* Berkeley: University of California Press.

Edwards, W. (1992). Sociolinguistic behavior in a Detroit inner-city Black neighborhood. *Language in Society, 21,* 93–116.

Ellison, C., Boykin, W., Towns, D., & Stokes, A. (1990). *Classroom cultural ecology: The dynamics of classroom life in schools serving low-income African American children.* Baltimore:

Center for Research on the Education of Students Placed at Risk, Johns Hopkins University and Howard University.

Fairclough, N. (1992a). *Critical language awareness.* London: Longman.

Fairclough, N. (1992b). *Discourse and social change.* Cambridge, England: Polity Press.

Farr, M. (1986). Language, culture, and writing: Sociolinguistic foundations of research on writing. In E. Rothkopf (Ed.), *Review of research in education* (Vol. 13, pp. 195–223). Washington, DC: American Educational Research Association.

Farr, M. (1993). Essayist literacy and other verbal performances. *Written Communication, 10,* 4–38.

Farr, M. (1994a). Biliteracy in the home: Practices among Mexicano families in Chicago. In D. Spener (Ed.), *Adult biliteracy in the United States.* Washington, DC: Center for Applied Linguistics.

Farr, M. (1994b). En los dos idiomas: Literacy practices among Chicago Mexicanos. In B. J. Moss (Ed.), *Literacy across communities.* Cresskill, NJ: Hampton Press.

Farr, M. (1994c). Echando relajo: Verbal art and gender among Mexicanas in Chicago. In *Proceedings of the 1994 Berkeley Conference on Women and Language.* Berkeley: Department of Linguistics, University of California.

Farr, M. (2000). Literacy and religion: Reading, writing, and gender among Mexican women in Chicago. In P. Griffin, J. K. Peyton, W. Wolfram, & R. Fasold (Eds.), *Language in action: New studies of language in society.* Cresskill, NJ: Hampton Press.

Farr, M., & Daniels, H. (1986). *Language diversity and writing instruction.* Urbana, IL: National Council of Teachers of English.

Farr, M., & Guerra, J. C. (1995). Literacy in the community: A study of Mexicano families in Chicago. *Discourse Processes, 19,* 7–19.

Farr Whiteman, M. (1981). Dialect influence in writing. In M. Farr Whiteman (Ed.), *Variations in writing: Functional and linguistic-cultural differences.* Hillsdale, NJ: Erlbaum.

Fasold, R. (1972). *Tense marking in Black English.* Washington, DC: Center for Applied Linguistics.

Ferguson, C., & Heath, S. B. (Eds.). (1981). *Language in the USA.* Cambridge, England: Cambridge University Press.

Ferreiro, E., & Teberosky, A. (1982). *Literacy before schooling.* Exeter, NH: Heinemann.

Fine, M. (1992). *Disrupting voices: The possibilities of feminist research.* Ann Arbor: University of Michigan Press.

Foucault, M. (1972). *The archaeology of knowledge* (A. Sheridan-Smith, Trans.). New York: Harper & Row.

Foucault, M. (1977). *Language, counter-memory, practice* (D. Bouchard, Trans.). Oxford, England: Basil Blackwell.

Foucault, M. (1979). *Discipline and punish* (A. Sheridan, Trans.). New York: Harper.

Foucault, M. (1980). *Power/knowledge* (C. Gordon, Ed., and C. Gordon, L. Marshall, J. Mepham, and K. Soper, Trans.). New York: Pantheon.

Freedman, S. W., Flower, L., Hull, G., & Hayes, J. R. (1995). *Ten years of research: Achievements of the National Center for the Study of Writing and Literacy.* Berkeley, CA: National Center for the Study of Writing.

Freedman, S. W., & Hechinger, F. (1992). *Writing matters.* Berkeley: University of California Press.

Gale, X. L. (1996). *Teachers, discourses, and authority in the postmodern composition classroom.* Albany: State University of New York Press.

Garcia, E. (1991). Effective instruction for language minority students: The teacher. *Journal of Education, 173,* 130–141.

Garcia, E. E. (1993). Language, culture, and education. In L. Darling-Hammond (Ed.), *Review of research in education* (Vol. 19, pp. 51–98). Washington, DC: American Educational Research Association.

Gee, J. P., & Green, J. L. (1998). Discourse analysis, learning, and social practice: A methodological study. In L. Darling-Hammond (Ed.), *Review of research in education* (Vol. 23, pp. 119–169). Washington, DC: American Educational Research Association.

Gilbert, P., & Taylor, S. (1991). *Fashioning the feminine.* Sydney: Allen & Unwin.

Gilmore, P., & Glatthorn, A. (Eds.). (1982). *Children in and out of school: Ethnography and education.* Washington, DC: Center for Applied Linguistics.

Goodlad, J. (1984). *A place called school.* New York: McGraw-Hill.

Goodson, I. (1994). Studying the teacher's life and work. *Teaching and Teacher Education, 10,* 29–37.

Goody, J., & Watt, I. (1963). The consequences of literacy. *Comparative Studies in Society and History, 5,* 304–345.

Grannis, J. C. (1979). *Classroom culture and the problem of control.* New York: ERIC Clearinghouse on Urban Education.

Grant, C. A., & Secada, W. G. (1990). Preparing teachers for diversity. In W. R. Houston (Ed.), *Handbook of research on teacher education* (pp. 403–422). New York: Macmillan.

Graves, D. (1983). *Writing: Children and teachers at work.* Exeter, NH: Heinemann.

Green, J. L., & Dixon, C. D. (1993). Talking knowledge into being: Discursive and social practices in classrooms. *Linguistics and Education, 5,* 231–240.

Green, J., & Wallat, C. (Eds.). (1981). *Ethnography and language in educational settings.* Norwood, NJ: Ablex.

Gulley, B., & Norwood, E. (1976). Critical aspects of open classroom. *Education, 96,* 207–208.

Gumperz, J. J. (1982a). *Discourse strategies.* Cambridge, England: Cambridge University Press.

Gumperz, J. J. (Ed.). (1982b). *Language and social identity.* Cambridge, England: Cambridge University Press.

Gumperz, J. J., & Hymes, D. (Eds.). (1972). *Directions in sociolinguistics: The ethnography of communication.* New York: Holt, Rinehart & Winston.

Gutierrez, K. D. (1992). A comparison of instructional contexts in writing process classrooms with Latino children. *Education and Urban Society, 24,* 244–262.

Gutierrez, K., Baquedano-Lopez, P., & Tejeda, C. (1999). Rethinking diversity: Hybridity and hybrid language practices in the third space. *Mind, Culture, and Activity, 6,* 286–303.

Halsted, D. L., Bober, A. M., & Streit, F. (1977). Open classroom: A panacea? *Educational Forum, 41,* 487–491.

Heath, S. B. (1983). *Ways with words: Language, life and work in communities and classrooms.* Cambridge, England: Cambridge University Press.

Heath, S. B., & Branscombe, A. (1985). "Intelligent writing" in an audience community: Teachers, students, and researcher. In S. Freedman (Ed.), *The acquisition of written language: Response and revision.* Norwood, NJ: Ablex.

Hicks, D. (1995). Discourse, learning, and teaching. In M. Apple (Ed.), *Review of research in education* (Vol. 21, pp. 49–95). Washington, DC: American Educational Research Association.

Hornberger, N. (1990). Creating successful learning contexts for bilingual literacy. *Teachers College Record, 92,* 212–229.

Hymes, D. (1972). Models of the interaction of language and social life. In J. Gumperz & D. Hymes (Eds.), *Directions in sociolinguistics: The ethnography of communication.* New York: Holt, Rinehart & Winston.

Hymes, D. (1974). *Foundations in sociolinguistics.* Philadelphia: University of Pennsylvania Press.

Hymes, D. (1995). *Education, linguistics, and narrative inequality.* London: Taylor & Francis.

Jackson, P. W. (1990). *Life in classrooms.* New York: Teachers College Press.

Klein, Z., & Eshel, Y. (1980). The open classroom in cross-cultural perspective: A research note. *Sociology of Education, 53,* 114–121.

Kochman, T. (Ed.). (1972). *Rappin' and stylin' out: Communication in urban Black America.* Urbana: University of Illinois Press.

Kochman, T. (1981). *Black and White styles in conflict.* Chicago: University of Chicago Press.

Kozol, J. (1992). *Savage inequalities: Children in America's schools.* New York: Harper Perennial.

Kreeft, J. P., & Shuy, R. W. (1985). *Dialogue writing: Analysis of student-teacher interactive writing in the learning of English as a second language.* Washington, DC: Center for Applied Linguistics.

Labbo, L., & Reinking, D. (1999). Negotiating the multiple realities of technology in literacy research and instruction. *Reading Research Quarterly, 34,* 478–492.

Labov, W. (1972a). *Language in the inner city: Studies in the Black English vernacular.* Philadelphia: University of Pennsylvania Press.

Labov, W. (1972b). *Sociolinguistic patterns.* Philadelphia: University of Pennsylvania Press.

Labov, W. (Ed.). (1980). *Locating language in time and space.* New York: Academic Press.

Ladson-Billings, G. (1995). Multicultural teacher education: Research, practice, and policy. In J. A. Banks & C. A. Banks (Eds.), *Handbook of research on multicultural education* (pp. 747–759). New York: Macmillan.

Langer, J., & Applebee, A. (1986). Reading and writing instruction: Toward a theory of teaching and learning. In E. Rothkopf (Ed.), *Review of research in education* (Vol. 13, pp. 171–194). Washington, DC: American Educational Research Association.

Leap, W. (1993). *American Indian English.* Salt Lake City: University of Utah Press.

Lee, C. D. (1992). Literacy, cultural diversity, and instruction. *Education and Urban Society, 24,* 279–291.

Lee, C. D. (1995). A culturally based apprenticeship: Teaching African American high school students skills in literary interpretation. *Reading Research Quarterly, 30,* 608–630.

Lemke, J. L. (1990). *Talking science.* Norwood, NJ: Ablex.

Lewis, M. G. (1993). *Without a word: Teaching beyond women's science.* New York: Routledge.

Lightfoot, S. L. (1978). *A question of perspective: Toward a more complex view of classrooms.* New York: Institute for Urban and Minority Education.

Lortie, D. C. (1975). *Schoolteacher: A sociological study.* Chicago: University of Chicago Press.

Lucas, C., & Borders, D. G. (1994). *Language diversity and classroom discourse.* Norwood, NJ: Ablex.

Luke, A. (1988). *Literacy, textbooks and ideology.* London: Falmer.

Luke, A. (1995). Text and discourse in education: An introduction to critical discourse analysis. In M. Apple (Ed.), *Review of research in education* (Vol. 21, pp. 3–48). Washington, DC: American Educational Research Association.

Mael, F. A. (1998). Single-sex and coeducational schooling: Relationships to socioemotional and academic development. *Review of Educational Research, 68,* 101–129.

Mahiri, J. (1994). African American males and learning: What discourse in sports offers schooling. *Anthropology and Education, 25,* 364–375.

McCarthy, C. C. (Ed.). (1993). *Race, identity and representation in education.* New York: Routledge.

McElroy-Johnson, B. (1993). Teaching and practice: Giving voice to the voiceless. *Harvard Educational Review, 63,* 85–104.

McGuire, M., & Weiner, G. (1994). The place of women in teacher education: Discourses of power. *Educational Review, 46,* 121–139.

McHoul, A. W., & Luke, A. (1989). Discourse as language and politics: An introduction to the philology of political culture in Australia. *Journal of Pragmatics, 13,* 323–332.

McPartland, J. M., & Epstein, J. L. (1977). Open schools and achievement: Extended tests of a finding of no relationship. *Sociology of Education, 42,* 133–144.

Means, B. (Ed.). (1991). *Teaching advanced skills to at-risk students: Views from research and practice.* San Francisco: Jossey-Bass.

Mehan, H. (1979). *Learning lessons.* Cambridge, MA: Harvard University Press.

Michaels, S. (1981). "Sharing time": Children's narrative styles and differential access to literacy. *Language in Society, 10,* 423–442.

Michaels, S., & Collins, J. (1984). Oral discourse styles: Classroom interaction and the acquisition of literacy. In D. Tannen (Ed.), *Coherence in spoken and written discourse* (pp. 219–224). Norwood, NJ: Ablex.

Moll, L. C. (1987). Change as the goal of educational research. *Anthropology and Education Quarterly, 18,* 300–311.

Moll, L. (1988). Some key issues in teaching Latino students. *Language Arts, 65,* 465–472.

Moll, L. (Ed.). (1990). *Vygotsky and education: Instructional applications of sociohistorical psychology.* Cambridge, England: Cambridge University Press.

Moll, L., & Diaz, R. (1987). Teaching writing as communication: The use of ethnographic findings in classroom practice. In D. Bloome (Ed.), *Literacy, language and schooling.* Norwood, NJ: Ablex.

Moss, B. (Ed.). (1994). *Literacy across communities.* Cresskill, NJ: Hampton Press.

Murphy, J., & Beck, L. (1995). *School-based management as school reform.* Thousand Oaks, CA: Corwin Press.

National Council of Teachers of English. (2000). *Trends and issues in secondary English.* Urbana, IL: Author.

Nielsen, H. D., & Moos, R. H. (1978). Exploration and adjustment in high school classrooms: A study of person-environment fit. *Journal of Educational Research, 72,* 52–57.

Nieto, S. (1992). *Affirming diversity: The sociopolitical context of multicultural education.* New York: Longman.

Oakes, J. (1985). *Keeping track.* New Haven, CT: Yale University Press.

Ochs, E., & Schieffelin, B. (1983). *Acquiring conversational competence.* London: Routledge & Kegan Paul.

Olson, D. (1977). From utterance to text: The bias of language in speech and writing. *Harvard Educational Review, 47,* 257–281.

Orfield, G., & Reardon, S. F. (1993). Race, poverty and inequality. In G. Orfield, S. Schley, & S. Reardon (Eds.), *The growth of segregation in American schools* (pp. 17–32). Alexandria, VA: National School Boards Association.

Osborne, D. (1977). *Whatever happened to the community control movement?* ERIC Document ED 152 921.

Page, R. (1991). *Lower track classrooms: A curricular and cultural perspective.* New York: Teachers College Press.

Philips, S. (1974). Participant structures and communicative competence: Warm Springs children in community and classroom. In C. Cazden, V. John, & D. Hymes (Eds.), *Functions of language in the classroom* (pp. 370–394). New York: Teachers College Press.

Pinnell, G. S. (1991). Oral language: Speaking and listening in the classroom. In J. M. J. J. Flood, D. Lapp, & J. R. Squire (Eds.), *Handbook of research on teaching of English language arts* (pp. 691–720). New York: Macmillan.

Popkewitz, T. S. (Ed.). (1993). *Changing patterns of power: Social regulation and teacher education reform.* Albany: State University of New York Press.

Poplack, S., & Tagliamonte, S. (1994). -S or nothing: Marking the plural in the African-American diaspora. *American Speech, 69,* 227–259.

Puar, J. K. (1994). Resituating discourse of "Whiteness" and "Asianness" in northern England. *Socialist Review, 24,* 21–54.

Quality Education for Minority Project. (1990). *Education that works: An action plan for the education of minorities.* Cambridge, MA: Massachusetts Institute of Technology.

Rand, G., & Rand, P. (1978). The effects of working atmospheres on creativity. *Scandinavian Journal of Educational Research, 22,* 91–106.

Read, C. (1975). *Children's categorization of speech sounds in English.* Urbana, IL: National Council of Teachers of English.

Redd, T. (1992, April). *Untapped resources: "Styling" in Black students' writing for Black audiences.* Paper presented at the annual meeting of the American Educational Research Association, San Francisco, CA.

Reed, C. (1981). Teaching teachers about teaching writing to students from varied linguistic social and cultural groups. In M. Farr Whiteman (Ed.), *Variation of writing: Functional and linguistic-cultural differences.* Hillsdale, NJ: Erlbaum.

Reid, L. G., & Jeffrey N. (Eds.). (1999). *Reflective activities: Helping students connect with texts: Classroom practices in teaching English.* Urbana, IL: National Council of Teachers of English.

Rogers, A. G. (1993). Voice, play and a practice of ordinary courage in girls' and women's lives. *Harvard Educational Review, 63,* 265–295.

Rose, R. (1989). Classroom action research: The teacher as researcher. *Journal of Reading, 33,* 216–218.

Rosenthal, R., & Jacobson, L. (1992). *Pygmalion in the classroom: Teacher expectation and pupils' intellectual development.* New York: Irvington.

Rosser, S. (1989). Creating an environment that is conducive to learning for the majority. *Journal of the Freshman Year Experience, 1,* 53–63.

Ruberg, L. F. (1996). Student participation, interaction, and regulation in a computer-mediated communication environment: A qualitative study. *Journal of Educational Computing Research, 14,* 243–268.

Ruddell, M. (2000). Dancing as fast as we can: Developing literacy, content, and curriculum in upper elementary grades. In M. McLaughlin & M. Vogt (Eds.), *Creativity and innovation in content area teaching* (pp. 281–298). Norwood, MA: Christopher-Gordon.

Santamaria, D. T. P. (1978). Effects of cooperation and teacher support on student attitudes toward decision making in the elementary science classroom. *Journal of Research in Science Teaching, 15,* 381–385.

Saravia-Shore, M., & Arvizu, S. (1992). *Cross-cultural literacy: Ethnographies of communication in multi-ethnic classrooms.* New York: Garland Press.

Saville-Troike, M. (1982). *The ethnography of communication: An introduction.* Oxford, England: Basil Blackwell.

Schauble, L., & Beane, D. (1996). *Outside the classroom walls: Learning in informal environments.* Mahwah, NJ: Erlbaum.

Schauble, L., & Glaser, R. (1996). *Innovations in learning: New environments for education.* Mahwah, NJ: Erlbaum.

Schieffelin, B., & Cochran-Smith, M. (1984). Learning to read culturally: Literacy before schooling. In H. Goelman, A. Oberg, & F. Smith (Eds.), *Awakening to literacy.* Exeter, NH: Heinemann.

Schieffelin, B., & Ochs, E. (Eds.). (1986). *Language socialization across cultures.* Cambridge, England: Cambridge University Press.

Schudson, M. A. (1981). A history of the *Harvard Educational Review.* In T. E. J. R. Snarey, C. Sienkiewicz, & P. Zodhiates (Eds.), *Conflict and continuity: A history of ideas on social equality and human development* (pp. 1–23). Cambridge, MA: Harvard Educational Review.

Schugurensky, D. (2002). *History of education: Selected moments.* Toronto: Ontario Institute for Studies in Education, University of Toronto.

Scollon, R., & Scollon, S. B. K. (1979). *Linguistic convergence: An ethnography of speaking at Fort Chipewyan.* New York: Academic Press.

Scollon, R., & Scollon, S. B. K. (1981). *Narrative, literacy, & face in interethnic communication.* Norwood, NJ: Ablex.

Scollon, R., & Scollon, S. W. (1995). *Intercultural communication.* Oxford, England: Basil Blackwell.

Scribner, S., & Cole, M. (1981a). Unpacking literacy. In M. Farr Whiteman (Ed.), *Writing: The nature, development, and teaching of written communication.* Hillsdale, NJ: Erlbaum.

Scribner, S., & Cole, M. (1981b). *The psychology of literacy.* Cambridge, MA: Harvard University Press.

Silberman, J. (1973). *The open classroom reader.* New York: Random House.

Sinclair, J. M., & Coulthard, R. M. (1975). *Towards an analysis of discourse: The English used by teachers and pupils.* London: Oxford University Press.

Sinclair, R. L. G., & Ward, J. (1979, April). *Views from the margins: Practical premises and modest priorities for curriculum improvement.* Paper presented at the annual meeting of the American Educational Research Association, San Francisco, CA.

Singer, J., Marx, R., Krajcik, J., & Chambers, J. (2000). *Designing curriculum to meet national standards.* Ann Arbor: University of Michigan.

Singh, P. (1993). Institutional discourse and practice: A case for the social construction of technological competence in the primary classroom. *British Journal of the Sociology of Education, 14,* 39–58.

Sirotnik, K. (1981). *What you see is what you get: A summary of observations in over 1,000 elementary and secondary classrooms.* Los Angeles: UCLA Graduate School of Education.

Sleeter, C. (2001). Epistemological diversity in research on preservice teacher preparation for historically underserved children. In W. G. Secada (Ed.), *Review of research in education* (Vol. 25, pp. 209–250). Washington, DC: American Educational Research Association.

Smitherman, G. (1994). "The blacker the berry, the sweeter the juice": African American student writers and the National Assessment of Educational Progress. In A. H. Dyson & C. Genishi (Eds.), *The need for story: Cultural diversity in classroom and community.* Urbana, IL: National Council of Teachers of English.

Spindler, G. (Ed.). (1982). *Doing the ethnography of schooling: Educational anthropology in action.* New York: Holt, Rinehart & Winston.

Staton, J., Shuy, R., Kreeft Payton, J., & Reed, L. (1988). *Dialogue journal communication: Classroom, linguistic, social, and cognitive views.* Norwood, NJ: Ablex.

Street, B. (1984). *Literacy in theory and practice.* Cambridge, England: Cambridge University Press.

Street, B. (Ed.). (1993). *Cross cultural approaches to literacy.* Cambridge, England: Cambridge University Press.

Sulzby, E. (1986) Writing and readings: Signs of oral and written language organization in the young child. In W. H. Teele & E. Sulzby (Eds.), *Emergent literacy: Writing and reading.* Norwood, NJ: Ablex.

Tannen, D. (Ed.). (1982). *Spoken and written language: Exploring orality and literacy.* Norwood, NJ: Ablex.

Tannen, D. (Ed.). (1984). *Coherence in spoken and written discourse.* Norwood, NJ: Ablex.

Tanner, M. (Ed.). (1992). *Classroom research by classroom teachers.* Flagstaff: Center for Excellence in Education, Northern Arizona University.

Taylor, D., & Dorsey-Gaines, C. (1988). *Growing up literate: Learning from inner-city families.* Portsmouth, NH: Heinemann.

Tjosvold, D., & Santamaria, P. (1978). Effects of cooperation and teacher support on student attitudes toward decision making in the elementary science classroom. *Journal of Research in Science Teaching, 15,* 381–385.

Valdés, G. (1992). Bilingual minorities and language issues in writing: Toward profession-wide responses to a new challenge. *Written Communication, 9,* 85–136.

Valdés, G. (1996). *Con respeto: Bridging the distances between culturally diverse families and schools.* New York: Teachers College Press.

Valdés, G., & Sanders, P. A. (1999). Latino ESL students and the development of writing abilities. In C. R. Cooper & L. Odell (Eds.), *Evaluating writing* (2nd ed., pp. 248–278). Urbana, IL: National Council of Teachers of English.

Valdez, C. (1981). Identity, power and writing skills: The case of the Hispanic bilingual student. In M. Farr Whiteman (Ed.), *Variations in writing: Functional and linguistic-cultural differences*. Hillsdale, NJ: Erlbaum.

Watson, K. (1975). Transferable communicative routines: Strategies and group identity in two speech events. *Language in Society, 4,* 53–72.

Watson-Gegeo, K., & Boggs, S. (1977). From verbal play to talk-story: The role of routines in speech events among Hawaiian children. In S. Ervin-Tripp & C. Mitchell-Kernan (Eds.), *Child discourse.* New York: Academic Press.

Wauters, J. K., Bruce, J. M., Black, D. R., & Hocker, P. N. (1989). Learning styles: A study of Alaska Native and non-native students [Special issue]. *Journal of American Indian Education, 28*(4).

Wayson, W. W. (1966). The political revolution in education, 1965. *Phi Delta Kappan, 47,* 333–339.

Weber, L. (1971). *The English infant school and informal education.* Englewood Cliffs, NJ: Prentice Hall.

Wertsch, J. V. (1991). *Voices of the mind: A sociocultural approach to mediated action.* Cambridge, MA: Harvard University Press.

Williams, G. (1992). *Sociolinguistics: A sociological critique.* London: Routledge.

Williams, P. C. (1994). *Colonial discourse and post-colonial theory.* New York: Columbia University Press.

Wolfram, W. (1969). *A sociolinguistic description of Detroit Negro speech.* Washington, DC: Center for Applied Linguistics.

Wolfram, W. (1974). *Sociolinguistic aspects of assimilation: Puerto Rican English in New York City.* Washington, DC: Center for Applied Linguistics.

Wolfram, W., & Christian, D. (1976). *Appalachian speech.* Washington, DC: Center for Applied Linguistics.

Wolfram, W., Christian, D., Potter, L., & Leap, W. (1979). *Variability in the English of two Indian communities and its effects on reading and writing.* Washington, DC: Center for Applied Linguistics.

Wolfram, W., & Fasold, R. (1974). *The study of social dialects in American English.* Englewood Cliffs, NJ: Prentice Hall.

Wolfram, W., & Hatfield, D. (1984). *The tense marking in second language learning: Patterns of spoken and written English in a Vietnamese community.* Washington, DC: Center for Applied Linguistics.

Zentella, A. C. (1981). *"Hablamos los Dos. We speak both": Growing up bilingual in El Barrio.* Unpublished doctoral dissertation, University of Pennsylvania.

Zentella, A. C. (1997). *Growing up bilingual: Puerto Rican children in New York.* Oxford, England: Basil Blackwell.

Chapter 4

Extracurricular and Other After-School Activities for Youth

JACQUELYNNE S. ECCLES AND JANICE TEMPLETON
University of Michigan

There is growing interest in the developmental consequences of extracurricular and after-school programs for youth, fueled by (a) concerns about the possible role of such activities in both promoting school achievement and preventing school dropout and school disengagement, (b) the continuing disparities in the school achievement of poor youth of all ethnic and racial groups relative to White middle-class youth, (c) the underachievement of American youth relative to youth in other industrialized countries, (d) concerns about whether youth are adequately prepared to enter an increasingly demanding and technical labor market, and (e) the amount of unsupervised time spent by so many youth (e.g., Cooper, Denner, & Lopez, 1999; Dryfoss, 1999; Eccles & Gootman, 2002; Gambone & Arbreton, 1997; Halpern, 1999; Larson, 1994; Lerner & Galambos, 1998; Pittman, Ferber, & Irby, 1999; Quinn, 1999; Scales, 1999). Other critical forces and events highlighting these concerns include the Carnegie Foundation's publication of *A Matter of Time* (1992), the growing interest in positive youth development among both youth advocates in the policy world and developmental and educational researchers interested in adolescence, the growing interest in positive psychology launched by Martin Seligman when he was president of the American Psychological Association, the publication of *When School Is Out* (1999) by the David and Lucile Packard Foundation in their Future of Children series, the increasing concern with violence at schools and declining school engagement among many youth as they move into and through secondary school, and the growing evidence of strong relations between school experiences and socioemotional development.

Added to this list is the growing interest in education outside of the school building and outside of normal school hours. As continued evidence of educational outcome

We would like to thank the members of the National Research Council community-level programs for youth committee for the many stimulating discussions that helped inform our perspective. We would also like to thank the National Research Council for funding a portion of Janice Templeton's time to do some of the research reported in this chapter. Jacquelynne S. Eccles's time was paid for by her research appointment at the Institute for Research on Women and Gender at the University of Michigan.

disparities between ethnic groups within the United States and continued evidence of weak performance by American students in comparison with students in other countries have accumulated, more and more people have discussed using the out-of-school hours for educational purposes. Although there are ongoing major debates about how best to use the out-of-school hours, school-based educators as well as positive youth development practitioners and policymakers are looking to programs both within and outside of school to understand what kinds of programs provide the best learning and developmental experiences for America's youth. Growth in the funds available for such programs through the federal government's 21st Century Learning Center initiative has accelerated the need for information. Finally, because these funds are targeted for collaborative efforts between schools and community-based organizations, school systems are being asked to play a major role in how the funds will be spent.

In this chapter, we review several bodies of work in an effort to identify the components of extracurricular and other out-of-school experiences that can facilitate the cognitive, psychological, and social aspects of positive youth development. We focus on three large bodies of work: studies of extracurricular activities, nonexperimental studies of after- and during-school programs housed both in and out of school buildings, and experimental evaluation studies of intervention and positive youth development programs housed in and out of school buildings. In the first section, we discuss the methodological issues we confronted as we conducted our review. In the subsequent three sections, we review the research in each of the three aforementioned bodies of empirical work on extracurricular and after-school programs for youth. Although many of these programs are housed in schools, none have academic instruction as their primary mission. In the final section, we draw upon all of the studies to offer some tentative conclusions regarding which features of these types of programs are likely to account for their impact on youth development.

METHODOLOGICAL ISSUES IN STUDYING NONACADEMIC AND OUT-OF-SCHOOL PROGRAMS FOR YOUTH

As we reviewed the work being done in each of the four aforementioned fields, we were struck by the heterogeneity in the following design features:

- characteristics of the youth being studied in terms of age, gender, sexual orientation, ethnicity, family social class, and place of residence
- research designs being used, including in-depth ethnographic studies of small and large local programs, cross-sectional and longitudinal survey-type studies of youth development across a diverse set of contexts, large- and small-scale experimental evaluations of both long-standing programs and new programs, descriptive studies of programs considered to be effective by the communities in which they reside, meta-analyses of other published articles, and more traditional summative reviews of both published and nonpublished reports

- the "outcomes" being studied, which ranged from such youth characteristics as increases in academic achievement, school engagement, mental health, and life skills to decreases in, or avoidance of, such problematic outcomes as teen pregnancy, alcohol and drug use/abuse, and involvement in delinquent and violent behaviors, as well as the quality of implementation of program goals
- level of study focus and analyses, which ranged from individual micro-level changes to much more macro-level changes (community or even city or state)

In addition to these variations, of course, were the variations associated with our initial goal, namely, to look at both school-based and community-based programs and to look at both prevention intervention and positive youth development programs. Being both optimists and intellectual "lumpers," we decided not to limit the scope of our review in hopes of providing as comprehensive a set of conclusions as possible at this point in time. Although we provide some discussion of the strengths and weaknesses of the methods we found, we do not want to focus too much attention on these problems because we found amazing convergence in the findings and conclusions across the various studies we reviewed. This convergence is made even more important by the diversity of methods used to gather the data.

Extracurricular Programs

As noted, a variety of methods have been used to study extracurricular and other after-school programs for youth. Most of the studies of extracurricular activities have relied on either cross-sectional or longitudinal survey methods that link participation in such activities to a variety of different individual-level outcomes, including indicators of school achievement and engagement, mental health, social development, and involvement in several different types of problem behaviors. Typically, the primary goal of such studies is to describe the relation between participation and other individual-level indicators of youth development. Few of these studies directly measure characteristics of the programs themselves (although more of this type of work is occurring in recent studies). Consequently, such studies tell us little about the actual characteristics of the programs that might explain any observed changes in participants' characteristics. Nonetheless, they represent a first step along the road toward more firm inferential conclusions. Sports psychologists have done a better job of assessing the specific features of sports programs in their work on effective coaches and effective programs. We include these studies in the extracurricular activities section.

Even the longitudinal studies of extracurricular activities and after-school activities are subject to selection concerns. Some of the recent longitudinal studies have included the most obvious third variables likely to provide an alternative selection bias explanation for longitudinal changes. Some have also gathered data consistent with the theory-based evaluation perspective outlined later in this section; in these studies, the researchers have measured the hypothesized mediators of participation in regard to individual change and then used causal modeling techniques to test these hypotheses. Such designs tell us more about the plausible "causes" of the longitudinal changes that might be associated with participation in the activity. Almost none of the studies of extracurricular activities have used random assignment, experimental intervention designs to pin down more definitively the consequences of activity participation. Those that have, such as the evaluations of the Teen Outreach Program's service learning experience, are included in our review of program evaluations.

After-School and Out-of-School Programs

Researchers studying after-school programs, whether in schools or in community organizations, have typically used two strategies: nonexperimental descriptive study strategies and experimental or quasi-experimental program evaluation strategies. In this chapter, we focus on two types of studies: nonexperimental studies of programs nominated as highly effective by the communities in which they reside and more formal evaluation studies that involve either experimental or quasi-experimental methods of evaluation. Although these latter methods are often considered the "gold standard" of program evaluation, they are quite expensive and difficult to implement. In addition, in our opinion, they often do not represent the best technique for studying community-based after-school programs. Given the controversy that rages regarding what constitutes legitimate evidence of program effectiveness, however, we feel compelled to say a little bit about this issue before reviewing the evidence from different methodologies.

In our opinion, the most appropriate method of studying after-school experiences depends on several factors. Most important, the method used depends on the question being asked. The method also depends on the nature of the "thing" being studied. As noted earlier, studies of these types of experiences have focused on at least four different levels: the individual across time, programs, organizations, and communities. Programs themselves are also composed of different specific types of activities. Similarly, organizations usually comprise a wide variety of programs and activities. They are also very heterogeneous themselves, including school-based after-school centers, parks and recreation centers and leagues, community centers, amateur sports leagues, faith-based centers, and the myriad places and opportunities developed by community-based and national youth organizations such as the YMCA, YWCA, 4-H, Boys' and Girls' Clubs, Girls Inc., Beacons, and the 21st Century Learning Centers. Community is the geographical and political place in which programs and organizations operate. Defining what constitutes a community is a complex and controversial task. The best method of investigation depends on which of these levels one wants to study.

Inherent in this levels perspective is the notion that "higher order levels" are composed of "lower order levels." For example, national organizations such as Boys' and Girls' Clubs and Girls Inc. comprise many different programs; programs are made up of activities, and activities can be broken down into specific activity components. Individuals usually select from the array of activities in both the program and the organization, and they typically manifest a unique pattern of participation. Many funders and stakeholders are interested in whether the "organization" is working rather in than the more specific programs and activities, because they usually fund specific organizations rather than specific programs and rely on the organization staff to make decisions about the programs or activities to include.

However, the most comprehensive theories about programming effects typically focus on either the program level or the activities within the program. Not surprisingly, most experimental and quasi-experimental program evaluations involve the same focus, for two major reasons: (a) Programs and activities are simple enough to allow for explicit theories regarding the nature of proposed effects on youth development, and (b) programs and activities are small enough to make random assignment to treatment and control groups possible. They are also usually sufficiently well developed that manuals and essential materials can be designed and disseminated to organizations throughout the country. The strongest examples of such evaluations are reviewed in the meta-analyses of mental health intervention programs and selected positive youth development programs such as the Teen Outreach Program, Big Brothers/Big Sisters, and the Seattle Social Development Project (also known as SOAR).

Randomized experimental evaluations are much more difficult to conduct at the organization and community levels. For example, there are a variety of challenges to using experimental designs to evaluate large nationally visible organizations such as 4-H and Boys' and Girls' Clubs. First, national organizations differ in their local programming. Consequently, even if one could successfully implement a truly randomized trial evaluation design for specific sites, it is not clear that the information gained would generalize to other sites. In addition, since these organizations are complex and offer a varied assortment of programs, the level of evaluation needs to be quite general. For example, one could assess whether an organization provides the kinds of general environmental conditions outlined in our concluding section and then whether participation in the organization leads to increases in very general outcomes such as community-level high school graduation rates.

One might also evaluate the organizational characteristics needed to support high-quality programming for youth by randomly assigning some of the organizational sites to one form of management and other sites to different forms of management. Such information would be very helpful in furthering our understanding of the reasons why organizations and programs often fail owing to inadequate political, economic, and community social supports as well as why programs found to be effective in one setting are not effective in other settings. But this information will tell us little about the specific aspects of the social context that produce positive developmental results for the participating children and adolescents.

Even evaluating programs within organizations can be quite difficult. Most after-school and in-school nonacademic programs are voluntary. Although parents may try to insist that their children attend, their ability to enforce their desires on their children declines as the children move into and through adolescence. In addition, as noted earlier, many community organizations for youth include a diverse array of programs from which to select. Often, young people's selections vary from week to week or day to day, making each individual youth's experiences quite unique.

Each of these program and organizational characteristics has implications for experimental program evaluation. For example, the voluntary nature of many community-based programs creates a problem with selection bias. When such programs are offered at school during the regular school hours, random assignment may be easier and more successful because the participants are more likely to attend regularly and complete the program. In contrast, the voluntary nature of joining and attending after-school community-based youth programs, particularly if they are situated in nonschool settings during nonschool hours, leads to more sporadic attendance and higher rates of dropping out. Consequently, researchers are faced with uncontrolled factors that influence attendance. In this case, rigid adherence to random assignment classification in analyzing one's results is likely to lead to underestimation of the program's effectiveness for those youth who are actually exposed to the program over an extended period of time.

Similarly, the diverse nature of many community programs for youth makes exact specification of the treatment problematic. Because individuals can select which parts of the programming to attend and how often, evaluators typically know little about each individual's exposure to various aspects of this programming. Such variation makes it difficult to determine which aspects of the programming are responsible for which developmental outcomes.

Finally, the evolving nature of many youth programs poses problems for evaluation. Experimental methods usually assume a static program. According to several nonexperimental studies of youth programs, the most highly respected and well-attended programs are dynamic shifting, for example, in response to seasonal activity structures, changing clientele, changing staff, and information derived from ongoing reflective practice and self-evaluation as well as from the youth themselves (McLaughlin, 2000; McLaughlin, Irby, & Langman, 1994). It is difficult to design random assignment experimental evaluations that capture this dynamic aspect of programs considered to be highly successful by community members.

Given these concerns, it is not surprising that some of the most careful studies of extracurricular and other after-school and positive youth developmental programs involve either nonexperimental methods or mixed methods in which small experiments are embedded as part of an action research agenda. We summarize some of these efforts in our section on nonexperimental studies. It is also not surprising that some of the strongest experimental evaluations of nonacademic programs for youth have been conducted on school-based programs often offered during regular school hours. Interestingly, even though such evaluations often assess programs' effects on academic as well as nonacademic indicators of positive development, the programs are often listed as prevention programs. We discuss this issue later as well.

Studying organized, systematic community-wide efforts at increasing the provision and accessibility of quality experiences for youth is even more challenging. Nonetheless, there is a growing interest in efforts at this level. Both researchers and policy advocates are coming to the conclusion that substantial and sustainable increments in the quantity and accessibility of high-quality after-school experiences for America's youth will require community-wide initiatives. We were struck with this new trend in our review of newly emerging programs. Many positive youth development advocates are now stressing the need for this approach to youth programming (e.g., Connell et al., 2000; Gambone, 1997; Greenberg, Domitrovich, & Bumbarger, 2001; Halpern, Barker, & Mollard, 2000; Walker, 2001). Individuals interested in whole-service schools also often advocate this perspective (e.g., Adelman & Taylor, 1997; Dryfoos, 1994, 1995; Holtzman, 1997; McMahon, Ward, Pruett, Davidson, & Griffith, 2000). It is unlikely that experimental randomized trial designs are appropriate for studying such community-wide initiatives. Instead, approaches are more closely linked to the new theory-based models of program evaluation (e.g., Connell et al., 2000; Gambone, 1997). We describe this approach next. However, we have not included research on these community-wide initiatives because they are beyond the scope of what we are trying to accomplish in this review.

Theory-Based Evaluation

Given the difficulties in implementing random assignment evaluations of youth-serving programs and organizations, some evaluators have suggested an alternative: theory-based evaluation (e.g., Connell et al., 2000). These scholars claim that theory-based evaluation can be used to study the effectiveness of social programs. They argue that many social and physical scientists test their causal hypotheses by comparing obtained data with predicted patterns of data. The predicted patterns are derived from strong theory. They propose that a similar strategy may be more useful than randomized trials in studying the effectiveness of many social programs, particularly those based on strong and complex theories of change. Although this remains a controversial claim, we believe that this approach provides a very useful alternative to random assignment evaluation, particularly when more complex organizations and community-wide initiatives are the target of study. In addition, we believe that the general strategy of using strong theoretical models to guide program design and study is important for both nonexperimental and experimental studies of all forms of youth-serving programs, including school-based learning programs and extracurricular activities at school as well as community-based out-of-school programs.

Advocates of theory-based evaluation acknowledge the importance of substantive theory, quantitative assessment, and causal modeling, but they do not require experimental or even quasi-experimental designs. Instead, they focus on causal modeling derived from a well-specified theory of change. First, the researchers, usually in collaboration with the program developers, work out a comprehensive model of change that specifies all of the relations (both mediated and moderated) among the various contextual characteristics and youth "outcome" characteristics. Often, these theoretical models include several layers of hypothesized relations between different aspects of the context as well as between different aspects of the relation of context to youth outcomes.

These models lay out a predicted sequence of contextual changes that must occur before one can expect to see changes in youth "outcomes." Thus, the models propose which contextual features must change first in order to produce changes in other contextual features as well as which contextual features are likely to produce changes in which specific youth "outcomes." Finally, these theoretical models sometimes specify how characteristics of the young people themselves, as well as of the program personnel, are likely to affect the relations outlined in the general model. For example, the most comprehensive of such models hypothesize differential effectiveness of program characteristics for various groups of youth and program personnel.

Measures are developed and then collected on all of the causal links between contextual or program characteristics and "outcomes." In the best of such designs, these measures are collected over time so that the hypothesized mediational and moderational relations can be tested as the program is implemented. The researchers then use the data collected from these measures to conduct causal analyses, typically using sophisticated longitudinal data-analytic techniques. If the causal modeling analyses indicate that the obtained data are consistent with the predictions of the program's theory, the researchers are willing to conclude that the theory is valid and that the program is successful for the reasons outlined in the theory.

Even if time does not permit assessing all of the postulated causal links, information on the quality of initial program implementation is typically gathered, because implementation variables are usually the first constructs in the causal model of the program. Thus, even if the hypothesized youth outcome results are not initially obtained, the early data provide some evidence about the extent to which the implementation is proceeding as predicted by the theory. Then the developmental outcomes can be assessed at a later stage when sufficient time has passed for the proposed mediating mechanisms to have their full effect on the proposed outcomes. Very few of the studies we found used this approach at any more than a superficial level. We will know much more about the impact of the specific aspects of programs on specific indicators of positive youth development, including those assets linked to school achievement and lifelong learning, when theory-based approaches are used in both experimental and nonexperimental designs.

EXTRACURRICULAR, SPORTS, AND LEISURE ACTIVITIES

The release of *A Matter of Time* by the Carnegie Corporation of New York (1992) focused attention on the role productive use of time might play in successful adolescent development and school achievement. It illustrated how much discretionary time adolescents have and how much of this time is spent on unstructured activities such as "hanging out" with friends, watching television, and listening to music. The authors argued that constructive, organized activities would represent a better use of adolescents' time because (a) doing good things with one's time takes time away from opportunities to get involved in risky activities, (b) one can learn good things while engaged in constructive activities (e.g., specific competencies, prosocial values and attitudes), and (c) involvement in organized activity settings increases the possibility of establishing positive social supports and networks that can facilitate both current levels of school engagement and achievement and subsequent educational and occupational attainment.

Four lines of work provide support for these suggestions: classic sociology studies of the relation of extracurricular activities to school achievement, research emerging from the newer field of leisure studies, research in sports psychology, and recent work emerging from interdisciplinary studies of adolescent development. Several sociological studies conducted during the 1970s documented a strong link between adolescents' extracurricular activities and adult educational attainment, occupation, and income, even after social class and cognitive ability had been controlled (Elliott & Voss, 1974; Hanks & Eckland, 1978; Landers & Landers, 1978; Otto, 1975, 1976; Otto & Alwin, 1977). Some of these studies also documented a protective association between extracurricular activity participation and involvement in delinquent and other risky behaviors (e.g., Elliott & Voss, 1974; Hanks & Eckland, 1978; Landers & Landers, 1978). Almost all of this work relied on survey methods used primarily at the descriptive level. Consequently, although these studies provide strong evidence for a link between participating in extracurricular activities and the aforementioned characteristics, they tell us little about the reasons for this association.

Research within both leisure studies and adolescent development has focused renewed attention on the probable benefits for youth of participating in the kinds of constructive leisure activities associated with extracurricular programs. In these fields, researchers stress the difference between relaxed leisure (enjoyable but not demanding activities) and constructive, organized activities that both require effort and provide a forum in which to express one's identity and passion (Agnew & Petersen, 1989; Csikszentmihalyi, 1991; Csikszentmihalyi & Kleiber, 1991; Fine, Mortimer, & Roberts, 1990; Grieves, 1989; Haggard & Williams, 1992; Kleiber, Larson, & Csikszentmihalyi, 1986; Larson, 2000; Larson & Kleiber, 1993; Larson & Richards, 1989). Like the authors of *A Matter of Time*, these researchers predict more beneficial outcomes for participation in constructive leisure precisely because constructive leisure provides opportunities (a) to acquire and practice specific social, physical, and intellectual skills that may be useful in a wide variety of settings, including school; (b) to contribute to the well-being of one's community and to develop a sense of agency as a member of that community; (c) to belong to a socially recognized and valued group; (d) to establish supportive social networks of both peers and adults that can help in the present as well as the future; and (e) to experience and deal with challenges.

Support for these predicted benefits is evident in the work of the researchers cited in the previous paragraph as well as new research being conducted by interdisciplinary scholars interested in adolescent development. For example, Mahoney and Cairns (1997) and McNeal (1995) found that participation in extracurricular activities during high school is associated with declines in the odds over time of school dropout, particularly during the early high school years and for high-risk youth (see also Mahoney, 2000). Furthermore, this link is linearly related to the number of years in which a youth participates in extracurricular activities (Eccles & Barber, 1999; Mahoney, Cairns, & Farmer, in press). Mahoney (1997, 2000) has also shown a connection between such experiences and reduced rates of criminal offending over time. In addition, adolescents involved in a broad range of activities that provide the opportunity for service report lower rates of substance use than their noninvolved peers (Youniss, McLellan, & Yates, 1999; Youniss, Yates, & Su, 1997). Finally, sports participation is linked over time to a lower likelihood of school dropout and higher rates of college attendance, particularly for low-achieving and blue-collar male athletes (Deeter, 1990; Eccles & Barber, 1999; Gould & Weiss, 1987; Holland & Andre, 1987; Howell & McKenzie, 1987; Kirshnit, Ham, & Richards, 1989; McNeal, 1995; Melnick, Vanfossen, & Sabo, 1988).

Participation in extracurricular activities is also linked to increases over time on such indicators of positive development as interpersonal competence, self-concept, high school grade point average, school engagement, and educational aspirations (Eccles & Barber, 1999; Elder & Conger, 2000; Lamborn, Brown, Mounts, & Steinberg, 1992; Mahoney et al., in press; Newmann, Wehlage, & Lamborn, 1992; Winne & Walsh, 1980). Again, these associations increase in strength with increasing numbers of activities. This is particularly true if one is involved in a leadership role. Similarly, involvement in high school extracurricular and service learning activities is predictive of such indicators of healthy adult development as higher educational achievement, better job quality at the age of 25 years, active participation in the political process and other types of volunteer activities, continued sport engagement, and better mental health (Barber, Eccles, & Stone, 2001; DeMartini, 1983; Glancy, Willits, & Farrell, 1986; Marsh, 1992; Youniss, McLellan, Su, & Yates, 1999; Youniss, McLellan, & Yates, 1997; Youniss, Yates, & Su, 1997). These relations hold even after the other obvious predictors of such outcomes are controlled, giving us some confidence that these effects do not simply reflect the selection factors that lead to participation in the first place.

Together, these studies provide good evidence that participating in extracurricular activities is associated with both short- and long-term indicators of positive development, including school achievement and educational attainment. However, they tell us less about the reasons for these associations. For the most part, the studies used either cross-sectional or longitudinal survey methods. These methods provide good evidence of an association but weak evidence of an actual causal inference and even weaker evidence regarding the actual features of the experience that might matter.

Because researchers using longitudinal designs typically assess change over time and include indicators of the most obvious third variables in their analyses, these studies provide stronger evidence that participation actually causes change. However, selection is still a concern. Evidence from recent studies suggests that there are both selection and participation effects. Youth who choose to participate in extracurricular activities are different from those who do not in ways that are predictive of better long-term developmental trajectories. These youth also appear to benefit from their participation (Barber et al., 2001; Mahoney et al., in press). More work needs to be done using experimental treatment designs as well as interrupted time series designs. Some of the data sets used in these studies have the information necessary at the individual level to conduct the latter type of analyses.

More problematic is the fact that few of the studies actually measured characteristics of the extracurricular activities themselves. Even the best longitudinal studies either did not collect measures of the activities themselves or collected very weak measures, making inferences about which specific aspects of the programs and activities might be responsible for change quite speculative. There is a presumption that such activity contexts provide the kinds of experiences that should promote positive development. But work in the field of sport psychology shows that some coaches and parents provide a more supportive context for sport engagement than others (e.g., Leff & Hoyle, 1995; Patrick et al., 1999; Pensgaard & Roberts, 2000; Roberts & Treasure, 1992; Smoll, Smith, Barnett, & Everett, 1993). We discuss this work in more detail later.

Similarly, high school sports participation has also been linked to higher levels of alcohol consumption and abuse during the high school years and to higher rates of truancy (Eccles & Barber, 1999; Lamborn et al., 1992). In addition, participation in activities in which a high proportion of the youth are involved in delinquent behavior is linked to increases in individual participants' involvement in such behavior (Dishion, McCord, & Poulin, 1999; Dishion, Poulin, & Burraston, 2001; Mahoney, Stattin, & Magnusson, 2001; Poulin, Dishion, & Burraston, 2001). Clearly, we need to know more about the specific characteristics of these programs that lead to positive as opposed to negative adolescent "outcomes."

Certainly, years of work on schooling demonstrate that certain types of classroom experiences are more effective than others in promoting learning as well as other aspects of positive development (e.g., see Eccles, Wigfield, & Schiefele, 1998; Maehr & Midgley, 1996). Although there are the beginnings of strong theoretical models regarding the specific characteristics of extracurricular activity settings that ought to matter as well as the mediating mechanisms through which these settings have their influence, more empirical work is badly needed to test these predictions. Recent studies are moving in this direction.

Recent Studies Focused on Mediating Mechanisms

Larson and Colleagues

Larson and his colleagues (e.g., Larson, 1994, 2000; Larson & Verma, 1999) have shown that young people report feeling both more challenge and enjoyment (as opposed to boredom) in organized out-of-school activity settings than in classrooms. Several different theoretical systems lead to the hypothesis that beneficial consequences should be associated with involvement in settings that elicit such reactions (e.g., effectance motivation theory [Harter, 1978], flow theory [Csikszentmihalyi, 1991; Csikszentmihalyi, Rathunde, Whalen, & Wong, 1993], goal theory [Maehr & Midgley, 1996], self-determination theory [Deci & Ryan, 1985; Ryan & Deci, 2000], the sport commitment model [Scanlan, 1999, 2000, 2002; Scanlan, Carpenter,

Schmidt, Simons, & Keeler, 1993; Scanlan & Simons, 1995], stage-environment fit theory [Eccles et al., 1993]). Similar emotional reactions have been reported as critical to continued participation by adolescents involved in both sports and instrumental music activities in the qualitative studies of Eccles and her colleagues (e.g., Fredricks et al., 2002). Larson and his colleagues are now studying these predictions as well as conducting more qualitative studies of young people's experiences in organized activity settings.

Eccles and Barber

Recent work by Eccles and Barber provides another example of an attempt to move beyond description to a theoretical analysis of the nature of experiences in extracurricular activities and the outcomes likely to result. In a series of analyses, these researchers assessed the links between involvement in a variety of extracurricular activities during the high school years and a range of indicators of both positive and problematic development during adolescence and young adulthood (Barber et al., 2001; Eccles & Barber, 1999). Their sample represented a socioeconomically diverse population of European and African American youth in southeastern Michigan. They began studying these youth when they were in the sixth grade; on average, the participants were 29 years of age in 2002.

Because these researchers were interested in the mechanisms that mediate the association between activity involvement and both positive and problematic adolescent development, they asked their participants two additional sets of questions, one focusing on identity and another focusing on the nature of one's peer group. The identity question asked the youth to select which of the five characters portrayed in the movie *Breakfast Club* they were most like. In the movie, these five characters labeled themselves "the jock," "the brain," "the criminal," "the princess," and "the basket case." The peer questions asked the participants to indicate what proportion of their friends had a series of characteristics related to being either academically oriented or involved in such risky behaviors as drinking and using drugs. The researchers hypothesized that activity involvement would influence behavior through its impact on identity formation and the social norms of one's peer networks.

In support of this prediction, the adolescents who participated in volunteer service and faith-based activities exhibited the most consistent pattern of positive outcomes: higher academic achievement in high school than one would predict based on family background characteristics and the individual's performance on a standardized academic achievement test administered in Grade 9 and lower rates of involvement in risky behaviors such as alcohol and drug use in high school and during their early 20s. They were also the group most likely to identify themselves as "brains" and the group that had the most friends who were academically oriented and the fewest who were engaged in risky behaviors.

A different pattern characterized youth involved in both team sports and school-spirit-related clubs and organizations. On one hand, these youth, both male and female, did better academically both in high school and after high school than one would have predicted based on their family's income and education and their own performance on a standardized test of academic abilities administered in ninth grade. On the other hand, these youth also engaged in more alcohol consumption and abuse than their noninvolved peers during both high school and young adulthood, particularly while they attended college. When asked their identity type, these youth selected "jock" and "princess," two groups that also reported both high rates of alcohol consumption and high academic achievement. When asked about their peer group, these youth reported having high proportions of friends who were both academically oriented and involved in relatively high levels of alcohol consumption. This pattern of convergence explained a substantial amount of the variance associated with high rates of both drinking and academic achievement during the high school and college years.

The critical mediating role of peer affiliations in the link between extracurricular activities and youth outcomes has also been documented by Eder and Parker (1987), Kinney (1993), and Youniss et al. (1999). These researchers suggest that peer affiliations influence development, either positively or negatively, through the social norms associated with the peer group culture, through reductions in social alienation, and through acquisition of improved social skills. Such suggestions are quite consistent with what is believed to be true about peer influence more generally (e.g., Brown, 1990; Dishion et al., 2001; Kinney, 1993).

Mahoney and Colleagues

These researchers have been doing work linking extracurricular activities and out-of-school programs to both positive and negative adolescent outcomes. Like many such studies, their early work took for granted that extracurricular activities are voluntary, structured, challenging, and connected to the school (e.g., Mahoney et al., in press). They argue that these characteristics should increase participation and retention as well as enjoyment, which in turn will increase learning of interpersonal skills, positive social norms, membership in prosocial peer groups, and emotional and social connections to school. These latter assets should increase mental health, school engagement, school achievement, and long-term educational outcomes and should decrease participation in problem behaviors, provided that problem behaviors are not endorsed by the peer cultures that emerge in these activities. Most of their work (as cited earlier) provides strong evidence of an association between participation and reductions in problem behaviors.

In a recent study, Mahoney et al. (in press) used longitudinal data to test the hypothesis that participation leads to increases in college attendance through its impact on interpersonal skills and educational aspirations. The structural equation modeling results provided strong support of this hypothesis. The data also supported the hypothesis that participation affects educational aspirations and college attendance through increasing the participants' popularity with peers; this relation, however, was true only for youth who already possessed good interpersonal skills. This work, then, provides preliminary evidence that extracurricular programs affect such outcomes as college attendance through their more immediate influences on adolescents' social skills and peer relationships. The work does not provide strong evidence regarding which particular aspects of the extracurricular activity context account for these effects.

Mahoney and his colleagues are studying the characteristics of leisure activities that are linked with both positive and negative youth outcomes. They have found that participating in highly structured and adult-supervised leisure activities is associated with less antisocial behavior than participating in low-structure leisure activities at youth recreation centers (Mahoney & Stattin, 2000). Also, they have found that participation in after-school activities is linked to lower levels of depressed affect primarily among those youth who perceive high social support from their activity leader (Mahoney & Stattin, 2002).

Sports Programs

More systematic work on the context of youth-serving programs has been done in the field of sports psychology. Typically, these studies use natural variations across coaches and programs to compare participants' motivation, performance, and continued involvement in particular sport activities. As is the case with Larson's work, these studies demonstrate that continued involvement is linked to the experience of high levels of enjoyment and challenge and low levels of anxiety while engaged in the sport activity in question (e.g., Brustad, Babkes, & Smith, 2001; Carpenter & Scanlan, 1998; Scanlan, Stein, & Ravizza, 1991; Scanlan et al., 1993; Smith, 1986; Weiss & Petlichkoff, 1989).

A few of the studies in this area have used experimental designs to test specific hypotheses about important contextual features. Some of these studies focus on elite adolescent athletes; others focus on normative populations of youth who participate in the many community-based sports programs across the country. Few of the studies actually measure the association of participation in sports programs with other types of youth outcomes such as school performance or engaging in problem behaviors. As noted earlier, however, studies of extracurricular sports participation do suggest that such links exist.

In general, these studies show that youth develop better mental health, motivation, and values in sports programs that emphasize skill acquisition rather than winning (e.g., Roberts & Treasure, 1992) and stress the importance of coaches providing strong emotional support (e.g., Smoll et al., 1993). Furthermore, using an experimental design, Smoll and colleagues demonstrated that youth who work with a coach who has completed a 3-hour training program focusing on emotional support show greater increases in their self-esteem than youth working with coaches who have not had this training.

These studies also document the importance of strong perceived social support from coaches, family members, peers, and the audience (Gould, Eklund, & Jackson,

1991, 1993; Gould, Finch, & Jackson, 1993; Scanlan, 2002; Scanlan & Lewthwaite, 1986). In each of the studies, the opportunity to form strong and supportive peer relationships was a strong motivator (e.g., Scanlan, Carpenter, Lobel, & Simons, 1993). These studies also provide strong correlational evidence of the importance of motivational scaffolding. Researchers interested in goal theory (e.g., Maehr & Midgley, 1996) stress the importance of mastery motivation as an individual characteristic and mastery motivational climates as classroom characteristics for optimal learning in the school context. These classroom characteristics include exposure to challenging activities in a climate of social acceptance and a focus on improvement and mastery rather than socially comparative performance. Sports psychologists have applied goal theory to the sports context and found strong evidence of similar dynamics at both the individual and contextual levels (e.g., Fox, Goudas, Biddle, Duda, & Armstrong, 1994; Scanlan, 2002; Stephens, 1998).

Summary

There is converging evidence from several different types of studies suggesting that involvement in constructive nonacademic activities both at school and in the community facilitates continued school engagement and academic achievement as well as other aspects of positive development during adolescence and into the early adulthood years. A few studies provide evidence regarding the particular aspects of these extracurricular and community-based activities that might account for such associations, including provision of challenging learning opportunities in structured settings, provision of opportunities to form strong social bonds with peers and adults, and support for a mastery motivational orientation.

The findings of Eccles and her colleagues, as well as the work conducted by Mahoney and his colleagues and by Dishion and his colleagues on the potential negative and positive effects of peers, also suggest a strong role for social norms. All three of these teams have shown that problematic behaviors on the part of peer participants in organized activity settings are linked over time to increases in involvement in such behaviors by many of the participants. However, much more research is needed before we will fully understand the impact of participation in extracurricular activities on positive youth development.

NONEXPERIMENTAL STUDIES OF YOUTH PROGRAMS

There have been a number of excellent nonexperimental studies of community-based programs for youth over the past 15 years, and there are several more in process. Probably the most comprehensive such study was conducted by Shirley Bryce Heath and Milbrey McLaughlin (e.g., McLaughlin, 2000; McLaughlin et al., 1994). Over the course of 10 years, these researchers used a variety of quantitative and qualitative methods to study approximately 120 youth-based organizations in 34 different cities and towns. They selected the organizations through nominations from youth and other community members of organizations that "work." Thus, they studied organizations that were widely regarded in their communities as successful by the community members themselves.

They also focused on organizations that serve a high proportion of youth living in high-risk neighborhoods or communities. Not surprisingly, then, the youth served in these organizations included a high proportion of those typically considered hard to reach and most likely to drop out of organized activity centers. McLaughlin and Heath used a variety of techniques to assess the influence of these centers on the participants, ranging from the young people's own reports to comparisons of their responses on several quantitative measures with the responses of a nationally representative sample of comparable youth.

Overwhelmingly, the youth in these organizations reported that their participation had changed their lives. These organizations had provided a sanctuary in what many youth felt was a hostile and nonresponsive world. They reported learning essential skills as well as building trusting relationships with adults and other youth. The testimonies of these young people about their experiences in these centers are truly inspiring.

A comparison of the participants' ratings of their experiences and feelings in these centers with identical ratings of their experiences and feelings in school was equally striking. Both the young men and the young women indicated that they were more likely to enjoy their time, to feel respected, to feel comfort and trust, and to feel supported at their center than at their school.

A similar picture of success is evident in the quantitative comparisons. On average, the youth in these programs exhibited better outcomes than comparable youth in a national sample (respondents from the National Educational Longitudinal Study) on several indicators of healthy development. They were more likely to report feeling good about themselves and being confident about their abilities to achieve their goals. They reported higher levels of self-worth, personal agency, and personal efficacy. They were more likely to report having received recognition for good academic performance at school and were 20% more likely to expect to go on to college. They were also more likely to be involved in their communities and to expect to continue to be involved in the future. Finally, in a follow-up study of 60 participants in three urban communities, the majority were in fact well on their way to what most would consider a successful transition into adulthood by their early 20s.

What did these organizations share that might help explain these positive youth outcomes? In *Community Counts*, McLaughlin (2000; see www.PublicEducation.org) sums up their communality in terms of the concept of intentional learning environments. She notes that the organizations differed in "nearly every objective way possible" (p. 8); what they shared in common corresponded "to the core elements of an effective learning environment as described by learning theorists" (p. 9). Such environments have three major components: They are youth centered, knowledge centered, and assessment centered. With regard to being youth centered, these organizations

- responded to diverse talents, skills, and interests by providing a rich array of activities that involved opportunities to participate at all levels of expertise
- identified and built on the strengths of the participating youth by providing opportunities for them to do what they could best do and to learn new skills
- used developmentally and cultural appropriate materials that allowed youth to grow in terms of skill and leadership within the specific activities
- provided extensive personal attention from the adults involved
- stressed youth leadership and voice
- actively recruited youth using a variety of locally appropriate methods

These organizations were knowledge centered in that they

- had clear learning foci (i.e., they were "about something in particular"; McLaughlin, 2000, p. 10)
- had quality content and exemplary instruction
- used the principles of embedded curriculum so that a range of academic competencies and life skills were being taught within each type of activity
- used many different types of "teachers," including the youth themselves

Finally, in terms of being assessment centered, the organizations had

- clearly articulated "cycles of planning, practice, and performance" (McLaughlin, 2000, p. 13)
- regular opportunities for feedback and recognition, often through public performances and other forms of celebration
- feedback focused on improvement and meeting individual specific objectives rather than competition and social comparison

In addition to these intentional learning environment characteristics, the organizations also stood out in the level of social support and care provided by the adults. The adults were passionate about the youth in their community. They were often available at all hours and regularly served as advocates for their members in a variety of situations. In this sense, they actively worked to expand their young people's social capital. Consequently, the youth were able to establish trusting relationships with these adults in a way that they were typically unable to do with their teachers.

These organizations were also characterized by physical and psychological safety, by clear rules that were consistently and fairly enforced, by positive social norms regarding respectful and civil behavior, and by a strong sense of shared responsibility for the organization among both adults and youth. In many of the centers, an explicit policy was in place according to which members were expected to support each other and to treat each other with respect, which meant that hostilities between members that existed outside of the organization were not to be expressed in the centers.

McLaughlin et al. (1994) noted that such a collection of contextual features is not common across the range of after-school programs in most communities. Not surprisingly, then, these centers often had large waiting lists, while other nearby centers and programs were unable to fill their available slots.

Several other nonexperimental program evaluation studies have yielded a similar picture of programs that appear to be successful in terms of several criteria. For example, in their study of literacy programs for children, Spielberger and Halpern (2002) found that the most engaging programs (a) involve literacy activities that are personally useful, are culturally relevant, and provide a balance of seriousness and play (i.e., they use principles of embedded curriculum); (b) provide opportunities for performance that allow both the children themselves and their parents, teachers, and other community members to share in their accomplishments; (c) use a variety of literacy activities so that children with different interests and talents can be engaged; (d) have high expectations for all of the children in terms of their capacity to learn; (e) have genuine enthusiasm for literacy activities; (f) provide strong social support and create comfortable, safe places for literacy activities; and (g) make use of a variety of community resources and expertise in planning literacy experiences.

Similarly, more quantitative nonexperimental studies conducted by Vandell and her colleagues (on quality after-school child care programs; e.g., Pierce, Hamm, & Vandell, 1999; Posner & Vandell, 1994, 1999; Vandell & Posner, 1999; Vandell & Ramanan, 1991; Vandell & Shumow, 1999), by the UC Links program (on after-school programs; www.uclinks.org/what/sum_report.html), and by other scholars (e.g., Howes, Olenick, & Der-Kiureghian, 1987; Marshall et al., 1997; Pettit, Laird, Bates, & Dodge, 1997; Sheley, 1984) document the importance of intentional learning environments; warm, supportive, and reliable adult staff; opportunities for choice and youth leadership; respectful interactions among the youth themselves; developmentally and culturally appropriate materials and activities; and safe, well-equipped space. Many of the positive effects shown in these studies are especially marked for low income or at-risk youth.

Interestingly, some of the after-school child care programs produced negative as well as positive results. For example, Pierce et al. (1999) found that first-grade boys in after-school care programs with positive emotional climates evidenced fewer problem behaviors and better academic performance than boys in programs with more negative emotional climates. Pierce and colleagues also looked at program structure and found that boys who attended programs that allowed more autonomy and choice had better social skills than boys who attended more regimented programs. Finally, Vandell and Pierce (1999) found that the strength of the beneficial associations depends on the extent of actual participation.

In summary, these nonexperimental studies suggest that the characteristics listed in Table 1 are likely to be important for positive youth development. A similar set of characteristics was suggested as representing critical contextual features in the recent National Research Council report *Community Programs to Promote Youth Development* (Eccles & Gootman, 2002). The characteristics presented in Table 1

TABLE 1 Contextual Features Likely to Support Positive Youth Development

- Adequate provisions for physical and psychological safety
- Developmentally appropriate levels of structure and adult supervision
- Strong social support from adults and peers
- Inclusive social networks and structures
- Strong positive social norms for behavior
- Intentional learning experiences designed to teach the skills necessary to do well in such social institutions as school and the workforce
- Motivational practices that support a mastery motivation focus
- Opportunities to make a real difference in and out of the organization—to experience leadership and mattering

are also consistent with most major theories of positive developmental contexts, including Csikszentmihalyi's work on flow (e.g., Csikszentmihalyi, 1991; Csikszentmihalyi et al., 1993); Deci and Ryan's work on self-determination theory (e.g., Deci & Ryan, 1985; Ryan & Deci, 2000); Eccles and colleagues' work on stage-environment fit (e.g., Eccles et al., 1993); Masten's work on resilience (e.g., Masten & Coatsworth, 1998); Midgley, Maehr, and Ames's work on goal theory (e.g., Maehr & Midgley, 1996); and Scanlan's work on sport commitment (e.g., Scanlan, 2002; Scanlan & Simons, 1995; Scanlan, Simons, Carpenter, Schmidt, & Keeler, 1993).

EXPERIMENTAL AND QUASI-EXPERIMENTAL
STUDIES OF YOUTH PROGRAMS

We found tracking down experimental and quasi-experimental evaluation studies of in- and out-of-school programs for youth quite challenging, because many of the best evaluations are not published in journals. Instead, they are often published as reports to the foundations and organizations that funded the evaluations. Consequently, we relied on either independently commissioned reviews of these reports or meta-analyses to identify the best experimental and quasi-experimental evaluation studies. We then contacted the sources and worked with a combination of the reviews and the materials we were able to obtain from these reviews. In this section, we summarize the findings of six major reviews of experimental and quasi-experimental evaluation studies of youth programs: two meta-analyses and four reviews of program evaluations focused on prevention programs and youth development programs. These reviews appeared in either published, professionally reviewed journals or highly reputable government documents between 1997 and 2002. In the latter category, we selected only government documents involving rigorous and well-specified methods of review in order to reduce the potential biases associated with reviews conducted by groups with high stakes in positive or negative conclusions. Programs cited in at least two of these reviews or characterized as model programs in any single review are summarized in Table 2.

(text continues on page 149)

TABLE 2   Effective Programs for Children and Adolescents

Program name/sample description	Program description	Postprogram outcomes/follow-up
Across Ages[1,2] n=562; 47%M, 53%F; 52.2%Bl, 9.1%Asn, 9%Lat, 15.8%Wh; 6th grade	Place: School, Community Components: Individual Intensity/Duration: Mentoring (2 hrs/wk), community service (1 hr every other week), social problem solving (26 1-hr sessions) over school yr Explicit Features: Mentoring by older adults, classroom-based life skills training, community service activities, workshops for parents Implicit Features: Social Support, Inclusion, Social Norms, Learning Focus, Motivational Scaffolding, Leadership/Mattering	Evaluation: Experimental ↑: Positive attitudes toward school, the future, older people, knowledge of elders, and community service ↓: School absence
Adolescent Transitions Project[1,3] (1) n=158 from 143 families; M=83, F=75; 95%Wh, 5%unspec; 10–14 yrs; 6th–8th grade (2) Irvine et al. (1999) n=303 families; 88%Wh; 61%M, 39%F; 12 yrs old	Place: Unspecified Components: Individual, Family Intensity/Duration: 12 over 18 hrs Explicit Features: Youth self-regulation skills training (teen focus group), parent management skills training (parent focus group), consultant to improve parent-youth communication (teen/parent focus group) Implicit Features: Learning Focus, Social Support, Inclusion, Social Norms, Motivational Scaffolding, Leadership/Mattering (2) Replication of the Parent Focus component only	Evaluation: Experimental ↑: Social learning ↓: Negative engagement with family, conflict, negative family events, youth aggression Follow-up: (1) ↑: School behavior problems for teen focus group (2) ↓: Child antisocial behavior

Big Brothers/Big Sisters[1,2] *n*=959; 60%Bl&Hisp combined, 40%unspec; 62.4%M; ages 10–16; low SES	Place: Community Components: Individual Intensity/Duration: 9–12 hrs/mth for 1 yr Explicit Features: Activities with mentor Implicit Features: Social Support, Inclusion, Social Norms, Motivational Scaffolding	Evaluation: Experimental ↑: GPA, parental trust ↓: Hitting behavior, likelihood of initiating alcohol and drug use, skipping school, lying to parents
Bullying Prevention Program[4] Grade: Norway: 4th–7th; *n*=2,500 in 42 schools; USA: 5th–8th; *n*=6,388	Place: School Components: Individual, Family, School Intensity/Duration: 9–12 hrs/mth for 1 yr Explicit Features: 32-page booklet included information on the scope, cause, and effects of school bullying and detailed suggestions for reducing and preventing bullying. Abbreviated bullying info to families with school-age children. A 25-minute video with vignettes of bullying situations. Students completed a brief bullying questionnaire related to bullying to increase awareness and promote discussion of the problem of bullying Implicit Features: Social Norms, Motivational Scaffolding, Learning Focus, Inclusion, Social Support	Evaluation: Quasi-experimental ↑: Satisfaction with school life, climate of order and discipline in the classroom, positive social relationships, positive attitude toward school and schoolwork ↓: Bullying, aggressive and antisocial behavior, 50% reduction in self-report of bullying and being bullied Follow-up: (20mths): Effects maintained US replication: Reduction in self-reported bullying, but not in being bullied

(continued)

TABLE 2 (*Continued*)

Program name/sample description	Program description	Postprogram outcomes/follow-up
Child Development Project[1,3] *n*=1,645; 24 schools from 6 districts; 3rd–6th grades; 11–12 yrs; 48%M, 52%F; 39–54%Wh, 17–23%Bl, 21–27%Hisp, 5–10%Asn, 2–3%other	Place: School Components: Individual, Family Intensity/Duration: Integrated curriculum over school year Explicit Features: Cooperative learning, reading and language arts, developmental discipline, school community building, home activities Implicit Features: Inclusion, Social Norms, Motivational Scaffolding, Leadership/Mattering, Social Support	Evaluation: Quasi-experimental ↑: Peer social acceptance ↓: Alcohol use, vehicle theft, loneliness, and social anxiety Analysis based on high, moderate, low implementation: High implementation group: (1st yr) ↓: Marijuana use, vehicle theft, carrying weapons; (2nd yr) ↓: Skipping school + 1st yr findings
Children's Aid Society Carrera Program[5] *n*=484; 45%M, 55%F; 56%Bl, 36%Hisp, 7%Bl/Hisp, 2%other; 13–15 yrs old, low SES	Place: Community youth serving organizations Components: Individual Intensity/Duration: 5 days/wk during school yr plus special sessions in summer through high school; mean of 16 hrs of participation/mth Explicit Features: Sex education, increase academic competency, work-related intervention, art and sports component. Also, mental and physical health care including contraception Implicit Features: Learning Focus, Leadership/Mattering, Motivational Scaffolding, Inclusion, Social Support, Social Norms	Evaluation: Experimental Follow-up: 3 yrs ↓: Initiation of sex, pregnancy, births ↑: Condom plus effective contraception method for girls (↓ for boys)

134

Children of Divorce Intervention Program[1,3] (3 evaluations)	Place: School	Evaluation: (1) Experimental
(1)[1,3] M=42, F=33 from 4 suburban schools; 100%Wh; 4th–6th grade	Components: Individual	↑: Adaptive assertiveness, peer sociability, following rules, frustration tolerance
(2)[3] n=104; F=46.5%; 69%Wh, 23%Bl, 5%Hisp, 3%other; 23% below poverty level	Intensity/Duration: (1,2,3) Multiple sessions	↓: Anxiety, learning problems
(3)[3] n=188; M=110, F=78 from 9 schools; 4th–6th grade; 56%Wh, 30%Bl, 10%Hisp, 3.6%Asn, 0.4%NatAm	Explicit Features: (1,2,3) Skill building in problem solving, communications, decision making, anger and anxiety management; (2) self-esteem session, (3) enhanced materials and more activities	(2) Quasi-experimental
		↑: Coping skills, positive feelings about family, competence, adjustment, assertive, peer social skills, frustration tolerance
	Implicit Features: Social Support, Social Norms, Learning Focus, Motivational Scaffolding	(3) Quasi-experimental
		↑: Coping skills, positive feelings about family, adjustment, positive divorce-related attitudes
		↓: Anxiety
Creating Lasting Connections[1,2] n=217 from 5 church communities; 77%Wh, 23%Bl; 12–14 yrs	Place: Church	Evaluation: Experimental
	Components: Individual, Family	↑: Youth use of community services, related action tendencies, perceived helpfulness
	Intensity/Duration: Youth (15 hrs); parents (55 hrs); volunteer service (18 hrs); follow-up and consultation support (1 yr)	↓: Onset of substance abuse delayed as parents changed their substance use beliefs and knowledge
	Explicit Features: Church community mobilization, parent and youth strategies to promote communication and self-management skills, follow-up case management service	
	Implicit Features: Social Support, Inclusion, Social Norms, Learning Focus, Motivational Scaffolding, Leadership/Mattering	

(continued)

TABLE 2 (*Continued*)

Program name/sample description	Program description	Postprogram outcomes/follow-up
Fast Track[1,3] n=898 in 385 classrooms at 4 sites; 66%M, 34%F; 50%Bl, 50%other; 1st–3rd grade	Place: School Components: Individual, Family Intensity/Duration: 3 20–30-min sessions per week through school yr + child/parental skill building (3-yr duration) Explicit Features: PATHS curriculum + 1st grade parent and child skill building for at-risk children, 2nd/3rd grade monthly meetings of parent and child groups Implicit Features: Social Support, Social Norms, Leadership/Mattering, Motivational Scaffolding, Inclusion, Learning Focus	Evaluation: Experimental ↑: Accepting authority, staying on task, appropriate emotional expression ↓: Oppositional/aggressive behavior, conduct problems, special education assignment
Incredible Years: Parent and Teacher Training Program n=328 families from 14 Head Start centers; 45.6%F (124), 54.4%M (148); 272 mothers; 19.1%Bl, 18%Hisp, 22.1%Asn, 1.5%NatAm, 2.2%unspec, 36.8%Wh; avg family income = $11,600	Place: Head Start Components: Individual, Family Intensity/Duration: 3 20–30-min sessions per week through school yr + child/parental skill building (3-yr duration) Explicit Features: PATHS curriculum + 1st grade parent and child skill building for at-risk children, 2nd/3rd grade monthly meetings of parent and child groups Implicit Features: Social Support, Social Norms, Leadership/Mattering, Motivational Scaffolding, Inclusion, Learning Focus	Evaluation: Experimental ↑: Accepting authority, staying on task, appropriate emotional expression ↓: Oppositional/aggressive behavior, conduct problems, special education assignment

Life Skills Training[1,4]
n=4,466 in 56 schools; 91%Wh, 9%unspec; 7th–9th grade

Place: School
Components: Individual
Intensity/Duration: 2 sessions/wk for 15 wks (Y1); 10 booster sessions (Y2); 5 booster sessions (Y3)
Explicit Features: Self-regulation skills (decision making, problem solving, anxiety coping), social skills, drug-related education, resistance training
Implicit Features: Social Norms, Social Support, Learning Focus, Motivational Scaffolding

Evaluation: Experimental
↑: Interpersonal skills, knowledge of smoking and substance abuse consequences
↓: Cigarette and marijuana smoking, alcohol intoxication and polydrug use
Follow-up: End of 12th grade
↓: Tobacco, alcohol, and marijuana use

Metropolitan Area Child Study[1]
(1) n=3,599; 40%Bl, 40%Hisp, 20%Wh; high-risk sample; 2nd/3rd & 5th/6th grades
(2) Eron et al. (2002)
n=1,518 high-risk; 60.7%M; 47.6%AfAm, 36.8%Hisp, 15.5%non-HispWh; 33–100% free lunch program

Place: School
Components: Individual, Family School
Intensity/Duration: (1) 40 1-hr sessions over 2 yrs; *YesICan* curriculum
(2) Conditions: (a) general classroom enhancement—teachers received 2 yrs of biweekly seminars; (b) above + small group meetings 1/wk for 28 wks over 2 yrs; (c) above + family intervention for 22 wks in 2nd yr
Explicit Features: (1,2) Teacher training program, social cognitive competency training, behavior management, family cohesiveness strategies

Evaluation: (1) Experimental
↑: Prosocial behavior
↓: Aggressive behavior in early intervention group, but increased aggression for one late intervention subgroup
(2) Longitudinal, quasi-experimental
↓: Aggressive behavior in (c) for early intervention (2nd, 3rd) in communities w/ adequate resources (effect size .59 SD); greater effect if 2nd exposure in 5th/6th grades (effect size .65 SD); inner-city children in (c) ↑ aggression (effect size .42 SD)
↑: Achievement for (a) early intervention (effect size = .83 SD)

(continued)

137

TABLE 2 (Continued)

Program name/sample description	Program description	Postprogram outcomes/follow-up
	(2) Conditions: (a) teacher training to promote emotional literacy, prosocial problem solving, self-regulation; (b) above + small group—prosocial beliefs/behavior; (c) Above + family intervention—family/ communication skills, build support networks, weekly phone calls, homework assignments Implicit Features: Social Support, Social Norms, Learning Focus, Inclusion, Motivational Scaffolding, Leadership/ Mattering	
Midwestern Prevention Project[1,2,4] n=4,153; 76.6%Wh, 19.2%Bl; 50.7%M; 6th–7th grade	Place: School, Community Components: Individual, Family, School, Community Intensity/Duration: School program (10 hrs), homework activities with parents (10 hrs) Explicit Features: Parent education about parent-child communication skills, resistance skills training for youth, community organization, mass media coverage Implicit Features: Social Norms, Social Support, Learning Focus, Motivational Scaffolding, Leadership/Mattering	Evaluation: Quasi-experimental ↓: Monthly, weekly, and heavy use of cigarettes, marijuana, and alcohol Follow-up: 3 yrs ↓: Monthly, weekly, and heavy use of cigarettes, marijuana, and alcohol 5 yrs: Less monthly drug use, weekly cigarette smoking

Penn Prevention Project[3]

(1) n=143; 5th/6th-grade students at risk for depression; 83%Wh, 11%Bl; 10–13 yrs old

(2) Pattison & Lynd-Stevenson (2001) n =66; 48%M, 52%F; 5th/6th grade in Australia

Place: School
Components: Individual
Intensity/Duration: 1.5 hrs/wk for 12 wks
Explicit Features: Cognitive behavioral; taught coping strategies to counteract cognitive distortions, specific focus on explanatory style
Implicit Features: Social Norms, Motivational Scaffolding, Learning Focus, Social Support

Evaluation:
(1) Quasi-experimental
↑: Improved classroom behavior
↓: Depressive symptoms, less likely to attribute negative events to stable, enduring causes (mediator)
Follow-up: 6 mths
↑: Parents reported improvements in children's home behavior
↓: Depressive symptoms 12, 18, 24 mths
↓: Depressive symptoms mediated by more optimistic explanatory style
(2) Quasi-experimental
Results from U.S. evaluation not replicated in Australia at end of program or at follow-up

Promoting Alternative Thinking Strategies (PATHS)[1,3]

n=200; 65%Wh, 21%Bl, 11%Asn, 7%Fil, 7%NatAm; 6–11 yrs (1st–3rd grade)

Place: School
Components: Individual
Intensity/Duration: 3 20–30-min sessions per week through school yr
Explicit Features: Enhance emotional intelligence, self-control, social competence, positive peer relations, and interpersonal problem-solving skills

Evaluation: Experimental
↑: Self-control, understanding of emotions, frustration tolerance, effective conflict-resolution strategies, thinking and planning skills
↓: Anxiety/depressive symptoms, conduct problems, aggression
Follow-up:

(continued)

TABLE 2 (*Continued*)

Program name/sample description	Program description	Postprogram outcomes/follow-up
	Implicit Features: Social Support, Social Norms, Learning Focus, Inclusion, Motivational Scaffolding	(1 yr) ↑: Emotional understanding and interpersonal problem-solving skills ↓: Depression/sadness symptoms, conduct problems (2 yr) ↓: Externalizing behavior, conduct problems
Project Northland[1,4] n=1,901 from 20 schools; 94%Wh, 4.5%NatAm; 6th–8th grade	Place: School Components: Individual, Family, Community Intensity/Duration: Weekly activities and/or training over 3 yrs Explicit Features: Youth skills and parent competence training, community organization Implicit Features: Social Norms, Social Support, Learning Focus, Motivational Scaffolding, Leadership/Mattering	Evaluation: Experimental ↑: Parent–youth communication, knowledge and attitudes for resisting peer influence, self-efficacy ↓: Tendency to use alcohol, use of alcohol in both the past week/month, frequency of the combination of alcohol and cigarette use, peer influence scores
Quantum Opportunities[1,2,4,5] n=170; 48%M, 52%F; 75%Bl, 14%Wh, 7%Hisp, 1%Asn, 2%other; 9th–12th grade; low SES	Place: Community youth serving agencies Components: Individual Intensity/Duration: Education-related activities (250 hrs), development activities (250 hrs), service activities (250 hrs) each year for 4 yrs	Evaluation: Experimental ↑: High school graduation rates, college or postsecondary school attendance, honors and awards, positive attitudes and opinions about life and future, volunteer community service work

	Explicit Features: Education activities, peer tutoring, community service activities, mentoring, life and family skills, incentives: hourly stipends and bonuses for completing program components Implicit Features: Social Support, Inclusion, Social Norms, Learning Focus, Motivational Scaffolding, Leadership/Mattering	↓: Trouble with police, high school dropout, number of children
Reach for Health and Community Youth Service Learning[5] n=195; 41%M, 59%F; 71%Bl, 26%Hisp, 3%other; low SES	Place: School Components: Individual Intensity/Duration: Health education (Reach for Health) curriculum plus 3 hrs/week for 30 weeks community service Explicit Features: Health education program—focus on substance use, violence and sexual behavior. Community service in 2 locations such as senior citizen homes, nursing homes, health centers, child day care centers Implicit Features: Social Norms, Social Support, Inclusion, Motivational Scaffolding, Learning Focus, Leadership/Mattering	Evaluation: Experimental (effects for community service group) ↓: Sexual activity, initiation of intercourse Follow-up (3 yrs): ↓: Initiation of intercourse, sex in previous month

(continued)

TABLE 2 (*Continued*)

Program name/sample description	Program description	Postprogram outcomes/follow-up
Reducing the Risk[1,5] (1) *n*=758; 47%M, 53%F; 62%Wh, 20%Lat, 9%Asn, 2%NatAm, 2%Bl, 5%unspec; 10th grade	Place: School Components: Individual, Family Intensity/Duration: 15 class periods plus unspecified parent/child time Explicit Features: Sex education program—focus on sexual antecedents[5]; cognitive-behavioral, teacher and peer role modeling, parent involvement, emphasis on avoiding unprotected sex either by abstinence or using protection Implicit Features: Social Norms, Motivational Scaffolding, Learning Focus, Social Support	Evaluation: Quasi-experimental (6-mth postintervention) ↑: Knowledge and communication with parents about contraception and abstinence, changes in normative belief (18th mth postintervention) ↓: Initiation of intercourse, ↑: contraceptive use for females and lower-risk youth, ↓: unprotected intercourse for sexually inexperienced at pretest
Responding in Peaceful and Positive Ways[1,5] (1) *n*=579; 96%Bl, 4%unspec; 6th grade from 3 urban schools (2) *n*=602; 50%M; 96%Bl; 11–12 yrs old; 6th grade	Place: School Components: Individual Intensity/Duration: 25 over school yr Explicit Features: Social/cognitive skill-building curriculum to promote nonviolent conflict resolution and positive communication; activities included team building and small group work, role playing, and relaxation techniques Implicit Features: Social Support, Social Norms, Learning Focus, Inclusion, Motivational Scaffolding	Evaluation: Experimental (1) ↑: RIPP knowledge and use of peer mediation, ↓: weapon carrying, in-school suspensions Follow-up: ↑: Knowledge and use of peer mediation, impulse control (boys) problem solving (girls); ↓: Violent behavior, anger suppression, frequency of hitting teacher, school suspensions, drug use, skipping school (2) ↓: In-school suspension, weapon carrying (after controlling for pretest group differences and attrition effects)

Safer Choices[5]
n=3,058 in 22 schools; 48%M, 52%F; 30%Wh, 27%Hisp, 17%Bl, 18%Asn, 7%other; 9th grade; urban and suburban areas; varied SES

Place: School
Components: Individual
Intensity/Duration: 25 over school yr
Explicit Features: Social/cognitive skill-building curriculum to promote nonviolent conflict resolution and positive communication; activities included team building and small group work, role playing, and relaxation techniques
Implicit Features: Learning Focus, Social Support, Social Norms, Motivational Scaffolding, Leadership/Mattering, Inclusion

Evaluation: Experimental
↑: Condom and contraception use at most recent intercourse
↓: Frequency of sex without condoms, number of sexual partners without condoms

Seattle Social Development Project[1,3,4,5]
n=643 from 18 schools; 52%M, 48%F; 44%Wh, 26%Bl, 22%Asn; 56% quality for school lunch program, 1st–5th grade

Place: School
Components: Individual, Family, School
Intensity/Duration: 7 sessions 1st/2nd grade; 5 in 2nd/3rd, 5 in 5th/6th, 4 in 6th
Explicit Features: Teacher training—classroom management, cooperative learning, interactive teaching; parent training—improve monitoring of child behavior, behavioral management, communication skills, teacher-parent relationship, build child resistance skills for drug use, social competence training for children

Evaluation: Quasi-experimental
Greatest effects for full intervention group (1st–5th) compared to late intervention group (5th–6th)
(Post 2nd grade)
↓: Aggression and externalizing behavior in Wh M only, self-destructive behaviors in Wh F only
(5th-grade posttest)
↑: Proactive family management, family communication, family cohesion, attachment/commitment to school

(continued)

143

TABLE 2 (*Continued*)

Program name/sample description	Program description	Postprogram outcomes/follow-up
	Implicit Features: Social Support, Social Norms, Inclusion, Motivational Scaffolding, Learning Focus	Follow-up: (end of 6th grade) ↓: Time with deviant peers (17, 18 yrs old) ↑: Attachment/commitment to school, self-reported achievement (no GPA, achievement test differences) ↓: School misbehavior, violent delinquent acts, alcohol use in past yr, sexual intercourse, multiple sex partners
Social Competence Program for Young Adolescents[1] n=421 from 4 schools; low/middle income families; M=210, F=211; Wh=178, Bl=167, Hisp=72, other=4; 5th–8th grades	Place: School Components: Individual, Family, School Intensity/Duration: 16, 45 min each over 12 weeks; teacher and aide training, consultation and coaching Explicit Features: Social competence promotion, family involvement Implicit Features: Social Support, Inclusion, Leadership/Mattering, Learning Focus, Social Norms, Motivational Scaffolding	Evaluation: ↑: Peer involvement, social acceptance, problem-solving, use of conflict resolution strategies, positive solutions ↓: Aggressive and passive solutions

Stay SMART[2,5]

n=273; 75%M, 25%F; 45%Wh, 42%Bl, 14%Hisp; mean age 13.6 yrs; low SES urban areas

Place: Boys and Girls Clubs of America
Components: Individual
Intensity/Duration: 12 sessions
Explicit Features: 9 sessions of life skills training (coping and resistance training); 3 sessions on postponing sexual involvement (discussions of sex in media, partner pressure to have sex, consequences of sex, role playing)
Boosters: 5 sessions at 1 yr; 4.5 hrs at 2 yrs (to reinforce resistance skills and knowledge and encourage older participants to be positive role models)
Implicit Features: Learning Focus, Social Norms, Motivational Efficacy

Evaluation: Quasi-experimental
↓: Marijuana, cigarette, and alcohol use; frequency of intercourse at 27 mths for pretest virgins

Success for All[1]

n=110 from 23 schools; K–5th grade; primarily Bl; 75–96% eligible for free lunch program in 1st grade

Place: School
Components: Individual, Family
Intensity/Duration: Daily, 8-wk assessments
Explicit Features: Cognitive competence, reading achievement, tutoring, parenting skills workshops
Implicit Features: Social Support, Learning Focus, Inclusion, Motivational Scaffolding

Evaluation: Quasi-experimental
↑: Reading competence
↓: Retained in grade

(continued)

145

TABLE 2 *(Continued)*

Program name/sample description	Program description	Postprogram outcomes/follow-up
Summer Training and Education Program (STEP)[2,4,5] *n*=4,800 from 5 urban areas; low SES; lagging behind academically; 48%M, 52%F; 49%Bl, 19%Asn, 18%Hisp, 14%Wh/other; 14–15 yrs old	Place: School, Community Components: Individual Intensity/Duration: 6–8 weeks during summer; half-time jobs (90 hrs), half-day academic classes (90 hrs), 2 mornings/wk in life skills training Explicit Features: Employment and academic classes, life-skills training, classroom time as well as work time Implicit Features: Social Norms, Learning Focus, Motivational Scaffolding	Evaluation: Experimental ↑: Reading and math test scores, knowledge tests of responsible social and sexual behavior (summer effects only; no effect for school year or long term)
Teen Outreach Program (TOP)[1,2,3,5] *n*=695 in 25 schools; 86%F; 17%Wh, 68%Bl, 13%Hisp, 2%other; 10th grade	Place: School or Community Components: Individual Intensity/Duration: (school year) 45 hrs volunteer service, weekly classroom discussions and activities Explicit Features: Small group classroom discussions of values, decision making, communication skills, parenting, life options and volunteer experiences; volunteer service in school or community Implicit Features: Social Support, Inclusion, Social Norms, Learning Focus: Knowledge, Motivational Scaffolding, Leadership/Mattering	Evaluation: Experimental ↓: School failure and suspension, teen pregnancy

Valued Youth Partnership[1]
n=194; 61/69%Hisp, 2/0%Wh, 37/37%unspec; 12 yrs

Place: School
Components: Individual, School, Family, Community
Intensity/Duration: 30 sessions over school yr, 4 hrs of tutoring/week
Explicit Features: Peer tutoring, stipends, leadership/mattering training, parent and business community involvement
Implicit Features: Social Support, Social Norms, Learning Focus, Leadership/Mattering, Motivational Scaffolding

Evaluation: Quasi-experimental
↑: Reading grades, positive self-concept, positive attitudes toward school
↓: School dropout rates

Woodrock Youth Development Project[1,2]
n=367; 53.1%M, 46.9%F; 44.4%Lat, 19.9%Wh, 11.4%Bl, 11.2%Asn, 9.3%other, 1.9%NatAm; 6–14 yrs

Place: School
Components: Individual, family, school, community
Intensity/Duration: Weekly classes and activities, daily mentoring, home visits and contacts
Explicit Features: Social competence promotion, life skills, human relations classes to develop resiliency skills, peer tutors, homework assistance, extracurricular activities (weekend retreats, after-school clubs, crisis intervention, summer program), parent training and involvement

Evaluation:
↑: Positive race relations, school attendance
↓: Drug use for past year (younger subgroup) and past month (older and younger subgroups)
Wrong direction outcome on attitudes toward drug use in older subgroup

(continued)

147

TABLE 2 (*Continued*)

Program name/sample description	Program description	Postprogram outcomes/follow-up
	Implicit Features: Social Support, Inclusion, Social Norms, Motivational Scaffolding, Leadership/Mattering	

Note. M/F: gender; ethnicity: African American (Bl), Asian (Asn), Latino/Hispanic (Lat), White (Wh), Native American (NatAm), Filipino (Fil); place: where program takes place; components: levels targeted by program; explicit features: program features described by evaluators; implicit features: program features implied by program description; ↓: decrease; ↑: increase. Adapted from Table 6-1, p. 150 in Eccles & Gootman (2002). Program reviews: [1]Catalano et al., [2]Roth et al., [3]Greenberg et al., [4]Blueprints (http://www.colorado.edu/cspv/blueprints/Default.htm), [5]Kirby et al.

148

After briefly describing the techniques used and the unique findings of each of these reviews, we summarize the consistent findings across the reviews in terms of the categories of supportive social contexts outlined in Table 1. We refer to these features as implicit features in Table 2. In this summary section, we add the results from recently published experimental evaluation studies and provide examples of some of the programs with the most consistent evidence of positive effects. We obtained and reviewed the materials and reports for each of these example programs.

Meta-Analyses
Durlak and Wells

Durlak and Wells (1997, 1998) conducted two meta-analytical reviews of 177 primary and 130 secondary prevention mental health programs that involved youth less than 19 years of age and were completed before 1992. Primary prevention programs intervene with normal populations to prevent problems from developing; secondary prevention programs target youth either at risk for problems or already exhibiting problems. Most of the primary prevention programs targeted children between and 7 and 11 years of age. Age distribution information was not provided in the case of the secondary prevention programs. Only programs with a control group of some type were included in these two meta-analyses. Randomized designs were used in 61% of the primary prevention program evaluations and 71% of the secondary prevention program evaluations. The majority of these programs took place in schools (72.9% of the primary prevention programs and 93.4% of the secondary prevention programs) during normal school hours. Durlak and Wells indicated that the intervention procedures and goals for the primary prevention programs were described in very general terms, making it difficult to determine which specific program components might explain the reported effects.

In general, the results suggest that preventive mental health programs based on well-established principles of clinical intervention can be effective across a variety of psychological outcome measures for periods of up to 2 years following the intervention exposure. They are particularly effective in increasing competencies such as assertiveness, communication, and cognitive skills; enhancing feelings of self-confidence; and reducing such problems as anxiety, behavior problems, and depressive symptoms. The most effective programs worked directly with individuals using techniques based on social learning theory (such as modeling and/or reinforcing appropriate behaviors) and other direct instructional approaches focused on educational and interpersonal problem solving.

Secondary prevention programs involving strategies based on cognitive-behavioral therapies were especially useful in reducing problem outcomes. In contrast, school-based primary prevention programs that focused on changing the psychological and social aspects of the classroom environment through increasing either interactive instructional techniques or effective classroom management techniques were more effective in increasing competencies than in reducing problems. Efforts to change parenting practices through parental training were not effective. Durlak and Wells (1998) also noted that some school programs actually produced increases in rates of problem behaviors. Recently, Dishion et al. (2001) concluded that such iatrogenic effects (effects in which the problem behaviors in the experimental group increase) are common when programs target and therefore include a large proportion of youth who are already heavily involved in problem behavior. Thus, in terms of the contextual features listed in Table 2, these programs were most successful when they included intentional learning experiences, motivational scaffolding, strong social supports from adults, and positive social norms.

Hattie et al.

Hattie, Marsh, Neill, and Richards (1997) conducted a meta-analysis of the effects of adventure programs. Common features of such programs include the following: wilderness or back-country settings; groups of less than 16; mentally and/or physically challenging objectives requiring effort, persistence, self-reliance, and cooperation; intense social interactions related to group problem solving and decision making; trained nondirective leaders; and an average duration of 2–4 weeks. Thus, these programs contain several of the contextual features we outlined in the earlier section on nonexperimental studies.

Outward Bound, one of the most popular adventure programs, consists of expeditions involving activities such as rock climbing, canoeing, rafting, backpacking, sailing, ropes courses, and cross-country skiing. Given the physical requirements of the expeditions, participants acquire physical fitness and skills. However, increases in physical skills are not the primary goal of these programs. The physical and mental challenges are the vehicles through which participants discover their strengths, manage their weaknesses, and use this knowledge, along with group cooperation, to master the outdoor challenges.

Hattie and colleagues stressed the challenge of finding good evaluations of adventure programs. Evaluations that went beyond anecdotal evidence often had correlational designs; evaluations using pretests/posttests or comparison groups often failed to reveal statistically significant differences, perhaps owing to the low statistical power of studies with small sample sizes. Because of the low statistical power in the individual studies, the authors chose to conduct a meta-analysis based on effect sizes rather than summarize statistically significant findings.

The authors chose studies for the meta-analysis based on sample size, use of controls, methodology descriptions, and the quality of instruments used in the study. Although they did not specify the exact criteria they used to judge quality, they did categorize studies as being of low, medium, or high quality; they eliminated nine studies that they categorized as low quality. They also did not include school-based outdoor education programs, because such programs typically are of very short duration and lack challenging experiences. Ninety-six studies published between 1968 and 1994 were included in their analysis; 53 were evaluations of Outward Bound (many from the Australian National School). The total sample size across all 96 studies was 12,057 (72% male and 28% female); the mean age was 22.28 years (range: 11–42 years). Average program duration was 24 days, with 72% of the programs lasting between 20 and 26 days.

The overall mean effect size immediately following the program was .34, with a follow-up overall mean effect size of .17 at an average of 5.5 months after the program. Many postprogram positive effects were maintained over time; some increased over time, the most notable of which involved decision-making skills, academic self-concept, values, and reduced aggression (see Table 3). The adventure programs had their greatest immediate effects on such psychological, emotional, and cognitive characteristics as self-control, confidence in one's abilities to be effective, decision making, school achievement, leadership, independence, assertiveness, emotional stability, social comparison, time management, and flexibility. Longer programs (more than 20 days) were more effective than shorter programs. Although a meta-analysis based on studies with significant methodological limitations is subject to criticism, the results provide additional support for the importance of such programs in terms of positive youth development and for the set of contextual characteristics outlined in Table 1. This claim is discussed more fully in our conclusion.

Prevention Programs

Three of the program reviews we considered focused on what are typically called prevention programs. These programs often take place in schools, and in some cases they occur during formal school hours. As can be seen from Table 2, the specific programs included in these reviews overlap with the programs selected in the youth development program reviews. This overlap suggests that the distinction between what is considered prevention and what is considered positive youth development is not all that clear in practice. Advocates of a positive youth development perspective have stressed the fact that preventing negative outcomes does not mean that youth are fully prepared (Pittman, Irby, & Ferber, 2000). Central to this distinction is the need for all programs to move beyond deficit-based goals if they are to support positive development as well. Interestingly, in practice, it appears that most prevention programs attempt to meet both of these goals and that this is particularly true of the most consistently successful programs.

Greenberg and Colleagues

Greenberg and colleagues (2001) reviewed 34 mental disorder prevention program evaluations for children and adolescents using a more conventional review process rather than meta-analysis. Their search concentrated on peer-reviewed journal databases as well as government reports, meta-analyses, reviews, Internet sources (e.g., Centers for Disease Control and Prevention), and relevant books. Of an

TABLE 3   Adventure Program Mean Effects on Outcome Variables

Outcome variable	Postprogram	Follow-up
Leadership	.38	.15
Conscientiousness	.46	-.28
Decision making	.47	.64
Leadership—general	.33	.16
Leadership—teamwork	.42	.16
Organizational ability	.44	.08
Time management	.46	.21
Values	.20	.32
Goals	.05	
Self-concept	.28	.23
Independence	.47	.27
Physical ability	.08	.37
Peer relations	.28	.20
General self	.28	.33
Physical appearance	.38	.32
Academic	.17	.30
Confidence	.33	.14
Self-efficacy	.31	.21
Family	.25	.10
Self-understanding	.31	.16
Well-being	.24	-.09
Academic	.46	.21
Academic—direct	.50	.30
Academic—general	.45	.13
Personality	.37	.14
Assertiveness	.42	.10
Reduction in aggression	.33	.72
Achievement motivation	.36	.15
Emotional stability	.49	.11
Femininity	.10	
Internal locus of control	.30	-.04
Maturity	.32	-.01
Neurosis reduction	.31	.24
Masculinity	.26	
Interpersonal	.32	.17
Behavior	.34	.01
Cooperation	.34	.31
Interpersonal communication	.13	.10
Relating skills	.26	.01

(continued)

TABLE 3　(*Continued*)

Outcome variable	Postprogram	Follow-up
Recidivism	.55	.10
Social competence	.43	.20
Adventuresome	.38	−.06
Challenge	.39	.08
Flexibility	.42	.08
Environmental awareness	.24	
Physical fitness	.40	−.26

Note. Adapted from Hattie et al. (1997, Table 13).

initial sample of 130 programs, 34 met the following criteria: randomized experimental design or quasi-experimental design with a comparison group, pretest and posttest measures, written manual specifying the theory and procedures used in the program intervention, clearly defined sample with adequate information about participants' behavior and social characteristics, and evidence of positive mental health outcomes. Follow-up assessments were preferred but not required. Many of the programs evaluated were school based, in part because experimental control is more feasible in this context.

Programs were categorized into three groups based on their target populations: broad unselected populations (universal prevention), youth already at risk for conduct disorders, and youth at risk for internalizing behaviors. Universal prevention programs produced either significant declines or slower increases in aggression, depression, anxiety, impulsiveness, cognitive skills, and/or antisocial behavior. Greenberg and colleagues concluded that several features were characteristic of effective universal prevention programs. For example, the content of effective programs focused on increasing social and emotional competence through cognitive skill development. Also, effective programs included efforts to intervene with schools, families, or both. The most effective programs usually lasted at least one school year and involved regular meetings to reinforce new attitudes and behaviors. These conclusions are consistent with those reached by Durlak and Wells (1997) in their meta-analysis of primary prevention programs in two ways: the focus on skill building as an important outcome and the focus on school-based interventions as effective vehicles for change. These conclusions differ from those of the Durlak and Wells report in one important way: Durlak and Wells concluded that intervention programs aimed at parents were not effective in either increasing children's skills or decreasing their involvement in problem behaviors.

Ten of the programs reviewed by Greenberg et al. (2001) targeted populations at risk for externalizing behaviors or conduct disorders. These programs ranged in focus from interventions aimed at individuals to interventions aimed at the parent-child relationship and interventions aimed at multiple contexts. Prevention or amelioration of externalizing behaviors and conduct disorders is especially desirable in that early conduct disorders often evolve into delinquency, substance abuse, and adult mental disorders, as well as school failure and school dropout. Greenberg et al. concluded that programs focusing only on either the children themselves or their parents involved smaller effects and that these effects were more likely to fade over time than the effects revealed among multicomponent programs. The effective multicomponent programs targeted the school, the family, and the community as well as the child, parents, teachers, and peers. Activities designed to build skills and competencies, particularly social and academic skills, were common features of successful programs. We describe one of these programs, the Adolescent Transitions Program, in our concluding comments. This program targeted both at-risk adolescents and their parents and was effective in lowering rates of problem behaviors and family conflict.

The third set of programs reviewed included programs that focused on children at risk for internalizing disorders such as depression and anxiety disorders. Of the 10 effective programs in this category, 2 reduced depressive symptoms, 1 reduced anxiety symptoms, and 1 reduced risk of suicide. These programs focused on improving young people's cognitive and behavioral coping skills so that they could more effectively deal with stressful periods in their lives. The other 5 programs were effective in helping youth deal with childhood stresses such as divorce and bereavement. Social support and instruction in specific problem-focused coping strategies were common characteristics of the effective programs.

The studies in the Greenberg et al. (2001) review provide strong support for the importance of skill building/competency promotion in preventing mental health disorders in children and adolescents. In a closer examination of individual programs (see Table 2), other implicit features emerge as likely to be important. For example, social norms for appropriate behavior and cognitions are inherent in programs targeting conduct disorders as youth are learning about appropriate social interactions with peers, with adults, and in the school environment. Likewise, knowledge building increases parents' ability to recognize early manifestations of problem behaviors; knowledge-building activities also help parents learn appropriate family management skills to support their children. Social support is implied in programs offering direct skill-building opportunities to youth as well as in programs that encourage caring parent-child relationships. Furthermore, motivational scaffolding is evident in the descriptions of the competency-building activities of effective programs. Concrete skills, such as how to cope with interpersonal conflict, are taught, and there are many opportunities for individuals to be successful in the learning process. Teaching strategies, including role-plays and written assignments, offer opportunities for individuals to receive positive feedback with an improvement focus.

Two of the features listed in Table 1, inclusion and leadership/mattering, were not as obvious in the program descriptions provided by Greenberg et al. (2001). However, Greenberg et al. concluded that programs of longer duration are more effective than programs of shorter duration. Because longer duration interventions tend to include the same group of individuals, they may be creating opportunities for inclusion even though this is not a specific program goal. Another reason why these features may not be as obvious is the lack of specificity in identifying and evaluating program characteristics, a flaw in most of the evaluation studies reviewed. A third explanation is that mental health promotion may not be as dependent upon these two program characteristics as other prevention and promotion areas. Given the evidence supporting all of the contextual characteristics in other effective programs, we believe that the mental health promotion field could benefit from assessing whether programs provide for inclusion, leadership, and mattering and add these elements if they are absent.

Blueprints Model Programs

The Center for the Study and Prevention of Violence at the University of Colorado in Boulder published a series of "Blueprints" describing program interventions effective in preventing violence. There is not a published, peer-reviewed violence prevention review of individual programs as comprehensive as the one that appears online. The best site for this review is http://www.colorado.edu/cspv/blueprints/Default.htm. Among the 450 delinquency, drug, and violence prevention programs reviewed, Blueprints highlighted 11 model programs that had statistically significant deterrent effects on delinquency, drug use, and/or violent behavior and also met most of the following criteria: experimental design with random assignment or a strong quasi-experimental design, at least one additional site replication involving an experimental design and demonstrated effects, and evidence that the deterrent effect was sustained for at least 1 year posttreatment.

Why are these programs successful? Elliott and Tolan (1999) looked for evidence that changes in risk or protective factors mediated changes in violent behavior. However, most of the evaluations had either not collected the necessary data to analyze the causal processes or had not reported these analyses. Furthermore, because these evaluations focused on entire program packages rather than specific components, Elliott and colleagues concluded that it was impossible to determine which particular aspects of the programs were responsible for the significant deterrent effects. Nonetheless, the programs do provide models of what can be done in communities to decrease rates of violence.

What characteristics did these programs share? Teaching life skills and providing strong adult social supports were common features of all of the programs. Mentoring was explicitly evaluated in one program. The other programs were more global in their orientation and included one or more of the following features: comprehensive educational services, mental health services, and development activities designed to help youth learn various life skills and develop confidence in themselves and financial incentives for attendance. Of the 11 model programs, 4 provided comprehensive, community-based, multifaceted programming; 5 provided family therapy aimed at involving families in changing those aspects of the young person's setting (i.e., peers, school, family, community) that contribute to the problem behavior.

These authors left unanswered a very important question: Are some characteristics more appropriate than others depending on the developmental stage of the individual? Using many of the same programs reviewed by Elliott and his colleagues, three other recent reviews have addressed this question as well as elaborating on the specific characteristics of effective programs. Samples and Aber (1998) reviewed school-based violence prevention programs and concluded that four school grade groupings were relevant to violence prevention programs: preschool (ages 2–5 years), elementary school (ages 6–11 years), junior high/middle school (ages 12–14 years), and high school (ages 15–18 years). These authors summarized what has been learned from the developmental and program evaluation literatures in terms of preventing violence.

In the preschool years, effective programs target the development of self-regulation and both social and cognitive competencies in children. In addition to the individual level, successful programs involve parents in the interventions to improve family functioning and increase parenting skills. Successful interventions reach the multiple contexts surrounding individuals. In elementary school, the limited evidence available suggests that the focus should be on social norms and interpersonal skill development, especially negotiation strategies. In junior high/middle school, changing classes with an assigned cohort and receiving instruction in small, personalized classrooms help youth form a stable peer group. These school strategies fall into the contextual feature categories of increasing social support and inclusion and possibly, depending on the teacher, encourage more opportunities for efficacy owing to the presence of small, inclusive groups.

Other school violence prevention researchers have made similar recommendations. Laub and Lauritsen (1998) described the importance of programs that help youth build social capital (social support) in their families, schools, and neighborhoods. Programs must also support development in recognizing and dealing with violent events. Fagan and Wilkinson (1998) concluded that role-playing strategies used by instructors to help youth break down and analyze the stages of violent situations (motivational scaffolding) are effective in violence prevention as well.

Kirby (1997, 2001)

Kirby (1997, 2001) reviewed evaluations of primary prevention programs designed to reduce sexual risk-taking behavior and teen pregnancy. The program evaluations met the following criteria: completed in 1980 or later, experimental or quasi-experimental design, minimum sample size of 100 in combined experimental and control groups, 12–18-year-olds as target group, conducted in the United States or Canada, and measurement of program impact on sexual or contraceptive behavior or pregnancy or birth rates. The earlier of the two reviews, *No Easy Answers* (Kirby, 1997), included only peer-reviewed publications. The new edition, *Emerging Answers* (Kirby, 2001), also includes unpublished studies involving rigorous evaluations and reviews studies published since the 1997 report.

In both reviews, Kirby divided programs into three groups based on whether they focused primarily on sexual behavior antecedents (i.e., age, gender, pubertal timing, attitudes and beliefs about contraception), nonsexual behavior antecedents (i.e., poverty, parental education, parental support, drug and alcohol use), or a combination of both. Sexual antecedent programs included curriculum-based sex education programs and other programs in the school or community designed to improve reproductive health care or access to contraceptives. In the paragraphs to follow, we summarize the conclusions from the more recent report in terms of what works in reducing teen pregnancy and risky sexual behavior.

Kirby identified 10 characteristics common to effective sexual antecedent curriculums, many of which match the contextual features listed in Table 1 as important for positive youth development. Examples of motivational scaffolding can be seen in several characteristics. For example, successful programs focused on a small number of behaviorally oriented goals, such as delaying initiation of intercourse or using condoms. Encouraging concrete behaviors in manageable numbers should increase young people's sense of personal efficacy about achieving the objectives. Effective programs also used a variety of teaching methods designed to make the curriculum content interactive and personally relevant. In addition, the behavioral goals, teaching methods, and informational materials were developed to be compatible with the age, level of sexual experience, and cultural background of the youth, and adequate time was given to complete activities, thereby encouraging mastery of the material.

Effective curriculums also had an intentional learning focus, incorporating both knowledge building and skill building. The programs built knowledge by providing basic and accurate information about the risks associated with sexual activity and about protective methods for avoiding pregnancy and sexually transmitted diseases. Skill building was accomplished through activities teaching youth how to identify and deal with social pressures about sexual behavior, including recognizing situations that may lead to sex. Effective programs also taught youth resistance skills by providing information about these skills, demonstrating them, and allowing them to be practiced through role-playing and written exercises (teaching strategies that also overlap with effective motivational scaffolding).

Positive social norms were conveyed through clear and consistent messages to the youth about correct sexual choices rather than providing pros and cons regarding choices. For example, abstinence programs provided clear messages that abstinence from sex is the correct choice. Contraceptive use programs stressed condom and other contraceptive use as the right choice and emphasized unprotected sex as the wrong choice.

Social support, including reinforcement of the social norms established in the program, came from leaders who believed in the program's objectives and who had received training in the implementation of the program. Lastly, effective programs incorporated theoretical knowledge about what is effective in reducing health-related risky behavior. For example, program goals targeted beliefs, attitudes, social norms, efficacy, and skills appropriate to achieving the desired behavior.

Contextual features not explicit in effective curriculum-based programs were opportunities for inclusion in social structures as well as opportunities for youth to experience leadership, mastery, and mattering. These characteristics were much more apparent in the non-sexual-antecedent category of successful programs. Non-sexual-antecedent programs included service learning, vocational education, and employment programs. These programs focused on improving education and life options as the means to reduce pregnancy and birth rates. The vocational education programs offered a combination of academic and vocational education and support services. However, although the vocational programs were quite intense, they were not very effective in decreasing pregnancy rates among disadvantaged youth. The vocational programs reviewed included the Summer Training and Education Program (STEP), the Conservation and Youth Service Corps, the Job Corps, and JOBSTART.

In contrast, there was strong evidence of positive effects for the service-learning programs. These programs provided opportunities for unpaid service time in the community as well as structured time for training, preparation, and reflection. Participants in the most extensively evaluated programs (the Teen Outreach Program and Reach for Health) reported lower rates of pregnancy than the control group during the school year in which they participated in the program intervention and in the few follow-up assessments currently available. Teen Outreach Program participants were less likely to fail in school as well. The service learning programs offered extensive opportunities for leadership, mattering, and contributions to one's community. Such opportunities were not typically offered in the vocational programs. It is likely that these types of opportunities for mattering also contribute to feelings of inclusion in one's community as well as teaching the positive social norms valued by the community.

The most promising program concentrating on both sexuality and positive youth development was the Children's Aid Society Carrera Program (Philliber, Kaye, Herrling, & West, 2000). Among the girls in this program, initiation of sex was delayed, contraceptive use increased, and pregnancy and births decreased for up to 3 years; there were no changes in risk-taking behaviors among boys, however. In addition, girls acquired more computer skills and job experience and were more likely to have visited a college. The Carrera Program includes sex and family life education, life skills training, academic help and counseling, work-related counseling and training, self-expression through the arts and athletics, and comprehensive mental and physical health services.

The programs concentrating on nonsexual antecedents of adolescent sexual behavior most closely exemplified the contextual characteristics related to social norms, social support, inclusion, leadership, and mattering. Interestingly, although these programs also were likely to provide skill and knowledge building opportunities as well as motivational scaffolding, these characteristics were not as central to goals as they were to the goals of programs targeting sexual antecedents. *Emerging Answers* (Kirby, 2001) identified programs in both categories that had positive effects on teen sexual behavior. These results suggest that not all contextual features are critical for positive effects. One other surprising observation made by Kirby is that programs focused on sexual antecedents had positive effects on risky sexual behavior but did not reduce teen pregnancy. In contrast, the programs focused on nonsexual antecedents of teen pregnancy reduced both risky sexual behavior and teen pregnancy. Although far more information is needed, one might speculate that positive youth development programs offer possibilities for alternative life choices that encourage avoiding a teen pregnancy that could limit life choices.

Positive Youth Development Programs

Over the past 10 to 15 years, increasing attention has been focused on the need for programs that stress promoting positive development rather than preventing problems (Public/Private Ventures, 2000). Many traditional youth-serving organizations, such as 4-H, Boys' and Girls' Clubs, and scouts, have always taken this perspective. Schools, of course, are also based on an orientation toward promotion rather than prevention. Despite the long history of both of these types of organizations, relatively little attention has been given to assessing their effectiveness in promoting positive youth development beyond the academic domain. Instead, a great deal of interest has focused on designing and evaluating programs aimed at preventing such negative developmental outcomes as school failure, school dropout, teen pregnancy, delinquency, and drug and alcohol consumption. In response to this research policy and funding climate, a growing group of youth advocates, foundations, and researchers have stressed the need for more programs and more program evaluations explicitly focused on promoting positive youth development. The results of the first generations of such evaluations are now becoming available.

Catalano, Hawkins, and Colleagues

In the mid-1990s, Catalano, Hawkins, and their colleagues were commissioned by the U.S. Department of Health and Human Services to review evaluation studies of positive youth development programs (see Catalano, Berglund, Ryan, Lonczak, & Hawkins, 1999). The authors solicited information on promotion/prevention programs from a wide variety of sources and collected more than 100 reports. From these, they first selected the 77 programs involving some form of systematic evaluation. From this set, they then selected the 25 "successful" programs that had included a control or strong comparison group, collected measures of behavioral outcomes, and claimed to be attempting to promote such positive youth development objectives as social bonding; psychological resilience; cognitive, emotional, social, behavioral, and moral competence; self-efficacy and self-determination; a clear and positive identity; optimism; spirituality; and prosocial values.

All 25 programs claimed to be promoting competence, self-efficacy, and prosocial norms; 76% stressed social bonding, and 86% provided opportunities for prosocial involvement and recognized positive behavior. The other major constructs (positive identify, self-determination, belief in the future, resiliency, and spirituality) were present in less than half of the programs. Eighty-eight percent had a school component, 60% had a family component, and 48% had a community component.

We can look for clues about the relative importance of specific contextual features by exploring the positive development characteristics prominent in the positive youth development review. As just noted, all 25 successful programs provided opportunities to develop competence in age-appropriate social, emotional, cognitive, behavioral, and moral skills. Ninety-six percent focused on building social or cognitive behavioral skills; 73% focused on decision-making and self-management skills; 62% focused on coping skills; and 50% focused on refusal-resistance skills. Acquiring such competencies should lead to increases in sense of self-efficacy. Descriptions of the ways in which both competencies and a sense of self-efficacy were facilitated by the programs also suggest that these programs provided intentional learning opportunities and strong mastery motivation scaffoldings.

Finally, all of the programs stressed positive social norms, defined as "healthy standards and clear beliefs." Programs delivered prosocial norm messages through adult and peer expectations and/or information about how to counteract negative peer influences. The prosocial norm definition included resistance training. The evaluations described in this review suggested that a learning focus on skill building, motivation scaffolding to increase sense of self-efficacy, and promotion of social norms are critical ingredients in effective positive youth development programs.

Two other characteristics were identified as salient in many of the successful programs; 76% of the programs stressed social bonding with adults and peers, and 86% provided opportunities for community involvement and recognized positive behavior. The prevalence of such opportunities in successful positive youth development programs provides evidence for the importance of leadership and mattering. Youth in many of these successful programs were provided opportunities to contribute to their "community" and were valued and recognized for those contributions.

Roth, Brooks-Gunn, and Colleagues

Roth, Brooks-Gunn, Murray, and Foster (1998; see also Roth & Brooks-Gunn, 2000) reviewed more than 60 evaluations of prevention and promotion intervention programs for adolescents. Of the 60 programs reviewed, 15 were selected for inclusion based on the following characteristics: positive youth development focus, experimental or quasi-experimental design, and focus on youth not currently demonstrating problem behaviors (see Table 2). Roth and colleagues both reviewed the materials they found for each program and talked directly with the program administrators in order to gather more complete details.

Roth and colleagues (1998) defined youth development programs as "developmentally-appropriate programs designed to prepare adolescents for productive adulthood by providing opportunities and supports to help them gain the competencies and knowledge needed to meet the increasing challenges they will face as they mature" (p. 427). They then grouped these programs into three categories based on how closely they matched a youth development framework: (a) positive-behavior-focused, competency/asset-enhancing programs; (b) problem-behavior-focused, competency/asset-enhancing programs; and (c) resistance-skills-based prevention programs.

Roth and colleagues categorized 6 of the 15 programs as positive-behavior-focused, competency/asset-enhancing programs. These programs offered a wide range of opportunities to develop positive psychological and social assets, skills, and competencies. Some of these programs also explicitly focused on providing caring relationships between youth and adults (e.g., mentoring programs). All 6 programs showed positive changes in attitudes and/or behaviors and improvements in competencies in areas such as educational achievement, school attendance and engagement, and interpersonal skills. Programs reaching out to more of the contexts in which the adolescents lived had more positive outcomes.

The problem-behavior-focused, competency/asset-enhancing programs focused on building competencies and assets as well, but the goal of these programs was reducing participation in problem behaviors. Four of these programs focused on reducing drug, alcohol, and tobacco use; one targeted reducing school dropout rates; and one focused on reducing school dropout and preventing teen pregnancy. Competency promotion in these programs focused on resistance skills training. Again, Roth and colleagues concluded that programs targeting multiple contexts, providing relational support, and enhancing youth competencies were most successful.

Roth and colleagues concluded that resistance skills–based prevention programs were least consistent with a positive youth development perspective. The three such programs that they reviewed promoted skill building through assertiveness training, resistance to peer pressure, skill development, and/or planning for the future. All three programs showed declines in problem behaviors. Caring adult relationships emerged as an important component of each of these programs. Roth and colleagues also concluded that more comprehensive programs with longer durations were the most successful.

Summary

Although many of the programs included in all of these reviews used a rigorous experimental or quasi-experimental design, few used a well articulated theory of change to guide program design, program implementation, selection of outcomes, or specification of the mediating and moderating conditions that might connect program characteristics to youth outcomes. There was very little attempt to theoretically link the program characteristics with the outcomes being assessed. Outcomes varied across studies and were quite idiosyncratic within each evaluation. Consequently, we do not know whether the programs might have affected other outcomes. Also, null findings were not reported, leaving us with little information about areas in which programs might not have an effect.

Few programs included high-quality implementation-evaluation techniques. Consequently, it is difficult to determine why most of these programs either succeeded or failed to support positive youth development, and, in the case of specific outcomes, it is often impossible to say what works. In addition, there was little overlap between the measures collected in most of the evaluations summarized in these reports and characteristics of settings outlined earlier. This reflects in part the scarcity of well-validated measures of these contextual characteristics; it also reflects in part the disconnection between research and practice traditions.

Despite these weaknesses, there is considerable convergence across the reviews on what works in general. Furthermore, there is considerable convergence in the findings of these experimental and quasi-experimental program evaluation studies and the findings of the nonexperimental studies of both extracurricular and leisure activities and youth organizations discussed earlier. Even though few of these studies explicitly looked at the contextual characteristics suggested in Table 1, the findings are quite consistent with these suggestions. We turn to this comparison in our concluding section.

CONCLUSION

We now turn to a more general discussion of the relation between studies of youth activity settings and programs and contextual characteristics we hypothesized to be important in Table 1. Mapping this framework of contextual features likely to promote child and adolescent development onto the youth-serving programs just reviewed, as well as the programs described in the earlier sections on extracurricular and leisure activities and nonexperimental studies, was a challenge. We know from the evaluations that such programs can be effective in promoting healthy development; we know much less about why. Programs typically consisted of several components and had varying characteristics that were usually not well measured. Consequently, there is rarely sufficient information in these reports to reach firm conclusions about which particular component or combination of components was responsible for any significant effects. Nonetheless, in this section we summarize our conclusions regarding the most likely contextual characteristics needed to support healthy development.

Developmentally Appropriate Structure

Many developmentalists stress the importance of developmentally appropriate contexts (e.g., Eccles et al., 1993). Few of the programs we reviewed provided information with which to determine whether this is true in youth-serving programs. Unfortunately, the best evidence is provided by the fact that youth drop out of these programs as they mature into adolescence (McLaughlin, 2000). In contrast, the success of programs that provide opportunities for adolescents to take on leadership roles as they mature and become more expert in the program areas provides descriptive evidence of the importance of programs responding in developmentally appropriate ways to the growing maturity of their participants. The programs studied by

McLaughlin and her colleagues provide numerous examples of how programs effectively use this strategy to retain adolescent participants.

The results of some of the longest lasting violence prevention programs also provide support for the importance of this component of good programs. Because some of these studies implemented experimental designs that included multiple age cohorts, they were able to document at what age particular programs were most effective. The Metropolitan Area Child Study (Eron et al., 2002; Huesmann et al., 1996) involved a multiyear, multicontext aggression prevention program aimed at children in either the early (Grades 2 and 3) or late (Grades 5 and 6) elementary school years. The program used skills and motivational training with all children in their classrooms, enhanced skill and motivational training, attempted to change peer social norms regarding acceptability of aggression among at-risk students in pull-out sessions, and used a family intervention to help parents of high-risk children recognize and reinforce prosocial behavior, improve peer group monitoring skills, improve family communication patterns, and provide general emotional and social support.

Schools were randomly assigned to one of four conditions (no intervention, universal classroom intervention, universal classroom intervention combined with pull-out experience for at-risk children, and all interventions). The children were exposed to these treatments over a 2-year period. The universal treatment was provided by the teachers in conjunction with intensive teacher training and support for implementation. Graduate students with advanced training provided the pull-out experiences once a week for 28 weeks, spread over 2 years. Trained clinicians provided the family intervention during the second year of the program, once a week for 22 weeks. Like most such programs, this program had major attrition problems over the course of the evaluation.

The results were quite mixed. The strongest positive impact on decreasing aggression occurred among boys who received the full set of interventions early in their elementary school years. The pull-out intervention actually led to increases in aggressiveness among boys who received the intervention late in their elementary school years. In one school district, the youth who received both the early and the late interventions showed increased aggression across all 6 years of participation. The results were similar for school achievement. Only those youth exposed to the universal classroom intervention early in their elementary school years showed increases in academic achievement; control students showed decreases in achievement. There were no effects on school achievement for the youth exposed to the more intense child or family interventions at either time period, and there were no effects of the universal treatment for those given the intervention in their late elementary school years.

Clearly, these results suggest that the developmental timing of a program is critical. In the early adolescent years, intensive exposure to aggressive peers, even in a pull-out program designed to reduce aggression, is likely to produce increases in aggressive behaviors. This finding is consistent with those reported by Dishion and his colleagues (see earlier discussion).

Social Support From Adults and Peers

Social and emotional support was a major implicit component of all of the programs investigated in both the nonexperimental and experimental studies we reviewed. Although mentoring activities are the most salient example of an effort to provide increased social and emotional support, most of the programs provided youth with some form of supportive contact with nonfamilial adults. In many programs, although "mentoring" was not explicitly stated as a program goal, adult-youth contact took the form of mentoring.

One of most carefully conducted experimental evaluations focused on a program specifically based on mentoring principles, namely, the evaluation of Big Brothers/Big Sisters (Grossman & Tierney, 1998). In this program, adult volunteers, referred to as big brothers or big sisters, are matched with a child, known as the little brother or little sister, with the hope that a caring and supportive relationship will develop. Professional staff match big brothers/big sisters and little brothers/little sisters based on factors such as shared interests, geographic proximity, and preferences for same-race matches, and there is a preference to match youth who have been waiting the longest. Orientations are conducted with youth and volunteers, and training is provided for volunteer mentors. Big Brothers/Big Sisters staff members supervise the matches between youth and volunteers by contacting all parties within 2 weeks of the initial match and then having monthly telephone contact with the volunteer for the first year of the program.

Big Brothers/Big Sisters staff members also contact the youth at least four times the first year. The matched pairs of mentors and youth spend 3–5 hours together each week for at least a 1-year period. Activity goals are identified in the initial interview with the child and parent/guardian; these goals are then used by a caseworker to develop an individualized case plan to help the matched pair develop a mutually rewarding relationship with regular contact.

According to telephone interviews with 1,101 mentors in 98 mentoring programs, youth focus groups, and youth interview data (Herrera, Sipe, & McClanahan, 2000), the matched pairs with the closest and most supportive relationships had more than 10 hours of contact per month, involved shared interests, and shared in decision making regarding activities. The most supportive relationships were between mentors and children of elementary school age. The positive effects of Big Brothers/Big Sisters included increases in grade point averages and parental trust as well as decreases in hitting behavior, skipping school, and lying to parents. Minority males were less likely to report initiation of alcohol and other drug use. Only self-reported measures were used in the evaluation.

Inclusive Social Networks and Social Organizational Arrangements

We hypothesized that healthy development is promoted by fostering a sense of belonging through inclusive social structures. This theme was evident in many of the programs investigated via both nonexperimental and experimental methods. It was a central component of the programs studied by McLaughlin and Bryce Heath, and it was also a critical component of the Quantum Opportunities Program (QOP), a program experimentally evaluated by Hahn, Leavitt, and Aaron (1994). Instilling a sense of belonging is at the core of the QOP mission. If participants stop attending QOP activities, program staff members track them down to find out what is wrong, to assure them they are still part of their QOP family, and to coax them back to the program. This attitude of refusing to give up on youth was considered by the evaluators (Hahn et al., 1994) to be a crucial component of the program.

The QOP (Hahn et al., 1994) is designed to provide adolescents from families receiving public assistance and living in high-risk neighborhoods with education, service, and development activities. Youth are paid to participate in the program, which begins in the ninth grade and continues through high school graduation. Participants receive 250 hours of education activities (e.g., taking part in computer-assisted instruction and peer tutoring) in order to enhance their basic academic skills. They also participate in 250 hours of developmental activities ranging from cultural enrichment to personal development, acquiring life/family skills, planning for college or advanced technical/vocational training, and job preparation. Finally, participants provide 250 hours of service in activities such as assisting in community service projects, helping with public events, and working as volunteers in various community agencies.

The centrality of inclusion in QOP is evident in its use of a family metaphor in guiding its programming. The program is explicitly designed to act as an extended family. Program staff track down youth when they skip school, follow them to new homes and neighborhoods and even prison, provide educational opportunities, and monitor their health and well-being much as a family cares for a child. The support system includes caring adult mentors and peers standing by the youth for a period of 4 years. The youth are given clear limits for behavior but are not expelled from the program regardless of their behavior. Finally, youth are placed into small groups of 25 to promote group bonding throughout the 4 years.

In the primary evaluation of this program, QOP youth, relative to the youth in the control group, were more likely to graduate from high school and attend college or other postsecondary schools; received more honors and awards; had more positive attitudes and opinions about life, including their futures; and were more likely to volunteer time to community service work (Hahn et al., 1994). They were less likely to drop out of school, had fewer children, and were in less trouble with the police than members of the control group.

Fostering inclusion in the early elementary years also has positive long-term results, as demonstrated by the Seattle Social Development Project. This project, a universal intervention for elementary school children developed by Hawkins, Catalano, and colleagues, is grounded in their social development theory (see Catalano & Hawkins, 1996). According to this theory, strong social bonds to family and school serve as protective factors against problem behaviors such as school misconduct and delinquency. The program is designed to foster strong social bonds in the early school years, including feelings of attachment and commitment to the school and school values, which in turn are predicted to protect against future problem behaviors.

One instantiation of this project began in 1981 with students entering the first grade in eight Seattle schools located in high crime areas. Teachers in the intervention group were trained in proactive classroom management, interactive teaching, and cooperative learning (Abbott et al., 1998). The intervention also included voluntary parent training focused on improving family management skills. In comparison with the control group, the student participants in the Seattle Social Development Project had greater school attachment, commitment, and achievement; less school misbehavior; and fewer delinquent acts and less alcohol use at follow-up (when they were 18 years of age) (Hawkins et al., 1992; Lonczak et al., 2001; O'Donnell et al., 1995). Greater effects were found for the full intervention group (first to fifth grade) than for the late intervention group (fifth and sixth grades). The positive long-term effects on youth participating in the project suggest the importance of fostering inclusion in the early school years to set children on a more positive trajectory through their high school years.

Strong and Clear Social Norms

Messages about social norms are a common feature of most of the programs reviewed. Many of the programs explicitly indicated that they promoted positive social norms to the youth. One program stands out for its efforts to influence social norms by casting a wide net that includes school, family, and community at large. The Midwestern Prevention Program (MPP; Chou et al., 1998; Pentz et al., 1989) is a comprehensive, community-wide intervention with the goal of preventing adolescent consumption of cigarettes, alcohol, and marijuana. The program is based on the theory that all environmental forces must work together to both reinforce resistance skills taught in school prevention curricula and promote community-wide norms regarding abstinence. The MPP consists of five components: (a) a school curriculum component with continuing school-based boosters for youth, (b) a media component, (c) a parent education and organization component, (d) a community organization component, and (e) a local policy change component regarding tobacco, alcohol, and other drugs.

One of the five components is implemented each year, except for the mass media component, which occurs throughout the 5 years of the program. The mass media component consists of an average of 31 news clips, commercials, and talk shows spots during the first 3 years of the program; the number of such media events decreases to an average of 10 per year in the fourth and fifth years. The media events are designed to educate the community on baseline drug use and the goals and intervention strategies of the program. Skill demonstrations and public recognition of participating students are also part of the mass media component.

In the first year of the program, students participate in a 10-session school curriculum teaching resistance to and counteraction skills for drug use influences and including prevention practice homework activities with parents. In the second year, participants receive a 5-session booster school program to maintain previous prevention skills during the transition to high school. Also in the second year, parents are trained in parent-child communication and prevention practice support skills. Parents are also involved in a parent-principal committee that meets regularly to review school drug policy and to provide parent-child communication training for parents.

In the high school years (Years 3–5), community organizations create task forces against drug use in the community. Tobacco and alcohol policy changes are targeted in the fourth and fifth years. All components involve regular meetings of respective stakeholders (e.g., community leaders) to review and refine programs. Through these five program components, the MPP delivers a strong anti-drug message to the youth in the community. In the Kansas City evaluation (Pentz et al., 1989), the program was effective in reducing use of cigarettes, marijuana, and alcohol at the 1-year follow-up, and cigarette use was also reduced at the 2-year follow-up. In Indianapolis (Chou et al., 1998), the program produced effects through the first follow-up period (6 months) for all three substances, and decreased alcohol use was also found at the 1.5-year follow-up.

Another program with both social norms and inclusion as central themes is the Bullying Prevention Program, which fosters inclusion by instilling clear social norms regarding intolerance of bullying behavior in the school setting. This 2-year school-based universal prevention program was developed and evaluated in Norway as part of a national campaign against bullying (Olweus, 1991, 1994a, 1994b). It focuses on reducing bullying problems by increasing awareness and knowledge of the problem, involving teachers and parents, establishing clear rules against bullying behavior, and providing support and protection for bullying victims. Thus, the intervention targets changes at the school, class, and individual levels that are designed to increase students' sense of inclusion and belonging in school through the reduction of bullying.

Prior to program implementation, each school administers the Bully/Victim Questionnaire, developed by Olweus, to determine the severity of the school's bullying problem by age and gender as well as to pinpoint physical locations where bullying incidents are likely to occur. At the school level, a bullying prevention committee composed of school administrators, teachers, counselors, parents, and students provides an infrastructure to support the intervention through coordinating activities, disseminating information to families and the community at large, and organizing adult supervision on the school grounds at nonclassroom times such as lunch and break periods.

In the classroom, trained teachers help students agree on specific rules about bullying and facilitate discussions about the problem. The rules target direct bullying (open attacks) as well as indirect bullying, such as intentional exclusion of specific individuals from peer groups and propagation of negative rumors. The following are examples of Bullying Prevention Program rules: "We will not bully other students"; "We will try to help students who are bullied"; and "We will make it a point to include all students who are easily left out." Teachers also lead weekly meetings to discuss bullying events during the week and review rules and consequences to foster a positive, inclusive classroom environment. At the individual level, interventions target individual bullies and include support for their victims. Teachers take the lead in finding solutions to the problem, and the parents of the bullies and victims are part of the discussions.

In the first evaluation of the Bullying Prevention Program in Norway, Olweus, Limber, and Mihalic (1999) reported a 50% reduction in student reports of bullying relative to preintervention baseline. The results were maintained at the 20-month follow-up. In addition, they found reductions in other antisocial behaviors, such as vandalism, fighting, theft, alcohol use, and truancy. Students also reported improvements in social relationships, discipline at school, and more positive attitudes toward school. The U.S. replication in South Carolina (Olweus et al., 1999) modified the program by establishing schoolwide rules against bullying behavior and involved the community in anti-bullying efforts. Students reported a decrease in bullying other children but not in being bullied (relative to the control group). Skilled involvement of teachers and other school staff is considered crucial for the success of the program.

Intentional Learning Experiences

Many programs provided opportunities for learning and skill building. This was the single most common aspect of the programs reviewed in the nonexperimental section. McLaughlin provides several excellent examples of this feature in her 2000 report. Most striking is the use of intentional learning strategies by athletic coaches:

Many coaches work academics into topics of great interest to their young athletes, such as nutrition and weight training. One year a basketball team had six-week units of study on the following topics: finances of the National Basketball Association, physics in the sport of basketball, and neurophysiology. Each of these units included original research, problem sets, discussion of ethics, and decision-making. For example, the unit on the NBA covered costs of health insurance, uniforms, travel, income from ticket sales, taxes on players' salaries, and using probability theory to illustrate the youngsters' chance of making it to the NBA. The neurophysiology unit discussed steroids, heart rate under exertion and under heat dehydration, and myths surrounding "chocolate highs" and "carbohydrate loading." (McLaughlin, 1990, p. 12)

The Life Skills Training (LST) program is a good example of the use of intentional learning experiences from the experimental evaluation studies. This program was designed to address substance abuse. It includes two aspects of intentional learning experiences: knowledge building and life skills building. The curriculum provides youth with factual information about cigarettes, alcohol, and marijuana, including discussions of common myths and misconceptions. The immediate and short-term effects of using these substances are stressed in order to provide experiences that match the cognitive developmental stage of early adolescence. For example, class experiments demonstrate the immediate effects of cigarette smoking on heart rate and head steadiness.

The knowledge building phase of the intervention is followed by the life skill building phase, in which youth develop informed decision-making skills and the social and personal skills needed to implement these decisions. In addition, youth learn self-control skills, anxiety management skills, self-improvement skills, and communication and other general social skills, as well as assertive verbal and nonverbal skills to help counteract peer pressure. The 3-year LST curriculum includes 15 sessions taught in the first year of the program, followed by 10 and then 5 booster sessions in Years 2 and 3, respectively. LST is typically implemented in middle schools in Grades 6–8 and in junior high schools in Grades 7–9.

Multiple studies have shown the program to be effective even with only the first-year intervention component (Botvin, 1998, 2000). These effects, however, are enhanced by the booster sessions. For example, studies have shown that the first year of LST reduced smoking by 56% to 67% without any additional booster sessions; however, smoking was reduced by as much as 87% when students received booster sessions (Botvin, Baker, Filazzola, & Botvin, 1990; Botvin, Baker, Dusenbury, et al., 1995).

The effects also appear to be long lasting (Botvin et al., 2000). Data collected 6.5 years after the initial pretest indicated that students who received life skills training during junior high school reported less use of illicit drugs than controls, implying that illicit drug use may be prevented by targeting the use of gateway drugs such as tobacco and alcohol. These results suggest that adolescents benefit from repeated reinforcement of knowledge and skill building in order to more fully internalize what they have learned. What program characteristics mediate these effects? Botvin (2000) summarizes work from several studies on mediating variables. Changes in perceived social norms, refusal skills, and risk taking mediate the effect of life skills training on tobacco, alcohol, and/or marijuana use.

Similar to LST, the Adolescent Transitions Program (Andrews, Soberman, & Dishion, 1995; Dishion & Kavanagh, 2000; Irvine, Biglan, Smolkowski, Metzler, & Ary, 1999) also targets skill building. However, unlike LST, it is a multilevel family-centered intervention. The three levels correspond to universal, selected, and indicated family designations. All families are targeted in the universal level, at-risk families in the selected level, and families with youth currently having problems in the indicated level. A family resource room is established in the school in the universal level of the intervention to create an infrastructure for collaboration between school and parents and to encourage good parenting practices. The space also becomes the setting for delivery of the other intervention levels. Brief home visits during the summer and parent self-assessments using videotaped examples and rating forms are also tools for parents at the universal level of the intervention. Youth participate in a 6-week health curriculum in the fall of the school year that promotes school success, reduced substance use, and reduced conflict. Students are graded on completing the homework with their parents.

The selected intervention helps parents accurately identify a child at risk and provides resources to help reduce risk factors and promote adjustment. In the next level, indicated intervention, parents are provided with professional support targeting family management practices. The Family Management Curriculum, based on the work of Patterson and colleagues (see Dishion & Kavanagh, 2000), consists of 12 weekly parenting group sessions of 90 minutes each. Family management skills are taught and reinforced through exercises, background knowledge, role-plays, and group discussion. The main skill focus is use of incentives for behavior change, limit setting and monitoring, and family communication and problem solving. Evaluations of the Adolescent Transitions Program have shown reductions in parent-child conflict and in the use of coercive strategies by parents, reductions in teacher ratings of high-risk antisocial behavior, and reductions in youth reports of substance use in the year following the program (Andrews et al., 1995; Dishion & Kavanagh, 2000).

Motivational Scaffolding

Another important contextual feature we looked for in programs was the opportunity for youth to develop a strong sense of personal efficacy and mastery motivation. Research in the field of educational psychology (see Eccles et al., 1998) suggests that acquisition of these assets is supported by the following learning context characteristics: focus on mastery rather than competitive performance, feedback focused on improvement, provision of challenging materials with many opportunities to demonstrate improvement and mastery of these materials, minimizing social comparison of current levels of competencies, and high mastery expectations for all participants. Adventure programs, such as Outward Bound, fit this description very well.

In their meta-analysis of adventure programs, Hattie and colleagues (1997) identified the key components of such programs. They take place in a back-country setting away from young people's typical environment, small groups are assigned mentally and physically challenging tasks to accomplish together, the duration is 2–4 weeks, group members are often involved in problem-solving and decision-making interactions, and the group is led by a trained, nonintrusive leader. The tasks, such as hiking a specific distance, provide demanding challenges for the group requiring cooperation, effort, determination, and self-reliance. Participants plan meals, prepare for the expedition, maintain the equipment, and plan and problem solve throughout the program. Initially, the leader's role is to build physical skills and group cooperation and communication skills, but as the program progresses the group operates largely independent of its leader and takes responsibility for all aspects of the expedition. The successful extracurricular activities, particularly the sports activities, also exemplify this contextual feature.

Opportunities to Experience Mattering and Leadership

Providing opportunities for youth to experience mattering, leadership, and challenge are common features of many of the organizations and programs investigated with both nonexperimental and experimental methods. Opportunities for community service provide the clearest examples. Several of the organizations reviewed provide such opportunities in activities ranging from direct service to the elderly and children to neighborhood clean-up projects. These organizations stand out as well in the extent to which the youth themselves are allowed to play a leadership role in selecting and overseeing these service activities. Many of the organizations also provide extensive opportunities for the youth to play leadership roles in the organizations themselves. Youth are expected to take "responsibility for the organization." Opportunities to move up in leadership and responsibility as the youth gain in both their maturity and expertise provide additional examples of the ways in which these programs provide their youth with a genuine sense that they matter to the organization.

Opportunities to offer meaningful service in one's community represent another effective way to provide adolescents experiences of mattering and leadership. This approach is exemplified in the Teen Outreach Program (TOP; Allen et al., 1990, 1994, 1997; Philliber & Allen, 1992). TOP, a national volunteer service program, is designed to both help adolescents understand and evaluate their future life options and develop life skills and autonomy in a context featuring strong social ties to adult mentors. Interestingly, even though its primary stated goal is prevention of teen pregnancy and risky sexual activity, neither of these outcomes are an explicit part of the programming. For example, less than 15% of the "official" curriculum deals with sexuality, and even these materials are often not used because of overlap with information offered in the school or because of conflicts with community values.

The three program components are supervised community service, classroom-based discussions of service experiences, and classroom-based discussions and activities related to social-developmental tasks of adolescence. Participants choose their volunteer activities with the assistance of trained staff who help match individuals' interests and skills with community needs. Examples of volunteer activities include aid work in hospitals and nursing homes, participation in walkathons, and peer tutoring. The TOP sites offer a minimum of 20 hours per year of volunteer service for each participant. In the evaluated programs, participants averaged 45.8 hours of volunteer service during their 9 months of involvement.

The TOP curriculum provides a framework for classroom meetings that include structured discussions, group exercises, role-playing exercises, guest speakers, and informational presentations. These discussions are designed to help students prepare for, and learn from, their service experiences by dealing with topics such as lack of self-confidence, social skills, assertiveness, and self-discipline. Trained facilitators lead discussions of such topics as values clarification, management of family relationships, and handling of close relationships. Participants are encouraged to discuss their feelings and attitudes.

Several evaluation studies have been done on TOP (e.g., Allen et al., 1990, 1994, 1997; Philliber & Allen, 1992). Although little direct attention is given to the program goals, the desired results of reductions in rates of pregnancy, school failure, and school suspension have been achieved in all evaluations. We can only guess as to the reasons for the program's success; however, community service appears to be a key component. The students who performed more volunteer service were at lower risk for course failure while they were involved in the program. Also, implementation quality of the TOP curriculum did not significantly influence program outcomes (Allen, Philliber, & Hoggson, 1990), suggesting that it is the community service and possibly the mentoring components that are most important.

172

Summary

In summary, there is growing evidence that youth programs focused on both prevention and promotion do increase positive outcomes and decrease negative outcomes for youth. Most interestingly, some programs not explicitly focused on academic instruction produce gains in academic achievement, school engagement, and high school graduation rates. These programs also show declines in school-related problem behaviors, particularly those related to violence and bullying as well as to dropping out. It is quite possible that some of the programs that did not measure these school-related outcomes would also show positive effects on such outcomes. It is also clear that effective programs can occur as extracurricular activities in schools, as nonacademic programs during and after school in the school building, as after-school programs in the school building, or as positive youth development programs in communities.

Although support is growing for the importance of the contextual features summarized in Table 1, more experimental studies that directly manipulate these features are needed before firm causal conclusions can be reached. There is also a major need for more theory-driven program design and evaluation. Staff of many of the organizations and programs studied did not use strong theory in designing their offerings. They did not develop a theoretically based rationale linking specific program features to specific youth outcomes. Instead, it seems as though they designed a program that they liked based on a variety of inputs. Too often, the evaluators of such programs then seemed to select outcomes that the evaluators believed would be convincing to funders and policymakers. Often, the interventions yielded mixed efficacy results. Too little attention was paid to finding out why specific components of the program or organization either worked or did not. Future program design and evaluation needs to overcome these limitations.

REFERENCES

Abbott, R. D., O'Donnell, J., Hawkins, J. D., Hill, K. G., Kosterman, R., & Catalano, R. F. (1998). Changing teaching practices to promote achievement and bonding to school. *American Journal of Orthopsychiatry, 68*, 542–552.

Adelman, H. S., & Taylor, L. (1997). Addressing barriers to learning: Beyond school-linked services and full-service schools. *American Journal of Orthopsychiatry, 67*, 408–421.

Agnew, R., & Petersen, D. M. (1989). Leisure and delinquency. *Social Problems, 36*, 332–350.

Allen, J. P., Kuperminc, G., Philliber, S., & Herre, K. (1994). Programmatic prevention of adolescent problem behaviors: The role of autonomy, relatedness, and volunteer service in the Teen Outreach Program. *American Journal of Community Psychology, 22*, 617–638.

Allen, J. P., Philliber, S., Herrling, S., & Kuperminc, G. P. (1997). Preventing teen pregnancy and academic failure: Experimental evaluation of a developmentally based approach. *Child Development, 68*, 729–742.

Allen, J. P., Philliber, S., & Hoggson, N. (1990). School-based prevention of teen-age pregnancy and school dropout: Process evaluation of the national replication of the Teen Outreach Program. *American Journal of Community Psychology, 18*, 505–524.

Andrews, D. W., Soberman, L. H., & Dishion, T. J. (1995). The adolescent transitions program for high-risk teens and their parents: Toward a school-based intervention. *Education and Treatment of Children, 18*, 478–498.

Barber, B. L., Eccles, J. S., & Stone, M. R. (2001). Whatever happened to the jock, the brain, and the princess? Young adult pathways linked to adolescent activity involvement and social identity. *Journal of Adolescent Research, 16,* 429–455.

Botvin, G. J. (1998). Preventing adolescent drug abuse through life skills training: Theory, methods, and effectiveness. In *Social programs that work* (pp. 225–257). New York: Russell Sage Foundation.

Botvin, G. J. (2000). Preventing drug abuse in schools: Social and competence enhancement approaches targeting individual-level etiologic factors. *Addictive Behaviors, 25,* 887–897.

Botvin, G. J., Baker, E., Dusenbury, L., Tortu, S., & Botvin, E. M. (1990). Preventing adolescent drug abuse through a multimodal cognitive-behavioral approach: Results of a 3-year study. *Journal of Consulting and Clinical Psychology, 58,* 437–446.

Botvin, G. J., Baker, E., Filazzola, A. D., & Botvin, E. M. (1990). A cognitive-behavioral approach to substance abuse prevention: One-year follow-up. *Addictive Behaviors, 15,* 47–63.

Botvin, G. J., Griffin, K. W., Diaz, T., Scheier, L. M., Williams, C., & Epstein, J. A. (2000). Preventing illicit drug use in adolescents: Long-term follow-up data from a randomized control trial of a school population. *Addictive Behaviors, 25,* 769–774.

Brown, B. B. (1990). Peer groups and peer cultures. In *At the threshold: The developing adolescent* (pp. 171–196). Cambridge, MA: Harvard University Press.

Brustad, R. J., Babkes, M. L., & Smith, A. L. (2001). Youth in sport: Psychological considerations. In R. N. Singer, H. A. Hausenblas, & C. M. Janelle (Eds.), *Handbook of sport psychology* (2nd ed., pp. 604–635). New York: Wiley.

Carnegie Corporation. (1992). *A matter of time: Risk and opportunity in the out-of-school hours.* New York: Author.

Carpenter, P. J., & Scanlan, T. K. (1998). Changes over time in the determinance of sport commitment. *Pediatric Exercise Science, 10,* 356–365.

Catalano, R. F., Berglund, M. L., Ryan, J. A. M., Lonczak, H. S., & Hawkins, J. D. (1999). *Positive youth development in the United States: Research findings on evaluations of the positive youth development programs.* New York: Carnegie Corporation.

Catalano, R. F., & Hawkins, J. D. (1996). The social development model: A theory of antisocial behavior. In *Delinquency and crime: Current theories* (Cambridge criminology series, pp. 149–197). New York: Cambridge University Press.

Chou, C. P., Montgomery, S., Pentz, M. A., Rohrbach, L. A., Johnson, C. A., Flay, B. R., & MacKinnon, D. P. (1998). Effects of a community-based prevention program in decreasing drug use in high-risk adolescents. *American Journal of Public Health, 88,* 944–948.

Connell, J. P., Gambone, M. A., & Smith, T. J. (2000). Youth development in community settings: Challenges to our field and our approach. In P. P. Ventures (Ed.), *Youth development: Issues, challenges and directions* (pp. 281–300). Philadelphia: Public/Private Ventures.

Cooper, C. R., Denner, J., & Lopez, E. M. (1999). Cultural brokers: Helping Latino children on pathways toward success. *Future of Children, 9,* 51–57.

Csikszentmihalyi, M. (1991). *Flow: The psychology of optimal experience.* New York: HarperPerennial.

Csikszentmihalyi, M., & Kleiber, D. A. (1991). Leisure and self-actualization. In B. L. Driver, P. J. Brown, & G. L. Peterson (Eds.), *Benefits of leisure* (pp. 91–102). State College, PA: Venture.

Csikszentmihalyi, M., Rathunde, K. R., Whalen, S., & Wong, M. (1993). *Talented teenagers: The roots of success and failure.* New York: Cambridge University Press.

Deci, E. L., & Ryan, R. M. (1985). *Intrinsic motivation and self-determination in human behavior.* New York: Plenum.

Deeter, T. E. (1990). Remodeling expectancy and value in physical activity. *Journal of Sport and Exercise Psychology, 12,* 83–91.

DeMartini, J. (1983). Social movement participation: Political socialization, generational, and lasting effects. *Youth and Society, 15,* 195–223.

Dishion, T. J., & Kavanagh, K. (2000). A multilevel approach to family-centered prevention in schools: Process and outcome. *Addictive Behaviors, 25,* 899–911.

Dishion, T. J., McCord, J., & Poulin, F. (1999). When interventions harm: Peer groups and problem behavior. *American Psychologist, 54,* 755–764.

Dishion, T. J., Poulin, F., & Burraston, B. (2001). Peer group dynamics associated with iatrogenic effects in group interventions with high-risk young adolescents. In *The role of friendship in psychological adjustment* (New directions for child and adolescent development, No. 91, pp. 79–92). San Francisco: Jossey-Bass.

Dryfoos, J. G. (1994). *Full-service schools: A revolution in health and social services for children, youth, and families.* San Francisco: Jossey-Bass.

Dryfoos, J. G. (1995). Full service schools: Revolution or fad? *Journal of Research on Adolescence, 5,* 147–172.

Dryfoos, J. G. (1999). The role of the school in children's out-of-school time. *Future of Children, 9,* 117–134.

Durlak, J. A., & Wells, A. M. (1997). Primary prevention mental health programs for children and adolescents: A meta-analytic review. *American Journal of Community Psychology, 25,* 115–152.

Durlak, J. A., & Wells, A. M. (1998). Evaluation of indicated preventive intervention (secondary prevention) mental health programs for children and adolescents. *American Journal of Community Psychology, 26,* 775–802.

Eccles, J. S., & Barber, B. L. (1999). Student council, volunteering, basketball, or marching band: What kind of extracurricular involvement matters? *Journal of Adolescent Research, 14,* 10–43.

Eccles, J. S., & Gootman, J. A. (Eds.). (2002). *Community programs to promote youth development.* Washington, DC: National Academy Press.

Eccles, J. S., Midgley, C., Wigfield, A., Buchanan, C. M., Reuman, D., Flanagan, C. & MacIver, D. (1993). Development during adolescence: The impact of stage/environment fit on young adolescents' experiences in schools and in families. *American Psychologist, 48,* 90–101.

Eccles, J. S., Wigfield, A., & Schiefele, U. (1998). Motivation. In N. Eisenberg (Ed.), *Handbook of child psychology* (Vol. 3, 5th ed., pp. 1017–1095). New York: Wiley.

Eder, D., & Parker, S. (1987). The cultural production and reproduction of gender: The effect of extracurricular activities on peer-group culture. *Sociology of Education, 60,* 200–213.

Elder, G. H. Jr., & Conger, R. D. (2000). *Children of the land: Adversity and success in rural America.* Chicago: University of Chicago Press.

Elliott, D. S., & Tolan, P. H. (1999). *Youth violence prevention, intervention and social policy.* Washington, DC: American Psychiatric Association.

Elliott, D., & Voss, H. (1974). *Delinquency and dropout.* Lexington, MA: Lexington Books.

Eron, L., Huesmann, R., Spindler, A., Guerra, N., Henry, D., & Tolan, P. (2002). A cognitive-ecological approach to preventing aggression in urban settings: Initial outcomes for high-risk children. *Journal of Consulting and Clinical Psychology, 70,* 179–194.

Fagan, J., & Wilkinson, D. L. (1998). Social contexts and functions of adolescent violence. In D. S. Elliott, B. A. Hamburg, & K. R. Williams (Eds.), *Violence in American schools: A new perspective* (pp. 217–252). New York: Cambridge University Press.

Fine, G. A., Mortimer, J. T., & Roberts, D. F. (1990). Leisure, work, and the mass media. In S. S. Feldman & G. R. Elliott (Eds.), *At the threshold: The developing adolescent.* Cambridge, MA: Harvard University Press.

Fox, K. M., Goudas, S., Biddle, S., Duda, J., & Armstrong, N. (1994). Children's task and ego profiles in sport. *British Journal of Educational Psychology, 64,* 253–261.

Fredricks, J. A., Alfeld-Liro, C. J., Hruda, L. Z., Eccles, J. S., Patrick, H., & Ryan, A. M. (2002). A qualitative exploration of adolescents' commitment to athletics and the arts. *Journal of Adolescent Research, 17,* 68–97.

Gambone, M. A. (1997). *Launching a resident-driven initiative: Community Change for Youth Development (CCYD) from site-selection to early implementation.* Philadelphia: Public/Private Ventures.

Gambone, M. A., & Arbreton, A. J. (1997). *Safe havens: The contributions of youth organizations to healthy adolescent development.* Philadelphia: Public/Private Ventures.

Glancy, M., Willits, F. K., & Farrell, P. (1986). Adolescent activities and adult success and happiness: Twenty-four years later. *Sociology and Social Research, 70,* 242–250.

Gould, D., Eklund, R. C., & Jackson, S. A. (1991). 1988 U.S. Olympic wrestling excellence: I Mental preparation, precompetitive cognition and affect. *The Sport Psychologist, 6,* 358–362.

Gould, D., Eklund, R. C., & Jackson, S. A. (1993). Coping strategies used by U.S. Olympic wrestlers. *Research Quarterly for Exercise and Sport, 64,* 83–93.

Gould, D., Finch, L. M., & Jackson, S. A. (1993). Coping strategies used by national champion figure skaters. *Research Quarterly for Exercise and Sport, 64,* 453–468.

Gould, D., & Weiss, M. R. (Eds.). (1987). *Advances in pediatric sport sciences: Vol. 2. Behavioral issues.* Champaign, IL: Human Kinetics.

Greenberg, M. T., Domitrovich, C., & Bumbarger, B. (2001). The prevention of mental disorders in school-aged children: Current state of the field. *Prevention and Treatment, 4,* 1–71.

Grieves, J. (1989). Acquiring a leisure identity: Juvenile jazz bands and the moral universe of healthy leisure time. *Leisure Studies, 8,* 1–9.

Grossman, J. B., & Tierney, J. P. (1998). Does mentoring work? An impact study of the Big Brothers Big Sisters program. *Evaluation Review, 22,* 403–426.

Haggard, L. M., & Williams, D. R. (1992). Identity affirmation through leisure activities: Leisure symbols of the self. *Journal of Leisure Research, 24,* 1–18.

Hahn, A., Leavitt, T., & Aaron, P. (1994). *Evaluation of the Quantum Opportunity Program (QOP): Did the program work?* Waltham, MA: Brandeis University, Heller Graduate School.

Halpern, R. (1999). After-school programs for low-income children: Promise and challenges. *Future of Children, 9,* 81–95.

Halpern, R., Barker, G., & Mollard, W. (2000). Youth programs as alternative spaces to be: A study of neighborhood youth programs in Chicago's West Town. *Youth and Society, 31,* 469–506.

Hanks, M., & Eckland, B. (1978). Adult voluntary associations and adolescent socialization. *Sociological Quarterly, 19,* 481–490.

Harter, S. (1978). Effectance motivation reconsidered: Toward a developmental model. *Human Development, 21,* 34–64.

Hattie, J., Marsh, H. W., Neill, J. T., & Richards, G. E. (1997). Adventure education and outward bound: Out-of-class experiences that make a lasting difference. *Review of Educational Research, 67,* 1943–1987.

Hawkins, J. D., Catalano, R. F., Morrison, D. M., O'Donnell, J., Abbott, R. D., & Day, L. E. (1992). The Seattle Social Development Project: Effects of the first four years on protective factors and problem behaviors. In *Preventing antisocial behavior: Interventions from birth through adolescence* (pp. 139–161). New York: Guilford Press.

Herrera, C., Sipe, C. L., & McClanahan, W. S. P. (2000). *Mentoring school-age children: Relationship development in community-based and school-based programs.* Philadelphia: Public/Private Ventures.

Holland, A., & Andre, T. (1987). Participation in extracurricular activities in secondary school: What is known, what needs to be known? *Review of Educational Research, 57,* 437–466.

Holtzman, W. H. (1997). Community psychology and full-service schools in different cultures. *American Psychologist, 52,* 381–389.

Howell, F., & McKenzie, J. (1987). High school athletics and adult sport-leisure activity: Gender variations across the life cycle. *Sociology of Sport Journal, 4,* 329–346.

Howes, C., Olenick, M., & Der-Kiureghian, T. (1987). After-school child care in an elementary school: Social development and continuity and complementarity of programs. *Elementary School Journal, 88,* 93–103.

Huesmann, L. R., Maxwell, C. D., Eron, L., Dalhberg, L. L., Guerra, N. G., Tolan, P. H., VanAcker, R., & Henry, D. (1996). Evaluating a cognitive/ecological program for the prevention of aggression among urban children. *American Journal of Preventive Medicine, 12*(Suppl. 5), 120–128.

Irvine, A. B., Biglan, A., Smolkowski, K., Metzler, C. W., & Ary, D. V. (1999). The effectiveness of a parenting skills program for parents of middle school students in small communities. *Journal of Consulting and Clinical Psychology, 67,* 811–825.

Kinney, D. A. (1993). From nerds to normals: The recovery of identity among adolescents from middle school to high school. *Sociology of Education, 66,* 21–40.

Kirby, D. (1997). *No easy answers: Research and findings on programs to reduce teen pregnancy.* Washington, DC: National Campaign to Prevent Teen Pregnancy.

Kirby, D. (2001). *Emerging answers: Research findings on programs to reduce teen pregnancy.* Washington, DC: National Campaign to Prevent Teen Pregnancy.

Kirshnit, C. E., Ham, M., & Richards, M. (1989). The sporting life. *Journal of Youth and Adolescence, 18,* 601–615.

Kleiber, D., Larson, R., & Csikszentmihalyi, M. (1986). The experience of leisure in adolescence. *Journal of Leisure Research, 18,* 165–176.

Lamborn, S. D., Brown, B. B., Mounts, N. S., & Steinberg, L. (1992). Putting school in perspective: The influence of family, peers, extracurricular participation, and part-time work on academic engagement. In F. M. Newmann (Ed.), *Student engagement and achievement in American secondary schools.* New York: Teachers College Press.

Landers, D., & Landers, D. (1978). Socialization via interscholastic athletics: Its effect on delinquency. *Sociology of Education, 51,* 299–301.

Larson, R. (1994). Youth organization, hobbies, and sports as developmental context. In R. K. Silberiesen & E. Todt (Eds.), *Adolescence in context.* New York: Springer-Verlag.

Larson, R. W. (2000). Toward a psychology of positive youth development. *American Psychologist, 55,* 170–183.

Larson, R., & Kleiber, D. (1993). Daily experience of adolescents. In *Handbook of clinical research and practice with adolescents* (Wiley series on personality processes, pp. 125–145). New York: Wiley.

Larson, R., & Richards, M. E. (Eds.). (1989). The changing life space of early adolescence [Special issue]. *Journal of Youth and Adolescence, 18,* 501–626.

Larson, R. W., & Verma, S. (1999). How children and adolescents spend time across the world: Work, play, and developmental opportunities. *Psychological Bulletin, 125,* 701–736.

Laub, J. J., & Lauritsen, J. L. (1998). The interdependence of school violence with neighborhood and family conditions. In D. S. Elliott, B. A. Hamburg, & K. R. Williams (Eds.), *Violence in American schools: A new perspective* (pp. 217–252). New York: Cambridge University Press.

Leff, S. S., & Hoyle, R. H. (1995). Young athletes' perceptions of parental support and pressure. *Journal of Youth and Adolescence, 24,* 187–203.

Lerner, R. M., & Galambos, N. L. (1998). Adolescent development: Challenges and opportunities for research, programs, and policies. *Annual Review of Psychology, 49,* 413–446.

Lonczak, H. S., Huang, B., Catalano, R. F., Hawkins, J. D., Hill, K. G., Abbott, R. D., Ryan, J., & Kosterman, R. (2001). The social predictors of adolescent alcohol misuse: A test of the social development model. *Journal of Studies on Alcohol, 62,* 179–189.

Maehr, M. L., & Midgley, C. (1996). *Transforming school cultures.* Boulder, CO: Westview Press.

Mahoney, J. L. (1997, April). *From companions to convictions: Peer groups, school engagement, and the development of criminality.* Paper presented at the biennial meeting of the Society for Research in Child Development, Washington, DC.

Mahoney, J. L. (2000). School extracurricular activity participation as a moderator in the development of antisocial patterns. *Child Development, 71,* 502–516.

Mahoney, J. L., & Cairns, R. B. (1997). Do extracurricular activities protect against early school dropout? *Developmental Psychology, 33,* 241–253.

Mahoney, J. L., Cairns, R. B., & Farmer, T. (in press). Promoting interpersonal competence and educational success through extracurricular activity participation. *Journal of Educational Psychology.*

Mahoney, J. L., & Stattin, H. (2000). Leisure activities and adolescent antisocial behavior: The role of structure and social context. *Journal of Adolescence, 23,* 113–127.

Mahoney, J. L., & Stattin, H. (2002). Structured after-school activities as a moderator of depressed mood for adolescents with detached relations to their parents. *Journal of Community Psychology, 30,* 69–86.

Mahoney, J. L., Stattin, H., & Magnusson, D. (2001). Youth recreation center participation and criminal offending: A 20-year longitudinal study of Swedish boys. *International Journal of Behavioral Development, 25,* 509–520.

Marsh, H. W. (1992). Extracurricular activities: Beneficial extension of the traditional curriculum or subversion of academic goals? *Journal of Educational Psychology, 84,* 553–562.

Marshall, N. L., Coll, C. G., Marx, F., McCartney, K., Keefe, N., & Ruh, J. (1997). After-school time and children's behavioral adjustment. *Merrill-Palmer Quarterly, 43,* 497–514.

Masten, A. S., & Coatsworth, J. D. (1998). The development of competence in favorable and unfavorable environments. *American Psychologist, 53,* 205–220.

McLaughlin, M. W. (2000). *Community counts: How youth organizations matter for youth development.* Washington, DC: Public Education Network.

McLaughlin, M. W., Irby, M. A., & Langman, J. (1994). *Urban sanctuaries: Neighborhood organizations in the lives and futures of inner-city youth.* San Francisco: Jossey-Bass.

McMahon, T. J., Ward, N. L., Pruett, M. K., Davidson, L., & Griffith, E. E. H. (2000). Building full-service schools: Lessons learned in the development of interagency collaboratives. *Journal of Educational and Psychological Consultation, 11,* 65–92.

McNeal, R. B. (1995). Extracurricular activities and high school dropouts. *Sociology of Education, 68,* 62–81.

Melnick, M. J., Vanfossen, B. E., & Sabo, D. F. (1988). Developmental effects of athletic participation among high school girls. *Sociology of Sport Journal, 5,* 22–36.

Newmann, F. M., Wehlage, G. G., & Lamborn, S. D. (1992). The significance and sources of student engagement. In F. M. Newmann (Ed.), *Student engagement and achievement in American secondary schools* (pp. 11–39). New York: Teachers College Press.

O'Donnell, J., Hawkins, J. D., Catalano, R. F., & Abbott, R. D. (1995). Preventing school failure, drug use, and delinquency among low-income children: Long-term intervention in elementary schools. *American Journal of Orthopsychiatry, 65,* 87–100.

Olweus, D. (1991). Bully/victim problems among schoolchildren: Basic facts and effects of a school based intervention program. In *The development and treatment of childhood aggression* (pp. 411–448). Hillsdale, NJ: Erlbaum.

Olweus, D. (1994a). Annotation: Bullying at school: Basic facts and effects of a school based intervention program. *Journal of Child Psychology and Psychiatry and Allied Disciplines, 35,* 1171–1190.

Olweus, D. (1994b). Bullying at school: Long-term outcomes for the victims and an effective school-based intervention program. In *Aggressive behavior: Current perspectives* (Plenum series in social/clinical psychology, pp. 97–130). New York: Plenum.

Olweus, D., Limber, S. P., & Mihalic, S. F. (1999). *Blueprints for violence prevention, Book 9: Bullying prevention program.* Boulder, CO: Center for the Study and Prevention of Violence.

Otto, L. B. (1975). Extracurricular activities in the educational attainment process. *Rural Sociology, 40,* 162–176.

Otto, L. B. (1976). Extracurricular activities and aspirations in the status attainment process. *Rural Sociology, 41,* 217–233.

Otto, L. B., & Alwin, D. (1977). Athletics, aspirations and attainments. *Sociology of Education, 50,* 102–113.

Packard Foundation. (1999). *When school is out* (Future of Children series, No. 9). Los Altos, CA: Author.

Patrick, H., Ryan, A. M., Alfeld-Liro, C., Fredricks, J. A., Hruda, L., & Eccles, J. S. (1999). Adolescents' commitment to developing talent: The role of peers in continuing motivation for sports and the arts. *Journal of Youth and Adolescence, 28,* 741–763.

Pensgaard, A. M., & Roberts, G. C. (2000). The relationship between motivational climate, perceived ability and sources of distress among elite athletes. *Journal of Sport Sciences, 18,* 191–200.

Pentz, M. A., Dwyer, J. H., MacKinnon, D. P., Flay, B. R., Hansen, W. B., Wang, E. Y., & Johnson, C. A. (1989). A multicommunity trial for primary prevention of adolescent drug abuse. *Journal of the American Medical Association, 261,* 3259–3266.

Pettit, G. S., Laird, R. D., Bates, J. E., & Dodge, K. A. (1997). Patterns of after-school care in middle childhood: Risk factors and developmental outcomes. *Merrill-Palmer Quarterly, 43,* 515–538.

Philliber, S., & Allen, J. P. (1992). Life options and community service: Teen Outreach Program. In *Preventing adolescent pregnancy: Model programs and evaluations* (Sage focus editions, Vol. 140, pp. 139–155). Thousand Oaks, CA: Sage.

Philliber, S., Kaye, J. W., Herrling, S., & West, E. (2000). *Preventing teen pregnancy: An evaluation of the Children's Aid Society Carrera Program.* Accord, NY: Philliber Research Associates.

Pierce, K. M., Hamm, J. V., & Vandell, D. L. (1999). Experiences in after-school programs and children's adjustment in first-grade classrooms. *Child Development, 70,* 756–767.

Pittman, K., Ferber, T., & Irby, M. (1999). *Developing and deploying youth leaders.* Takoma Park, MD: International Youth Foundation.

Pittman, K., Irby, M., & Ferber, T. (2000). Unfinished business: Further reflections on a decade of promoting youth development. In *Youth development: Issues, challenges and directions* (pp. 17–64). Philadelphia: Public/Private Ventures.

Posner, J. K., & Vandell, D. L. (1994). Low-income children's after-school care: Are there beneficial effects of after-school programs? *Child Development, 65,* 440–456.

Posner, J. K., & Vandell, D. L. (1999). After-school activities and the development of low-income urban children: A longitudinal study. *Developmental Psychology, 35,* 868–879.

Poulin, F., Dishion, T. J., & Burraston, B. (2001). Three-year iatrogenic effects associated with aggregating high-risk adolescents in cognitive-behavioral preventive interventions. *Applied Developmental Science, 5,* 214–224.

Public/Private Ventures. (2000). *Youth development: Issues, challenges and directions.* Philadelphia: Author.

Quinn, J. (1999). Where need meets opportunity: Youth development programs for early teens. *Future of Children, 9,* 96–116.

Roberts, G. C., & Treasure, D. C. (1992). Children in sport. *Sport Science Review, 1,* 46–64.

Roth, J. & Brooks-Gunn, J. (2000). *What do adolescents need for healthy development?: Implications for youth policy* (Social Policy Report 16). Ann Arbor, MI: Society for Research in Child Development.

Roth, J., Brooks-Gunn, J., Murray, L., & Foster, W. (1998). Promoting healthy adolescents: Synthesis of youth development program evaluations. *Journal of Research on Adolescence, 8,* 423–459.

Ryan, R. M., & Deci, E. L. (2000). Self-determination theory and the facilitation of intrinsic motivation, social development, and well-being. *American Psychologist, 55,* 68–78.

Samples, F., & Aber, L. (1998). Evaluations of school-based violence prevention programs. In D. S. Elliott, B. A. Hamburg, & K. R. Williams (Eds.), *Violence in American schools: A new perspective* (pp. 217–252). New York: Cambridge University Press.

Scales, P. C. (1999). Increasing service-learning's impact on middle school students. *Middle School Journal, 30,* 40–44.

Scanlan, T. K. (1999, August). *Sources of athletes' commitment.* Lecture presented at the Australian Institute of Sport and University of Canberra, Canberra, Australia.

Scanlan, T. K. (2000, April). *Presenting a new interview methodology designed to test, modify, and expand theory using the sport commitment model as an exemplar.* Paper presented at the Achievement Motivation and Engagement in Different Domains symposium, Winchester, England.

Scanlan, T. K. (2002). Social evaluation and the competition process: A developmental perspective. In F. L. Smoll & R. E. Smith (Eds.), *Children and youth in sport: A biopsychosocial perspective* (2nd ed.). Dubuque, IA: Kendall/Hunt.

Scanlan, T. K., Carpenter, P. J., Lobel, M., & Simons, J. P. (1993). Sources of sport enjoyment for youth sport athletes. *Pediatric Exercise Science, 5,* 275–285.

Scanlan, T. K., Carpenter, P. J., Schmidt, G. W., Simons, J. P., & Keeler, B. (1993). An introduction to the sport commitment model. *Journal of Sport and Exercise Psychology, 15,* 1–15.

Scanlan, T. K., & Lewthwaite, R. (1986). Social psychological aspects of the competitive sport experience for male youth sport participants: IV. Predictors of enjoyment. *Journal of Sport Psychology, 8,* 25–35.

Scanlan, T. K., & Simons, J. P. (1995). The construct of sport enjoyment. In *Motivation in sport and exercise* (pp. 199–215). Champaign, IL: Human Kinetics.

Scanlan, T. K., Simons, J. P., Carpenter, P. J., Schmidt, G. W., & Keeler, B. (1993). The sport commitment model: Measurement development for the youth-sport domain. *Journal of Sport and Exercise Psychology, 15,* 16–38.

Scanlan, T. K., Stein, G. L., & Ravizza, K. (1991). An in-depth study of former elite figure skaters: III. Sources of stress. *Journal of Sport and Exercise Psychology, 13,* 103–120.

Sheley, J. F. (1984). Evaluation of the centralized, structured, after-school tutorial. *Journal of Educational Research, 77,* 213–218.

Smith, R. E. (1986). Toward a cognitive-affective model of burnout. *Journal of Sport Psychology, 8,* 36–50.

Smoll, F. L., Smith, R. E., Barnett, N. P., & Everett, J. J. (1993). Enhancement of children's self-esteem through social support training for youth sport coaches. *Journal of Applied Psychology, 78,* 602–610.

Spielberger, J., & Halpern, R. (2002). *The role of after-school programs in children's literacy development.* Chicago: Chapin Hall Center for Children.

Stephens, D. E. (1998). The relationship of goal orientation and perceived ability to enjoyment and value in youth sport. *Pediatric Exercise Science, 10,* 236–247.

Vandell, D. L., & Pierce, K. (1999, April). *Can after-school programs benefit children who live in high-crime neighborhoods?* Paper presented at the biennial meeting of the Society for Research in Child Development, Albuquerque, NM.

Vandell, D. L., & Posner, J. K. (1999). Conceptualization and measurement of children's after-school environments. In *Measuring environment across the life span: Emerging methods and concepts* (pp. 167–196). Washington, DC: American Psychological Association.

Vandell, D. L., & Ramanan, J. (1991). Children of the National Longitudinal Survey of Youth: Choices in after-school care and child development. *Developmental Psychology, 27,* 637–643.

Vandell, D. L., & Shumow, L. (1999). After-school child care programs. *Future of Children, 9,* 64–80.

Walker, G. (2001). *The policy climate for early adolescent initiatives.* Philadelphia: Public/Private Ventures.

Weiss, M. R., & Petlichkoff, L. M. (1989). Children's motivation for participation in and withdrawal from sport: Identifying the missing links. *Pediatric Exercise Science, 1,* 195–211.

Winne, P. H., & Walsh, J. (1980). Self-concept and participation in school activities reanalyzed. *Journal of Educational Psychology, 72,* 161–166.

Youniss, J., McLellan, J. A., Su, Y., & Yates, M. (1999). The role of community service in identity development: Normative, unconventional, and deviant orientations. *Journal of Adolescent Research, 14,* 248–261.

Youniss, J., McLellan, J. A., & Yates, M. (1997). What we know about engendering civic identity. *American Behavioral Scientist, 40,* 619–630.

Youniss, J., McLellan, J. A., & Yates, M. (1999). Religion, community service, and identity in American youth. *Journal of Adolescence, 22,* 243–253.

Youniss, J., Yates, M., & Su, Y. (1997). Social integration: Community service and marijuana use in high school seniors. *Journal of Adolescent Research, 12,* 245–262.

Chapter 5

The Effects of Welfare Reform on the Educational Outcomes of Parents and Their Children

MARIKA N. RIPKE AND DANIELLE A. CROSBY
University of Texas at Austin

E conomic well-being and educational attainment go hand in hand. Linked to future employability and financial well-being, education is often considered the primary way to "get ahead" in society. It is ironic, then, that even as the Bush administration touts the importance of education, particularly for disadvantaged children, education for low-income adults has taken a back seat in recent years to the "work-first" approach of welfare reform. The Personal Responsibility and Work Opportunity Reconciliation Act (PRWORA) of 1996 effectively ended 61 years of federally guaranteed cash assistance to poor families and, in its place, created a time-limited program focused primarily on reducing welfare caseloads and increasing employment. Many consider the law to be the single most important welfare legislation since the inception of the system in 1935. The 1996 legislation differs from previous legislation primarily because it emphasizes the rapid movement from welfare to work and thereby greatly reduces opportunities for welfare recipients to engage in such human capital development activities as education and job training.

Proponents of the "work-first" philosophy of welfare reform argued that getting parents into the workforce quickly would benefit families by providing important work experience for adults, positive role models for children, and possibly increased family income. Opponents, on the other hand, worried that strong employment requirements coupled with few supports would greatly exacerbate hardship for families already at risk. Now, years after the passage of PRWORA, the impact of welfare reform on poor families continues to be widely discussed, and it appears that policymakers on each side of the debate have had some of their objectives, as well as some of their fears, realized.

We thank Greg Duncan, our consulting editor, for his insightful comments and suggestions. We are also grateful to Aletha Huston for reviewing an earlier version of this chapter and providing valuable feedback.

Faced with new participation mandates, sanctions, and time limits—and in the context of a strong economy—significant numbers of welfare recipients entered the workforce during the first 5 years of PRWORA. A dramatic 51% reduction in caseloads between 1994 and 2000 led many to describe welfare reform as an unmitigated "success." While it is clear that changes brought about by the 1996 legislation have been partly responsible for national caseload reductions and higher employment rates among former welfare recipients (Blank & Schmidt, 2001), it is much less clear what these changes have meant for the daily lives of families and children. A rapidly growing body of literature on the effects of reform policies on family and child well-being suggests somewhat of a "mixed" picture. Some national indicators of child well-being have improved in the post-1996 years. For example, teen fertility rates have decreased, and high school completion rates have increased (see Duncan & Chase-Lansdale, 2001).

Moreover, the percentage of children living in poverty declined by about 17% between 1996 and 1999 (Primus, Rawlings, Larin, & Porter, 1999). It is unclear, however, whether these shifts have been driven primarily by the 1996 legislation or by other factors such as a strong economy. Notably, the decline in child poverty rates has not matched the dramatic reduction in welfare receipt (Primus et al., 1999).

Fewer children may be living below the official poverty line than a decade ago, yet there are now many more children living in *working poor* families. In his 1999 state of the union address, President Bush claimed that "when America works, America prospers." Recent findings suggest that this does not ring true for everyone. While the higher employment rates spurred by welfare reform decreased the number of people receiving public assistance, they have not translated into substantial increases in income or standard of living for most former welfare recipients. As a result, many families continue to struggle (see Zuckerman, 2000).

Some believe that children are suffering academically, socially, and emotionally under the new welfare legislation. Not only are child advocates concerned about the well-being of the large number of recipients who have left the welfare rolls only to acquire low-wage jobs that do not include benefits and do not raise families out of poverty, but they are also worried about how former recipients who have lost welfare benefits and not yet found employment are supporting themselves and their children. These potentially detrimental circumstances are likely to be exacerbated by the softening economy and recipients' loss of benefits owing to time limits.

In this chapter, we examine how the set of policies contained under the umbrella of welfare reform has affected the educational experiences and outcomes of poor adults and their children. We begin our review with a discussion of the political debates surrounding welfare reform, including the motivating factors behind the 1996 legislation. Although a comprehensive review of the changes initiated by PRWORA is beyond the scope of this chapter (see Greenberg, 2002), we provide an overview of the fundamental changes, particularly as they affect (or have the potential to affect) the educational outcomes of parents and children. We outline briefly the potential processes by which effects occur, discuss related methodological issues, and provide a general overview of how families have fared under the new system.

In the second and third sections of the chapter, we review existing research concerning welfare reform policies and education. We first examine the effects of the "work-first" approach on parents' educational activities and outcomes, as well as its impact on the field of adult education. Next, we review the data on children's educational outcomes, including a discussion of their relationship to effects on parents' educational outcomes. The findings reported in this chapter are relatively short term; however, hypotheses regarding the long-term consequences of welfare reform for children (i.e., 10 or 15 years after families participate in welfare programs) are also of interest and discussed herein.

In the final section of the chapter, we identify key issues of debate in welfare policy and discuss the current challenges facing policymakers, program administrators, and educators. Because this topic is of interest to a wide audience, we draw from a variety of literatures related to employment and income, poverty, education, child development, and family functioning and well-being. A multidisciplinary approach not only provides a comprehensive review of the research findings but also highlights the diverse and often conflicting goals surrounding this timely and important topic. Finally, we conclude with several recommendations for policy and research.

OVERVIEW OF THE 1996 WELFARE REFORM LEGISLATION

Motivating Forces

During the years preceding PRWORA, there was a growing desire across the political spectrum to reduce dependency on government assistance, increase self-sufficiency, and discourage out-of-wedlock births. The largely bipartisan passage of the 1996 reform act reflected widespread dissatisfaction with the former welfare system (see Weaver, Shapiro, & Jacobs, 1995). Many Democrats and Republicans agreed that the Aid to Families with Dependent Children (AFDC) program did little to help poor families improve their circumstances. The specific provisions of the act and its intended consequences, however, have been intensely debated, and discussions have been steeped in competing rhetoric. A key point of disagreement is whether the root cause of dependency on welfare stems from individual responsibility or structural barriers (Jayakody & Stauffer, 2000).

Conservatives, on the one hand, generally argued that poor young women, submerged in a "welfare culture," viewed public assistance as a rightful means to have and support children (Coley, Kuta, & Chase-Lansdale, 2000). Furthermore, many believed that the AFDC system helped to create an intergenerational cycle of dependence on welfare. Research demonstrating that girls whose mothers are on welfare are more likely to be on welfare themselves as adults (Martin, 1999) was cited as evidence that unemployed mothers portray negative messages about work to their children. Proponents of this theory argued that having a parent working in *any* job is better than not working at all. Thus, one intention of the new welfare law was to communicate to young people that parents should be solely responsible for the economic well-being of their families through active participation in the workforce. Through its adoption of a "work-first" approach, the 1996 welfare legislation sought to eliminate the "culture of welfare" believed to encourage out-of-wedlock childbirth and discourage working as a way to support a family (Zuckerman & Kalil, 2000).

Democrats, on the other hand, focused on features of the old welfare system that created strong employment disincentives. For example, before the 1996 legislation, entitlements to Medicaid and child care subsidies were linked to welfare (AFDC) receipt; hence, there was little or no incentive for parents to leave welfare and attain a low-wage job that did not provide these important benefits. While they were in favor of improving existing welfare policies, liberals were concerned about the effects that strict sanctions, time limits, and the absence of a "safety net" would have on poor families. Moreover, they argued that poverty reduction should be an explicit goal of welfare reform, particularly since the benefits provided through the current welfare system were too low to lift many families out of poverty. Ultimately, however, poverty reduction was not articulated as a specific goal of the final legislation.

The Personal Responsibility and Work Opportunity Reconciliation Act of 1996

Although the overarching theme of PRWORA is clearly self-sufficiency through employment, the legislation itself is complex, and there have been several interpretations of its major goals, which include promotion of two-parent families and reductions in out-of-wedlock births (for a detailed review, see Greenberg, 2002; Haskins, 2001). Here we summarize the major changes brought about by the 1996 bill, giving particular attention to those most relevant to the educational outcomes of parents and children.

The 1996 legislation effectively ended federally guaranteed cash assistance to low-income mothers and children, and in its place established Temporary Assistance for Needy Families (TANF) block grants to states. The inclusion of "temporary" in the new program's name reveals one of the key changes in the system. Whereas the previous AFDC system did not limit benefits to a certain period of receipt, the current legislation stipulates that federally funded cash benefits can be received only for a maximum of 5 years in the lifetime of a parent. States have some options with regard to time limits. Individual states may impose a shorter time limit (20 states have done this), may exempt up to 20% of their caseload from the limit (by "stopping the clock" on the 5-year limit or by extending benefits), or may use state funds to continue providing benefits after 5 years.

In line with its strong emphasis on rapid employment and time-limited assistance, PRWORA significantly reduced opportunities for educational development (particularly for nonteen parents) by restricting the types of allowable "work" activities. States were given a fair amount of discretion in defining "work" and some flexibility to establish separate educationally focused programs outside of the TANF system.

The devolution of welfare to state authority reflects one of the most significant changes enacted by PRWORA. Some have argued that this flexibility is a positive change because it allows state and local governments to design programs that best meet their particular needs. Certainly, PRWORA has brought about a significant diversification of programs at the state and county levels. While some states have moved toward very stringent time limits and work requirements, others have chosen to maintain more generous and accessible benefits. Increased variability has led to some concern that recipients may migrate to states where benefits are more generous, resulting in a potential "race to the bottom" as states attempt to reduce caseloads and costs. There is also concern that, in the absence of strong federal standards, benefits may be distributed unfairly at the discretion of individual policymakers and caseworkers. Variations in how states have responded to the new federal guidelines are discussed in the next section.

The welfare reform bill also changed the structure and funding for states' provision of child care assistance. Under PRWORA, four separate funding streams were combined into a single child care and development block grant known as the Child Care Development Fund (CCDF). The creation of the new block grant included increased funding for child care in recognition of the fact that increased maternal employment would likewise increase the need for child care. CCDF provides states with increased flexibility and discretion regarding how to structure their subsidies and allocate funds. In addition to changing child care assistance policies, PRWORA included provisions that denied welfare benefits to most noncitizens, created penalties for states failing to meet work participation goals, and made eligibility requirements for the Supplemental Security Income (SSI) program for disabled children more restrictive.

The flexibility that PRWORA grants to the states in creating and administering their welfare programs makes it difficult to speak consistently or broadly of the effects of "welfare reform" on families because there is no single "welfare reform" package. While the 1996 legislation put into place policies and requirements that all states must meet (e.g., work participation rates and caseload reduction goals) to avoid sanctions, there are many exceptions to these policies and wide variations in how states interpret, adjust, allow for, and react to these broader regulations. Furthermore, there are many contextual factors (e.g., environmental and familial) that can play a role in how families are affected by welfare reform. These factors include (a) local unemployment rates and job markets, (b) the availability of government and nongovernment services and supports in the community, (c) racial and gender discrimination, and (d) the circumstances and characteristics of families (e.g., mental health, disabilities, domestic violence, language/cultural barriers). Therefore, throughout this chapter we discuss effects of "welfare reform" generally but also, as much as possible, relate effects to specific contexts and policies.

Pathways of Influence

Figure 1 illustrates the potential pathways by which welfare reform may affect the educational outcomes of adults and children. The adult outcomes most directly affected by welfare reform are likely to be those targeted by policies, primarily

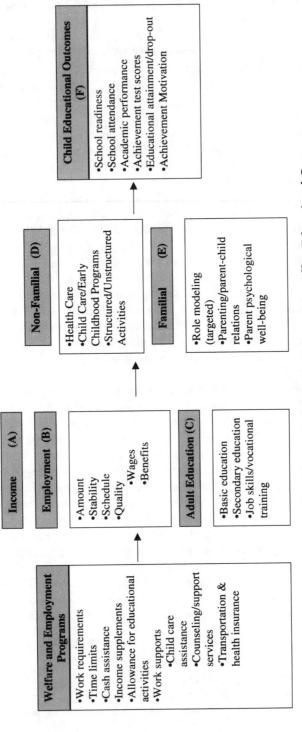

FIGURE 1 Pathways by Which Welfare Reform May Affect Educational Outcomes

employment and income (Boxes A and B). We also include adult education in this set of outcomes because welfare reform policies include stipulations concerning educational activities (Box C). Nonfamilial (i.e., access to resources) and familial outcomes generally not targeted by reform policies, but nonetheless likely to be affected, are shown in Boxes D and E. These variables have been identified in the literature as potential mediators between parent outcomes and the child outcomes shown in Box F. As we review the literatures relevant to these pathways, we discuss the possible mechanisms in more detail.

Measuring the Effects of Welfare Reform

Given that two primary goals of the welfare legislation were to increase employment and reduce reliance on public assistance, the initial "wave" of research evaluating its effects focused mainly on these outcomes. An analysis of 30 state evaluation plans at the time PRWORA was enacted revealed a general lack of attention to measuring effects on children, despite the fact that historically a key purpose of the welfare system has been to ensure the well-being of children in low-income families (Collins & Aber, 1996). In the last several years, however, a second "wave" of research has considered more broadly the effects of reform policies on family well-being and children's social, academic, and behavioral outcomes.

The data discussed in this chapter were derived from several sources, namely (a) national surveys (e.g., the National Survey of American Families [NSAF] and the National Longitudinal Study of Youth [NLSY]), (b) state welfare "leaver" studies, (c) time-series data, and (d) a set of random assignment experiments designed largely to evaluate state waiver programs begun prior to 1996. These data sources vary in the populations to which they pertain (e.g., welfare leavers vs. the broader low-income population), the outcomes they examine (e.g., adult, family, or child), and the rigorousness of their methodology (e.g., nonexperimental vs. experimental designs). The first two types of research provide the most extensive data on employment, earnings, and welfare receipt; the latter two have been important sources of information on family and child well-being.

On the one hand, the diversity of these studies provides valuable information about the various mechanisms that do or do not affect families; on the other hand, the conclusions that can be drawn from these data are often limited in several ways. For instance, not all of the studies use sufficiently detailed or standardized measures, conceptualize or measure outcomes in similar ways, account for the same demographic or preexisting variables in their analyses, or use the same research design. For these reasons, making comparisons across studies is often difficult (Moffitt & Ver Ploeg, 1999).

Time-series data can provide useful information when one is examining the effects of welfare reform policies on children's outcomes; yet, drawing conclusions from simplistic comparisons of indicators before and after welfare reform should be done with caution. Time-series data on such outcomes as poverty, teen fertility, and high school dropout rates after welfare reform reveal a fairly benign picture (see Duncan & Chase-Lansdale, 2001). Unfortunately, less is known about educational outcomes for children. Few studies exist that use preform and postreform measures of children's cognitive development or school achievement.

According to the Panel on Data and Methods for Measuring the Effects of Changes in Social Welfare Programs (see Moffitt & Ver Ploeg, 1999), nonexperimental designs are currently the most common evaluation method of PRWORA. One problem with disentangling the impacts of welfare reform, however, is that underlying characteristics may affect outcomes for welfare recipients as well as their children. For example, parental depression may simultaneously increase the likelihood of welfare receipt for parents and negative outcomes for children. Failure to control for these preexisting characteristics might lead to false conclusions about the relationship between participation in welfare programs and family and child outcomes. Therefore, randomized experimental methodologies provide the strongest test of causation. Assignments to "treatment" and "control" groups ensure that the two groups will have, on average, similar observed and unobserved characteristics, thereby permitting stronger causal inference (Currie, 1997; Huston, 2002).

Most of the random assignment experiments discussed in this chapter began prior to the welfare reform legislation of 1996, but all include policies adopted or considered by states in response to PRWORA. The programs differed in the generosity of supports provided to parents (e.g., earning supplements, health care, child care subsidies), the extent to which employment was mandated, and whether time limits were placed on assistance. Making comparisons across these experimental studies is particularly valuable given that such large variations exist at the state level (and even the community level) in the administration of welfare. Comparing these welfare and employment programs and their effects can help identify which policy components make a difference for families (see Table 1 for a brief description of the major experimental studies reviewed in this chapter). In the next section, we briefly review general findings about how families have fared in the wake of "welfare reform" before moving on to a more focused discussion of the effects on educational activities and outcomes for adults and children.

How Are Adults and Children Generally Faring Under Reform Policies?

Given the major goals of PRWORA, the most abundant and detailed data on the effects of welfare reform have focused on adult employment and economic outcomes. Converging evidence from welfare leaver and experimental waiver studies demonstrates that "work-first" policies can substantially increase employment in the context of a healthy economy. National indicators suggest a similar story; between 1993 and 2000, unemployment rates fell from 7% to 4% (U.S. Department of Labor, 2000). In addition, the sizable reduction in welfare caseloads—from approximately 13.7 million in 1995 to 5.8 million recipients in 2000—surprised PRWORA's opponents and proponents alike and has been the basis for widespread claims of success. During this same time period hourly wage rates increased, and the earned income tax credit (EITC) program was expanded to provide additional financial incentives for low-wage work. Few would dispute that these trends have been positive; yet, there are indications that the extensiveness and sustainability of these effects may be limited.

The "work-first" philosophy of PRWORA was predicated in part by the belief that work experience would eventually lead to higher wages and job advancement for low-income workers. This hypothesis has not been borne out, as many have left welfare for jobs marked by low wages, few benefits, nonstandard work schedules, and limited opportunities for advancement (Harris, 1996; Mishel & Bernstein, 1994; Polit et al., 2001). The first national welfare leaver study indicates that about 60% of leavers were employed in 1997; 28% worked night shifts, and only 23% had employer-sponsored health insurance (Loprest, 1999). "Leavers" who work tend to do so full time and earn an average of $7 an hour or less, meaning income levels often hover near or below the poverty line despite full-time employment (Acs & Loprest, 2001). These leaver studies suggest that many former welfare recipients continue to have difficulty providing sufficient food to their families and paying rent and utility bills. In other words, most former welfare recipients have joined the ranks of the working poor. In 1999, 70% of welfare workers and their counterparts (those with comparable skills and sociodemographic characteristics but not receiving welfare) did not earn enough to lift a family of three out of poverty (Johnson & Tafoya, 1999).

Unfortunately, welfare reform has not had the major impact on income that some predicted it would; for many families, leaving welfare has not meant leaving poverty or hardship (see Zuckerman, 2000). A report evaluating 20 welfare and employment programs found that many families continue to struggle under the new policies (Michalopoulos, Schwartz, & Adams-Ciardullo, 2000). Because families often lose benefits (e.g., food stamps) when they leave welfare (owing to ineligibility or misinformation about eligibility), increased earnings have not translated into substantial gains in disposable income. Disposable income upon leaving welfare may actually decline if families forgo such benefits as food stamps and child care and health care subsidies. However, the fact that families are often simply trading a welfare check for a paycheck is an expected and acceptable outcome to those who considered caseload reduction the primary goal of welfare reform (Zuckerman, 2000).

Many of those who left welfare after 1996 have had difficulty maintaining their jobs and have cycled between employment and welfare or been unemployed without welfare benefits (see Danziger, Corcoran, et al., 2000). Nearly half of the women exiting welfare rolls return within 1 year, and 60% do so in 2 years (Pavetti, 1995). This is not entirely surprising given that the low-wage jobs likely to be held by welfare leavers are marked by high instability. It is estimated that only 35% to 40% of former welfare recipients remain employed for the entire year after they leave welfare (Acs & Loprest, 2001). Recent data suggest that cycling between employment and unemployment may be particularly detrimental to children (Kalil, Dunifon, & Danziger, 2001). Finally, a

(*text continues on page 194*)

TABLE 1 Brief Summary of Experimental Projects

	Purpose	General research	Key policy
Canadian Self-Sufficiency Project (SSP): 1992–2001	To implement a program providing an earnings supplement to single parents (a small group of long-term recipients receive voluntary services as well) who have been on public assistance for at least the full preceding year, and who agree to leave welfare and maintain full-time employment, and to evaluate the program's take-up rate and effectiveness	Largest random assignment study of increased work incentives Intensive technical assistance provided to administration systems Includes two provinces: British Columbia and New Brunswick	Make-work-pay strategies
Connecticut Jobs-First Program (CT Jobs-First): 1996–2002	To evaluate a program that includes one of the nation's shortest time limits on welfare receipt (21 months) and a generous financial work incentive; also one of the first programs to impose a time limit in major urban areas	Random assignment design Program that includes time limits and financial work incentives Sites include New Haven and Manchester Special study of focal children aged 0 to 11 at study entry	Participation mandate Make-work-pay strategies Time limit Services

| Florida's Family Transition Program (FTP): 1994–2000 | To evaluate one of the first operational programs including time limits on AFDC receipt, financial work incentives, and enhanced employment, training, and social services | Random assignment design
Program that includes time limits, financial work incentives, and enhanced employment services
Special study of focal children aged 1 to 8 at study entry | Participation mandate
Make-work-pay strategies
Time limit
Services |
| Milwaukee's New Hope Project (New Hope): 1994–2002 | To evaluate an anti-poverty program with financial incentives to work and a stated goal of reducing the social costs of welfare and poverty | Random assignment design
Program linking income support to full-time employment; technical assistance in project design and implementation
Targeted to and eligible for all households with incomes below 150% of poverty line with an adult willing to work 30 hours a week or more
Special study of focal children aged 2 to 10 at time of study entry | Participation mandate
Make-work-pay strategies
Child care and health care subsidies |

(continued)

191

TABLE 1 Brief Summary of Experimental Projects

	Purpose	General research	Key policy
Minnesota's Family Investment Program (MFIP Full & MFIP Incentives): 1993–2000	To evaluate separately the effects of changing financial incentives to work and mandatory case management services	Random assignment design Anti-poverty program with large financial work incentives for cases and intensive case management Includes 3 urban and 4 rural counties Special study of focal children aged 2 to 9 at study entry	Participation mandate Make-work-pay strategies Services
National Evaluation of Welfare-to-Work Strategies (NEWWS): 1989–2001 (control group embargo varied by site)	To evaluate the differential effects of programs that emphasize work first and those that emphasize education/training, implemented under the federal JOBS program in a variety of sites across the country	Random assignment design 50,000 AFDC and AFDC-UP cases Innovative procedures to test effects of different JOBS approaches 11 programs in 7 sites nationwide Special study of focal children aged 3 to 5 at study entry	Participation mandate Services

New Chance Demonstration (New Chance): 1986–1997	To develop and test a mix of educational, personal development, employment-related, and support services aimed at helping 16- to 22-year-old mothers on welfare become more self-sufficient, and to encourage the healthy development of their children	Random assignment design Process, impact, and benefit-cost analyses of program serving teen parents on welfare Explicitly two-generational in focus and design Over 16 sites in the U.S.	Services Child care provided on site or nearby
Vermont's Welfare Restructuring Project (WRP and WRP Incentives): 1994–2002	To evaluate an employment-focused program that includes participation mandates and financial incentives	Random assignment design Program that includes work requirements and financial work incentives	Participation mandate Make-work-pay strategies

national study revealed that one in seven recipients who leave welfare are not working, have no working spouse, and are not receiving any sort of disability payments (Zedlewski & Loprest, 2001). Other studies suggest that 25% to 40% of women who leave welfare are not working (Greenberg, 2001; Moffitt, 2002). This raises questions about how these families are managing and what the implications are for their children.

In addition to economic outcomes, welfare reform policies have the potential to affect psychological well-being and family functioning. One of the arguments behind the 1996 reforms was that work in and of itself would improve parents' self-esteem and optimism and decrease depression. In general, entry into the workforce does not appear to have had these effects. Experimental studies reveal few effects on psychological well-being and parenting; when they do occur, effects appear to be mixed (Morris et al., 2001). Some "make work pay" programs that increased employment and income report a handful of positive effects on parent well-being and parent-child relationships. A recent review of experimental data on mandatory programs noted impacts on depression in 7 of the 20 samples examined; depressive symptoms increased in 5 of the programs and decreased in 2 of the programs (Ahluwalia, McGroder, Zaslow, & Hair, 2001). Of interest in their own right, effects in these domains are also potentially important in understanding how children's educational outcomes are affected by the policies aimed at their parents.

Data regarding the effects of welfare reform on children's educational outcomes are limited; yet, the existing literature on employment programs (e.g., welfare-to-work and anti-poverty demonstration programs) provides some important information concerning effects on children's outcomes and offers insights as to what may be happening as a result of the 1996 reforms. Examining time-series data from before and after welfare reform also sheds light on how children have been faring since the enactment of PRWORA. For instance, 1988 to 1999 time-series data indicate a decline in deep poverty (i.e., family income less than 50% of the poverty threshold) among children, a slight decrease in academic performance for children 6–8 years of age, and a fairly stable dropout rate for teens in Grades 10 to 12 (U.S. Bureau of the Census, 2002).

Research thus far demonstrates that the most successful welfare reform policies in terms of child well-being are those that improve parental income and economic security through strongly encouraging *and* rewarding work. A review of 16 welfare experiments designed to encourage work showed that only some succeeded in raising family income, while others reduced income and increased poverty. All programs that raised participants' income by at least 5% had primarily positive effects on children, while those that reduced income by at least 5% had primarily negative effects on child outcomes (Sherman, 2001). The bottom line from these studies is that income is a critical determinant of how welfare and employment policies affect children.

For a number of reasons, it is premature at this point to conclude that reform policies pose no harm to families and children. In general, welfare reform does not appear to have been as detrimental as many once feared; however, the economy was strong in the years immediately following the passage of the PRWORA. Notably, few data are available concerning families that have been sanctioned or have reached time limits; further research on the effects of these policies is needed, especially in the context of a weakening economy. There is also evidence suggesting that effects differ in important ways across subgroups of families and children. Moreover, given the narrow focus of many studies on adult economic outcomes, data exist for a relatively limited set of indicators of child well-being. A more detailed discussion of the demonstrated and potential effects of welfare reform on educational outcomes for adults and children follows.

EDUCATION FOR ADULTS IN THE "WORK-FIRST" ERA OF WELFARE REFORM

Low-income adults, especially those receiving welfare, typically have low levels of education and skills. The average welfare recipient reads at a sixth- to eighth-grade level (Barton & Jenkins, 1995), approximately 50% to 60% of recipients lack a high school diploma or general equivalency degree (GED) (Harris, 1996; Olson & Pavetti, 1996; Spalter-Roth, Burr, Hartmann, & Shaw, 1995), and as many as 40% may have a learning disability (Nightingale, 1991). These educational deficits present a serious obstacle to the type of employment and earnings needed to sustain a family above poverty. Adults with low education levels are less likely to be employed, have lower wages when they do work (Cohen, 1998a; Holzer, 1996; Strawn, 1998), and are likely to cycle between welfare and employment (Bane & Ellwood, 1994; Harris, 1993, 1996; Olson & Pavetti, 1996).

Given the demonstrated links between education and economic well-being, efforts to increase employment and self-sufficiency among low-income adults have often focused on human capital development strategies (particularly in the years prior to the 1996 legislation). During the 1980s, several states and localities implemented programs offering basic education and skill building as an alternative to job search with the reasoning that these activities would have positive effects on job quality, stability, and earnings. Some also argued that educationally based programs would benefit children because parents would serve as role models and might become more involved in their children's schoolwork as well. The Family Support Act of 1988 further encouraged states to invest in educational services for low-income adults. As part of this act, the Job Opportunities and Basic Skills Training (JOBS) program introduced mandatory basic skills training for welfare recipients with either weak skills or no high school diploma. During these years, many states also chose to emphasize education and training more broadly as an important component of their early reform efforts (along with job search and work experience). The overhaul of the national welfare system in 1996, however, dramatically changed the educational landscape for welfare recipients.

Policy Changes Affecting Educational Opportunities

Evaluations of early human capital development programs during the 1980s suggested that despite some positive effects on employment and earnings (especially for voluntary programs offering intensive services), education and training were not substantially more successful than job search activities and were considerably more expensive to operate (see review by Gueron & Pauly, 1991). As a result, many states redirected their efforts and dollars toward "work-first" strategies. The passage of PRWORA intensified this shift and created incentives for states to invest in programs that placed people into jobs quickly and with minimal costs. Along with removing the requirement that states provide any educational services, PRWORA went much further and included changes to the work requirement and the definition of allowable "work" activities that directly curtailed opportunities for education and training. States now had to meet new requirements for work participation and caseload reduction or face sanctioning of their federal funds. The introduction of time limits on federal assistance under PRWORA further reduced the likelihood that welfare recipients would be allowed or encouraged to pursue educational activities. Postsecondary degree programs may be particularly incompatible with time-limited assistance, because they often require several years to complete.

In 1997, 25% of single parents were required to work 20 hours per week and 25% of two-parent families were required to work 35 hours per week to receive benefits. These requirements have increased each year to the current level of 50% of single parents (who must now work 30 hours per week) and 90% of two-parent families. Allowable work activities under TANF include employment, on-the-job training, 6 weeks of job search, "community service," "work experience," and "vocational educational training." The latter three activities are defined by states but are restricted in duration to 12 months and permissible for only 30% of the TANF caseload. Recipients may also be engaged in employment-related education or job skills training or in a high school or GED program; however, these activities count toward only a portion of the weekly hour requirement (e.g., in 2000, these activities were allowable for 10 of the required 30 hours). It is estimated that half of those participating in such activities are teens (Cohen, 1998a). In a departure from the "work-first" approach applied to adult welfare recipients, PRWORA requires minor, unmarried, custodial teen parents with an infant 12 weeks of age or older to pursue a high school degree (or equivalent) or engage in alternative education or training as approved by the state.

The Welfare-to-Work grant program under the Balanced Budget Act of 1997 and the enactment of the Workforce Investment Act (WIA) in 1998 also changed the landscape of adult education and training. The Welfare-to-Work grants provided an additional $3 billion to states (outside of TANF) to pursue the goals of PRWORA specifically for long-term welfare recipients with significant barriers to employment, including no high school diploma, a substance abuse problem, or a poor work history. The goal of WIA was to create a "one-stop" workforce development system integrating job training, adult education and literacy, and vocational rehabilitation programs. The WIA mirrors the "work-first" objectives of PRWORA by emphasizing job search activities as the first step for participants; only those unsuccessful in finding work are considered for "intensive services" or training. As such, WIA primarily increased postemployment opportunities for education and training.

Adolescents represent a special segment of the low-income population targeted by welfare reform policies. First, adolescents with children may be welfare recipients themselves and therefore subject to the rules and regulations of the new TANF system. In a departure from the "work-first" approach applied to adult welfare recipients, PRWORA requires teen parents to pursue a high school degree (or equivalent) or engage in alternative education or training as approved by the state. Educational outcomes are particularly tenuous for adolescent mothers, who complete less education than do older mothers (Upchurch & McCarthy, 1990). The argument is that increased education and skill levels will lead to better employment opportunities and reduce welfare use in adulthood. This requirement for teens to focus on school and to complete their high school degree or equivalent stands in contrast to the requirements for adult recipients—many of whom have less than a high school education—who have generally been shunted away from education and training toward employment.

Combining parenthood and schooling may be particularly difficult for teens. In an attempt to facilitate continued education for young mothers, PRWORA requires adolescent recipients to live in adult-supervised settings (e.g., with the adolescent's parent) in order to qualify for benefits. The effects of this type of mandated living arrangement are unclear. Co-residing adults might be subject to work requirements themselves and thus may not be available for child care. Co-residing with the baby's grandmother has been associated with poorer educational outcomes but reduced economic strain as well (Kalil & Danziger, 2000). Moreover, adolescent mothers are likely to suffer from depression, child care difficulties, and domestic violence (Kalil & Danziger, 2000), posing serious challenges to improving educational outcomes for this group.

Second, adolescents are targeted more broadly by welfare policies as the next generation of potential recipients. The preamble to PRWORA clearly states as one of its goals the transformation of views held by "young people making the transition into adulthood." The idea is that more stringent policies send a signal to adolescents that time-unlimited welfare is no longer an option. One of the few studies to examine this "signaling" effect suggests that stringent state welfare policies may influence the decisions of low-income youth regarding full engagement in school (Hao, Astone, & Cherlin, 2001). All things being equal, the stricter the welfare policies in a state, the less likely low-income youth are in that state to take (and keep) a job while in school. Welfare policies may further influence adolescents because the low-wage, low-skill retail and service sector jobs usually attained by welfare recipients moving to work are the jobs typically held by adolescents. Thus, one potential effect of welfare reform is a reduction in the formal employment of teens.

To the extent that reduced employment results in greater school engagement, reform policies may help low-income youth gain human capital, thereby improving their long-term economic outcomes. Alternately, adolescents—particularly those in deep poverty—may be harmed by missing out on attaining "soft skills" from a formal job (e.g., work experience, important contacts/networking, opportunities for advancement); acquiring these skills can be particularly decisive for youth who are not college bound. Hao and colleagues also report that low-income dropouts in stringent states are more likely to stay out of school as well as the labor market. This impact is clearly detrimental. Adolescents experiencing difficulties in school and perhaps considering dropping out may be even more inclined to do so with the enactment of more stringent welfare policies.

State Responses to PRWORA

Increased state discretion under PRWORA has led to increased diversity in state welfare-to-work programs, including to what extent education and training are a part of these programs. States generally decide (a) how many hours TANF recipients must be engaged in work activities, (b) how to define work activities, (c) whether to limit participation to certain groups, (d) whether to require that educational activities be combined with work, (e) the maximum allowable duration of an activity, and (f) whether a specific sequence of activities must be followed. While some states have chosen to define "work activities" broadly, allowing for a range of such activities as basic skills education, postsecondary education, and work-study programs, other states have implemented more stringent policies that focus on rapid entry into work and severely restrict opportunities for education and training.

The "work-first" model has clearly dominated the post-1996 years, given the widespread policy goals of quickly reducing dependence and cutting costs; yet, most states (44) authorize at least some type of educational activity directly related to employment (another 2 states leave this up to local authority). Approved work activities may include subsidized employment, vocational training, adult basic education, English as a second language, education related to employment, on-the-job training, job skills training, unpaid community service, unpaid work experience, and job readiness. Fourteen states limit participation in education and training to certain groups (e.g., primarily those with no high school diploma or GED); 34 have some requirement that education be combined with other activities (e.g., if needed to meet hourly requirements or after a certain time period); and 26 place no time limit on participation, 7 have a limit of 18–36 months, and 4 limit participation to 12 months or less (State Policy Demonstration Project [SPDP], 2001). Twenty states require a fixed sequence of work activities (e.g., job search prior to an assessment and referral to other activities), 24 states do not require such a sequence, and in 7 states this decision is made at the community level (SPDP, 2001).

PRWORA created particular disincentives to the pursuit of higher education as a means to self-sufficiency. "Job skills training" and "education directly related to employment" can include vocational courses offered by a postsecondary institution; however, nonvocational postsecondary education is not an approved activity under PRWORA. The larger than expected decline in caseloads has provided some flexibility to states because those meeting the work requirement may allow participation in postsecondary education and, moreover, may use TANF funds for this purpose. In fiscal year 2000, 21 states allowed recipients to participate in postsecondary degree programs as part of the state work requirement for longer than 12 months; 9 of these states required recipients to combine participation with some amount of work, while the remaining 12 allowed postsecondary education as a stand-alone activity. Thirteen states allowed postsecondary education to count toward the work requirement for up to 12 months, another 13 did not authorize postsecondary education at all, and 4 states left this decision to counties (SPDP, 2001).

Maine and Wyoming have been particularly supportive of higher education and have incurred federal penalties as a result. In Maine, the Parents as Scholars program provides TANF-like support for low-income parents wishing to attend 2- or 4-year colleges (including aid for transportation, child care, cash assistance, and other services as if they had been TANF recipients). Wyoming has a similar program and allows some college attendance within TANF.

Finally, many states provide some type of postemployment services to those who have left TANF, 34 states offer case management to former recipients, and 16 states support education and training. Five states (Florida, Michigan, New York, Ohio, and Washington) and the District of Columbia have expanded their programs to serve the working poor more generally rather than restricting services to former welfare recipients. They offer a range of services, including education and training, tuition assistance, individual training accounts, transportation aid, case management, employment services, and financial assistance for expenses associated with emergencies.

As states have implemented TANF, the effects of reform policies on educational opportunities have become apparent. Between 1996 and 1999, the percentage of welfare recipients participating in education and training activities decreased from approximately 5.8% to 2.7% (Strawn, Greenberg, & Savner, 2001). The impact of reform policies has been most negative for postsecondary education. Nationally, the number of welfare recipients attending college dropped from more than 650,000 in 1996 to fewer than 360,000 in 1999 (Price, 2000). In New York City, work-fare policies have contributed to a 50% reduction in the number of recipients pursuing higher education (Casey, 1998). In Milwaukee County, Wisconsin, technical colleges saw their enrollment of welfare recipients decline 95% in the year the county's welfare-to-work program began (Johnson, 1998). Although some of the decline in educational enrollment of welfare recipients may be due to caseload reductions, it is certain that the new emphasis on rapid employment has redirected many adults from pursuing educational activities to employment.

What Research Reveals About What Works and for Whom

Historically, evidence that adult education programs can be effective in improving outcomes for low-income adults has been weak at best. D'Amico (1997) suggests several possible reasons for minimal program success. Literacy and adult education programs often lack adequate funding, a full-time professional teaching staff, well-defined program goals, and a systematic method of documenting outcomes. Student retention also presents a problem; most students do not spend a substantial amount of time in such programs, and completion rates are often low. Despite these challenges, research in this area demonstrates some potential positive effects depending on the types of services that are being offered and for whom. Our review of this literature is organized around the three main types of educational services accessed by low-income adults: basic education (including adult basic education, literacy, and English as a second language), vocational training, and postsecondary education (including certification and degree programs).

Basic Education

Basic education is designed for adult students without a high school diploma or a GED. It includes adult basic education, which provides basic instruction in reading and math (typically at the elementary school level) and GED preparation. For welfare recipients, a high school diploma increases their likelihood of leaving the welfare rolls and decreases their likelihood of reentry into the system (Harris, 1993, 1996; Olson & Pavetti, 1996). Despite this association, basic education programs have had little demonstrable effect on employment and earnings among welfare recipients (see review by Pauly, 1995).

A review of 18 evaluations of adult education-focused programs aimed at AFDC recipients during the 1980s and early 1990s indicates that programs increased participation in education and GED/high school diploma attainment but did not improve achievement on standardized tests (Pauly, 1995). Similarly, the New Chance program (a comprehensive program targeted to poor young mothers and their children) had a positive effect on GED attainment but had no impact on literacy, basic skill level, welfare receipt, or employment (Quint, Bos, & Polit, 1997). The usefulness of a GED in the labor market has been questioned (see Cameron & Heckman, 1993; Murnane, Willett, & Boudett, 1995); analyses suggest that it is not equivalent to a high school diploma in terms of employment and wage rates or job mobility (see Fishman, Barnow, Gardiner, Murphy, & Laud, 1999). This may be a reason why welfare recipients seem to benefit only slightly from adult basic education. A review of 18 evaluations of adult education-focused programs aimed at AFDC recipients during the 1980s and early 1990s indicates that programs increased participation in education and GED/high school diploma attainment but did not improve achievement on standardized tests (Pauly, 1995). Similarly, the New Chance program (a comprehensive program targeted to poor young mothers and their children) had a positive effect on GED attainment but had no impact on literacy, basic skill level, welfare receipt, or employment (Quint, Bos, & Polit, 1997). The usefulness of a GED in the labor market has been questioned (see Cameron & Heckman, 1993; Murnane, Willett, & Boudett, 1995); analyses suggest that it is not equivalent to a high school diploma in terms of employment and wage rates or job mobility (see Fishman, Barnow, Gardiner, Murphy, & Laud, 1999). This may be a reason why welfare recipients seem to benefit only slightly from adult basic education.

During the 1990s, the National Evaluation of Welfare-to-Work Studies (NEWWS) provided the first large-scale test of the relative benefits of labor force attachment (LFA) versus human capital development (HCD) strategies by examining several JOBS sites. As part of the NEWWS random assignment study, more than 40,000 single parents (mostly mothers) and their children were followed over 5-year periods between 1991 and 1999 (depending on site). Participants at six sites (Atlanta, Detroit, Columbus, Grand Rapids, Oklahoma City, Riverside) were assigned to a control group with no services, a program group with rapid employment-focused services (LFA), or a program with an education and training component (HCD). Participants at a seventh site (Portland, Oregon) were assigned to either a control group with no services or a program group eligible for a mix of employment and education services. In general, education-focused programs operated by placing large percentages of participants into initial skill-building activities (mostly GED preparation and basic education); none of the HCD programs made assignments to or emphasized college. Also, NEWWS programs used a variety of institutions to provide educational service; however, it is important to note that site visits and surveys suggest that few providers altered their curricula to address the specific needs of welfare-to-work participants (Bos, Scrivener, Snipes, & Hamilton, 2001). During the 1990s, the National Evaluation of Welfare-to-Work Studies (NEWWS) provided the first large-scale test of the relative benefits of labor force attachment (LFA) versus human capital development (HCD) strategies by examining several JOBS sites. As part of the NEWWS random assignment study, more than 40,000 single parents (mostly mothers) and their children were followed over 5-year periods between 1991 and 1999 (depending on site). Participants at six sites (Atlanta, Detroit, Columbus, Grand Rapids, Oklahoma City, Riverside) were assigned to a control group with no services, a program group with rapid employment-focused services (LFA), or a program with an education and training component (HCD). Participants at a seventh site (Portland, Oregon) were assigned to either a control group with no services or a program group eligible for a mix of employment and education services. In general, education-focused programs operated by placing large percentages of participants into initial skill-building activities (mostly GED preparation and basic education); none of the HCD programs made assignments to or emphasized college. Also, NEWWS programs used a variety of institutions to provide educational service; however, it is important to note that site visits and surveys suggest that few providers altered their curricula to address the specific needs of welfare-to-work participants (Bos, Scrivener, Snipes, & Hamilton, 2001).

The 2- and 5-year results of the NEWWS suggest that basic education programs are not generally effective in increasing employment and earnings (Gueron & Hamilton, 2002). Human capital development programs were able to maintain longer periods of participation than those focused on labor force attachment; however, employment-focused programs moved people into jobs more quickly and were less expensive to operate (costs were 40% to 90% higher for HCD programs). Notably, neither the HCD nor LFA approach led to significant improvements in economic well-being.

Most families realized few changes in total income, as earnings and EITC simply replaced welfare and food stamp benefits.

Relative to control group levels, education-focused programs increased job search somewhat and increased enrollment in education and training programs substantially. Among those with a high school diploma or GED upon entering the program, increases in vocational training were minimal. Only the Atlanta program had success in terms of increasing education credentials (e.g., trade license or certificate) for this group of participants. Among those without a high school degree or GED, increases in basic education were large; the average participant in adult education received two thirds of a year of high school education. Despite the fact that most participants who entered adult education as part of the NEWWS programs expressed no desire to do so, their receipt of education increased (more than double the participation of the control group and triple the number of participation hours). Moreover, it does not appear that mandated participation had different effects than voluntary participation. There were few overall positive effects of participating in educational activities for this sample.

Recent nonexperimental work provides more detail about the experiences of the most disadvantaged NEWWS participants (i.e., no high school diploma or GED) in the human capital development programs (Bos et al., 2001). A small proportion of the participants received a GED, and there were few improvements in reading and math skills. Those most likely to obtain a GED had relatively high reading and math skills to begin with and were probably close to being able to pass the exam when they entered the program. Reading levels improved only among the minority of students who participated for longer than a year, whereas improvements in math skills occurred primarily during the first 6 months of education. Teachers' experience and education levels were positively associated with the effects on reading and math. The small group of participants who obtained a GED, increased their reading and math skills, or participated in postsecondary programs realized substantial earning and employment gains. Earning a GED predicted postsecondary education, which in turn was associated with positive employment and earning effects.

Therefore, although there may be benefits in doing so, few participants in mandatory welfare-to-work programs successfully obtain a high school diploma or GED. Fewer than 25% of the NEWWS participants who lacked credentials upon entering the program had obtained them 5 years later. Hamilton and Brock (1994) assert that this happens because people leave welfare-to-work programs before completing classes, people cannot forgo the income that a job would provide, and many recipients report that they would prefer skill-building or job search assistance over basic education. Evaluations of successful basic skills programs indeed suggest that they should be shorter, more intensive, and more closely tied to work or training (Murphy & Johnson, 1998).

Vocational Training

Training programs have typically targeted those with a high school diploma or GED (i.e., not the most disadvantaged students). Vocational activities often are not combined with basic education or linked to local job markets. Work-based training programs, however, have generally had more success than short-term classroom education and training alone. A national evaluation of the Job Training Partnership Act revealed no increase in earnings for short periods of classroom training (Orr et al., 1996) but suggested that formal on-the-job training and vocational training in technical and professional fields may be the most cost-effective strategy for disadvantaged recipients, particularly those who are younger and who have little or no work experience (Heinrich, 1998). Strong positive effects of on-the-job training on welfare recipients' employment and earnings have been reported elsewhere (see Bloom, 1997; Orr et al., 1996; Strawn, 1998), as has evidence that vocational training programs can increase wages and hours of employment (Friedlander & Burtless, 1995; Gueron & Pauly, 1991). Census data indicate that fewer than 10% of TANF recipients were engaged in training in 1998.

Postsecondary Education

The assumption that entry-level employment is adequate for self-sufficiency is flawed; many single mothers and their families require an income that typically comes only with the types of jobs held by those with a postsecondary education (Bos, 1996). Wages for those without a high school degree have declined since 1980, while, during the same period, wages for those with a college degree have increased (Mare, 1995; Wetzel, 1995). It is estimated that by 2006 nearly a third of all new jobs will require education and skills beyond the high school graduate level; yet, only 7% of welfare recipients are at this level (Carnevale & Desrochers, 1999).

Postsecondary education is a much less frequent activity for low-income adults than either basic education or vocational training. This is not surprising given the educational barriers faced by this population and the fact that PRWORA effectively discouraged this type of activity among welfare recipients. Welfare recipients with basic skills comparable to a high school diploma need approximately 200 hours of additional education and training to move up to advanced-skilled jobs (Carnevale & Desrochers, 1999).

If low-income adults are able to pursue a postsecondary education, data suggest potential employment and earnings payoffs. Returning to school can benefit displaced workers by leading to increased wages. For example, LaLonde (2001) reports that a year of community college translates into a 5% increase in earnings. Returns appear to be greater among more skilled workers and for focused, as opposed to general, coursework. Effects on earnings appear to exist regardless of degree completion (Kane & Rouse, 1995). As with basic education and GED preparation, the majority of low-income workers do not complete the academic year (LaLonde, 2001; McPherson & Shapiro, 1999).

Approximately 15% of the NEWWS HCD participants received postsecondary services during the 2-year follow-up; those who did averaged 7 months of instruction. This sample had higher earnings and lower rates of welfare usage but not typically until after the third year following an initial spell of adult education, suggesting that current time limits may be too restrictive. Because having only a GED limits employment and earning potential, links to postsecondary education or training should be strengthened to maximize effects. The NEWWS report suggests that states could benefit in the long run from supporting low-income workers' participation in postsecondary education because welfare-related expenses could decline, despite evidence that programs concentrating on human development are twice as costly as those emphasizing work. The report further shows that most of these costs are borne by nonwelfare agencies.

Advocates of a pro-college viewpoint believe that it will ensure the job stability and wage rates needed to reduce poverty. They argue that postsecondary programs should be a more accessible option for parents trying to meet the participation mandates of PRWORA. Under the current law, many mothers must juggle working 20–30 hours per week, going to school, and caring for their young children. Opponents, on the other hand, argue that it is unfair to subsidize a college education for welfare recipients, that most educational activities are more effective once a person has held a job, and that the data do not provide clear evidence of improved outcomes for welfare recipients.

Mixed Models

"Mixed" models have had somewhat more success than those focused exclusively on human capital development or labor force attachment. Programs that include education and training along with a strong work focus have produced more positive and longer lasting effects on earnings than those involving job search services only (Hamilton et al., 2001). The NEWWS program that had the most substantial and longest lasting effects on employment and earnings (the Portland site) offered a mix of services; while some recipients were assigned to very short-term education or training, others were assigned to job search. Moreover, case managers used job developers, encouraged participants to wait for a good job, and had experience operating job search programs.

The NEWWS Riverside-GAIN program was similar to that of Portland in its flexibility regarding initial activities, enforced participation, experienced administrators, strong focus on employment, and use of "job developers." The Portland program, however, urged participants to wait for a job with good earning potential and stability, whereas the Riverside program urged recipients to move as quickly as possible into any job. Both had typical enrollments of 6 months or less. Those deemed "not work ready" were assigned to basic education, short-term life skills classes, or occupational training; those with a high school diploma or GED were usually assigned to job search or life skills classes, vocational training, or work experience; and those already attending postsecondary programs were allowed to continue if they could obtain their degree in a short time period. Portland partnered with the community college system to design and implement courses and provide case management services. The Riverside-GAIN program was administered solely through the welfare department and relied more on adult education schools than community colleges to provide education and training services. Riverside also paid service providers based on measures of students' performance.

The New Visions study (currently being conducted by Abt Associates) experimentally tests a mixed-strategy approach and is the first to rigorously evaluate a college-based program for welfare recipients. Participants who are randomly assigned to the program must work at least 20 hours a week and are enrolled in a 24-week core curriculum that includes remedial instruction and guidance. The course schedule is flexible and individualized, with courses offered in 3-hour blocks (repeated three times per day) four times a week. After completing the core program, participants attend an occupational mini-program (e.g., early childhood education) at a community college, resulting in certification and academic credits. Five-year effects of the New Visions program will be evaluated in 2004.

Issues Facing Policymakers, Program Administrators, Educators, and Students

Policymakers preparing to debate the reauthorization of TANF are faced with a serious set of challenges, intensified by a slowing economy and impending or expiring time limits. The consistent finding that many recipients who made the transition to work during the 1990s are not much better off than they were on welfare—working in jobs with low wages, few benefits, and little stability or possibility for advancement—has prompted increased attention to questions of how states can best promote self-sufficiency and simultaneously reduce poverty among low-income families. Many states are reconsidering the role that education and training services can play in meeting these goals.

Proponents of expanding educational opportunities argue that work requirements and time limits should be eased to accommodate more educational activities with the goal of improving wages and long-term sufficiency (e.g., see Greenberg, 2001). Opponents argue that such changes will undermine the work requirements and increase short-term costs (e.g., see Mead, 2001). Some also argue that expansion is not warranted given the lack of support for the effectiveness of human capital development strategies. Next, we consider some of the specific questions facing lawmakers and administrators and reflect on how research can inform policy and programmatic decisions.

What Role Should Education and Training Play in the Next "Phase" of Welfare Reform?

In the debate over "employment-focused strategies" versus "education," data suggest that neither has been substantially effective on its own in reducing poverty, despite effects on employment. Both types of approaches have had difficulty showing sustained positive effects on employment or earnings. Instead of framing the discussion of these strategies as "either-or," one possibility is to consider how the two models can be combined effectively. For example, even though basic education activities have the lowest returns in terms of employment and earnings, basic educational skills are a prerequisite for most other employment-related activities, suggesting that they should perhaps be combined with vocational training. Work and training packaged together may increase opportunities to meet work requirements, improve the effectiveness of education, and increase earning potential. This approach, however, may also require more hours and thus entail more child care costs than education or work alone.

Empirically, approaches that link education to specific employment appear to be somewhat effective. Nonexperimental analyses of the NEWWS data demonstrate that obtaining a GED, and especially a GED with some vocational training, can increase employment and earnings (Bos et al., 2001). There is also some evidence of the benefits of postsecondary education for low-income workers; however, programs have rarely been evaluated adequately. Grubb and colleagues (1999) suggest that postsecondary programs designed to serve welfare recipients and other low-income workers are most effective when they understand labor market needs and target jobs with strong employment growth; integrate basic education, occupational skills training, and "on-the-job" experiences; offer flexible scheduling while maintaining adequate intensity and duration; provide opportunities for further education; and provide a variety of support services.

Alternative approaches to simple integration of the traditional "education-first" and "work-first" models should also be considered given the generally minimal success of such models. Also, training low-income women for nontraditional jobs could be effective in increasing wages. When asked about their occupational aspirations and expectations, women have talked almost exclusively about female-dominated, low-skill, and low-wage positions (e.g., medical clerical, hospitality, customer service, or child care provider) (Scott, London, & Edin, 2000). Traditionally male-dominated jobs (e.g., truck driver, warehouse worker, electrician, and automotive technician) typically pay higher wages. Increasing access to and information about these jobs among women may improve their earning potential (Negrey, Golin, Lee, Mead, & Gault, 2001).

Who Should Receive Education and Training Services? How Can Different Groups Be Motivated to Participate in and Benefit From Such Services?

In the years prior to 1996, low-income individuals could participate voluntarily in a range of educational and training activities, and many no doubt benefited from these experiences. Welfare reforms under PRWORA at once limited these activities for some and mandated them for others. Making activities mandatory may mean that a certain segment of those receiving education and training services are not as motivated as those who would have participated voluntarily. Studies indicate that few welfare recipients express a desire to resume basic education; many have had negative schooling experiences, feel alienated from the educational system, and would prefer to acquire job-related skills (D'Amico, 1999). This may be one way in which welfare recipient students may differ from the "traditional" students of adult education programs. In addition, welfare recipients themselves are often skeptical of publicly funded training programs and perceive that they will lead only to low-wage, unsteady work (Grubb, 1996; Merrifield, 1997). Single mothers receiving welfare reveal desires to complete 2–4-year training programs that will prepare them for jobs that pay a living wage (Edin & Lein, 1997).

The literature consistently demonstrates the heterogeneity of the welfare population; therefore, successful programs must take into account the diverse needs and circumstances of subgroups. Those who have moved into the workforce need skills and training for progression and wage growth and may benefit from educational services while working. Those not yet working need basic skills, support for work-study programs, and options for part-time and full-time education. Empirically, subgroup findings support the notion that certain individuals or groups have been affected differentially by the reforms and by participation in education and training activities. Generally, those with lower educations have fared worse under PRWORA. In some of the NEWWS sites, 5-year effects on financial well-being were negative for the subgroup of participants without a high school diploma or GED at baseline (Hamilton et al., 2001). Training appears to be most effective for recipients with 12 or more years of prior education (see Zambrowski & Gordon, 1993) and basic math, literacy, and study skills (Schweber, 1997).

On the other hand, an analysis of the 2-year NEWWS evaluation suggests no additional impact of participating in human capital development activities for those recipients who had a high school diploma or GED. In fact, the basic pattern of effects in NEWWS was consistent across subgroups based on skill level, work history, and race and ethnicity. Those who were the most educationally disadvantaged (lacking a diploma or GED) did not benefit any more from these services than other groups. Overall, there were few improvements in reading or math abilities or in employment or earnings, perhaps in part because most recipients only participated for a short time. Low attendance and completion rates are common for welfare recipients in general (Pauly, 1995).

Programs may have limited success for the most educationally disadvantaged partly because few programs are appropriate for learning disabled participants or those with limited English skills. It is estimated that between 25% and 50% of the welfare population has a learning disability (Strawn, 1998). In addition, one analysis indicates that the skill gap between those receiving welfare and those not receiving welfare is not completely explained by lower educational attainment, age, gender, language, and/or physical and mental disabilities. This finding suggests that welfare recipients may be struggling with challenges that are not easily identifiable (Johnson & Tafoya, 1999). Furthermore, it is increasingly likely that those left on the welfare rolls are the "hard to serve" and include many who lack education credentials and have poor skills (Danziger et al., 2000)

In sum, there is still much to be learned about which types of human capital development strategies work best for whom in the context of welfare reform. Preliminary evidence suggests that targeted and flexible programs that use a "mix" of education- and employment-based strategies may be the most effective. The Portland NEWWS program succeeded in increasing earnings and wages among single, low-income women by providing training with a strong link to the local job market, an integrated education and training curriculum, and easily accessible child care. This program was also more flexible in terms of its courses, unlike many programs that rigidly assign certain groups to one set of activities (e.g., basic education before skills training). It is clear that innovative approaches are needed to improve upon the largely ineffective single-focus programs of the last few decades.

Who Should Provide Services?

State and local agencies can choose among a variety of providers in developing education and training programs: nonprofit community organizations, for-profit schools, school districts, and community colleges. Agencies and providers may choose to integrate their services in a comprehensive delivery system, or each entity might provide specialized services in the context of collaborative partnerships in a network system (Knell, 1998). Local welfare or workforce development agencies, a private industry council, or community colleges can coordinate services.

In many states, community colleges have played a central role in developing a diverse set of innovative programs. For example, California has allocated $65 million annually to the community college system as part of its welfare reform efforts. Funds have been used for curriculum development, child care services, work-study programs, job development and placement services, and coordination with programs and agencies. In 1999, community colleges were authorized to provide assistance to adults who had been off welfare for 2 years and who currently worked in low-wage and/or temporary employment or were employed with no benefits.

According to Cohen (1998b), there are four models of how community colleges can provide and coordinate vocational training and other employment services. First, community colleges statewide can participate in the development and management of the welfare-to-work system as a partner with the welfare and workforce development agencies. Second, community colleges can be contracted as case managers for all or part of a welfare-to-work program. Third, community colleges can be contracted to deliver education or training. Finally, community colleges can house a one-stop job center that comprises all workforce development services, including welfare-to-work programs.

States need to consider the strength of community colleges, their experience in dealing with the welfare population, and the extent to which their resources are being underused as a result of declining college attendance by welfare recipients. Community colleges have been the traditional provider of "off-hour and employer-based education." In addition, local businesses can join with agencies to create programs that will meet local employment needs and the continuing education needs of workers (Friedman, 1999). Workforce development boards may be key in bringing together educators and employers and in clearly identifying program goals. As part of the Learn, Earn, Advance and Prosper (LEAP) program—a collaboration between the Tucson Medical Center and the Arizona State Department of Employment—participants spend 4 days a week in on-the-job training and 1 day (or more if desired) in classroom training provided by a community-based organization. Graduates of the program may become employed by the hospital and continue their training for up to 24 months, at which time they can advance to a higher paying position (see Friedman, 1999, for a discussion of this program and others). In another example of a public-private partnership, United Parcel Service (UPS) offers welfare recipients a variety of skill building and job training activities to build and strengthen its workforce.

When Should Services Be Provided and for How Long?

Education and training programs can be considered a last resort for people who cannot find employment or as a way to increase earning potential for welfare recipients preparing for employment (preemployment) and those already employed (postemployment). Typically, in the years following PRWORA, states have not provided education or training services prior to job search, although many are now providing postemployment training. Data on the co-occurrence of multiple barriers to employment (e.g., low human capital in combination with physical and mental health problems) in a substantial proportion of welfare-reliant women suggest that human capital development activities may be appropriate prior to job search for certain recipients (Danziger, Kalil, & Anderson, 2000).

Another consideration in the design of programs is their duration. Given evidence that recipients have trouble completing degree programs and may have difficulty following a typical college schedule, states can work with community colleges to develop shorter term training and compress existing programs by increasing the number of class hours per week. Questions exist, however, about the effectiveness of shorter term training (see Stanley, 1995). As Grubb (1999) strongly cautions, in the wake of welfare reform many community colleges have shifted their focus from certificate and associate degree programs to short-term, nondegree training programs, despite substantial evidence that such programs have had little success in the past.

What Supports Are Needed for Recipients to Pursue Education and Training Successfully?

As time limits take effect, transitional benefits expire, and the economy shifts downward, the challenge of combining welfare-to-work activities and parenting will become increasingly difficult. Like all working parents, welfare recipients need several supports to manage work and family responsibilities—among the most important are affordable, convenient, and quality child care; reliable transportation; and accessible health care.

Subsidies for these supports are typically not as available to parents involved in education as they are to those involved in job search activities or those making the transition to employment. For example, many states do not authorize child care subsidies for students receiving welfare. Yet, parents' success in education and training programs has been linked to their perceptions of the adequacy of child care for their children (see review by Silva, Cahalan, & Lucierno-Paquet, 1998). In addition to expanding access to subsidies, programs providing on-site or nearby child care may increase participation and retention. Child care centers situated within high schools may be an important resource for adolescent parents trying to complete their degree.

Along with basic support services, parents pursuing a postsecondary education could benefit from assistance with tuition, other educational costs and fees, and living costs (Friedman, 1999). Federal aid programs such as Pell grants, the HOPE scholarship, and the Lifetime Learning tax credit cover educational expenses (or lend money for these purposes) but cannot be used for support services. Access could be increased by providing larger grants and scholarships, making tax credits refundable, and expanding work-study opportunities. Alternatively, eligibility requirements could be changed to reduce eligibility conflicts with other programs. Pell grant deadlines could be extended or structured as "rolling" to improve access to students in nontraditional programs. Also, resources are typically less available for short-term or part-time educational activities, although these are more likely to be approved under TANF.

A substantial number of low-income parents face considerable challenges (e.g., depression, substance abuse, parent or child health problems, domestic violence) and most likely require additional support services (Danziger et al., 2000). For example, survey data suggest high levels of depressive symptoms in 25% to 57% of female welfare recipients (Lennon, Blome, & English, 2001).

What Are States' Options for Expanding Education and Training, Either Within or Outside the TANF System?

At the federal and state levels, important decisions need to be made about whether education and training services should be expanded under PRWORA. Expansions could be accomplished either within the TANF system (e.g., allowing more educational activities to count toward the work requirement) or outside the system (e.g., providing non-TANF support).

States have a range of options for expanding opportunities for postsecondary education. They may (a) allow TANF recipients to participate in postsecondary education only after putting in the required amount of time in approved work activities and not provide support services, (b) require a minimum number of hours in approved work activities but provide support services or other assistance for those in college as well, or (c) allow and support college as a stand-alone activity. To avoid financial penalties, a state must either have enough people in approved activities to meet federal requirements or create a separate state program to finance this education, thus removing college students from the participation calculations.

Currently, states have flexibility in using maintenance-of-effort money for postsecondary education, but federal funds are limited. Vocational training qualifies as work, but only 30% of the caseload (including teen parents) can be counted, and participation is limited to 12 months. It has been argued that the 5-year limit may not provide enough time to complete programs for those just beginning or those combining work with school and child rearing. Suggested changes include expanding the definition of "work" to include some or all postsecondary education, counting work hours in proportion to credits earned, extending the 12-month time limit, extending time limits for those in postsecondary education making progress, and "stopping the clock" for students who maintain a certain grade point average. In collaboration with state and local efforts, colleges can package work and education together by using federal work-study funds or making community service opportunities available through Americorps or state and local community service programs. They can also develop internship programs that are coordinated with academic programs.

How Should Education and Training Initiatives Be Evaluated?
What Are Important Areas for Future Research?

Research findings on education and training services are mixed. Some evaluations of these programs suggest positive results, but most have not been intensive or extensive enough to yield conclusions. Despite the consistent finding of better economic outcomes for those with higher levels of education, it has been unclear whether providing or even mandating educational activities for low-income adults can significantly increase employment and earnings and reduce welfare dependence.

Information regarding effective education and training initiatives remains limited because of the relatively small number of evaluations that exist and because of limitations in their design. Traditionally, there have been accountability problems in the field of adult education because of insufficient data on adult students, validity issues in the assessments used, and a lack of clear program goals (U.S. General Accounting Office, 1995). Also, follow-up periods may not have been adequate to assess long-term effects of human capital development strategies; only a few studies have long-term data on the years following the program's end (see Bloom, 1997; Pauly, 1995).

Providing educational services for low-income parents may have benefits for children (outside of effects on employment and earnings). Parents involved in educational activities may provide a role model for children and may be more likely to be involved with their own children's schooling. The very limited literature on this topic is discussed in the next section concerning children's educational outcomes; it is important to note here, however, that this topic should be considered when evaluating education programs for parents.

Given the large variations in programs across states and even communities, evaluations of specific programs and innovative approaches are needed. At the same time, it will be important to establish a set of criteria to evaluate these programs on a broader level to allow estimations of whether they can be implemented successfully on a larger scale.

Summary

Since the early 1980s, the welfare policy pendulum has swung alternately between an emphasis on education and an emphasis on work. The welfare reform legislation of 1996 signaled a clear shift toward the policy goals of caseload reduction and self-sufficiency through rapid entry into employment. Most states responded initially to PRWORA by limiting educational opportunities for welfare recipients. However, in light of a potential recession, job instability, limited advancement, and persistent poverty, many states recently have reconsidered the role of education in improving outcomes for the working poor. The research reviewed in this chapter provides tentative support for the notion that certain education and training efforts (especially those linked to specific jobs) can be effective in increasing welfare recipients' employment and earnings. This review also highlights the challenges facing policymakers, administrators, and educators given the unique issues of adult education in the context of welfare reform.

Research suggests that discussions of "work-first" versus "education-and-training-first" approaches should instead focus on how these two approaches can be combined or improved upon. Strict work-first programs have moved people into jobs quickly and at a relatively low cost; however, these jobs are largely low wage, unstable, and of low quality. Although strict education-and-training-first programs have also produced long-term effects on employment, they have had difficulty boosting incomes or improving family and child outcomes. Programs that have achieved the most success appear to strike a balance between these two approaches and share the following characteristics: "comprehensive, individualized services; a consistent focus on employment; close relationships with local employers; rapid skill development through time-intensive training; high expectations for participation; and developed collaboratively with all stakeholders in the work force development arena" (D'Amico, 1997, as cited in Immel, 1998, p. 1). It has recently been suggested that programs should integrate basic education and skills training, engage local employers, and provide needed support services (Gueron & Hamilton, 2002).

Welfare reform policies make the challenge of effective education and training at once more difficult and more pressing. There are indications that an increasing number of jobs created in next few years will require at least a high school diploma (Carnevale & Desrochers, 1999). Ironically, the "marriage" of adult education and welfare-to-work programs could weaken adult education efforts because of time limits and the focus on rapid entry into employment. On the other hand, integration could increase effects, because the welfare package often includes support services as well as requirements and expectations for participation.

Finally, welfare reform has had important implications for the field of education as the goals for adult education have become increasingly intertwined with policymakers' goals for low-income adults. In the context of welfare-to-work programs, goals of adult education that extend beyond employment and self-sufficiency can be obscured. Yet, adult learners usually identify goals relevant not only to employment but to their roles as citizens and family members as well (Stein, 1997).

PRWORA and WIA have ushered in a new phase of federal involvement in adult education. Policy debates within the field are now driven in large part by the new focus of welfare policy on employment outcomes (Immel, 1998). Some have argued that the movement toward subsuming adult basic education and vocational education under the umbrella of workforce development has oversimplified and distorted the relationships among literacy, adult education, and welfare-to-work efforts (see discussion in D'Amico, 1999). Despite research demonstrating that education level is only one of a host of factors influencing employment and earnings, education programs for low-income adults are often evaluated solely on the basis of their success in improving these outcomes. Furthermore, the participation of adult educators in policy discussions at the local and state levels may be determined by their ability to meet the goals of workforce development. This creates tensions for educators attempting to incorporate current policy goals for low-income people in terms of research, policy stands, and programmatic decisions.

IMPLICATIONS OF WELFARE REFORM FOR CHILDREN'S EDUCATIONAL OUTCOMES

Although welfare reform was intended to primarily affect parents' outcomes (e.g., increase employment, reduce dependency, increase self-sufficiency), children represent the majority of public assistance recipients (Children's Defense Fund, 2001). In 1999, approximately two thirds of TANF recipients were children, the majority were under 11 years of age, and half were under age 6 (Knitzer & Cauthen, 1999). The importance of examining the impact of welfare reform policies on children's educational outcomes can be highlighted by the fact that, by age 10, more than one third of all children will have lived in a welfare household. The rate is even higher for Black, non-Hispanic children (Levine & Zimmerman, 2000).

The total number of children living in poverty has decreased in the period since the enactment of PRWORA, dropping by 1.2 million from 1995 to 1998; yet, there has been an increase in the percentage of children living in poverty whose parents are meeting the work requirements set by welfare reform. Thus, even during the "economic boom" that occurred during 1995–1998, working full time did not raise a large number of families out of poverty. The percentage of poor children living in working families increased from 34% in 1995 to 37% in 1997 and 42% in 1998. Translating these percentages to numbers, the number of children in working poor families increased from 4.9 million in 1995 to 5.6 million in 1998 (Dalaker, 1999; Wertheimer, 2001). Currently, more than 12 million children live in poverty in the United States, proportionally more than any other westernized nation (Newberger, 2001), leading many to express concern for this "poverty amidst plenty."

In his 2002 state of the union address, President Bush spoke of his role in creating what he referred to as "historic education reform" legislation that would help ensure that no child is left behind in America. He resolved to accomplish this task by improving Head Start and early childhood development programs and by placing quality teachers in every classroom. While these are both important steps in "leaving no child behind," this list of solutions ignores the role of families' economic well-being. Part of ensuring that no child is left behind educationally is ensuring that no child lives in poverty.

In the previous sections, we provided an overview of how families are faring after welfare reform. We also discussed the effects PRWORA has had—and could potentially have—on two of the primary targeted outcomes for adults (income and employment), as well as the educational outcomes of adults (though not a targeted outcome). In this section, we examine the relations among income, welfare receipt, employment and maternal education, and children's educational outcomes. Furthermore, we examine the pathways by which these targeted and nontargeted outcomes affect children's educational outcomes. We close with conclusions and recommendations for future research and policy.

Economic Well-Being and Children's Educational Outcomes

Relations Among Family Income, Welfare Receipt, Maternal Employment, and Children's Educational Outcomes

It should be noted that, just as policies enacted by welfare reform can affect adults differently according to preexisting characteristics such as their education and skill levels, the effects of welfare reform can differ for children according to particular demographic characteristics, the most important of which is probably age. For instance, a consistent finding (and for the most part unexpected) from the synthesis of evaluations of welfare-to-work demonstration programs is that while programs generally have a positive effect for elementary school children (including school performance), they may be detrimental to adolescents (e.g., school problems and risky behaviors) (Duncan & Chase-Lansdale, 2001; Morris et al., 2001). These developmental differences are highlighted throughout this section. In order to examine how changes brought about by welfare reform can affect children's educational outcomes, it is important to first discuss the associations among family income, welfare receipt, and parental employment and children's educational outcomes.

Family income. Economic hardship has been found to affect a wide variety of child outcomes. There is a large body of research demonstrating that poverty significantly interferes with healthy development (physical and cognitive), including intellectual functioning and academic achievement (Duncan & Brooks-Gunn, 1997; Huston, 1991). Children growing up in poverty are at risk for exposure to various environmental and biological risk factors that are harmful to their development, including their outcomes in school and later experiences with jobs (Duncan & Brooks-Gunn, 1997).

Families' economic resources affect the quality of the home, child care, and school and community environments to which children are exposed (see Huston, 2002). Poverty limits children's access to safe, nurturing learning environments, as well as limiting opportunities to engage in warm and responsive interactions with adults

(Rosenbaum, 1992). Material deficiencies related to poverty (e.g., malnutrition, inadequate health and child care, homelessness or unsafe housing conditions and neighborhoods, and insufficient schools) have detrimental effects on children's motivation and ability to learn, and they can contribute to social and emotional difficulties and hamper learning, academic performance, and cognitive development (Korenman, Miller, & Sjaastad, 1995; Kotch & Shackelford, 1989).

Children from low-income families perform worse academically than children from higher income families (see Corcoran, 1995; Duncan & Brooks-Gunn, 1997; Haveman & Wolfe, 1994; Zill, Moore, Smith, Stief, & Coiro, 1991). Seventy-nine percent of all children in low-performing schools are from families in poverty. Poor children are much more likely to experience problems with school readiness and achievement (National Center for Children in Poverty, 1999) and are at least twice as likely to be kept back in school as nonpoor children. Conversely, children in families with better resources are healthier and perform better in school, are more likely to complete high school, and have higher incomes as adults (Mayer, 1997).

Research shows that children's early experiences have profound effects on their overall development and future achievement. In terms of intellectual development, family income has been considered to be more critical during the early ages (0–5 years) than at later ages (Smith, Brooks-Gunn, & Klebanov, 1997). Children who experience economic deprivation in early childhood may be limited in terms of their successive achievement (Duncan, Dunifon, Doran, & Yeung, 1998). Inadequate nutrition (which is associated with poverty) during the brain's critical formative years is related to much lower scores on tests of reading, vocabulary, and mathematics (National School Boards Association, 1999).

Welfare receipt. With clear associations between poverty and child outcomes, some have investigated whether welfare receipt in and of itself has negative implications for children. Using two nationally representative data sets from periods before welfare reform (early 1970s and early 1990s), Duncan and his colleagues (2001) found large differences between welfare families and middle-class families in terms of their time use, mental health, and expenditures, adjusting statistically for differences in demographic characteristics such as mother's age and education level. Often, the outcomes favored middle-class families (e.g., lower levels of maternal depression, lower family tension, greater involvement in youth activities); on other measures, however, there were no differences between the two groups (e.g., parental attitudes regarding monitoring, parent-teacher involvement). As Duncan and his colleagues (1998) point out, welfare reform is unlikely to raise low-income families into the middle class, and thus it may be more fruitful to make comparisons between low-income families receiving welfare and low-income families not receiving welfare. When these comparisons are made, for the most part, there are few differences between the two populations.

Many argue that a "welfare culture" exists that has detrimental effects on the motivation of children exposed to this lifestyle. The influence of welfare per se on children's educational outcomes (as opposed to lack of resources) is difficult to tease apart, since welfare families have the lowest incomes of all families. However, studies examining well-being among children living in poor families that did and did not receive welfare (as well as comparing families that were and were not poor) showed that, for the most part, children's achievement differed by poverty level and not welfare (AFDC) receipt (Zill et al., 1991). This conclusion is consistent with other research. In general, when background characteristics are taken into account (including levels of child development), differences in children's achievement and cognitive test scores in welfare versus nonwelfare families disappear (Menaghan, Jakielek, Mott, & Cooksey, 1998), and, to the extent that welfare increases family income, children's cognitive outcomes may be improved by welfare receipt (see Duncan & Brooks-Gunn, 1997).

Levine and Zimmerman (2000) examined the impact of children's exposure to the welfare system through their mothers' benefit receipt prior to adolescence on several developmental outcomes using data from the National Longitudinal Survey of Youth (NLSY). They found that children in households headed by welfare mothers, and especially those who were on welfare a good deal of the child's life, scored lower on tests of cognitive development and had more behavior problems than other children. Using three methodological strategies to examine whether this association was attributable to welfare receipt per se or other characteristics of mothers (observed or unobserved), they found no causal links between welfare receipt in and of itself and children's outcomes. They concluded that welfare receipt does not affect how much mothers invest in their children; instead, it seems to play a more direct role in changing the constraints faced by families by providing income supplements.

Other studies indicate that changes in children's cognitive development are most affected by changes in family income, not the source of that income (Chase-Lansdale & Brooks-Gunn, 1995; Zill & Schoenborn, 1990). In one study, children in welfare families completed significantly less schooling (ranging between 1 and 2 years) than children in nonwelfare families and children of single working mothers of low socioeconomic status (SES); however, controlling for variables such as mother's race and educational level, number of children, city size, mother's age, and unemployment rate reduced these differences substantially, leading the researchers to conclude that the differences were more a function of demography than of welfare receipt itself (Duncan et al., 1998). In a review of several experimental welfare-to-work evaluations, increases in school achievement came consistently from those programs that also supplemented wages, though not for children whose parents were least educated or who had little job experience (Morris et al., 2001). Findings such as these imply that the welfare-to-work transition will not have much of an impact on children's achievement if changes in some of these other variables do not also occur (e.g., maternal education level).

There are a few exceptions to the general conclusion that amount of income matters more than the source of that income for children's educational outcomes. For instance, results from one study demonstrated that, after background characteristics (including parental schooling, race, household composition, marital status, income, and residential location) had been controlled, women from poor families who received welfare were more likely to be on welfare themselves as adults than those from poor families who did not receive welfare (Martin, 1999). One possible explanation for this finding is that adolescents whose parents receive welfare are more likely to have a child themselves by the age of 18 (Gottschalk, 1992); these teens may require more of a safety net than those not having children before the age of 18.

Some research suggests that welfare receipt in the early or middle childhood years may have more sustained and negative effects on children's academic outcomes than later in life. Welfare receipt in early childhood is related to lower high school graduation rates, higher grade failure rates, and lower literacy scores, even after control for school readiness (Baydar, Brooks-Gunn, & Furstenberg, 1993; Brooks-Gunn, Guo, & Furstenberg, 1993; Guo, Brooks-Gunn, & Harris, 1996). Welfare receipt in the middle childhood years (roughly ages 5–12) has been associated with more negative outcomes in the adolescent years (see Duncan, Dunifon, Doran, & Yeung, 2001).

Most studies have focused on how welfare receipt in early adolescence affects later schooling and demographic behavior, particularly in late adolescence and early adulthood. For example, after controlling for personal and family characteristics, Gottschalk (1992) found that rates of childbearing by the age of 18 were 50% higher among Whites and 100% higher among Black and Hispanic adolescents whose parents received welfare than among those whose parents did not receive welfare. Early childbearing may dampen adolescents' educational attainment.

In addition, there is some evidence suggesting that duration of welfare receipt may matter. In one sample, children in families receiving welfare for less than 2 years had better scores on tests of school readiness than children in families receiving AFDC for more than 2 years (Zaslow, McGroder, Cave, & Mariner, 1999). Prereform research indicates that child age influences families' length of and need for welfare receipt and benefits. One study showed that the transition from welfare (AFDC) to work was likely to occur more frequently among families with older children. This finding is consistent with other results showing that families with very young children are most in need and likely to remain on AFDC longer than those with older children (U.S. Department of Health and Human Services, 2000).

On the other hand, results from some studies suggest positive effects of welfare receipt. For instance, children whose families receive welfare are more likely to have health insurance and better health (Wertheimer, 2001), which are both important factors exhibiting positive associations with school attendance and achievement (see Schwarz & Liu, 2000).

Collectively, existing data provide evidence for what is known as the "correlated disadvantages hypothesis"; that is, other factors lead to both welfare receipt and lower achievement, and therefore it is not necessarily welfare receipt in and of itself that causes negative outcomes for children. This lack of association between welfare receipt per se and child outcomes offers little support for the hypothesis that role modeling is the critical pathway by which welfare receipt affects children. In sum, although research findings overall indicate that welfare receipt in and of itself does not appear to have negative effects on children's educational outcomes, it is important to note that there is some research suggesting that living in a welfare family (as opposed to a nonwelfare family), particularly during adolescence or for extended periods of time, is better avoided.

Maternal employment. Most of the research examining the links between maternal employment and children's school achievement has involved middle-class samples. The data available on low-income families show that, when main effects are found, maternal employment is related to better achievement in elementary and middle school (Alessandri, 1992; Vandell & Ramanan, 1992). However, virtually no data exist about the implications of *mandatory* maternal employment for children. Research on this topic is especially needed now given welfare reform's work requirements for all mothers. There are some potentially harmful implications of mothers who have young children moving from welfare to work (see Loprest, 1999). A few studies show negative outcomes for children in low-income families when employment begins during the first year of children's lives (see Baydar & Brooks-Gunn, 1991).

Data show that maternal employment is associated with positive school achievement for elementary school children but not adolescents (Vandell & Ramanan, 1992) and is linked with negative outcomes, such as delinquency, in adolescence (Sampson & Laub, 1994). Using data on more than 450 White and African American children from the NLSY, Han, Waldfogel, and Brooks-Gunn (2001) found that maternal employment in the first year of children's lives has significant negative effects on children's cognitive (math, vocabulary, and reading) achievement at age 3 or 4 that persist up to age 7 or 8; however, these findings were only for White children.

The linkages between parental employment and child outcomes as a result of welfare reform are complex. In general, it appears to be a matter of trade-offs. For example, increases in employment may lead to increases in income but may also lead to decreases in the amount of time parents spend interacting with and supervising children. This lack of supervision may be especially harmful for older children and adolescents for reasons discussed later in this chapter.

Previous research on maternal employment and children's cognitive outcomes in low-income families suggests neutral to positive effects. Reductions in time and supervision spent with children appear to be offset by economic and psychological benefits associated with being employed (Haveman & Wolfe, 1994; Moore & Driscoll, 1997; Parcel, 1998; Vandell & Ramanan, 1992; Zaslow & Emig, 1997).

Increased income that *may* come from working in a job with higher wages as opposed to receiving welfare is likely to positively affect children and families in various ways. In addition to income, the effects of employment on parents' and children's well-being depend on the characteristics of parents' jobs, such as wages, work schedule, occupational complexity, and fringe benefits. Researchers have found (e.g., Hofferth, Smith, McLoyd, & Finkelstein, 2000) that leaving welfare may be beneficial to children *if* parents' wages increased upon leaving the rolls. For instance, a study of former AFDC recipients showed that children had higher scores on math achievement tests if their mothers earned higher wages upon leaving welfare (Moore & Driscoll, 1997).

Low-income jobs often require working fluctuating or nighttime hours (Presser & Cox, 1997; Silvestri, 1995). Jobs with nonstandard schedules are associated with reduced parent contact with school-aged children, poor cognitive skills, and more mental health problems in children (Barton, Aldridge, & Smith, 1998; Presser, 2000; White & Keith, 1990). Data from the NLSY indicate that even when income, parent education level, marital status, and number of hours worked by parent were controlled, evening or nighttime work hours increased, children's math and reading achievement scores decreased, and the likelihood of children repeating a grade or being suspended from school increased (Heymann, 2000).

Occupational complexity refers to the opportunities provided by a job for self-direction, cognitive stimulation, and engaging in a variety of tasks, as opposed to monotonous, routine tasks with high levels of supervision. A job's occupational complexity has been shown to be related to parenting behaviors, home environments, and children's verbal skills, independent of maternal and child background factors such as maternal education level, although little of this research has involved low-income families (e.g., Menaghan & Parcel, 1990, 1995; Parcel & Menaghan, 1994, 1997). For instance, research shows that the quality of home environments declines when mothers start jobs involving low wages and unstimulating tasks (Menaghan & Parcel, 1995). This may be explained, at least in part, by the fact that occupational complexity is positively associated with mothers' cognitive skills and, thus, the home environment they are able to provide (e.g., level of cognitive stimulation)—both of which affect children's verbal abilities and capacities (Parcel & Menaghan, 1994). A 1999 Urban Institute report based on data from the 1997 National Survey of America's Families (NSAF) indicates that women who have left the welfare rolls are working in low-wage jobs, and 25% of these women work primarily at night.

Research has demonstrated that welfare-to-work and employment programs can have positive impacts on parents' job quality. For example, the Portland site of the NEWWS produced immediate impacts on employment and earnings, as well as increased job quality. Specifically, it produced significant increases in participants' average hourly wages and the proportion of participants who attained jobs with employer-provided health benefits. These findings were widespread, occurring for participants who had few as well as many barriers to employment (Scrivener et al., 1998). Thus, to the extent that welfare programs can significantly increase parents' job quality, this may translate into positive achievement outcomes for children (as well as adults).

It is important to note that, unlike income, which was positively associated with child well-being on various academic and social measures, data from experimental welfare-to-work and employment programs show that employment alone does not appear to have a positive impact on child outcomes; in fact, those that increased employment without simultaneously increasing income had mostly mixed or negative effects on child outcomes (Children's Defense Fund, 2001). If welfare reform does not raise families out of poverty (i.e., make work pay) and ensure access to benefits, it is unlikely that children's prospects will improve by families working but remaining poor. Future research should pay more attention to the characteristics of jobs that parents obtain under mandatory welfare requirements and how these job characteristics affect their, and their children's, well-being.

Relations Between Maternal Education Level and Children's Educational Outcomes

Research on links between low-income parents' educational level and child outcomes has focused primarily on maternal education, given that a majority of welfare families are headed by single parents, mostly mothers. In general, parents with higher education levels display more effective parenting behaviors, which in turn have positive implications for their children (see Chase-Lansdale & Pittman, 2002). There is a fair amount of evidence that maternal education is linked to children's intellectual development (Desai, Chase-Lansdale, & Michael, 1989; Duncan, Brooks-Gunn & Klebanov, 1994). According to the National Assessment of Educational Progress, parents' education level is the single greatest determinant of children's reading achievement. Level of maternal education is also strongly associated with children's later academic success (see Haveman & Wolfe, 1994). Duncan et al. (1998) found that mothers' education levels and test scores when their children were born were associated with the children's completion of schooling. McGroder, Zaslow, Papillo, Ahluwalia, and Brooks (2001) found that one of the strongest predictors of children's cognitive outcomes was maternal literacy; interestingly, this was also the most consistent "barrier" to mothers' employment.

Children in working poor families are less likely to have at least one parent who has completed at least 12 years of education (Wertheimer, 2001). Zaslow and her colleagues (2002), in their synthesis of results from welfare-to-work demonstrations, discovered that maternal educational progress was associated more closely with positive child outcomes than was economic progress; specifically, increases in education resulted more consistently in positive outcomes for children than did increases in family employment and income.

One study found that family process or mental health measures did not predict children's schooling success as strongly as mother's education level, test scores, and age when child was born. Given the limited variability in maternal education levels in low-SES samples, the fact that mothers' educational levels predicted children's educational outcomes points to the significance of mothers' education in children's academic development (Duncan et al., 1998).

An important question regarding welfare reform that has not been adequately addressed in the current era of the "work-first" approach is the following: Does improving maternal education levels lead to improvements in children's academic outcomes? While we know strong relationships exist between maternal education level and children's educational outcomes, surprisingly little research has been conducted that explores the causal nature of such relationships. Some data suggest that increases in maternal education might translate into improvements in children's educational outcomes. For instance, a nonexperimental study showed that a mother's enrollment in school during the first 3 years of her child's life has a significant positive effect on the child's vocabulary achievement test scores (Rosenzweig & Wolpin, 1994).

The only experimental study examining how increases in maternal education affect children's development used data from the NEWWS. Magnuson and McGroder (2001) found that increases in maternal education were significantly positively related to children's academic school readiness and negatively related to their academic problems. Their findings were strong in comparison with studies investigating other influences on children's school readiness (Bee et al., 1982). These findings are especially important because school readiness has been shown to be an important predictor of future success in school (Entwisle & Alexander, 1993).

Many researchers and child advocates contend that the reduction in educational opportunities prompted by the 1996 welfare legislation has had, and will continue to have, negative implications for the educational outcomes of parents and their children. As Weiss and Halpern (1991) note, the primary rationale for community support and education programs for poor families is that parents are the "window" into the lives of their children. Especially in early childhood, parents hold primary responsibility for their children's environments; thus, because maternal education is positively associated with the quality of environments provided to children, and in turn positively related to children's educational outcomes, welfare policies aimed at improving maternal education provide an important opportunity to improve the educational outcomes of children.

Some studies have shown beneficial results for welfare-to-work programs that were educationally focused versus work focused. For instance, in the NEWWS child outcomes study, overall child effects did not differ systematically according to whether mothers were involved in work-focused programs or education-focused programs (neither had consistently favorable or consistently unfavorable effects), but children who were at high versus low risk for poor development had more favorable outcomes (at two of the three sites) when their mothers were assigned to education-focused programs (Hamilton, Freedman, & McGroder, 2000).

Focusing on the "How": Pathways by Which Income, Employment, and Welfare Receipt Affect Child Outcomes

The results are clear that income, welfare receipt, maternal employment, and educational level all have the potential to significantly affect children's educational outcomes; what is less clear is "how?" What are the pathways by which these characteristics affect children's educational development and achievement? The fact that welfare programs have shown mixed effects on children stems, in part, from the differing characteristics across differing family ecologies (Zaslow, Tout, Smith, & Moore, 1998) but also suggests the existence of mediating or moderating effects (Rosman & Yoshikawa, 2001).

On the basis of existing research (Duncan & Chase-Lansdale, 2001; Moore, 2001; Zaslow, Tout, et al., 1998), we have outlined the ways in which welfare reform programs can affect children according to nonfamilial and familial pathways (see Figure 1). The most obvious pathway by which welfare reform can affect children's educational outcomes is through its impact on parents' employment, earnings, and income (as just discussed), which in turn can affect the amount of resources available for children's development (Wilson, Ellwood, & Brooks-Gunn, 1995; Zaslow et al., 1995; Zaslow, Tout, et al., 1998). As represented in Box D of Figure 1, parents' welfare receipt may affect children through the amount of material resources available outside of the family (i.e., nonfamilial), including child care, health care, and out-of-school structured and unstructured activities (Haveman & Wolfe, 1995).

It is often debated whether it is low income levels (and thus less access to material resources) or personal and family characteristics (e.g., family composition, educational levels and skills, mental health, and genetics) that are most important in influencing developmental outcomes of poor children (Duncan & Brooks-Gunn, 1997; Huston, McLoyd, & Garcia Coll, 1994; Mayer, 1997; Rowe & Rodgers, 1997). Research demonstrates that there are multiple pathways, both economic and noneconomic, by which the transition from welfare to work can affect children's development (e.g., Duncan et al., 1994; Huston et al., 2001; Zaslow, Tout, et al., 1998). Welfare employment programs can initiate changes in family life that are important to children's educational outcomes, including—but also extending beyond—changes in maternal educational level and family income (Quint et al., 1997). Therefore, we also examine the role of familial processes, including role modeling, parental psychological well-being, and parent-child relationships (Figure 1, Box E).

Nonfamilial Pathways

Availability of material resources. Interestingly, research to date suggests that nonfamilial processes may be more crucial than familial processes to children's academic outcomes. The most prevalent theory regarding how welfare reform can affect children is through the impact of mandatory employment on the targeted economic outcomes of welfare reform (i.e., adults' employment, earnings, and income) and, in turn, the availability of material resources, which can affect children's development either positively or negatively (McGroder et al., 2001; Wilson et al., 1995; Zaslow et al., 1995; Zaslow, Tout, et al., 1998). Poverty limits children's opportunities for and access to high-quality services that can promote healthy development, including child care, health care, and early education experiences (Knitzer & Cauthen, 1999).

Welfare programs that raise parents' incomes may have a positive impact on children's educational outcomes if parents are able to invest more in educational resources (e.g., books, computers, education programs, tutoring). As Hofferth and her colleagues point out (2000), to the extent that welfare reform—and, in many cases, loss of cash receipt—causes low-income parents to have less money (which research shows is indeed the case for many families), less money will be available to invest in educational activities and materials for children, and children's cognitive skills and levels of completed schooling may suffer as a result.

Health care. Leaving welfare rolls often results in loss of health care subsidies, since most jobs entered upon leaving welfare pay minimum wage and offer no benefits. Children in working poor families are less likely to have health insurance and much less likely to receive food stamps or benefits under TANF (Wertheimer, 2001). On almost every indicator of health, children in low-income families are worse off than children in higher income families (Besharov & Germanis, 2002). Zill and his colleagues (1991) discovered that children of welfare recipients (AFDC), through their automatic eligibility for Medicaid programs, are better off than children of parents not receiving welfare benefits with respect to health insurance coverage and access to medical care. Since parents moving off welfare often obtain jobs that do not provide benefits, child health insurance is a significant issue. Findings from the Three Cities Study indicate that the longer families are off welfare, the less likely they are to be covered by any type of health insurance (Angel, Lein, Henrici, & Leventhal, 2001).

Lack of health insurance can affect children's achievement. Children's health is linked to school attendance and academic performance. Children who suffer from illnesses without access to sufficient care are often unable to keep up in school, and they are more likely to miss school than insured children (Florida Healthy Kids Corporation, 1997). In Delaware, an examination of the Prospects Study, involving a nationally representative sample of third and seventh graders, showed that absenteeism is greater for welfare children than other children, with income differences accounting for a large share of this gap (Fein, Lee, & Schofield, 1999). National data compiled from parent and teacher reports and school records suggest that absenteeism is significantly more prevalent among welfare than nonwelfare children. Welfare children miss more school because they are sick and truant more often than other children, with illnesses accounting for most of this difference. Obviously, children cannot progress educationally if they are not in school. Thus, welfare policies that seek to improve public health and health care for low-income children can have a positive impact on children's school outcomes.

Child care and early childhood education. The work requirements set forth by PRWORA have dramatically increased the number of children who require care while parents are working. Whereas the AFDC-based welfare system was intended to allow single (mostly widowed) mothers to remain home to care for young children, the new TANF-based system is motivated by a much different set of policy goals. As a result, low-income parents, especially those of very young children, are working more than ever before. One provision of the 1996 legislation was the lowering of the child age exemption. Until the late 1980s, welfare-reliant mothers with children less than 6 years of age were exempt from participation requirements and mandates. The Family Support Act of 1988 lowered this exemption to age 3 and further gave states the option of exempting only mothers of infants less than 1 year of age.

Under PRWORA, the federal exemption has been reduced to 1 year of age, and states may now require parents of infants as young as 3 months to participate in employment activities; in 1999, 11 states had this most limited exemption in place (SPDP, 2000). As a result of PRWORA, an estimated additional 1 million preschool-aged children have entered child care settings (Fuller & Kagan, 2000). Existing research suggests that experiences in these care settings have important consequences for academic development and are thus one pathway by which parents' participation in welfare-to-work programs can affect children's educational outcomes.

The nature and extent of these effects depend in part on such characteristics of care as type, duration, stability, and, perhaps most important, quality. Child care quality usually encompasses (a) the child-provider relationship (e.g., amount of verbal and cognitive stimulation, responsiveness, stability), (b) structural and caregiver characteristics (e.g., ratios, group size, caregiver education, physical environment/materials), and (c) health and safety provisions (Lamb, 1997; Vandell & Wolfe, 2000). The primary challenge in examining the relationship between child care quality and child outcomes is that child care is a naturally occurring event rather than part of a well-controlled experiment (i.e., where children are assigned to different types of care). Families who choose different types of care are likely to differ in many ways, making it difficult to disentangle the effects of care on children. Despite methodological challenges, child care research over the past two decades has provided a fairly consistent and convincing argument that child care matters for developmental outcomes (Galinsky, Howes, Kontos, & Shinn, 1994; Kisker, Hofferth, Phillips, & Farquhar, 1991; Moore, Zaslow, Miller, & Magenheim, 1996; Zaslow, 1991).

A growing body of research highlights the importance of quality (Phillips & Adams, 2001; Vandell & Wolfe, 2000) and suggests that high-quality care can contribute positively to children's academic functioning. High-quality child care is associated with better cognitive outcomes (e.g., language, reading, and math skills) (see review by Isaacs, 2002), and several longitudinal studies demonstrate that this relationship persists even after demographic and parenting characteristics have been controlled (Lamb, 1997; NICHD Early Child Care Network, 2000). Alternatively, low-quality care can have negative consequences for development. Poor-quality care can deprive children of intellectual stimulation and is often associated with delayed language and reading skills. Effects of child care quality on cognitive functioning and school achievement have been linked specifically to levels of engagement between children and caregivers (Shonkoff & Phillips, 2000).

Low-income children, usually at risk academically, may benefit in particular from high-quality early childhood care environments (Moore, Zaslow, Coiro, & Miller, 1996). In other words, high-quality care may serve as a protective factor, while low-quality care may compound other risk factors (National Research Council and

Institute of Medicine, 2000). Both experimental and nonexperimental studies suggest that high-quality programs for infants and preschool-aged children from low-income families can affect measures of intelligence (Bianci & McArthur, 1993; Collins & Brick, 1993), support school readiness (Zaslow, Oldham, Moore, & Magenheim, 1998), lead to short- and long-term improvements in school performance (Barnett, 1995; Lazar, Darlington, Murray, Royce, & Snipper, 1982; Ramey & Campbell, 1991; Ramey et al., 2000), and promote school progress (Lazar et al., 1982).

The size and endurance of these effects are not yet clear. For example, the positive effects of early interventions may not endure if children go on to attend poor-quality schools. It is important to note that the strongest evidence for the potential of high-quality early childhood programs comes from experimental evaluations of small-scale, intensive programs. With the exception of Head Start, there are few large-scale demonstrations to inform federal policies concerning child care quality.

Head Start is one of the largest and oldest early childhood intervention programs. Begun in 1965, this federally funded preschool program was designed to improve the school readiness, social skills, and health of children from low-income families. As part of the Head Start program, parents also receive a range of services and supports. Over the years, evaluations of Head Start have shown generally positive short-term effects on children's academic performance and IQ, as well as long-term effects on cognitive ability, achievement, social adjustment, grade retention, and educational attainment (Barnett, 1995; Currie & Thomas, 2000). The long-term effects of Head Start are somewhat tenuous and appear to depend in part on children's ethnicity and their school experiences in the years after program participation (Currie & Thomas, 2000).

Historically, Head Start has not been considered a child care program because of its half-day schedule and involvement of parents; however, with increased pressure on low-income parents to work (and to work full time), there have been some efforts to expand Head Start to better meet the needs of working poor families. In some cases, "wrap-around" child care services are now provided to extend the program to a full day. In 1995, Early Head Start was also initiated to provide child and family development services from birth to 3 years of age. An initial evaluation of Early Head Start demonstrates small but positive effects on children's cognitive, language, and social-emotional development after 1 to 2 years of program participation (U.S. Department of Health and Human Services, 2002).

One question often asked by parents and debated by researchers, policymakers, and practitioners is whether certain types of care are more beneficial to children than others (e.g., formal, center-based vs. home-based arrangements). Given the large variations in quality across types of arrangements, this question is not straightforward. When quality is held constant, center-based care during the infant, toddler, and preschool years is associated with better cognitive, language, and school performance than home-based care (NICHD Early Child Care Research Network, 2000). One study showed that low-income children 3–5 years of age placed in high-quality child care centers performed better on measures of school readiness than children in home-based child care settings (Zaslow, McGroder, Moore, & LeMenestral, 1999).

The advantages of center care over home-based care in terms of cognitive and intellectual development may due to the fact that they are uniformly subject to state-specific regulations on group size, child-to-staff ratios, and safety, whereas this is case for only some home-based arrangements (primarily family day care homes). Centers are also more likely to have developmentally appropriate materials and may have staff trained in child development and early education. Unregulated providers have less education, less training, and are less "child focused" in their caregiving than are regulated child care providers (Galinsky et al., 1994). Using data from the Three Cities Study, researchers rated 80% of unregulated child care settings, including relative care, as "minimal" or "inadequate." Most lacked books and appropriate materials for children to play with, and they often had unsanitary or dangerous conditions and poor nutrition. In contrast, 80% of regulated centers were rated as "good" quality.

One of the most consistent findings regarding low-income families and child care is the disproportionate use by these families of informal, or home-based, arrangements (Brown-Lyons, Robertson, & Layzer, 2001; Hofferth et al., 1991), and this appears to be the case for most families leaving welfare as well (Schumaker & Greenberg, 1999). Parents at all income levels choose child care arrangements based on a complex combination of their preferences and the constraints they face. For low-income parents, these constraints are often substantial.

Poor families are less likely to use paid care, but when they do pay for care they spend five times more of their income on care than families who are not poor (Smith, 2000). As a result, child care often represents the second or third greatest expense for low-income working families (Isaacs, 2002). Recent studies indicate that a large proportion of families will turn to informal, unlicensed child care when trying to fulfill new work requirements, because such settings offer more flexible hours and are less expensive; this type of care, however, is often of lower quality than regulated settings (Kontos, Howes, Shinn, & Galinsky, 1995).

Availability issues place additional constraints on the types of care families can use. Care for infants and school-aged children is often more difficult to find than care for preschool-aged children. For example, the current supply of school-aged child care is estimated to meet less than 25% of the demand in urban areas (U.S. General Accounting Office, 1997). Market supply conditions vary greatly across states and communities. In general, the supply of child care tends be lower in low-income neighborhoods than in higher income neighborhoods, and it may be particularly scarce during nonstandard hours and for children with special needs (U.S. General Accounting Office, 1997). Only 10% of centers and 6% of family child care homes offer care on weekends (Phillips, 1995), and fewer offer care during nighttime hours. Low-income parents, especially those who have left welfare, are much more likely than other parents to work evenings, early mornings, weekends, and rotating or inconsistent shifts (Hofferth, 1995; Mishel & Bernstein, 1994).

Despite research demonstrating its importance for child development, high-quality care is not readily available; on average, care in the United States is rated as poor to mediocre in quality. It is estimated that 40% of infants in child care centers experience care that jeopardizes their health, safety, and development and that one third of family child care homes are of inadequate quality (see Vandell & Wolfe, 2000). In general, children from more disadvantaged homes receive lower quality care, with the exception that the working poor and families just above the poverty line experience the lowest quality because they have only limited access to child care subsidies and intervention programs such as Head Start.

Recognizing that the new TANF requirements would intensify the need for child care, policymakers increased funding for child care subsidies as part of the reforms. Despite the wider availability, however, only 12% of children who were eligible for subsidies in 1999 received them (U.S. Department of Health and Human Services, 1999). The extent to which this figure reflects low take-up by families versus inadequacies of the subsidy system has been debated; low usage rates are probably the result of multiple factors. First, not all families who are eligible for subsidies use paid care; some families may prefer types of care that are free or low cost (i.e., care by friends or relatives). Subsidies generally can be used for informal or home-based arrangements, as well as formal arrangements, though many states require that the care be certified or regulated (i.e., meeting minimum safety and health standards). Second, families may not know they are eligible for assistance, particularly if they are not receiving welfare. Parents who have recently made the transition from welfare to work appear to be largely unaware of the availability of subsidies.

Third, the structure of subsidy systems often makes it difficult for parents to use them. Most states require parents to make a copayment, and the process of obtaining and maintaining subsidies can involve several administrative hurdles. Requirements that parents maintain a continuous level of employment and an income below a set level do not fit with the sporadic nature of low-wage work. Thus, parents whose work hours fluctuate can cycle between eligibility and ineligibility, making it difficult to maintain a stable subsidized arrangement. Working poor families have even less access to child care subsidies than families just leaving welfare and those on welfare because of these issues of eligibility, copayment and reimbursement policies, and cumbersome administrative processes (Fuller et al., 2002). Finally, subsidy reimbursement rates are usually lower than market rates and therefore not necessarily sufficient to pay for quality care. As a result, children from low-income families are often excluded from the high-quality care that could attenuate the risks of living in poverty.

There is some indication that provision of child care subsidies expands parents' options; families who receive subsidies are more likely to use center-based care than those who do not (Schumaker & Greenberg, 1999). Moreover, experimental programs in the Next Generation study that offered expanded child care assistance increased families' use of center-based care, whereas those that provided the same assistance to program and control groups increased only use of home-based care (Crosby, Gennetian, & Huston, 2001; Gennetian, Crosby, & Huston, 2001). Generous and well-structured child care assistance also appears to increase families' use of subsidies and decrease child care problems related to parents' finding and maintaining employment (Gennetian, Crosby, Huston, & Lowe, 2002).

Although it is clear that child care has the potential to benefit or impede development, relatively little is known about issues of quality and the link to child outcomes in the context of welfare reform. Much of the recent research describes families' child care usage and examines policy influences on child care decisions. It is clear that more children are in care in the post-PRWORA years, often in multiple arrangements for a substantial number of hours (Cappizano & Adams, 2000a, 2000b). It is also apparent that despite the increased availability of subsidies, many parents' needs in caring for their children remain unmet. Experimental evaluations indicate that the extent and quality of child care assistance offered in welfare and employment programs can influence the types of care parents choose (formal vs. home-based arrangements) (Crosby et al., 2001; Gennetian et al., 2001). Ironically, these same data suggest that welfare-to-work programs do not increase (and in some cases decrease) families' use of Head Start, the primary early education federal program for at-risk children.

Considerably less attention has been given to the *quality* and *stability* of care available to families working to meet the new requirements and how children are faring as a result of increased time spent in these settings. Many argue, however, that in the absence of strong evidence of the long-term impacts of care, policy changes that impose federal regulations on quality are unlikely. Future research should be based on scientific criteria such as random assignment, strong documentation of intervention, long-term effects, and replication, and the outcomes of interest must demonstrate improvements of interest to policymakers (e.g., school achievement, IQ, lower rates of delinquency and crime).

Structured and unstructured activities. In discussions of child care, it is often assumed that such factors as type of care, quality, and supervision level matter only for young children. However, older children also need supervised and structured settings for positive, healthy development. After-school programs and activities are important ways these types of settings may be provided to adolescents. School-aged children and adolescents are often ignored when policymakers think about which supports should be available to help ease families' transitions from welfare to work. A fair amount of attention has been paid (in research and policy) to parents' employment as it affects preschool children. Much less attention has been given to the types and quality of arrangements used by low-income families for school-aged children and how these arrangements might affect cognitive and academic outcomes.

How children spend out-of-school time has important implications for development; engagement in structured activities, in particular, may provide opportunities for learning and developing competencies (Bronfenbrenner, 1979; Larson & Verma, 1999; Weisner, 1987). Evidence exists suggesting that children from economically disadvantaged families spend more time in informal and unstructured activities than their more advantaged counterparts (Medrich et al., 1982; Posner & Vandell, 1999). Specifically, the lower their families' socioeconomic status, the less school-aged children read, the less they are involved in sports, and the more they watch television (Larson & Verma, 1999; Medrich et al., 1982; Timmer et al., 1985). Low-income children also spend more time playing outdoors and less time indoors playing with toys and games (Newson & Newson, 1976). A study involving low-income children in the first and third grades showed that children who spent more time on their own (i.e., in self-care) exhibited lower academic performance as sixth graders than children who spent less time in self-care (Pettit, Laird, Bates, & Dodge, 1997).

Time spent in unstructured and unsupervised activities (e.g., hanging out with friends) provides children and youth with opportunities to engage in delinquent or risk-taking behaviors (Osgood, Wilson, Bachman, O'Malley, & Johnston, 1996; Posner & Vandell, 1999). McHale, Crouter, and Tucker (2001) found that time spent hanging out and playing outdoors was associated with lower school grades and more conduct problems. Hanging out has also been associated with delinquency in adolescence (e.g., Osgood et al., 1996). Research conducted by McHale and her colleagues suggests that the negative implications of "hanging out" are due to fact that children often do so with peers in unsupervised settings (i.e., no adults). However, some unsupervised activities can promote positive development, such as reading. For instance, reading is positively linked with academic achievement (Allen, Cipielewski, & Stanovich, 1992; McHale et al., 2001).

Recent findings of McHale and her colleagues (2001) lend support to previous results that children's activity participation and indicators of social class are strongly associated, with parents' education level being the most consistent correlate. Watching TV and "hanging out" were associated with lower SES, while participation in sports and time spent reading were associated with higher SES. These results suggest that children's participation in structured activities (e.g., hobbies, lessons, sports) is the most "development-enhancing" way for them to spend their time.

For older children, such organized activities as sports, lessons, youth groups, and community and recreation centers provide supervision, structure, learning and practicing skills, and instruction. Formal after-school arrangements that provide cognitive stimulation and positive adult interactions have been associated with higher academic achievement among low-income children (Pierce, Hamm, & Vandell, 1999; Posner & Vandell, 1994, 1999). Werner (1993) notes the importance of structured activities (e.g., hobbies) in accounting for children's differential reactions to stressful family circumstances. Thus, participation in structured activities may be especially important for children living in poverty because of their increased risk of experiencing family stress. Unfortunately, research indicates that low-income children are the least likely to engage in these types of structured activities. Children from more affluent families are more likely to be enrolled in lessons, organized sports, or clubs than children from low-income families (Hofferth et al., 1991). Low-income parents rely more on community centers and such national youth-serving organizations as the Boys' and Girls' Clubs and the YMCA as out-of-school arrangements (Halpern, 1999; Pettit et al., 1997).

Middle- and upper-income parents have greater resources to place their children in more expensive enrichment programs during their out-of-school time (Vandell & Posner, 1999). Higher income parents also are more likely to avail themselves of school-based programs or lessons for their children's out-of-school time (Halpern,

1999; Pettit et al., 1997). In addition to low-income parents lacking the monetary resources to place their children in structured activities, there may also be a limited amount of opportunities to engage in structured activities in the communities where these children live, either because these communities lack the necessary resources to offer such activities or because of other barriers such as transportation or perceived safety. The types of activities that are available to low-income children, the environments in which low-income children spend their time when their mothers work, and how these environments affect their development need more attention in both research and policy arenas.

Familial Pathways

Role modeling. Perhaps the most common familial process theory driving the 1996 welfare legislation was the idea that parents who work would provide a positive model of work for their children. Some believe that, in comparison with children not raised in welfare households, children raised in a household that receives welfare may be less likely to attach a stigma to participation in the welfare system, will be more knowledgeable of how the system operates, and will thus be more likely to receive welfare themselves as adults and less likely to invest in human capital (Levine & Zimmerman, 2000).

Therefore, a motivating force behind the 1996 welfare legislation was the idea that moving parents from welfare to work would present children with role models of work and self-sufficiency, a concept some call the "family reinforcing effect" (Hao et al., 2001), as opposed to promoting a welfare culture that encourages dependency. Welfare receipt has been hypothesized as influencing the attitudes and values of parents and their motivation for employment. Some believe that this "welfare culture" emphasizes deviant values, attitudes, and behaviors about work that are transmitted to children through the parenting process (see Hofferth et al., 2000). Some fear that children whose parents do not work may not realize the importance of links between school completion and career attainment and thus may be less motivated to complete school themselves. However, existing research suggests that *level* of income, rather than the *source* of that income, is the most important determinant of children's educational outcomes.

Findings that children whose parents participated in welfare and employment programs that provided wage supplements if they worked part or full time did better in school than children whose mothers were working but not receiving extra money (Morris et al., 2001) suggest that presenting children with models of work is not sufficient to produce positive effects on their academic outcomes and reinforce the idea that income matters most. Thus, the existing data suggest that role modeling is not the primary way in which effects on parents translate to positive educational effects for children.

Given the current emphasis by educators and policymakers alike regarding the importance of educational attainment for children's future success, it is interesting that the notion of parents serving as role models for their children encompasses only work activities and is not extended to parents' engagement in educational activities as part of welfare reform policy. As pointed out by Shields and Behrman (2002), providing children with a model for education (i.e., parent going to school) may be as important as or more important than seeing a parent go to work. This hypothesis was used to support the creation of several state programs (primarily in California) that offered basic education and skill building as an alternative to job searches. The effects of these types of programs on children's educational outcomes, however, were never examined.

Many believe that role modeling is a primary pathway through which the "cycle of dependency" could be broken and children's attitudes and values toward work positively affected (i.e., moving parents into work would provide their children with positive role models for work). Others have argued that having a parent working in *any* job may do more harm than good for both parents and their children, particularly if job quality (e.g., wages, complexity, benefits) is low. For example, if parents are working significantly more after welfare reform in order to make ends meet, there may be adverse effects on parent well-being (e.g., increases in stress and depression) as well as parent-child interactions (e.g., amount of time spent at home monitoring, supervising, and interacting with children). Thus, others have concentrated on familial processes such as parenting and parents' psychological well-being (rather than role modeling) as the critical pathway to children's academic motivation and performance.

Parenting and parent-child relationships. It follows from an ecological perspective on human development (Bronfenbrenner, 1979) that agencies, institutions, and social policies aimed at the family environment have strong influences on parenting processes and parent-child relationships (Weiss & Halpern, 1991). Welfare reform can affect children's development through the behavior of parents (Zill & Schoenborn, 1990), and specifically parent-child interactions (Zaslow, Tout, et al., 1998).

Some argue that welfare participation produces or encourages a sort of complacency in parents that becomes reflected in the home environment (Rector & Fagan, 2001), such as a lack of motivation to invest in the developmental needs of their children. In turn, children's early success in school may be negatively affected because of problems with self-control or ability to delay gratification (Levine & Zimmerman, 2000). In contrast, others argue that the "work-first" approach may interfere with effective parenting and positive parent-child relationships.

The transition from welfare to work has many potential benefits for parents and children, but it may also have negative implications for family functioning, parental well-being (e.g., stress, self-esteem), parenting styles (e.g., warmth, cognitive stimulation), and child outcomes (e.g., social and cognitive outcomes, achievement, health). Experiences at work influence parents' expectations for their children's future, parenting practices, the quality of the home environment, and the behaviors and values parents encourage in their children (Bronfenbrenner, 1986; Kohn & Schooler, 1982; McLoyd, 1989; Menaghan & Parcel, 1995; Zaslow & Emig, 1997).

The degree to which parents influence their children's development has been a highly controversial issue in recent years (see Harris, 1998; Rowe, 1994), although research suggests that parents can have a significant effect on children's cognitive development. In addition to economic security and access to other supports and services (e.g., education, health and child care), children's educational development is also promoted by positive and stable parent-child relationships (Collins & Aber, 1997). Thus, it is important that families have the time and capacity to form these relationships, which may be hindered by the stress and time that accompany working 40 hours or more to make ends meet.

Income and education gains often lead to changes in the home environment. For example, parents may provide more cognitive stimulation to their children through increased material resources and activities (Bradley et al., 1994), both of which are linked to positive educational outcomes for children. Research shows that books, computers, and trips make a difference to children's achievement in the summer, when high-SES children improve their academic skills and low-SES children lose ground (Entwisle, Alexander, & Olson, 1997). The relationship between the home environment and such educational outcomes as school readiness, language development, intelligence, and achievement in reading and math persists even after control for numerous family and demographic characteristics (Duncan, Brooks-Gunn, & Klebanov, 1994; NICHD Early Child Care Network, 2000; Zaslow, McGroder, Cave, & Mariner, 1999; Zaslow, McGroder, et al., 1999). Furthermore, quality of home environment predicts participation in early childhood programs; specifically, the more cognitive stimulation and emotional support children receive, the more likely they are to be involved in early childhood programs, even when maternal literacy, education, and employment are controlled (Zaslow et al., 1998).

Research on children's early development, including brain development, demonstrates that the quality of parent-child relationships has a significant impact on later developmental outcomes, including social competence and performance in school (Shore, 1997), which in turn are predictive of later adult outcomes such as success with employment. In addition, mothers' warmth and engagement in cognitive stimulation activities are positively associated with cognitive development (e.g., school readiness scores) (Greenstein, 1995; McGroder, 2000; Moore et al., 1995). Furthermore, low parental warmth has been associated with lower achievement (Baldwin, Baldwin, & Cole, 1990; Clark, 1983; Jarrett, 1995; Smith & Brooks-Gunn, 1997).

If having to work more hours postwelfare disrupts family life (e.g., working irregular hours and weekends), negative effects could ensue. However, the income generated by employment may offset negative effects such as decreased parental time and supervision (Desai et al., 1989; Zaslow & Emig, 1997; Zaslow, Rabinovich, & Suwalsky, 1991).

Supports provided by welfare and employment programs may have positive effects on parent-child relationships. One might expect that welfare receipt allows parents to spend more time with children, and this in turn ensures better developmental outcomes for children with a welfare system in place than without one (Gruber, 2000).

Conversely, if a program decreases the amount of time parents are at home with their children, they may be less able to monitor, supervise, and help with or encourage children's engagement in homework, which could result in negative effects on children's educational development.

Research to date has shown that welfare-to-work demonstrations implemented before welfare reform have had minimal effects on parenting (see Morris et al., 2001), although a few findings suggest positive impacts. For instance, among those employed full time at random assignment, the New Hope program appeared to increase quality of parent-child interactions. In their review of seven welfare-to-work programs, Zaslow and her colleagues (2002) found moderate positive effects on parenting coupled with increased family income. Those programs that included a parenting component produced increases in levels of parenting-related activities, but effects on children's growth and development were not measured; however, one could assume that the positive impacts on parenting would translate into positive impacts for children's educational development.

Poor single parents are more punitive, unresponsive, and inconsistent in their parenting (McLoyd & Wilson, 1991), which could have negative effects on children's educational development. For instance, research has shown that this kind of parenting often leads to learning disabilities (see Collins & Aber, 1997). One of the major findings from the New Chance study, which involved observational measures of affective and behavioral qualities of mother-child relationships, was that mothers assigned to the experimental group demonstrated less coercive and punitive behavior toward children than control group mothers, thus suggesting that the New Chance program reduced harsh treatment of children by mothers (Weinfield, Egeland, & Ogawa, 1998). More research is needed to examine whether, within these studies, the increases in positive parent-child relationships translated to improved educational outcomes for children.

In 1994, as part of the "Goals 2000: Educate America Act" (www.ed.gov/pubs/G2KReforming/), a national education goal was set that all children enter school ready to learn. One way in which early childhood programs have attempted to achieve this national goal is by strengthening parent-child relationships; another would be including parenting programs and supports in welfare reform policies. The good news is that some states are indeed using their welfare funds for initiatives whose direct purpose is to improve parenting; these initiatives include home visits to new parents and parenting classes (see www.welfareinfo.org). The policy debates surrounding welfare reform must be broadened beyond employment and income; policymakers should focus on a full array of both basic and specialized supports needed to ensure positive development of low-income children and families. Research suggests that child development programs that are high quality *and* include family-focused supports can reduce the likelihood of poor outcomes for low-income children (Gomby, Larner, Stevenson, Lewit, & Behrman, 1995).

Unfortunately, the debates surrounding welfare reform contained little or no discussion about how the new welfare legislation would affect adolescents. The implied assumption was that younger children would be more affected by single parents moving into the workforce than would older children. However, recent research suggests that welfare reform may have negative implications for adolescents, including their educational development and engagement in deviant behavior. A review of welfare-to-work programs showed that teens in families in which parents worked were more likely than teens in welfare families to be involved in delinquent activities, to have behavior problems at school, and to be suspended at school (Morris et al., 2001).

Specifically, older children in the program groups of the Minnesota Family Investment Program (MFIP), the Self Sufficiency Project (SSP), and the New Hope project (all of which were income supplement programs) were slightly more likely to have declining achievement scores and more behavior problems, including delinquency and suspensions from school. Results from the SSP suggest that participation in the program group hurt adolescents' school performance and resulted in problem behaviors such as drinking and smoking. The MFIP showed similar results for parent-reported school performance among children who entered the program at 10 years of age and older. These recent findings are in line with results of experimental studies conducted in the 1960s and 1970s in which receipt of a guaranteed minimum income had positive effects on school performance and attendance among some children of elementary school age but not among high school adolescents (Mallar & Maynard, 1981; Maynard & Murnane, 1979).

These negative adolescent effects have been primarily attributed to decreases in parental supervision and monitoring and increases in responsibilities in the home (Brooks, Hair, & Zaslow, 2001). When parents work, adolescents receive less supervision from adults, may face greater strains from sharing household responsibilities and caring for younger siblings, or may also work themselves to supplement family income (Children's Defense Fund, 2001). Maternal employment may be linked with poorer outcomes for adolescents because of lack of parental monitoring at a time when peer influences increase, along with independence and temptations (McLoyd, 1993).

Thus, moving parents from welfare to work as a result of PRWORA could have negative impacts through what is referred to as a "family change effect." Specifically, if families' daily routines change dramatically, this may impose increasing stressors on adolescent children and cause reductions in time spent with parental supervision, particularly between the end of school and dinnertime, which is often considered a period in which adolescents may engage in high-risk behavior (Hao et al., 2001). In the case of older children, then, family economic resources may not be enough to promote positive development; instead, supervision, parent-child relationships, and opportunities for mentoring may be just as (or more) critical. This has important implications for policy; specifically, older children may require additional supports and services, such as after-school programs or more income support, as part of welfare policies (Children's Defense Fund, 2001). A key consideration for policymakers should be how to simultaneously support the positive development of adolescents and ensure the economic self-sufficiency of parents.

Parent expectations. Two of the most consistent predictors of children's academic achievement and motivation are parents' expectations and confidence in their children's abilities (Parsons, Adler, & Kaczala, 1982). In fact, parental expectations are stronger predictors of children's academic performance (Parsons et al., 1982) and competence beliefs than are academic grades (Eccles, 1983; Phillips, 1987). Parents who experience economic hardship are less optimistic about the future of their children, which in turn may lower children's own future expectations (McLoyd, 1989). Employment in jobs with reasonable wages, hours, and benefits may raise parents' expectations about their children's futures by increasing not only their optimism and awareness regarding the importance of education for occupational success but also their ability to provide economic support for their children's educational pursuits. Conversely, negative job experiences could lower expectations as a result of parents' awareness of the economic and psychological difficulties facing their children in the future.

There is some research that supports this theory. Ripke, Huston, and Mistry (2001) found that parents' job characteristics (wages, benefits, and work hours) were positively associated with both parents' educational expectations for their children and the children's own aspirations and expectations. Specifically, the more benefits parents' jobs provided and the higher their wages, the higher parents' educational expectations were for their children, and the higher children's occupational aspirations and expectations were for themselves.

In addition, some research shows that mothers who experience substantial increases in income after leaving welfare report feeling more hopeful about their children's futures. Unfortunately, most parents who have left welfare have moved into low-wage jobs with little chance for advancement. This may affect their expectations for their children's future. In other words, data on the types of jobs that people hold after leaving welfare (i.e., low wage, part time, unstable, few benefits) do not offer much hope that parents' expectations for their children will rise upon leaving the welfare rolls.

Psychological well-being. Research has demonstrated that a major way in which family income affects children's developmental outcomes is through its impact on parents' psychological well-being. Living conditions that are pervasively stressful as a result of inadequate income and absence of entitlements and services from welfare programs pose major obstacles for adults' ability to provide attentive parenting (Weiss & Halpern, 1991). Low-income parents face high levels of stress and depression, which may affect parenting styles (Collins & Aber, 1997). Parents' psychological well-being affects their relationship with their children, and research demonstrates that the stress of poverty increases the likelihood of abuse and neglect (Veltkamp & Miller, 1994; Videka-Sherman, 1991). The increased stress placed on low-income families related to time limits, losing cash assistance, and new work requirements may lead to abuse and other forms of maltreatment.

If welfare reform does not increase employment for parents, or if parents are unable to attain and keep a job, their stress and anxiety may increase. Some research suggests that unemployment is associated with more stress than employment, especially for single moms (McLoyd, Jayaratne, Ceballo, & Borquez, 1994). Similarly, if upon leaving welfare parents do find employment, but their job hours are erratic and inconsistent and their wages are low, then their psychological well-being may also decline. Research suggests that the low wages many parents have upon obtaining employment postwelfare may have negative implications for their psychological well-being and parent-child relationships in addition to preventing access to resources. If parents are earning less as a result of the transition from welfare, an increase in parental stress is likely (Menaghan & Parcel, 1995).

To the extent that welfare reform leads to more employment, and employment then leads to more structure and consistency in families' lives through scheduling of time around work, parents' self-efficacy and self-esteem may improve. Development theory suggests that accomplishments such as completing a training program and improved employment prospects for welfare mothers may lead to improvements in their psychological well-being, including increased self-esteem and motivation (Zuckerman & Kalil, 2000). Thus, if working in and of itself (or working in a high-quality job, which is unlikely for most leaving welfare) has a positive impact on parental well-being, then more positive parenting behavior may follow. Some hypothesize that this may be the reason for findings from a study demonstrating that children had higher scores on reading and math in the early years of elementary school when their mothers had been employed than when they had not (Vandell & Ramanan, 1992).

The effects of parents' mental health on their relationships with their children have been well documented (McLoyd & Wilson, 1991). An important factor that might influence the way in which welfare reform policies affect children is maternal depression (Quint et al., 1997), particularly since depression is more prevalent among the poor. Low-income women are approximately twice as likely as higher income mothers to be depressed, and mothers' depression is shown to negatively affect children's cognitive abilities (Alpern & Lyons-Ruth, 1993; Downey & Coyne, 1990). Poor families experience more stress than families that are economically secure (Conger & Elder, 1994; McLoyd, 1990). This increased stress is associated with parental depression, irritability, and less responsive parenting, as well as more punitive, harsh, and inconsistent parenting practices (McLoyd, 1990). The impacts of these parenting styles often lead to psychological problems, learning disabilities, and behavioral disturbances for children. For instance, research shows that children of depressed mothers have difficulties in meeting academic demands (Lennon et al., 2001) and exhibit lower school readiness than children of nondepressed mothers (Estrada, Arsenio, Hess, & Holloway, 1987; McGroder, 2000).

More than two decades of research demonstrates that maternal depression detrimentally affects children by compromising parents' ability to respond to their children and places children at risk for developmental difficulties at all ages, including difficulties in meeting social and academic demands (see Lennon et al., 2001). Stresses associated with depression include poverty (Belle, 1990), unemployment

(Broadhead, Blazer, George, & Tse, 1990; McLoyd, 1993), and lack of social support (Turner, 1999). Women on welfare experience multiple stresses, and welfare reform now poses the threat of benefit loss should they fail to find employment (Lennon et al., 2001).

Using national AFDC data, Zill and colleagues (1991) found lower self-esteem among welfare recipients than nonpoor mothers but no difference between welfare mothers and other poor mothers. For the most part, data suggest few differences between welfare families and low-SES working families in regard to mothers' psychological well-being, suggesting that it is poverty and not welfare use that affects parents' psychological outlook. Mothers in low-income, single-parent working families are just as depressed as women receiving welfare, are just as likely to feel they lack control of their fate and to display hostile parenting, and spend similar amounts of time reading to their children and helping them with homework (Duncan et al., 1998).

Thus far, we have discussed the various pathways by which income, employment, and maternal education may affect a wide array of familial processes, but it should be kept in mind that often many of these processes go hand and hand. In other words, it is very likely that one or more of these processes are operating simultaneously. It is not surprising, then, that research shows that children fare worse when parents have several of these strikes against them, such as low education and income levels, unfavorable work histories, and low levels of psychological well-being (Moore et al., 1995, as cited in Knitzer & Cauthen, 1999).

Overall, the existing data suggest that supported work affects children's educational outcomes more through extrafamilial processes (e.g., child care and after-school programs) than through family processes (e.g., role modeling, psychological well-being, parenting) (see Duncan & Chase-Lansdale, 2001). However, the role of familial processes should not be overlooked. Thus, to the extent that welfare and employment programs can increase the range of supports provided to parents (e.g., income-related as well as parenting and counseling supports), both parents and children will fare more positively. Unfortunately, welfare reform has primarily focused on adults as providers of *economic* support for children. There has not been much of an emphasis in welfare policy on helping parents as providers of *emotional* support for children, including an absence of supports designed to improve parents' own psychological well-being, which in turn would have positive implications for their children's development.

Summary

Findings from research thus far demonstrate that, for children, the most successful welfare reform programs are those that improve parental income and economic security through strongly encouraging and rewarding work. Programs such as New Hope demonstrate that a package of earning supplements, health and child care benefits, and full-time job opportunities can result in modest changes in income, employment, and family resources and thus significantly affect children's educational outcomes. It should be kept in mind, however, that a narrow focus on economic outcomes might understate the effects of programs such as New Hope, whose benefits extend beyond economic outcomes. Those programs that increased employment but failed to raise income did more harm than good for children; therefore, income-reducing programs can be harmful to children.

Programs that target services directly to children have the largest measured effects, while unrestricted cash transfer programs have the smallest, perhaps because their benefits are more diffused or because the amounts of money involved are typically quite small (Currie, 1997). Welfare and employment programs that raise families' income and offer other work supports to parents *and* children, including child care subsidies and financial supports, have the most positive effects on children's overall educational outcomes.

Existing data demonstrate that welfare reform policies have the potential to significantly enhance the achievement of children. Changes outside of the family, such as enrollment in child care and after-school programs, appear to have more positive effects on children than do changes within the family, such as parenting, parental mental health, or other aspects of the home environment (Duncan & Chase-Lansdale, 2001).

It must be kept in mind, however, that welfare reform is not likely to affect all low-income families and children equally. While some may benefit, others may be harmed. For instance, an important conclusion drawn from the existing research is that welfare reform packages affect children differently according to their age or developmental stage. There is significant evidence that welfare policies can be an important factor in enhancing children's achievement in preschool and elementary school; however, in the case of adolescents, lack of adult supervision may compromise their achievement and behavioral outcomes. On average, demonstration programs show more negative outcomes for adolescents than for younger children.

These findings call into question the former conclusion that parents with younger children may require more supports. Instead of parents needing differing *amounts* of support based on the age of their children, it appears that it is the *types* of supports parents need that vary. Thus, states need to be cognizant of how policies can affect children of different ages and make necessary supports available. For instance, allowing exemptions for parents who have children below a certain age and ensuring the availability of after-school programs for teens could help.

There is an ongoing debate between those individuals having a primarily economic perspective and individuals with a child development perspective regarding whether investments in the future economic productivity of children (e.g., child care, early childhood education and interventions) should be evaluated by the extent to which they can produce long-term effects on adult attainment (including educational attainment and income) or whether quality of life during childhood should be a sufficient goal in its own right. Although academics, child advocates, and public educators acknowledge the importance of children's achievement in terms of later adult outcomes and future productivity, they also agree that children have the right to experience quality environments in childhood, whether or not they ultimately demonstrate positive, measurable achievement outcomes 10 to 20 years later (Huston, 2002). Thus, Huston (2002) poses the following question: Is it enough to say that investments in children are worthy in their own right, or must outcomes be documented 10 to 20 years later in order to be "policy relevant" or worthy of attention and funding from policymakers?

Referring to welfare reform as an "overwhelming success" for parents and children is premature. While some random assignment experiments have shown positive effects for low-income children whose parents work full time, a few important points must be kept in mind. First, many of the studies reviewed here included work supports more generous than existing state policies. Second, as Duncan and Chase-Lansdale point out (2001), the success of some of these programs in helping to reduce poverty and promote children's health and development should not mask the fact that numerous problems (e.g., poor psychological and physical health, domestic violence) still exist in many of the families that engaged in programs offering work supports. Thus, we still need to address these families' most pressing issues (e.g., barriers to employment, low education levels).

Furthermore, the policy picture changes when welfare reform is examined with the needs of young children and adolescents in mind. Although children may benefit from the increased family income that leaving welfare for work may provide families—which research shows is *not* the case for many families—children may be simultaneously harmed by reductions in parental supervision and the quality of parent-child relationships. Thus, additional measures must be taken to ensure children's positive development in the context of welfare reform (see Collins & Aber, 1997). Low-income children, as do all children, need regular health care and positive learning experiences, as well as nurturing parent-child relationships (Cauthen & Knitzer, 1999). Older children need adult supervision and monitoring at a time in their lives when peer and delinquent behaviors are most influential.

The good news is there is a large body of research over the last decade demonstrating that for children at risk, including those living in poverty, child development and family support programs can make a difference by promoting successful school performance and reducing the risk of involvement with special education (Gomby et al., 1995). Thus, supports offered via welfare programs could provide opportunities to improve and foster positive educational outcomes for children.

The interconnectedness of parental employment, educational levels, and child well-being should not be ignored, and steps to improve each of these should not be approached independently. Currently, one of the main goals of educators and policymakers in this country is for all children to enter school ready to learn. If this goal is to be achieved, it is important that we address issues critical to ensuring families' economic well-being (e.g., parental employment) and human capital (e.g., maternal education level). Because there is evidence suggesting that increases in maternal education levels will lead to improvements for both mothers and their children, welfare policies that include opportunities for increasing maternal education levels would seem to involve payoffs for parents as well as children. More experimental studies such as the one conducted by Magnuson and McGroder (2001) are needed.

Policymakers may be persuaded to mix a "work-first" approach with opportunities for educational development if a causal link can be established between gains in maternal education and improved educational outcomes for children. Regardless of the pathways by which children's educational outcomes are affected (i.e., familial, nonfamilial, or both), family income and maternal education level—and not welfare receipt per se (role modeling, welfare culture, lack of motivation attitudes)—appear to have the largest impacts on children's academic outcomes; thus, welfare policies designed with the opportunity to increase at least one, but ideally both, would produce the most beneficial outcomes for children.

RECOMMENDATIONS AND CONCLUSION

What Lies Ahead: Recommendations for the Next Stage of Welfare Reform

In the first 6 years of PRWORA's implementation, rates of entry into the labor force were unexpectedly high, and caseloads declined precipitously. The new work-focused policies in combination with a robust economy were credited with making the first wave of welfare reform a "success." Few families, however, are financially better off today than under the old AFDC system. Evidence suggests that a majority of welfare leavers are in low-wage, low-quality jobs with few benefits, and they are likely to cycle between welfare and such jobs. Moreover, although child poverty rates have declined in the past few years, the number of children in "working poor" families has increased. Finally, in 2002, more than 2 million families remain on welfare and at risk of having their benefits terminated. The next stage of welfare reform therefore holds several challenges for policymakers and program administrators. How can the welfare system evolve more fully into an effective work-support system? And, provided that improving the well-being of low-income families and children is indeed a goal of reform policies, what else must be done?

The present review of how welfare policy intersects with education has several implications for policy and research. A growing body of literature demonstrates that work-based welfare policies have the potential to either benefit or harm low-income families and children, although widespread effects in either direction have not been found. A popular belief at the outset of PRWORA was that work in and of itself would benefit families, but it is clear that the effects on families of the federal, state, and community policies described broadly as "welfare reform" are much more complicated. Research efforts designed to clarify the processes by which these effects occur are ongoing, yet emerging findings suggest that how families fare in welfare-to-work programs depends in part on the specific policies or policy packages facing families (these vary greatly across states and communities); the types of employment, earnings, and noncash benefits secured by families under these policies; and the types of child care and out-of-school activities children experience as a result of changes in parental employment and family resources.

Recommendations for Policy

Ongoing debates concerning the future of welfare reform include the following: level of federal funding for TANF block grants to states, extent and definition of work requirements, amount of flexibility afforded to states, time limits, level of funding for such work supports as health care and child care, and benefits for immigrant families. There is also growing support on both sides of the political spectrum to make child well-being an explicit goal of welfare policy.

"Work-Focused" Adult Education and Training

Serious questions exist about the ability of welfare recipients to find and maintain employment and about the quality of this employment. The low-wage jobs that many welfare leavers obtained during the post-TANF years are *not* likely to lead to self-sufficiency in the short term or to increased wages or better jobs in the long term (Burtless, 1995; Danziger et al., 2000; Edin & Lein, 1997). Reauthorization discussions should therefore consider strategies to improve job quality, job retention, and advancement, particularly if poverty reduction is added as a goal of reform efforts.

States' initial responses to PRWORA were to limit educational opportunities. The demanding work requirements, narrow definition of allowable activities, and stringent time limits created disincentives for states to invest in education and training programs for low-income adults. However, in light of persistent poverty despite employment, evidence of cycling, and the possibility of a recession, many states are now reconsidering the role of education and training in improving outcomes for the working poor. In fact, in its policy position on welfare reauthorization, the National Governors Association asserts that states need to do more to promote job retention, job advancement, and wage growth and identifies expanded education and training initiatives as an important tool for doing so.

Historically, efforts to increase human capital for welfare recipients have focused on basic education and skills; although necessary, these are most likely insufficient to improve employment and earning prospects. Several recent studies suggest that "mixed" approaches may be more effective than either "work-first" or "education-first" approaches alone. Such approaches have often led to increased employment and earnings, and they may even be more effective and less costly than "work-first" strategies in the long run. Recent data suggest that increasing parents' education has positive effects on children's achievement. Therefore, families and children may receive benefits from human capital development that go beyond effects on parental employment and earnings.

States currently have several options for expanding education and training opportunities. Within the TANF system, states have had some flexibility in defining allowable "work activities," and because of the large decline in caseloads, they have been able to use TANF/Maintenance of Effort funds to suspend time limits and to provide cash assistance, tuition assistance, and supports (e.g., child care and health care) to those involved in education and training. Another suggestion for funding would be to help colleges and other educational providers redesign their curricula to address the needs of low-income students.

Postsecondary education appears to have been an underused option during the first wave of welfare reform. Postsecondary education is not always accessible or practical for working parents, and furthermore, the PRWORA legislation included no incentives for states to support this type of educational activity. To encourage postsecondary education, states could expand financial aid to low-income students; provide outreach and financial incentives for enrollment and completion; provide supports for child care, housing, and transportation (especially for work in the evenings or on weekends); establish mentoring programs; and involve employers in program design as well as training and retention initiatives. States, agencies, and colleges can create partnerships and coordinate funding streams to accomplish several of these goals (see Golonka & Matus-Grossman, 2001, for examples).

Although proposals to do some of these things have received support from policymakers and program administrators, including the National Governors Association (2002), President Bush's budget proposal for fiscal year 2003 included deep cuts (totaling $309.8 million) to employment and job training programs. Moreover, the White House proposal included a stricter work requirement (a proposed increase from 30 to 40 hours per week with up to 2 days a week allowed for educational activities) and greater work participation rates (a proposed increase from 50% to 70% of caseloads by 2007). The proposed changes to the work requirement and participation rates are likely to force most states to devote extensive amounts of energy and funds to moving even more people into the workforce in a short time period. Therefore, despite the allowance of 16 hours for education and training, it is unclear how this will be carried out and how many resources states will have left to develop human capital development initiatives.

Education and training are clearly not the only strategies needed to improve the well-being of families, and specifically the educational outcomes of children. Substantial experimental data indicate that programs that improve children's academic functioning feature strong financial incentives for work (e.g., income supplements), coupled with such work supports as child and health care subsidies. Parental employment without these kinds of supports, however, does not appear to benefit children and may in fact be detrimental to some groups of families and children (particularly adolescents). The benefits provided in the financial incentive programs evaluated in these studies are more generous than what is currently provided in most states, suggesting that federal and state policies have not yet gone far enough to ensure that families will indeed be better off financially (and otherwise) after leaving welfare.

Reconsidering Time Limits

Early estimates suggested that a large proportion of families would be affected by the new time limits on cash assistance (Duncan, Harris, & Boisjoy, 1997; Pavetti, 1995). It was predicted that the loss of income assistance and supports would increase the number of families unable to provide basic food and shelter for children (National Center for Children in Poverty, 1999). Preschoolers in families who have lost benefits owing to time limits or sanctions have been found to perform worse on cognitive achievement tests than other low-income children, including those who are still on welfare. Because time limits have largely taken effect only recently, their full impact on children and families remains unclear and will be an important topic for research in the coming years.

There is little evidence to suggest that welfare receipt in and of itself is harmful; living in poverty affects children similarly regardless of whether families' income comes primarily from cash assistance or wages (Chase-Lansdale & Brooks-Gunn, 1995; Zill & Coiro, 1989). In fact, many families cycle between employment and welfare or combine the two (especially in states with high "earning disregards") in order to sustain themselves. If child well-being is of interest, the notion of definitively removing the "safety net" for poor families after an arbitrary time period must be reconsidered.

Cross-study comparisons as part of the Next Generation project suggest that programs that provided financial supports (e.g., earning supplements) for at least 3 years had more positive effects on children than those with time-limited benefits (Morris, Knox, & Gennetian, 2002). Time limits are intended to induce families to leave welfare quickly or at least to reduce long-term dependence. The Next Generation findings, however, underscore the notion that working poor families most likely need, and can benefit from, continued financial assistance.

Work Supports

Like all parents, low-income parents require certain support services to effectively meet both work and family responsibilities. Parents need to have safe, nurturing, and reliable care for their children; transportation to and from work and child care settings; and access to basic health care for themselves and their children. Low-income, single mothers (the primary population affected by welfare reform) face considerable challenges to securing all of the resources needed to successfully obtain and maintain employment while adequately caring for their children. The 1996 legislation, as well as states' implementation of the new law, included some recognition of the need for work supports. Notably, funding for child care tripled, and subsidies for such supports as transportation have often been available. Many of these supports, however, are often only "transitional" in nature, expiring a year or two after a parent has become employed. This is the case even though many low-income parents will not exhibit significant earning gains because of job instability and limited opportunities for advancement in the low-wage job sector. Also, available supports and services are not at a level that is sufficient to meet demand; for example, many states maintain waiting lists for child care subsidies.

It has already been mentioned that extension of time limits may be one way to address the continued need for supports among the growing population of working poor families. Another recommendation is to effectively separate these supports from the TANF system. Although families are typically eligible for such work supports as food stamps, Medicaid, and child care subsidies regardless of TANF receipt, research suggests that many are not receiving these supports. Parents are often confused or misinformed about their eligibility and are often dissuaded from applying given the substantial administrative hurdles that often exist. Outreach is needed to ensure that eligible families receive the supports and services that are critical to their self-sufficiency efforts. In addition, the evolution of the welfare system into a work-support system surely necessitates increased funding for these supports.

Child care as a component of welfare reform has recently received increased attention in research and policy arenas because of its dual role as a support for parental employment and a context for child development. In this review, we have highlighted the importance of early childhood care environments for children's academic development and have discussed several recommendations for policy. On the basis of experimental data of how welfare policies can affect family and child well-being, it is clear that the welfare policy debate can and should be broadened beyond the outcomes of employment and income. The consistent finding that programs with the most generous work supports benefited children the most suggests that states must go beyond work mandates and supply rewards or supports for mandated work. At this time, it remains unclear which particular features of these programs promoted children's achievement; however, as suggested by Duncan and Chase-Lansdale (2001), it may be unnecessary to identify the specific pathways of influence to implement successful programs on a larger scale. In fact, the success of programs such as New Hope may be due in part to their offer of a wide variety of flexible supports. In other words, pathways of influence may differ across diverse families and circumstances.

Finally, in addition to the work supports discussed earlier, many low-income families require interventions for such specialized needs as mental health issues, substance abuse, and domestic violence. Not only do these issues represent serious barriers to employment, but they also have obvious implications for parental and child well-being. Because it is apparent that welfare-to-work transitions are unlikely to produce large, favorable changes in family functioning and child development, the essential issue of welfare reform may be one of more selective supports for the subsets of families whose transition from welfare to work will be the most difficult (Duncan et al., 1998).

Recommendations for Research

Evaluations of the effects of welfare reform on families and children are still in their infancy, and continued research efforts are needed to understand the long-term effects of the new (and ever changing) policies. As we have already noted, it will be particularly important to follow what happens as families are sanctioned and reach time limits. Here we identify some specific gaps in the literature and suggest topics for future research.

More data are clearly needed concerning the effectiveness of a range of human capital development strategies in improving the types of jobs people obtain as they leave welfare. Initiatives that strongly link education and training to work seem promising but need to be further evaluated (preferably using random assignment experiments). There is also a need to further evaluate two-generation programs that address the educational needs of parents and children. Such programs as Head Start may increase parents' earning capacities, while they also provide high-quality early childhood services to children. The literature suggests that successful programs have dealt with the child as part of the family and with the family as part of a community.

A second general area for ongoing and future research concerns the specific ways policies help or harm children and why. In other words, what are the pathways of influence? Currently, more support exists for a resource model suggesting that environments outside the home (child care and activities) play a role in how children are affected by welfare and employment polices; however, much more information is needed. Related to questions about pathways, more research is needed on how characteristics of parents' jobs (e.g., quality, schedule, stability, wages, complexity, satisfaction) affect children's educational outcomes. Also, what is the link between a mother's educational activities and her children's outcomes? Specifically, we know little about how policy-induced changes in the former affect the latter. A recent nonexperimental analysis of the child outcome sample in the NEWWS suggests that children benefit academically from program-induced increases in their mothers' education level (Magnuson & McGroder, 2001).

More research is also needed on how the effects of welfare and employment policies differ for different kinds of families and under different circumstances. Groups of interest include adults with several barriers to employment and self-sufficiency (specifically human capital barriers, and those beyond mental and physical limitations), different age groups (e.g., adolescents), and immigrant families and their children.

Immigrant families have been placed in a position of increased risk because of the 1996 reforms, which denied benefits to most noncitizens. Approximately 27% of poor children are either immigrants or children of immigrants (Greenberg, 2001). Latinos already have the lowest education levels and highest dropout rates. The diversity of living situations in immigrant families often jeopardizes poor children's access to services. Children may be eligible citizens even if their parents are not, or children may be legally in the country but not eligible for benefits (although parents are eligible). Siblings may also differ in their citizenship (Brady, 1998). A report from the Urban Institute on immigrant outcomes indicates that between 1994 and 1997, benefit use dropped by 35% for noncitizen households with children, as compared with 14% for citizen households with children (Capps et al., 2002). In the Three-City Study, native-born children of noncitizen immigrants received less cash assistance (TANF) in all three cities (2,400 low-income families), and a larger percentage of Mexican Americans than African Americans and other Hispanics lacked health coverage for children.

Substantial diversity exists not only in the families affected by welfare reform but also in the contexts in which these families live. Policies and their effects are by no means uniform across states or localities; indeed, one of the major legacies of PRWORA is the devolution from federal to state authority. State- and community-level differences in policy and context (e.g., employment markets and resource availability) are likely to have important implications for how families are faring. National data sources and welfare waiver evaluations do not provide an adequate or thorough understanding of the effects of state-specific programs; in addition to these, child and family outcome data at the state level are needed. The Project on State-Level Child Outcomes, sponsored by the U.S. Department of Health and Human Services through the Administration for Children and Families and the Office of the Assistant Secretary for Planning and Evaluation, represents an important new data source on how children and families have been affected by state-specific policies (Le Menestrel, Tout, McGroder, Zaslow, & Moore, 1999).

As mentioned earlier, a recommendation for both policy and research is that the two be more interconnected. In addition to the research community, other "voices" should also be included in the policy debates. Program administrators interacting with this population have important insights. For example, Knitzer and Cauthen (1999) argue that early childhood programs should have the opportunity to participate in policy discussions of TANF and to coordinate with state and community welfare administrators given their direct contact with the families and children being affected by reform policies. Adult educators are another potentially important resource often left out of the discourse.

Concluding Remarks

While attention to the educational outcomes of poor adults decreased post-1996 given PRWORA's emphasis on rapid employment, the educational outcomes of poor children have received increased attention in recent years. The current administration has placed improving education at the top of the domestic agenda. In the interest of future employability and self-sufficiency, President Bush emphasizes that we must "leave no child behind." It is clear, however, that children's outcomes depend heavily on what is happening to the adults in their families. The welfare and employment behavior of parents appears to affect children primarily via the pathways of income and education, rather than through effects on parent psychological well-being or parent-child relations, including role modeling. As such, the "new" educational goals for children cannot and will not be met without improving the financial and human capital resources of families.

President Bush claimed that the work component of the 1996 law "dramatically improved" the lives of poor people and ended generations of dependence; however, this assertion overlooks the fact that many families—working families—are not better off and still live in poverty. If "the overall goal of TANF reauthorization is child well-being," as the administration has suggested, poverty reduction must be a priority. To accomplish this, policies could (a) provide the educational and support services needed to ensure the type of employment and earnings necessary to sustain families above poverty, (b) ensure that the jobs that people are able to take pay a living wage (and research has shown that they do not), and (c) acknowledge and address the continued need for cash assistance if wages are not increased. Income supplements may be appropriate given the lack of wage growth in these types of jobs. The appropriateness of time limits must also be reconsidered; time limits mean that the cycling pattern characteristic of low-wage work will no longer be an option for families.

There are many trade-offs for families struggling to balance family and work demands in the context of the new welfare system. Parents may be working more and relying less on public assistance, but it does not appear to be generally the case that they (or their children) face fewer constraints, stresses, or risks as a result. In theory, employment and financial independence could free low-income parents from the stigma and limitations of relying on welfare. In ethnographic interviews during the early years of PRWORA, many welfare recipients were optimistic. They expressed their own eagerness to work and leave welfare, but they also expressed concerns about the effects on family life and, most important, on their children (Scott, Edin, London, & Mazelis, 2001). In reality, a growing body of research suggests that many families are facing difficult trade-offs between work and family demands.

The key components of the 1996 welfare reform law focused heavily on changing the *behaviors* rather than the *resources* of welfare recipients. The underlying assumption is that poverty and joblessness are caused by negative personal characteristics (e.g., lack of effort). This sentiment is communicated further through policies that focus on the formation of two-parent, married families as the primary way to ensure positive outcomes for children. As D'Amico (1999) points out, these assumptions ignore the influence of such structural factors as the employment market and the lack of national child care and health care systems.

We are currently in a "critical period" concerning federal policies aimed at low-income families. In the next stage of welfare reform, states will likely face increased federal work participation requirements. As the economic growth of the 1990s slows, many states may be faced with difficult decisions of how to allocate resources between their remaining welfare caseloads (likely to include the most disadvantaged families) and support programs for a now sizable number of working poor families. Poor families may be entering a period of particular vulnerability as the safety net shrinks, the economy weakens, and federal time limits on assistance take effect.

At the same time, however, the future of welfare reform need not be so bleak. Policymakers and program administrators have access to a substantial and growing body of research that identifies ways to move beyond the initial goals of caseload reduction and self-sufficiency to reduce poverty and actually improve the well-being of disadvantaged families and children. Increased access to education and opportunities for educational success not only benefit individuals but contribute to the well-being and productivity of society.

248

REFERENCES

Acs, G., & Loprest, P. (2001). *Initial synthesis report of the findings from ASPE's leavers' grants.* Washington, DC: U.S. Department of Health and Human Services, Office of the Assistant Secretary for Planning and Evaluation.

Ahluwalia, S. K., McGroder, S. M., Zaslow, M. J., & Hair, E. C. (2001). *Symptoms of depression among welfare recipients: A concern for two generations.* Washington, DC: Child Trends.

Alessandri, S. M. (1992). Effects of maternal work status in single-parent families on children's perception of self and family and school achievement. *Journal of Experimental Child Psychology, 54,* 417–433.

Allen, L., Cipielewski, J., & Stanovich, K. E. (1992). Multiple indicators of children's reading habits and attitudes: Construct validity and cognitive correlates. *Journal of Educational Psychology, 84,* 489–503.

Alpern, L. & Lyons-Ruth, K. (1993). Preschool children at social risk: Chronicity and timing of maternal depressive symptoms and child behavior problems at school and at home. *Development and Psychopathology, 5,* 371–387.

Angel, R., Lein, L., Henrici, J., & Leventhal, E. (2001). *Health insurance coverage for children and their caregivers in low-income neighborhoods.* Austin: University of Texas.

Baldwin, A. L., Baldwin, C., & Cole, R. E. (1990). Stress-resistant families and stress-resistant children. In J. Rolf, A. S. Masten, D. Chichetti, K. H. Neuchterlein, & S. Weintraub (Eds.), *Risk and protective factors in the development of psychopathology* (pp. 257–280). New York: Cambridge University Press.

Bane, M. J., & Ellwood, D. T. (1994). *Welfare realities: From rhetoric to reform.* Cambridge, MA: Harvard University Press.

Barnett, W. S. (1995). Long-term effects of early childhood programs on cognitive and school outcomes. *Future of Children, 5,* 25–50.

Barton, J., Aldridge, J., & Smith, P. (1998). The emotional impact of shift work on the children of shift workers. *Scandinavian Journal of Work, Environment and Health, 24,* 146–150.

Barton, P. E., & Jenkins, L. (1995). *Literacy and dependency: The literacy skills of welfare recipients in the United States.* Princeton, NJ: Educational Testing Service.

Baydar, N., & Brooks-Gunn, J. (1991). Effects of maternal employment and child-care arrangements on preschoolers' cognitive and behavioral outcomes: Evidence from the children of the National Longitudinal Study of Youth. *Developmental Psychology, 27,* 932–945.

Baydar, N., Brooks-Gunn, J., & Furstenberg, F. F. (1993). Early warning signs of functional literacy: Predictors in childhood and adolescence. *Child Development, 64,* 815–829.

Bee, H. L., Barnard, K. E., Eyres, S. J., Gray, C. A., Hammond, M. A., Spietz, A. L., Snyder, C., & Clark, B. (1982). Prediction of IQ and language skill from perinatal status, child performance, family characteristics, and mother-infant interaction. *Child Development, 53,* 1134–1156.

Belle, D. (1990). Poverty and women's mental health. *American Psychologist, 45,* 385–389.

Besharov, D. R., & Germanis, P. (2002). Introduction. In D. R. Besharov (Ed.), *Family well-being after welfare reform.* College Park: Maryland School of Public Affairs, Welfare Reform Academy.

Bianchi, S., & McArthur, E. (1993). *Characteristics of children who are "behind" in school.* Paper presented at the annual meeting of the American Statistical Association, San Francisco, CA.

Blank, R., & Schmidt, L. (2001). Work, wages, and welfare. In R. M. Blank & R. Haskins (Eds.), *The new world of welfare.* Washington, DC: Brookings Institution.

Bloom, D. (1997). *After AFDC: Welfare-to-work choices and challenges for states.* New York: Manpower Demonstration Research Corporation.

Bos, J. (1996). *Effects of education and educational credentials on the earnings of economically disadvantaged young mothers*. New York: Manpower Demonstration Research Corporation.

Bos, J. M., Scrivener, S., Snipes, J., & Hamilton, G. (2001). *Improving basic skills: The effects of adult education in welfare-to-work programs*. Washington, DC: U.S. Departments of Education and Health and Human Services.

Bradley, R. H., Whiteside, L., Mundfrom, D. J., Casey, P. H., Kelleher, K. J., & Pope, S. K. (1994). Early indications of resilience and their relation to experiences in the home environments of low birthweight, premature children living in poverty. *Child Development, 65,* 346–360.

Brady, S. A. (1998). *ONE IN TEN: Protecting children's access to federal public benefits under the new welfare and immigration laws*. Washington, DC: National Association of Child Advocates.

Broadhead, W. E., Blazer, D. G., George, L. K., & Tse, C. K. (1990). Depression, disability days and days lost from work in a prospective epidemiological survey. *Journal of the American Medical Association, 264,* 2524–2528.

Bronfenbrenner, U. (1979). *The ecology of human development: Experiments by nature and design*. Cambridge, MA: Harvard University Press.

Bronfenbrenner, U. (1986). Ecology of the family as a context for human development: Research perspectives. *Developmental Psychology, 22,* 723–742.

Brooks, J. L., Hair, E. C., & Zaslow, M. J. (2001). *Welfare reform's impact on adolescents: Early warning signs*. Washington, DC: Child Trends.

Brooks-Gunn, J., Guo, G., & Furstenberg, F. (1993). Who drops out and who continues beyond high school? A twenty-year follow-up of Black urban youth. *Journal of Research on Adolescence, 3,* 271–294.

Brown-Lyons, M., Robertson, A., & Layzer, J. (2001). *Kith and kin—Informal child care: Highlights from recent research*. New York: Columbia School of Public Health, National Center for Children in Poverty.

Burtless, G. (1995). Employment prospects of welfare recipients. In D. Smith Nightingale & R. H. Haveman (Eds.), *The work alternative: Welfare reform and the realities of the job market*. Washington, DC: Urban Institute Press.

Cameron, S., & Heckman, J. (1993). The nonequivalence of high school equivalents. *Journal of Labor Economics, 11,* 1–47.

Cappizano, J., & Adams, G. (2000a). *The hours that children under five spend in child care: Variation across states*. Washington, DC: Urban Institute Press.

Cappizano, J., & Adams, G. (2000b). *The number of child care arrangements used by children under five: Variation across states*. Washington, DC: Urban Institute Press.

Capps, R., Leighton, K., Fix, M. E., Furgiulel, C., Passel, J. S., Ramchand, R., McNiven, S., & Perez-Lopez, D. (2002). *How are immigrants faring after welfare reform? Preliminary evidence from Los Angeles and New York City*. Washington, DC: Urban Institute.

Carnevale, A. P., & Desrochers, D. M. (1999). *Getting down to business: Matching welfare recipients' skills to jobs that train*. Princeton, NJ: Educational Testing Service.

Casey, T. (1998). *Welfare reform and its impact in the nation and in New York*. New York: Federation of Protestant Welfare Agencies.

Cauthen, N. K., & Knitzer, J. (1999). *Beyond work: Strategies to promote the well-being of young children and families in the context of welfare reform* (Children and Welfare Reform Issue Brief 6). New York: Columbia School of Public Health, National Center for Children in Poverty.

Chase-Lansdale, P. L., & Brooks-Gunn, J. (1995). *Escape from poverty: What makes a difference for children*. New York: Cambridge University Press.

Chase-Lansdale, P. L., & Pittman, L. D. (2002). Welfare reform and parenting: Reasonable expectations. *Children and Welfare Reform, 12,* 167–185.

Children's Defense Fund. (2001). *Issue basics: Children and welfare.* Retrieved from http://www.cdfactioncouncil.org

Clark, R. (1983). *Family life and school achievement: Why poor Black children succeed or fail.* Chicago: University of Chicago Press.

Cohen, M. (1998a). Education and training under welfare reform. *Education and Training, 2*(2), 1–10.

Cohen, M. (1998b). Post-secondary education under welfare reform. *WIN Issue Notes, 2*(8). Retrieved November 16, 2001, from http://www.welfareinfo.org/vocational%20ed.htm

Coley, R., Kuta, A., & Chase-Lansdale, L. (2000). An insider view: Knowledge and opinions of welfare from African American girls in poverty. *Journal of Social Issues, 56*, 707–726.

Collins, A., & Aber, J. L. (1996). *State welfare waiver evaluations: Will they increase our understanding of the impact of welfare reform on children?* New York: Columbia School of Public Health, National Center for Children in Poverty.

Collins, A., & Aber, J. L. (1997). *How welfare reform can help or hurt children* (Children and Welfare Reform Issue Brief 1). New York: Columbia School of Public Health, National Center for Children in Poverty.

Collins, M. A., & Brick, J. M. (1993). *Children's academic progress and school adjustment.* Ft. Lauderdale, FL: American Statistical Association.

Conger, R. D., & Elder, G. H. Jr. (1994). *Families in troubled times: Adapting to change in rural America.* New York: Aldine de Gruyter.

Corcoran, M. (1995). Rags to rags: Poverty and mobility in the United States. *Annual Review of Sociology, 21*, 237–267.

Crosby, D. A., Gennetian, L. A., & Huston, A. C. (2001). *Does child care assistance matter? The effects of welfare and employment policies on child care for preschool and young school-aged children.* New York: Manpower Demonstration Research Corporation.

Currie, J. (1997). *The effect of welfare on child outcomes: What we know and what we need to know* (Economic Growth and Policy Working Paper Series ECWP-108). Toronto: Canadian Institute for Advanced Research.

Currie, J., & Thomas, D. (2000). School quality and the longer-term effects of Head Start. *Journal of Human Resources, 35*, 755–774.

Dalaker, J. (1999). *Poverty in the United States: 1998* (Current Population Reports, No. P60-207). Washington, DC: U.S. Government Printing Office.

D'Amico, D. (1999). *Politics, policy, practice and personal responsibility: Adult education in an era of welfare reform.* Cambridge, MA: National Center for Adult Learning and Adult Literacy.

Danziger, S., Corcoran, M., Danziger, S., Heflin, C. M., Kalil, A., Levine, J., Rosen, D., Seefeldt, K., Siefert, K., & Tolman, R. (2000). *Barriers to the employment of welfare recipients.* Retrieved January 10, 2002, from http://www.jcpr.org/wpfiles/Danziger.barriers.update2-21-2000.PDF

Danziger, S., Kalil, A., & Anderson, J. (2000). Human capital, health and mental health of welfare recipients: Co-occurrence and correlates. *Journal of Social Issues, 54*, 637–656.

Desai, S., Chase-Lansdale, P. L., & Michael, R. T. (1989). Mother or market? Effects of maternal employment on the intellectual ability of 4-year-old children. *Demography, 26*, 545–562.

Downey, G., & Coyne, J. C. (1990). Children of depressed parents: An integrative review. *Psychological Bulletin, 108*, 50–76.

Duncan, G. J., & Brooks-Gunn, J. (1997). *Consequences of growing up poor.* New York: Russell Sage Foundation.

Duncan, G. J., Brooks-Gunn, J., & Klebanov, P. K. (1994). Economic deprivation and early childhood development. *Child Development, 65*, 296–318.

Duncan, G., & Chase-Lansdale, L. (2001). Welfare reform and children's well-being. In R. Blank & R. Haskins (Eds.), *The new world of welfare.* Washington, DC: Brookings Institution.

Duncan, G., Dunifon, R., Doran, M. W., & Yeung, W. J. (1998). *How different ARE welfare and working families? And do those differences matter for children's achievements?* Paper presented at the Joint Center for Poverty Research conference, Chicago, IL.

Duncan, G., Dunifon, R., Doran, M. W., & Yeung, W. J. (2001). *How different are welfare and working families? And do those differences matter for children's achievements?* In G. Duncan & P. L. Chase-Lansdale (Eds.), *For better and for worse: Welfare reform and the well-being of children and families* (pp. 103–131). New York: Russell Sage Foundation.

Duncan, G., Harris, K. M., & Boisjoy, J. (1997). *Time limits and welfare reform: New estimates of the number and characteristics of affected families* (Working Paper 1). Chicago: Joint Center for Poverty Research.

Eccles, J. S. (1983). Expectancies, values, and academic behaviors. In J. T. Spence (Ed.), *Achievement and achievement motives: Psychological and sociological approaches* (pp. 75–146). San Francisco: Freeman.

Edin, K., & Lein, L. (1997). *Making ends meet: How single mothers survive welfare and low-wage work.* New York: Russell Sage Foundation.

Entwisle, D. R., & Alexander, K. L. (1993). Entry into school: The beginning school transition and educational stratification in the United States. *Annual Review of Sociology, 19,* 401–423.

Entwisle, D. R., Alexander, K. L., & Olson, L. S. (1997). *Children, schools, and inequality.* Boulder, CO: Westview Press.

Estrada, P., Arsenio, W. F., Hess, R. D., & Holloway, S. D. (1987). Affective quality of the mother-child relationship: Longitudinal consequences for children's school-relevant cognitive functioning. *Developmental Psychology, 23,* 210–215.

Fein, D. J., Lee, W. S., & Schofield, E. C. (1999). *The ABC evaluation: Do welfare recipients' children have a school attendance problem?* Cambridge, MA: Abt Associates.

Fishman, M. E., Barnow, B. S., Gardiner, K. N., Murphy, B. J., & Laud, S. A. (1999). *Job retention and advancement among welfare recipients: Challenges and opportunities.* Baltimore: Johns Hopkins University.

Florida Healthy Kids Corporation. (1997). *Facts on uninsured children.* Retrieved December 5, 2001, from http://www.amsa.org/cph/CHIPfact.cfm

Friedlander, D., & Burtless, G. (1995). *Five years after: The long-term effects of welfare-to-work programs.* New York: Russell Sage Foundation.

Friedman, P. (1999). Post-secondary education options for low-income adults. *Issue Notes, 3*(12). Retrieved November 16, 2001, from http://www.welfareinfo.org/postseced2.htm

Fuller, B., & Kagan, S. L. (2000). *Remember the children: Mothers balance work and child care under welfare reform.* Berkeley, CA: Growing Up in Poverty Project.

Fuller, B., Kagan, S., Caspary, G. L., & Gauthier, C. (2002). Welfare reform and child care options for low-income families. *Children and Welfare Reform, 12,* 97–120.

Galinsky, E., Howes, C., Kontos, S., & Shinn, M. (1994). *The study of children in family child care and relative care.* New York: Families and Work Institute.

Gennetian, L., Crosby, D., & Huston, A. (2001). *Does child care assistance matter? The effects of welfare and employment programs on child care for very young children* (Next Generation Working Paper No. 2). New York: Manpower Demonstration Research Corporation.

Gennetian, L., Crosby, D., Huston, A., & Lowe, T. (2002). *How child care assistance in welfare and employment programs can support the employment of low-income families* (Next Generation Working Paper No. 11). New York: Manpower Demonstration Research Corporation.

Golonka, S., & Matus-Grossman, L. (2001). *Opening doors: Expanding education opportunities for low-income workers.* New York: Manpower Demonstration Research Corporation.

Gomby, D. S., Larner, M. B., Stevenson, C. S., Lewit, E. M., & Behrman, R. (1995). Long term outcomes of early childhood programs: Analysis and recommendations. *Future of Children, 5*(3), 6–24.

Gottschalk, P. (1992). The intergenerational transmission of welfare participation: Facts and possible causes. *Journal of Policy Analysis and Management, 11,* 254–272.

Greenberg, M. (2001). Welfare reform and devolution: Looking back and forward. *Brookings Review, 19*(3), 20–24.

Greenberg, M. (2002). Bush's blunder. *American Prospect, 13*(13). Retrieved June 25, 2002, from http://www.prospect.org/print/V13/13/greenberg-m.html

Greenstein, T. (1995). Are the most advantaged children truly disadvantaged by maternal employment? Effects on child cognitive outcomes. *Journal of Family Issues, 16,* 149–169.

Grubb, N. (1996). *Learning to work: The case for reintegrating job training and education.* New York: Russell Sage Foundation.

Grubb, N. (1999). *From isolation to integration: Occupational education and the emerging system of workforce development.* Berkeley, CA: National Center for Research in Vocational Education.

Grubb, W. N., Badway, N., Bell D., & Castellano, M. (1999). *Community colleges and welfare reform: Emerging practices, enduring problems.* Retrieved November 16, 2001, from http://www.c-wic.org/calcommunitycollege.htm

Gruber, J. (2000). Cash welfare as a consumption smoothing mechanism for divorced mothers. *Journal of Public Economics, 75,* 157–182.

Gueron, J., & Hamilton, G. (2002). *The role of education and training in welfare reform* (Welfare Reform Brief 20). Washington, DC: Brookings Institution.

Gueron, J. M., & Pauly, E. (1991). *From welfare to work.* New York: Russell Sage Foundation.

Guo, G., Brooks-Gunn, J., & Harris, K. M. (1996). Grade retention and persistent economic deprivation among urban Black children. *Sociology of Education, 69,* 217–236.

Halpern, R. (1999). After-school programs for low-income children: Promises and challenges. *Future of Children, 9*(3), 81–95.

Hamilton, G., & Brock, T. (1994). *The JOBS evaluation: Early lessons from seven sites.* Washington, DC: U.S. Department of Health and Human Services, Administration for Children and Families, and U.S. Department of Education.

Hamilton, G., Freedman, S., Gennetian, L., Michalopoulos, C., Walter, J., Adams-Ciardullo, D., & Gassman-Pines, A. (2001). *National evaluation of welfare-to-work strategies: How effective are different welfare-to-work approaches? Five-year adult and child impacts for eleven programs.* Washington, DC: U.S. Department of Health and Human Services, Administration for Children and Families, and U.S. Department of Education.

Hamilton, G., Freedman, S., & McGroder, S. M. (2000). *National evaluation of welfare-to-work strategies: Do mandatory welfare-to-work programs affect the well-being of children?* Washington, DC: U.S. Department of Health and Human Services, Administration for Children and Families, and U.S. Department of Education.

Han, W., Waldfogel, J., & Brooks-Gunn, J. (2001). The effects of early maternal employment on children's later cognitive and behavioral outcomes. *Journal of Marriage and the Family, 63,* 336–354.

Hao, L., Astone, N. M., & Cherlin, A. J. (2001). *Adolescents' school enrollment and employment: Effects of state welfare policies.* Baltimore: Johns Hopkins University Press.

Harris, J. R. (1998). *The nurture assumption: Why children turn out the way they do.* New York: Free Press.

Harris, K. M. (1993). Work and welfare among single mothers in poverty. *American Journal of Sociology, 99,* 317–352.

Harris, K. M. (1996). Life after welfare: Women, work and repeat dependency. *American Sociological Review, 61,* 407–426.

Haskins, R. (2001). Effects of welfare reform on family income and poverty. In R. Blank & R. Haskins (Eds.), *The new world of welfare.* Washington, DC: Brookings Institution.

Haveman, R., & Wolfe, B. (1994). *Succeeding generations: On the effects of investments in children.* New York: Russell Sage Foundation.

Haveman, R., & Wolfe, B. (1995). The determinants of children's attainments: A review of methods and findings. *Journal of Economic Literature, 33,* 1829–1878.

Heinrich, C. J. (1998). *Aiding welfare–to-work transitions: Lessons from JTPA on the cost-effectiveness of education and training services.* Chicago: Northwestern University and University of Chicago, Joint Center for Poverty Research.

Heymann, J. (2000). *The widening gap: Why America's working families are in jeopardy and what can be done about it.* New York: Basic Books.

Hofferth, S. L. (1995). Caring for children at the poverty line. *Children and Youth Services Review, 17,* 61–90.

Hofferth, S. L., Brayfield, A., Ceich, S., & Holcomb, P. (1991). *National Child Care Survey, 1990.* Washington, DC: Urban Institute Press.

Hofferth, S. L., Smith, J., McLoyd, V. C., & Finkelstein, J. (2000). *Achievement and behavior among children of welfare recipients, welfare leavers, and low income single mothers.* Ann Arbor: Institute for Social Research, University of Michigan.

Holzer, H. (1996). *What employers want: Job prospects for less educated workers.* New York: Russell Sage Foundation.

Huston, A. C. (1991). *Children in poverty: Child development and public policy.* New York: Cambridge University Press.

Huston, A. C. (2002). Children and welfare reform: Reforms and child development. *Future of Children, 12*(1). Retrieved from http://www.futureofchildren.org

Huston, A. C., Duncan, R. G., Bos, J., McLoyd, V., Mistry, R., Crosby, D., Gibson, C., Magnuson, K., Romich, J., & Ventura, A. (2001). Work-based antipoverty programs for parents can enhance the school performance and social behavior of children. *Child Development, 72,* 318–336.

Huston, A., McLoyd, V., & Garcia Coll, C. (1994). Children and poverty: Issues in contemporary research. *Child Development, 65,* 275–282.

Imel, S. (1998). *Welfare reform: What's at stake for adult and vocational education.* Washington, DC: Office of Educational Research and Improvement, U.S. Department of Education.

Isaacs, J. (2002). Mothers' work and child care. In D. J. Besharov (Ed.), *Family well-being after welfare reform.* College Park: Maryland School of Public Affairs, Welfare Reform Academy.

Jarrett, R. L. (1995). Growing up poor: The family experiences of socially mobile youth in low-income African American neighborhoods. *Journal of Adolescent Research, 10,* 111–135.

Jayakody, R., & Stauffer, D. (2000). Mental health problems among single mothers: Implications for work and welfare reform. *Journal of Social Issues, 56,* 617–634.

Johnson, H. P., & Tafoya, S. (1999). *The basic skills of welfare recipients: Implications for welfare reform.* San Francisco: Public Policy Institute of California.

Kalil, A., & Danziger, S. K. (2000). How teen mothers are faring under welfare reform. *Journal of Social Issues, 56,* 775–798.

Kalil, A., Dunifon, R., & Danziger, S. K. (2001). Are children's behavior problems affected by their mothers' work participation since welfare reform? In G. Duncan & P. L. Chase-Lansdale (Eds.), *For better and for worse: Welfare reform and the well-being of children and families* (pp. 154–178). New York: Russell Sage Foundation.

Kane, T. J., & Rouse, C. E. (1995). Labor-market returns to two- and four-year colleges. *American Economic Review, 85,* 3.

Kisker, E. E., Hofferth, S. L., Phillips D., & Farquhar, E. (1991). *A profile of child care settings: Early education and care in 1990.* Washington, DC: U.S. Department of Education.

Knell, S. (1998). *Learn to earn: Issues raised by welfare reform for adult education, training and work.* Retrieved November 16, 2001, from http://www.nifl.gov/nifl/fellowship/reports/sknell.htm

Knitzer, J., & Cauthen, N. K. (1999). *Beyond work: Strategies to promote the well-being of young children and families in the context of welfare reform* (Children and Welfare Reform Issue Brief No. 6). New York: Columbia School of Public Health, National Center for Children in Poverty.

Kohn, M. L., & Schooler, C. (1982). *Work and personality: An inquiry into the impact of social stratification.* Norwood, NJ: Ablex.

Kontos, S., Howes, C., Shinn, M., & Galinsky, E. (1995). *Quality in family child care and relative care.* New York: Teachers College Press.

Korenman, S., Miller, J. E., & Sjaastad, J. E. (1995). Long-term poverty and child development in the United States: Results from the NLSY. *Children and Youth Services Review, 17,* 127–155.

Kotch, J., & Shackelford, J. (1989). *The nutritional status of low-income preschool children in the United States: A review of the literature.* Washington, DC: Food Research and Action Center.

LaLonde, R. (2001). *The returns of going back to school for displaced workers.* Chicago: University of Chicago, Center for Human Potential and Public Policy.

Lamb, M. E. (1997). Nonparental child care: Context, quality, correlates, and consequences. In I. Sigel & K. A. Renninger (Eds.), *Child psychology in practice* (5th ed., pp. 73–134). New York: Wiley.

Larson, R., & Verma, S. (1999). How children and adolescents around the world spend time: Work, play, and developmental opportunities. *Psychological Bulletin, 125,* 701–736.

Lazar, I., Darlington, R., Murray, H., Royce, J., & Snipper, A. (1982). Lasting effects of early education: A report from the Consortium for Longitudinal Studies. *Monographs of the Society for Research in Child Development, 47*(2–3, Serial No. 195).

Le Menestrel, S. M., Tout, K., McGroder, S. M., Zaslow, M., & Moore, K. (1999). *An overview and synthesis of the project on state-level child outcomes.* Washington, DC: Child Trends.

Lennon, M. C., Blome, J., & English, K. (2001). *Depression and low-income women: Challenges for TANF and welfare-to-work policies and programs.* New York: Columbia School of Public Health, National Center for Children in Poverty.

Levine, P., & Zimmerman, D. (2000). *Children's welfare exposure and subsequent development.* Chicago: Northwestern University and University of Chicago, Joint Center for Poverty Research.

Loprest, P. (1999). *Families who left welfare: Who are they and how are they doing?* Washington, DC: Urban Institute.

Magnuson, K., & McGroder, S. (2001). *The effect of increasing welfare mothers' education on their young children's academic problems and school readiness.* Chicago: Northwestern University and University of Chicago, Joint Center for Poverty Research.

Mallar, C. D., & Maynard, R. A. (1981). The effects of income maintenance on school performance and educational attainment. In A. Khan & E. Sirageldin (Eds.), *Research in human capital and development* (Vol. 2). Greenwich, CT: JAI Press.

Mare, R. (1995). Changes in educational attainment and school enrollment. In R. Farley (Ed.), *State of the union.* New York: Russell Sage Foundation.

Martin, M. (1999, August). *The intergenerational relationship of welfare participation.* Paper presented at the annual meeting of the American Sociologist Association, Chicago, IL.

Mayer, B. W. (1997). Cognitive complexity in group performance and satisfaction. *Dissertation Abstracts International, 57A,* 4882.

Maynard, R. A., & Murnane, R. J. (1979). The effects of a negative income tax on school performance: Results of an experiment. *Journal of Human Resources, 14,* 463–476.

McGroder, S. M. (2000). Parenting among low-income, African American single mothers with preschool-age children: Patterns, predictors, and developmental correlates. *Child Development, 71,* 752–771.

McGroder, S. M., Zaslow, M. J., Moore, K. A., Hair, E. C., & Ahluwalia, S. K. (2001). The role of parenting in shaping the impacts of welfare-to-work programs on children. In J. G. Borkowski, S. Landesman, & M. Bristol-Power (Eds.), *Parenting and the child's world: Influences on academic, intellectual and socio-emotional development* (pp. 283–310). Mahwah, NJ: Erlbaum.

McGroder, S. M., Zaslow, M. J., Papillo, A. R., & Ahluwalia, S. K. (2001, April). *Do mandatory welfare-to-work programs eliminate selection into maternal employment?* Paper presented at the meeting of the Society for Research in Child Development, Minneapolis, MN.

McHale, S. M., Crouter, A. C., & Tucker, C. J. (2001). Free-time activities in middle childhood: Links with adjustment in early adolescence. *Child Development, 72,* 1764–1778.

McLoyd, V. C. (1989). Socialization and development in a changing economy: The effects of paternal job and income loss on children. *American Psychologist, 44,* 293–302.

McLoyd, V. C. (1990). The impact of economic hardship on Black families and children: Psychological distress, parenting, and socioemotional development. *Child Development, 61,* 311–346.

McLoyd, V. C. (1993). Employment among African American mothers in dual-earner families: Antecedents and consequences for family life and child development. In J. Frankel (Ed.), *The employed mother and the family context* (pp. 180–226). New York: Springer-Verlag.

McLoyd, V. C., Jayaratne, T. E., Ceballo, R., & Borquez, J. (1994). Unemployment and work interruption among African American single mothers: Effects on parenting and adolescent socioemotional functioning. *Child Development, 65,* 562–589.

McLoyd, V. C., & Wilson, L. (1991). The strain of living poor: Parenting, social support, and child mental health. In A. C. Huston (Ed.), *Children in poverty: Child development and public policy* (pp. 105–135). New York: Cambridge University Press.

McPherson, M., & Shapiro, M. (1999). *Reinforcing stratification in American higher education: Some disturbing trends.* Stanford, CA: National Center for Postsecondary Improvement.

Mead, L. (2001). The politics of conservative welfare reform. In R. Haskins & R. M. Blank (Eds.), *The new world of welfare.* Washington, DC: Brookings Institution.

Medrich, E. A., Roizen, J. A., Rubin, V., & Buckley, S. (1982). *The serious business of growing up: A study of children's lives outside school.* Berkeley: University of California Press.

Menaghan, E., Jakielek, S., Mott, F., & Cooksey, E. (1998). *Work and family circumstances and child trajectories: When (and for what) does AFDC receipt matter?* Chicago: Northwestern University and University of Chicago, Joint Center for Poverty Research.

Menaghan, E. G., & Parcel, T. L. (1990). Parental employment and family life: Research in the 1980s. *Journal of Marriage and the Family, 52,* 1079–1098.

Menaghan, E. G., & Parcel, T. L. (1995). Social sources of change in children's home environments: The effects of parental occupational experiences and family conditions. *Journal of Marriage and the Family, 57,* 69–84.

Merrifield, J. (1997). If job training is the answer, what is the question? Research with displaced women textile workers. In G. Hull (Ed.), *Changing work, changing workers: Critical perspectives on language, literacy and skill* (pp. 273–293). Albany: State University of New York Press.

Michalopoulos, C., Schwartz, C., & Adams-Ciardullo, D. (2000). *What works best for whom: Impacts of 20 welfare-to-work programs by subgroup.* New York: Manpower Demonstration Research Corporation.

Mishel, L., & Bernstein, J. (1994). *The state of working America, 1994–95.* Armonk, NY: Sharpe.

Moffitt, R. A. (2002). *From welfare to work: What the evidence shows.* Washington, DC: Brookings Institution.

Moffit, R. A., & Ver Ploeg, M. (1999). *Evaluating welfare reform: A framework and review of current work.* Washington, DC: Panel on Data and Methods for Measuring the Effects of Changes in Social Welfare Programs, National Research Council.

Moore, K. A. (2001). *How do state policymakers think about family process and child development in low-income families?* Washington, DC: Child Trends.

Moore, K. A., Coiro, M. J., Blumenthal, C. S., & Miller, S. M. (1995). *Home environments and the developmental status of children in AFDC families.* Paper presented at the biennial meeting of the Society for Research in Child Development, Indianapolis, IN.

Moore, K. A., & Driscoll, A. K. (1997). Low-wage maternal employment and outcomes for children: A study. *Future of Children, 7,* 122–127.

Moore, K. A., Zaslow, M. J., Miller, S. M., & Magenheim, E. (1996). *The JOBS evaluation: How well are they faring? AFDC families with preschool–aged children in Atlanta at the outset of the JOBS evaluation.* Retrieved November 16, 2001, from http://aspe.hhs.gov/hsp/cyp/jobchdxs.htm

Morris, P. A., Huston, A. C., Duncan, G. J., Crosby, D., & Bos, J. M. (2001). *How welfare and work policies affect children: A synthesis of research.* New York: Manpower Demonstration Research Corporation.

Morris, P., Knox, V., & Gennetian, L. (2002). *Welfare policies matter for children and youth: Lessons for TANF reauthorization.* New York: Manpower Demonstration Research Corporation.

Murnane, R. J., Willett, J. B., & Boudett, K. P. (1995). Do high school dropouts benefit from obtaining a GED? *Educational Evaluation and Policy Analysis, 17,* 133–147.

Murphy, G., & Johnson, A. (1998). *What works: Integrating basic skills training into welfare-to-work.* Washington, DC: National Institute for Literacy.

National Center for Children in Poverty. (1999). *Young children in poverty: A statistical update.* New York: Author.

National Governors Association. (2002). *Welfare reform policy.* Retrieved from http://www.nga.org/nga/legislativeUpdate/policyPositionDetailPrint/1,1390,554,00.html.

National Research Council and Institute of Medicine. (2000). Growing up in child care. In J. P. Schonkoff & D. A. Phillips (Eds.), *From neurons to neighborhoods: The science of early childhood development* (pp. 297–327). Washington, DC: National Academy Press.

National School Boards Association. (1999). *Ten critical threats to America's children: Warning signs for the next millennium.* Retrieved December 10, 2000, from http://www.nsba.org/highlights/ten_threats.htm

Negrey, C., Golin, S., Lee., S., Mead, H., & Gault, B. (2001). *Working first but working poor: The need for education and training following welfare reform.* Washington, DC: Institute for Women's Policy Research.

Newberger, J. (2001). *Barely getting by: Working families in America.* Retrieved from http://www.connectforkids.org

Newson, J., & Newson, E. (1976). *Seven years old in the home environment.* London: Allen & Unwin.

NICHD Early Child Care Research Network. (2000). The relation of child care to cognitive and language development. *Child Development, 71,* 960–980.

Nightingale, D. (1991). *Supportive services for youth.* Philadelphia: Public/Private Ventures.

Olson, K., & Pavetti, L. (1996). *Personal and family challenges to the successful transition from welfare to work.* Washington, DC: Urban Institute.

Orr, L. L., Bloom, H. S., Bell, S. H., Doolittle, F., & Lin, W. (1996). *Does training for the disadvantaged work? Evidence from the National JTPA Study.* Washington, DC: Urban Institute.

Osgood, D. W., Wilson, J. K., Bachman, J. G., O'Malley, P. M., & Johnston, L. D. (1996). Routine activities and individual deviant behavior. *American Sociological Review, 61,* 635–655.

Parcel, T. (1998). Working mothers, welfare mothers: Implications for children in the 21st century. In D. Vannoy & P. Dubeck (Eds), *Challenges for work and family in the 21st century* (pp. 125–141). New York: Aldine de Gruyter.

Parcel, T. L., & Menaghan, E. G. (1994). Early parental work, family social capital, and early childhood outcomes. *American Journal of Sociology, 99,* 972–1009.

Parcel, T. L., & Menaghan, E. G. (1997). Effects of low-wage employment on family well-being. *Future of Children, 7*(1), 116–121.

Parsons, J. E., Adler, T., & Kaczala, C. M. (1982). Socialization of achievement attitudes and beliefs: Parental influences. *Child Development, 53,* 322–329.

Pauly, E. (1995). *The JOBS evaluation: Adult education for people on AFDC—A synthesis of research.* Washington, DC: U.S. Department of Education and U.S. Department of Health and Human Services, Office of the Assistant Secretary for Planning and Evaluation.

Pavetti, L. (1995). *And employment for all: Lessons from Utah's Single Parent Employment Demonstration Project.* Paper presented at the 17th Annual Research Conference of the Association for Public Policy and Management, Washington, DC.

Pettit, G. S., Laird, R. D., Bates, J. E., & Dodge, K. A. (1997). Patterns of after-school care in middle childhood: Risk factors and developmental outcomes. *Merrill-Palmer Quarterly, 43,* 515–538.

Phillips, D. A. (1987). Socialization of perceived academic competence among highly competent children. *Child Development, 58,* 1308–1320.

Phillips, D. A. (1995). *Child care for low-income families: A summary of two workshops.* Washington, DC: National Academy Press.

Phillips, D. A., & Adams, G. (2001). Child care and our youngest children. *Future of Children, 11,* 35–51.

Pierce, K. M., Hamm, J. V., & Vandell, D. L. (1999). Experiences in after-school programs and children's adjustment in first-grade classrooms. *Child Development, 70,* 756–767.

Polit, D. F., Widom, R., Edin, K., Bowie, S., London, A. S., Scott, E. K., & Valenzuela, A. (2001). *Is work enough? The experiences of current and former welfare mothers who work.* New York: Manpower Demonstration Research Corporation.

Posner, J. K., & Vandell, D. L. (1994). Low-income children's after-school care: Are there beneficial effects of after-school programs? *Child Development, 65,* 440–456.

Posner, J. K., & Vandell, D. L. (1999). After-school activities and the development of low-income urban children: A longitudinal study. *Developmental Psychology, 35,* 868–879.

Presser, H. B., & Cox, A. G. (1997). The work schedules of low-educated American women and welfare reform. *Monthly Labor Review, 120,* 25–34.

Presser, H. B. (2000). Nonstandard work schedules and marital instability. *Journal of Marriage and the Family, 62,* 93–110.

Price, C. (2000). *Welfare reform and the college option: A national conference: A summary of conference proceedings.* New York: Howard Samuels State Management and Policy Center.

Primus, W., Rawlings, L., Larin, K., & Porter, K. (1999). *The initial impacts of welfare reform on the incomes of single-mother families.* Washington, DC: Center on Budget and Policy Priorities.

Quint, J. C., Bos, J. M., & Polit, D. F. (1997). *New Chance: Final report on a comprehensive program for young mothers in poverty and their children.* New York: Manpower Demonstration Research Corporation.

Ramey, C. T., & Campbell, F. A. (1991). Poverty, early childhood education, and academic competence: The Abecedarian experience. In A. C. Huston (Ed.), *Children in poverty: Child development and public policy* (pp. 190–221). New York: Cambridge University Press.

Ramey, C. T., Campbell, F. A., Burchinal, M. R., Skinner, M. L., Gardner, D. M., & Ramey, S. L. (2000). Persistent effects of early childhood education on high-risk children and their mothers. *Applied Developmental Science, 4,* 2–14.

Rector, R., & Fagan, P. (2001). *The good news about welfare reform.* Retrieved January 13, 2002, from http://www.heritage.org/library/backgrounder/bg1468.html

Ripke, M., Huston, A., & Mistry, R. (2001). *Parents' job characteristics and children's occupational aspirations and expectations in low-income families.* Poster session presented at the biannual conference of the Society for Research in Child Development, Minneapolis, MN.

Rosenbaum, S. (1992). Effects of poverty and the quality of the home environment on changes in the academic and behavioral adjustment of elementary school-age children. *American Journal of Public Health, 88,* 1371–1373.

Rosenzweig, M. R., & Wolpin, K. I. (1994). Are there increasing returns to the intergenerational production of human capital? Maternal schooling and child intellectual achievement. *Journal of Human Resources, 29,* 670–694.

Rosman, E. A., & Yoshikawa, H. (2001). Welfare reform's effects on children of adolescent mothers: Moderation by race/ethnicity, maternal depression, father involvement, and grandmother involvement. *Women and Health, 32,* 253–290.

Rowe, D. C. (1994). *The limits of family influence: Genes, experience, and behavior.* New York: Guilford Press.

Rowe, D. C., & Rodgers, J. L. (1997). Poverty and behavior: Are environmental measures nature and nurture? *Developmental Review, 17,* 358–375.

Sampson, R. J., & Laub, J. H. (1994). Urban poverty and the family context of delinquency: A new look at structure and process in a classic study. *Child Development, 65,* 523–540.

Schumaker, R., & Greenberg, M. (1999). *Child care after leaving welfare: Early evidence from state studies.* Washington, DC: Center for Law and Social Policy.

Schwarz, C., & Liu, E. (2000). *The link between school performance and health insurance: Current research.* Retrieved from http://www.consumersunion.org/pdf/hiresearch.pdf

Schweber, H. (1997). *Teaching work: Vocational education, workforce preparation, and the future of welfare reform.* Paper presented at the Odyssey Forum conference, Washington, DC.

Scott, E. K., Edin, K., London, A. S., & Mazelis, J. (2001). My children come first: Welfare-reliant women's post-TANF views of work-family tradeoffs and marriage. In G. J. Duncan & P. L. Chase-Lansdale (Eds.), *For better or for worse: Welfare reform and the well-being of children and families.* New York: Russell Sage Foundation.

Scott, E. K., London, A. S., & Edin, K. (2000). Looking to the future: Welfare-reliant women talk about their job aspirations in the context of welfare reform. *Journal of Social Issues, 56,* 727–746.

Scrivener, S., Hamilton, G., Farrell, M., Freedman, S., Friedlander, D., Mitchell, M., Nudelman, J., & Schwartz, C. (1998). *National evaluation of welfare-to-work strategies: Implementation, participation patterns, costs, and two-year impacts of the Portland (Oregon) welfare-to-work program.* Washington, DC: U.S. Department of Health and Human Services, Administration for Children and Families.

Sherman, A. (2001). *How children fare in welfare experiments appears to hinge on income.* Washington, DC: Children's Defense Fund.

Shields, M. K., & Behrman, R. E. (2002). Children and welfare reform: Analysis and recommendations. *Future of Children, 12*(1). Retrieved from http://www.futureofchildren.org

Shonkoff, J. P., & Phillips, D. A. (2000). *From neurons to neighborhoods: The science of early childhood development.* Washington, DC: National Academy Press.

Shore, R. (1997). *Rethinking the brain: New insights into early development.* New York: Families and Work Institute.

Silva, T., Cahalan, M., & Lucierno-Paquet, N. (1998). *Adult education participation decisions and barriers: Review of conceptual frameworks and empirical studies* (Working Paper 98-10). Washington, DC: U.S. Department of Education, National Center for Education Statistics.

Silvestri, G. T. (1995). Occupational employment to 2005. *Monthly Labor Review, 118,* 60–87.

Smith, J. R., & Brooks-Gunn, J. (1997). Correlates and consequences of harsh discipline for young children. *Archives of Pediatric and Adolescent Medicine, 151,* 777–786.

Smith, J. R., Brooks-Gunn, J., & Klebanov, P. K. (1997). Consequences of living in poverty for young children's cognitive and verbal ability and early school achievement. In G. J.

Duncan & J. Brooks-Gunn (Eds.), *Consequences of growing up poor* (pp. 132–189). New York: Russell Sage Foundation.

Smith, K. (2000). *Who's minding the kids? Child care arrangements* (Current Population Reports, No. P70-70). Washington, DC: U.S. Bureau of the Census.

Spalter-Roth, R., Burr, B., Hartmann, H., & Shaw, L. (1995). *Welfare that works: The working lives of AFDC recipients.* Washington, DC: Institute for Women's Policy Research.

Stanley, M. (1995). *What's working and what's not.* Washington, DC: U.S. Department of Labor, Office of the Chief Economist.

State Policy Demonstration Project. (2000). *Employability plans: Exemptions and sanctions.* Retrieved November 5, 2001, from http://www.spdp.org/tanf/applications/applicepexsanc.pdf

State Policy Demonstration Project. (2001). *State policies regarding TANF work activities and requirements.* Retrieved January 13, 2002, from http://www.spdp.org/tanf/work/worksumm.htm

Stein, S. G. (1997). *Equipped for the future: A reform agenda for adult literacy and lifelong learning.* Washington, DC: National Institute for Literacy.

Strawn, J. (1998). *Beyond job search or basic education: Rethinking the role of skills in welfare reform.* Washington, DC: Center for Law and Social Policy.

Strawn, J., Greenberg, M., & Savner, S. (2001). *Improving employment outcomes under TANF.* Washington, DC: Center for Law and Social Policy.

Timmer, S. G., Eccles, J. S., & O'Brien, K. (1985). How children use time. In F. T. Juster & F. P. Stafford (Eds.), *Time, goods, and well-being* (pp. 353–382). Ann Arbor: Institute for Social Research, University of Michigan.

Turner, R. J. (1999). Social support and coping. In A. V. Horwitz & T. L. Scheid (Eds.), *A handbook for the study of mental health: Social contexts, theories, and systems* (pp. 198–210). New York: Cambridge University Press.

Upchurch, D. M., & McCarthy, J. (1990). The timing of a first birth and high school completion. *American Sociological Review, 55,* 224–234.

U.S. Bureau of the Census. (2002). *Work and work-related activities of mothers receiving Temporary Assistance for Needy Families: 1996, 1998, and 2000.* Washington, DC: Author.

U.S. Department of Health and Human Services. (1999). *Access to child care for low-income families.* Retrieved August 29, 2001, from http://www.acf.dhhs.gov/news/press/ccreport.htm

U.S. Department of Health and Human Services. (2000). *Monitoring the child and family social program outcomes: Dynamics of children's movement among the AFDC, Medicaid, and foster care programs prior to welfare reform: 1995–1996, March.* Washington, DC: Author.

U.S. Department of Health and Human Services. (2002). *Study shows positive results from Early Head Start Program.* Washington, DC: Author.

U.S. Department of Labor. (2000). *Statistical information.* Retrieved from http://www.bls.gov/cps/home.htm

U.S. General Accounting Office. (1995). *Child care subsidies increase likelihood that low-income mothers will work.* Washington, DC: U.S. Government Printing Office.

U.S. General Accounting Office. (1997). *Welfare reform: Implications of increased work participation for child care.* Washington, DC: U.S. Government Printing Office.

Vandell, D. L., & Posner, J. K. (1999). Conceptualization and measurement of children's after-school environments. In S. L. Friedman & T. D. Wachs (Eds.), *Assessment of the environment across the lifespan.* Washington, DC: American Psychological Association.

Vandell, D. L., & Ramanan, J. (1992). Effects of early and recent maternal employment on children from low-income families. *Child Development, 63,* 938–949.

Vandell, D. L., & Wolfe, B. (2000). *Child care quality: Does it matter and does it need to be improved?* Madison: Institute for Research on Poverty, University of Wisconsin.

Veltkamp, L. J., & Miller, T. W. (1994). *Clinical handbook of child abuse and neglect.* New York: International Universities Press.

Videka-Sherman, L. (1991). Child abuse and neglect. In A. Gitterman (Ed.), *Handbook of social work with vulnerable populations* (pp. 345–381). New York: Columbia University Press.

Weaver, R. K., Shapiro, R. Y., & Jacobs, L. R. (1995). Trends: Welfare. *Public Opinion Quarterly, 59,* 606–627.

Weinfield, N. S., Egeland, B., & Ogawa, J. R. (1998). *Promises to keep: Assessing affective and behavioral qualities of mother-child relationships in the New Chance Observational Study.* Chicago: Joint Center for Poverty Research, Northwestern University, and University of Chicago.

Weisner, T. S. (1987). Socialization for parenthood in sibling caretaking societies. In J. B. Lancaster & J. Altmann (Eds.), *Parenting across the life span: Biosocial dimensions* (pp. 237–270). Hawthorne, NY: Aldine.

Weiss, H., & Halpern, R. (1991). *Community-based family support and education programs: Something old or something new? A broad look at family support and education programs for low-income parents.* New York: Columbia School of Public Health, National Center for Children in Poverty.

Werner, E. E. (1993). Risk, resilience, and recovery: Perspectives from the Kauai Longitudinal Study. *Development and Psychopathology, 5,* 503–515.

Wertheimer, R. (2001). *Working poor families with children: Leaving welfare doesn't necessarily mean leaving poverty.* Washington, DC: Child Trends.

Wetzel, J. R. (1995). Labor force, unemployment and earnings. In R. Farley (Ed.), *America in the 1990s.* New York: Russell Sage Foundation.

White, L. D., & Keith, B. (1990). The effect of shift work on the quality and stability of marital relations. *Journal of Marriage and the Family, 52,* 453–464.

Wilson, J. B., Ellwood, D. T., & Brooks-Gunn, J. (1995). Welfare-to-work through the eyes of children. In P. L. Chase-Lansdale & J. Brooks-Gunn (Eds.), *Escape from poverty: What makes a difference.* New York: Cambridge University Press.

Zambrowski, A., & Gordon, A. (1993). *Evaluation of the minority female single parent demonstration: Fifth year impact at CET.* Princeton, NJ: Mathematica Policy Research.

Zaslow, M. J. (1991). Variation in child care quality and its implications for children. *Journal of Social Issues, 47,* 125–138.

Zaslow, M. J., & Emig, C. A. (1997). When low-income mothers go to work: Implications for children. *Future of Children, 7,* 110–115.

Zaslow, M. J., McGroder, S. M., Cave, G., & Mariner, C. L. (1999). Maternal employment and measures of children's health and development among families with some history of welfare receipt. In R. Hodson & T. L. Arcel (Eds.), *Research in the sociology of work: Vol. 7. Work and family* (pp. 233–259). Stamford, CT: JAI Press.

Zaslow, M., McGroder, S., & Moore, K. (2002). *The National Evaluation of Welfare-to-Work Strategies: Impacts on young children and their families two years after enrollment.* Washington, DC: U.S. Department of Health and Human Services, Administration for Children and Families, Office of Child Support Enforcement.

Zaslow, M. J., McGroder, S. M., Moore, K. A., & LeMenestral, S. M. (1999). *Behavior problems and cognitive school readiness among children in families with a history of welfare receipt: Diverging patterns and their predictors.* Paper presented at the meeting of the Society for Research in Child Development, Albuquerque, NM.

Zaslow, M. J., Moore, K. A., Morrison, D. R., & Coiro, M. J. (1995). The Family Support Act and children: Potential pathways of influence. *Children and Youth Services Review, 17,* 231–249.

Zaslow, M. J., Oldham, E., Moore, K. A., & Magenheim, E. (1998). Welfare families' use of early childhood care and education programs, and implications for their children's development. *Early Childhood Research Quarterly, 13,* 563.

Zaslow, M. J., Rabinovich, B. A., & Suwalsky, J. T. (1991). From maternal employment to child outcomes: Preexisting group differences and moderating variables. In J. V. Lerner & N. L. Galambos (Eds.), *Employed mothers and their children* (pp. 237–282). New York: Garland.

Zaslow, M. J., Tout, K., Smith, S., & Moore, K. (1998). Implications of the 1996 welfare legislation for children: A research perspective. *Social Policy Report: Society for Research in Child Development, 12,* 1–34.

Zedlewski, S. R., & Loprest, P. (2001). Will TANF work for the most disadvantaged families? In R. Blank & R. Haskins (Eds.), *The new world of welfare* (pp. 311–334). Washington, DC: Brookings Institution.

Zill, N., Moore, K., Smith, E., Stief, T., & Coiro, M. J. (1991). *The life circumstances and development of children in welfare families: A profile based on national survey data.* Washington, DC: Child Trends.

Zill, N., & Schoenborn, C. A. (1990). *Health of our nation's children: Developmental, learning, and emotional problems, United States, 1988.* Hyattsville, MD: National Center for Health Statistics.

Zuckerman, D. M. (2000). The evolution of welfare reform: Policy changes and current knowledge. *Journal of Social Issues, 56,* 811–820.

Zuckerman, D. M., & Kalil, A. (2000). Introduction: Welfare reform: Preliminary and unanswered questions. *Journal of Social Issues, 56,* 579–586.

Chapter 6

Reducing School Violence: Strengthening Student Programs and Addressing the Role of School Organizations

R. MATTHEW GLADDEN

Consortium on Chicago School Research

We also know that in too many American schools there is a lawlessness where there should be learning. . . . Make no mistake, this is a threat not to our classroom, but to America's public school system and, indeed, to the strength and vitality of our nation. (President Clinton, as cited in Astor, Meyer, & Behre, 1999, p. 4)

Shootings in Columbine, Colorado; Santana, California; and Jonesboro, Arkansas, have ignited concern over school violence. In May 1999, a national poll showed that 52% of parents feared for their children's safety at school (Brooks, Schiraldi, & Ziedenberg, 2000). Although a consensus exists that too much violence occurs in America's schools, some assert that public schools are safe havens for youth (Brooks et al., 2000). In the first section of this chapter, I examine these claims by sketching the scope of school violence and assessing how schools are both safe and unsafe.

High schools have responded to public concern by implementing violence prevention programs that instruct students in social-cognitive skills such as anger management, installing zero tolerance polices that expel or suspend students for being involved in fights or carrying a weapon to school, and heightening school security (Gottfredson, 2001). Evaluating and reflecting on the strengths and weakness of these initiatives has important public policy implications because the vast majority of schools operate a growing number of programs (Gottfredson, Gottfredson, & Czeh, 2000; Small et al., 2001). Although fair and consistent application of school rules and social-cognitive prevention programs can reduce school violence, the promise of these initiatives is diminished by weak implementation (Gottfredson et al., 2000; Office of the Surgeon General, 2001).

Also, zero tolerance policies that were designed to exclude extremely violent students from schools are being widely applied to a range of student misbehavior and have contributed to large increases in out-of-school suspensions. The widespread use of suspensions is deeply troubling, because suspensions have not been shown to

---

I would like to thank Michelle Fine and the reviewers of this chapter for their insightful comments and critique. These comments significantly enhanced the quality of the chapter.

modify behavior, can undermine students' academic achievement and attachment to school, and are disproportionately applied to minority students (Advancement Project and Civil Rights Project, 2000; Skiba, 2000; Skiba, Michael, Nardo, & Peterson, 2000; Skiba & Peterson, 2000).

Both prevention and discipline initiatives implicitly assume that school violence emerges from students' aggressive tendencies and problems in their communities. Adults and the structure of schools are invisible (Fine & Smith, 2001). Fostering student engagement in school through interesting academic programs and personal connections with adults is hypothesized to reduce students' propensity to become involved in violence by making them respect and value school. Although this relationship exists (Blum & Rinehart, 1997; Resnick et al., 1997), programs that increase student engagement and academic performance often fail to reduce school violence (Gottfredson, 2001).

The inconsistent effects of prevention, discipline, and environmental initiatives highlight the need for a broader theoretical framework. The present review argues that strong relationships among and between students and teachers, a broad commitment to teach students nonviolent behavior, effective instruction, and responsiveness to students' culture and community work together and in tension to make schools safe. Responding to concerns about the atheoretical nature of environmental strategies (Baker, 1998), the second half of the review speculates on how these four factors shape interactions among and between adults and students to reduce school violence. The conclusion briefly discusses how the organization of high schools facilitates or undermines the establishment of these conditions.

The review focuses on middle schools and high schools, because youth are most likely to commit their first serious violent act between 12 and 20 years of age, and teens nationally are 2.5 times more likely to be victims of violence than people more than 20 years old (Office of the Surgeon General, 2001). Also, school victimization rates are highest in middle schools and high schools (Kaufman et al., 2001).

SCHOOL VIOLENCE

There are many misconceptions about the prevalence of youth violence in our society and it is important to peel back the veneer of hot-tempered discourse that often surrounds the issue . . . statistically speaking, schools are among the safest places for children to be. (Bi-Partisan Working Group on Youth Violence, 106th Congress, cited in Brooks et al., 2000, p. 1)

School violence statistics clash with public perceptions (Brooks et al., 2000; Schiraldi & Ziedenberg, 2001). An *NBC Nightly News/Wall Street Journal* telephone poll conducted after the school shootings in Jonesboro, Arkansas, showed that 71% of American citizens thought a school shooting was likely or very likely to happen in their community (Brooks et al., 2000). Although gruesome images of multiple school shootings have inspired widespread fear of such events, only 1% of youth homicides were committed in schools during the 1998–1999 school year (Kaufman et al., 2001). This translates to only a 1 in 2 million chance that a school-aged child would die at school (Brooks et al., 2000).

Also, serious violent crimes such as aggravated assault and rape are less likely to occur in schools than outside of schools. In 1998–1999, about 30% of serious violent crimes reported by 12- to 18-year-olds occurred on school property or while the students were en route to school. Student victimization at school also declined between 1992 and 1999, from 48 to 33 violent incidents[1] per 1,000 students, a drop of 31% (Kaufman et al., 2001). Homicides are extremely rare in schools, and serious violent crimes are less likely to occur inside of schools. In these important ways, America's public schools are extremely safe and getting safer.

Media representations of school violence contribute to the discrepancy between public perceptions and documented occurrences of school violence. Over the last decade, the media has increased coverage of violence by 240% (Brooks et al., 2000; Schiraldi & Ziedenberg, 2001). The majority of youth appearances on the evening news are connected with violence, even though less than one half of 1% of juveniles were arrested for a violent crime in 2000. This skewed coverage of youth fuels misconceptions. Americans believe that young people are responsible for 43% of homicides, when they actually perpetrate only 9% of such crimes (Schiraldi & Ziedenberg, 2001). A more accurate and balanced portrayal of youth in the media is needed.

Although homicides are extremely rare in America's schools, schools are deeply troubled by harassment, bullying, and fighting. A 2001 national survey revealed that 38% of parents, 26% of teachers, and 32% of students thought bullying/harassment was a very or somewhat serious problem in their high school (Johnson, Duffett, Farkas, & Collins, 2002). Also, 22% of seniors reported being physically threatened at school over the past 6 months (National Center for Education Statistics, 1998). Sometimes bullying/harassment is ignored in schools because it is perceived as "boys being boys" or as part of the high school experience (Aronson, 2000; Casella, 2001). This type of attitude is harmful because incidents of disrespect, bullying, and harassment often trigger more serious violence (Devine, 1996; Noguera, 2001; Skiba & Peterson, 2000). Bullying that meets the legal definitions of harassment in the workplace has played a major role in a number of school shootings over the past 20 years (Vossekuil, Reddy, Fein, Borum, & Modzeleski, 2000).

Both the teachers and students I interviewed were generally in agreement that most physical confrontations were the result of previous verbal exchanges or harassments. For many students, being disrespected was considered the crucial ingredient that led to serious violence, including weapon violence in schools. To deal with weapon violence or fights without dealing with issues of respect sets the stage for, at best, a quick fix with a short life span. (Casella, 2001, p. 33)

Harassment and bullying often target students' race/ethnicity, gender, or sexual orientation. In 1999, 13% of students 12–18 years of age reported being called a derogatory name based on these characteristics over the previous 6 months (Kaufman et al., 2001). This type of harassment has negative implications for individuals, schools, and society in general. High school students who believe students at their school are prejudiced report higher levels of emotional distress[2] (Blum & Rinehart, 1997). At the school level, high levels of racial or sexual harassment may violate students' civil rights by creating a hostile or offensive school environment (Casella, 2001). Also, harassment is symptomatic of rifts of intolerance across race, gender, and sexuality that challenge democratic values. If the purpose of education is to prepare students to participate in democracy (Dewey, 1916/1970), confronting prejudicial feelings and behaviors in students is an important goal of schooling.

Fights erupt as a result of bullying or harassment, and the frequent occurrence of fights makes the threats encased in harassment or bullying potent (Casella, 2001). In 1999, 14% of high school students reported being involved in a fistfight on school property. Fighting is part of the experience of many high school students, especially male students, and it tends to occur at rates similar to those in students' communities. One 1999 study showed that, unlike serious violent crime, simple assaults among 12- and 18-year-olds were slightly more likely to occur in schools (26 vs. 21 incidents per 1,000 students) (Kaufman et al., 2001).

The interaction of three factors in schools—frequent fistfights, students carrying weapons,[3] and the occurrence of a few serious violent incidents—fuels fear of fatal school violence even though its occurrence is extremely rare. In 1999, 7% of high school students reported carrying weapons on school property in the previous 30 days (Kaufman et al., 2001); in 1996, 5% of seniors reported being injured with a weapon at school in the past 12 months (National Center for Education Statistics, 1998). Because weapons are present in schools, teachers and students may fear that each scuffle or argument has the potential to escalate into a serious incident.

Also, middle schools and high schools experience enough serious violent incidents, 7 per 1,000 students, to justify fear of serious violence. In a 1996 survey of school social workers, 71% reported the occurrence of at least one potentially fatal assault in their school during the previous academic year. In high-poverty inner-city communities, this percentage jumped to 87% (Astor, Behre, Fravil, & Wallace, 1997). Although public fears of school shootings are inflated by media representations, high levels of fighting punctuated by a few very serious assaults justify concern over school violence. Recent multiple shootings in schools have made concerns more acute, because the possible harm caused by a single event can be tragically high.

High levels of fighting in schools have negative effects on students' educational opportunities. In 1999, 5% of students reported missing one or more days of school during the preceding 30 days because they felt too unsafe to go to school (Centers for Disease Control and Prevention, 2002). High levels of school violence also contribute to a chaotic school environment in which teaching and learning are more difficult (Devine, 1996). In a 1998 national survey, 40% of adolescents reported that the behavior of other students in their school interfered with their performance (Park, 1998). In addition, students attending schools with moderate or high levels of violence are less likely to graduate from high school or attend a 4-year college, even after a range of student and school characteristics have been controlled (Grogger, 1997).

Fear of violence and victimization also produces more violence. The majority of youth who carry a gun outside of their home and into school do so for protection and not intimidation (Casella, 2001; Sheley & Wright, 1998). For instance, Sheley and Wright (1998) found that young people who had been threatened with a weapon, had attended a social event at which shots were fired, or feared neighborhood violence were more likely to carry a gun outside of their home. According to Casella (2001), the line between victim and victimizer is blurred, and perpetrators of violence are also often victims. An environment characterized by harassment and fighting fuels more violence by pressuring students to act tough and protect themselves.

In terms of homicides and serious violent crimes such as aggravated assault, schools are one of the safest places for youth. However, schools are still violent places. According to recent national surveys, the average high school serving 1,000 students should expect approximately 140 fistfights and 7 serious violent incidents (e.g., rape or aggravated assault) to occur during a given school year.

Relatively speaking, young people may in fact be far safer in school than they are in their neighborhoods. For many parents and students, the fact that schools are relatively safe provides little solace, given the expectation that schools should be absolutely safe and therefore should not be judged by the same standards we used to gauge security in other public, or even private, places. (Noguera, 1995, p. 191)

RESPONSES TO SCHOOL VIOLENCE

School violence emerges from deeper problems in American society such as high levels of poverty among children, high levels of domestic violence, the prevalence of firearms, and high rates of imprisonment and recidivism (Casella, 2001; Lawrence, 1998; Spina, 2000; Wilson, 1996). For instance, the level of violence in communities surrounding schools strongly predicts school safety (Gottfredson, 2001; National Education Association, 1996; Sebring, Bryk, Roderick, & Camburn, 1996). The long-term success of violence prevention initiatives relies on addressing broader societal problems and community violence (Casella, 2001; Spina, 2000). Recognizing the broader causes of school violence, however, does not diminish the responsibility of schools to create safe environments. If there are to be quality educational opportunities for all students regardless of their background, they need access to safe schools. Because schools have almost universal access to youth, schools are also the site of many youth violence prevention programs and an important resource in broader community and governmental efforts to reduce violence (Leone, Mayer, Malmgren, & Meisel, 2000; Office of the Surgeon General, 2001). High schools have responded to the problem of school violence primarily through three types of strategies: prevention, discipline, and environmental. In the next several sections, the scope, rationale, and effectiveness of these strategies are described.[4]

Prevention and disciplinary approaches assume that school violence emerges from students' aggressive impulses and problems outside of school (Baker, 1998; Gottfredson, 2001; Sandler, Wong, Morales, & Patel, 2000). Prevention programs address this perceived deficit by training students in social-cognitive skills such as anger management and conflict negotiation (Astor, Meyer, & Behre, 1999). Discipline strategies increase surveillance, security, and punishments in order to reduce the opportunity for violence to occur, deter it with harsh punishments, and exclude students committing violence.

Proponents argue that the high levels of violence in American society justify these strategies. Comparisons of homicide rates of countries across the world reveal that "the United States is the most violent of developed nations and one of the most violent of all nations" (Short, 1997, p. 12). Fighting is part of the experience of many adolescents, especially male adolescents. In 1999, 44% and 27% of high school–aged males and females, respectively, reported being involved in a physical fight over the previous 12 months (Kaufman et al., 2001). In addition, Gellert (1997) estimated that 2 to 4 million children were abused or neglected in 1991. High rates of violence perpetuate the idea that violence is an effective method for solving conflict. Aronson (2000) found that, in comparison with teenagers from 10 other countries, American teenagers were more likely to complete a story about conflict with a violent conclusion.

Violence, poverty, and other factors lead students to enter school with personal problems that put them at risk of school failure and striking out violently. A Phi Delta Kappa study involving more than 22,000 elementary and high school students showed that between 25% and 35% of "typical" students experience disruptive or traumatic events such as sexual abuse, attending three or more schools over a 5-year period, living with a family member who uses drugs, or misbehaving in school to a severe enough degree to be suspended (Frymier & Gansneder, 1989). Other students' school experiences are also intermittently affected by family tragedies such as divorce or death. These experiences may have an impact on student performance and behavior.

In the following, findings on and criticisms of prevention and discipline strategies are delineated. Also, general criticisms lodged against the rationale underlying these strategies are described.

Prevention Strategies

In 2000, almost 90% of high schools reported having a required course that taught students social-cognitive skills such as anger management and conflict resolution techniques (Small et al., 2001). Prevention programs that teach students social-cognitive skills can reduce school violence. More specifically, social-cognitive programs that are longer in duration (i.e., more than a few sessions), reinforced across grade levels, and taught through interactive instructional techniques such as role modeling tend to be more effective (Gottfredson, 2001; Office of the Surgeon General, 2001). The Office of the Surgeon General (2001) lists specific programs whose effectiveness has been validated by quasi-experimental research.

Social-cognitive programs have been criticized for failing to model skills (Devine, 1996) and for being weakly implemented (Gottfredson, 2001; Gottfredson et al., 2000). Students primarily learn social skills by observing and interacting with people in their lives (Bandura, 1986; Thorton, Craft, Dahlberg, Lynch, & Baer, 2000).

The most basic flaw in promoting violence-prevention and conflict-resolution curricula within schools is . . . it consists of substituting the hypothetical for the real . . . adolescents learn behaviors more through an osmotic process of daily interaction than through theoretical talk about ethics. Violence prevention deals with past behavior, conflict resolution with future behavior, and both are convenient ways of escaping behavior in the present. It is one thing for a principal to add violence-prevention courses to the curriculum; it is a totally different thing for a principal to challenge all the teachers—and the entire school community—to adopt and enforce a uniform code of conduct. (Devine, 1996, p. 164)

Also, a national survey of prevention programs showed that only about 20% of prevention programs were very well implemented. "It may be that the quality of implementation of prevention programs matters more than the type of prevention intervention" (Gottfredson et al., 2000, p. 4-1). Poor implementation and limited social modeling diminish the effectiveness of prevention programs.

Discipline Strategies

Increasing the fairness and consistency of school rules and implementing deterrence strategies such as zero tolerance, suspension, and school surveillance are two discipline strategies used by schools to reduce school violence.

Fair and Consistent School Rules

A consensus exists that safer schools possess and fairly enforce clear expectations for student behavior (Dwyer & Osher, 2000; Gottfredson, Gottfredson, & Hybl, 1993; Learning First Alliance, 2001; National Institute of Education, 1978; Verdugo & Schneider, 1999). Quasi-experimental research confirms that improving the consistency of discipline policies spurs reductions in school violence (Gottfredson, 2001). Little attention, however, has been paid to what types of school policies foster perceptions of fairness and consistency among students.

After an arrest, people's adherence to the law is more likely to increase when they feel their perspective is considered in the administering of sanctions (Sherman, 1993). Similarly, some researchers have argued that school discipline is most effective when it is tailored to the causes and severity of the event and the response involves a range of sanctions (Curwin & Mendler, 1997; Mayer, 1999; Noguera, 2001; Skiba & Peterson, 2000). Because serious school violence is linked to bullying and harassment, a variety of research has identified the need to consistently address and respond to misbehavior in schools (Casella, 2001; Noguera, 2001; Skiba & Peterson, 2000). These findings suggest that discipline policies need to be consistent in addressing misbehavior and fair by making punishments responsive to the circumstances of the event. Although the link between safer schools and fair and consistent discipline policies has been established, very little work has explored what types of discipline policies produce subjective feelings of fairness and consistency and how culture or community contexts affect these perceptions.

Similar to prevention programs, the implementation of discipline policies has proved problematic. Although most schools have recently revised their disciplinary policies, almost half have inconsistent disciplinary policies (Gottfredson et al., 2000). Also, sound discipline policies do not ensure sound discipline practices. The consistency of discipline practices relies on their enactment in classrooms, hallways, and the lunchroom.

The consistent use of incentives and consequences is critical to successful management of behavior at the school level. . . . *Consistency does not happen.* It is usually due to school-level strategic planning, team building, professional development, and ongoing discussion and evaluation. (Dwyer & Osher, 2000, p. 12)

Zero Tolerance and School Security

Adapting strategies from the criminal justice system, schools have tried to deter school violence by suspending and expelling misbehaving students, expanding school surveillance, and criminally prosecuting students for incidents previously handled in schools (Ayers, Ayers, & Dohrn, 2001; Brooks et al., 2000; Casella, 2001). Although field research has shown that these policies can have negative effects on students and schools, very little survey or quasi-experimental research has directly evaluated their effectiveness (Skiba, 2000; Skiba & Peterson, 2000). Field research, however, highlights the need to question and challenge the assumption that heightening security and severity of punishment makes schools safe. Although interconnected, zero tolerance policies and heightened school security are examined separately here because each represents a unique approach to school violence.

Zero tolerance. Possession of firearms greatly affects the chance that serious violence will occur (Thorton et al., 2000). In an attempt to address the problems of weapons in schools, the federal government passed the Gun-Free Schools Act in 1994. The law mandates a 1-year expulsion for possession of a firearm,[5] referral of a violating student to the criminal justice system, and the ability of the chief administrative officer of each school district to modify these types of expulsions on a case-by-case basis (Skiba, 2000). Because receipt of federal education funds is contingent on compliance to the law, almost all public schools have zero tolerance policies for weapons (Sheley & Wright, 1998).

In practice, zero tolerance policies have been applied to an increasingly broad range of student misbehavior, the majority of which is nonviolent (Brooks et al., 2000; Gottfredson et al., 2000; Skiba, 2000). For instance, 60% of suspensions in Maryland during 1998 and 1999 were for attendance violations, disrespect of authority, cheating, and property crime (Brooks et al., 2000). Incidents of overzealous application of zero tolerance policies, including a 10-day suspension of a student who said that a French teacher could not speak French during morning announcements (Skiba, 2000), the expulsion of a ninth-grade student for having sparklers in her book bag (Brooks et al., 2000), and many similar published incidents (see Ayers, Dohrn, & Ayers, 2001), are symptomatic of the tendency of schools to severely punish minor infractions. Zero tolerance has grown beyond its legal intent of preventing severe violence into a disciplinary strategy for a wide range of behaviors (Skiba, 2000).

While the use of expulsions remains relatively rare, suspensions are one of the most commonly used punishments (Skiba, 2000). Nationally, the growing use of zero tolerance policies is evidenced by the doubling of student suspension rates between 1974 and 1997, from 3.7% to 6.8% (Brooks et al., 2000). In urban areas, suspension rates are often much higher (Sandler et al., 2000). For instance, a 1999 report on Milwaukee's schools found that 50% of all middle school students and 33%

of all high school students have been suspended at least once (Milwaukee Catalyst and Designs for Change, 1999, as cited in Advancement Project and Civil Rights Project, 2000). In addition, 97% of Milwaukee's suspensions are for nonviolent offenses. The growing use of suspensions raises the question of whether suspensions are justifiable responses to minor misbehavior and effective in making schools safer.

Zero tolerance policies are hypothesized to make schools safer by changing students' behavior through punishment, excluding students exhibiting violent behavior from school, and deterring future violence by making "examples" of misbehaving students. Contemporary field and survey research challenge the veracity of these arguments. Punishment alone is unlikely to change behavior and can increase misbehavior (Kaplan & Johnson, 1991; Sherman, 1993; Skiba, 2000; Skiba & Peterson, 2000). Suspensions and expulsions weaken relationships that are necessary to manage students' behavior and improve their academic achievement (McEnvoy & Welker, 2000). Poor academic performance and misbehavior are strongly related and tend to reinforce one another by undermining students' perceptions of the utility of school and interrupting their opportunity to learn (McEnvoy & Welker, 2000). Suspensions tend to fuel instead of interrupt this cycle by causing students to fall behind academically, devalue school, be labeled "bad" students, and seek out peers who misbehave (Kaplan & Johnson, 1991; Sandler et al., 2000). For instance, young people who have faced public punishment report higher levels of delinquency than similar nonlabeled youth (Pepler & Slaby, 1994). Suspensions and expulsions also increase students' odds of dropping out (Gordon, Piana, & Keleher, 2001; Sandler et al., 2000). Exclusionary practices such as suspensions can worsen instead of address misbehavior.

Zero tolerance strategies assume that suspension and expulsion of a few "violent" students make schools safe for the remaining students. In fact, suspensions and expulsions sometimes are used to push misbehaving students to drop out of school (Skiba, 2000). Indeed, "analysis of school referral data confirms the perceptions of school personnel that a relatively small proportion of students may be responsible for much of the disruption and violence in a given school" (Skiba, 2000, p. 15). In rare instances, a student exhibiting very violent behavior will need to be educated in an alternative setting. However, the high and increasing number of school suspensions and expulsions is unlikely to make schools safe, because such actions do not address the environmental or individual problems fueling student behavior, are influenced by environmental factors as much as students' behavior, and prejudicially classify minority students as "violent."

Zero tolerance does not address why students are misbehaving, and thus chronic individual and school problems may go unaddressed. For instance, one school attempted to increase its orderliness and academic performance by segregating the 20 most disruptive students in a special classroom. The initiative failed. Teachers reported that other students in their classes became disruptive after the removal of the 20 students. After this failure and the observation that some teachers did not have discipline problems, the school turned to trying to understand environmental, academic, and relationship problems that were triggering student misbehavior (Noguera, 2001). Zero tolerance is based on a logic similar to that of the original intervention and assumes that exclusion solves misbehavior.

Schools once claimed to use zero tolerance as a statement of their commitment to respond aggressively to the intolerable. Now the words too often are an excuse to punish without thought, to remove the troublemakers without guilt or responsibility, or to sound tough without doing the tough work to finding real solutions. . . . Our extensive work in school discipline over 15 years has proven to us that behavior and problems worsen when the solutions or consequences are based on formulas rather than circumstances, motivations, and needs. The motivation for behavior and the way students make choices is the central factor that should determine the selection of consequences to teach responsibility. (Curwin & Mendler, 1997, p. x)

Zero tolerance policies are applied inconsistently across classrooms and schools. For instance, Skiba (2000) showed that, in one middle school, two thirds of all disciplinary referrals came from 25% of the school's teachers. A study of four schools in the Miami-Dade school system that served students from similar demographic backgrounds revealed that their out-of-school suspension rates varied greatly, even though the schools were under the same zero tolerance policy (Browne, 2001). These studies show that students' classroom and school assignments determine their chance of being suspended as much as their behavior (Skiba, 2000). Researchers need to investigate factors that contribute to inconsistent and overly harsh or lenient practices.

As discussed earlier, many adolescents will be involved in a fight sometime in their school career, and the distinction between violent and general education students made by zero tolerance policies is false. The high and growing rates of suspension are testament to the fact that many students become caught in a disciplinary web of suspension and expulsion for mistakes that many adolescents make. Unquestionably, fighting needs to be punished and students held accountable. Punishment, however, should focus on changing behavior and forcing students to take responsibility for their actions, not excluding students from school (Ayers, Ayers, & Dohrn, 2001). The tendency of many students to be involved in fights, coupled with the questionable ability of suspensions to change behavior, indicates the need to explore other strategies. "There are not enough police or metal detectors in the world to solve this [the problem of students carrying firearms]. . . . We need to deal with more relationships" (Education Secretary Rod Paige, as cited in CNN.com, 2001).

Disturbingly, minority students and students with disabilities are disproportionately punished (Advancement Project and Civil Rights Project, 2000; Brooks et al., 2000; Gordon et al., 2001; Sandler et al., 2000; Skiba, 2000, 2001; Skiba & Peterson, 2000). A 1998 Department of Education report showed that African America children account for 32% of out-of-school suspensions, even though they represent only 17% of public school enrollees (Advancement Project and Civil Rights Project, 2000). Among Latino students, the story varies by region of the country. Latino students are proportionately suspended in some areas and disproportionately in others (Gordon, Piana, & Keleher, 2000).

The disproportionate punishment of African American students suggests a systematic bias in school suspension and expulsion policies. Income discrepancies between White and African American families and actual student behavior, two popular alternative explanations of the punishment discrepancy, fail to explain it (Skiba, 2001; Skiba et al., 2000). "African-American males from the wealthiest families are almost as likely to be expelled or suspended as white males form the poorest families" (Losen & Edley, 2001, p. 231). An analysis of the rate and reason students were referred for discipline and suspension showed that African American students were referred more often than White students for subjective reasons such as disrespect, excessive noise, threat, and loitering (Skiba et al., 2000).

Nor can we explain away black-white disparities in discipline through black students' misbehavior: if anything, African-American students may be referred and suspended for less objective and less serious reasons. As more of the rationalizations for a black-white discrepancy in school discipline are ruled out, we are eventually left with a simple question: What else besides discrimination can racial disproportionality be? (Skiba, 2001, p. 184)

Field and survey research has shown that safe schools are characterized by an atmosphere of respectful relationships among and between adults, coupled with a strong academic mission (Bryk & Driscoll, 1988; Noguera, 1995). The broad use of zero tolerance makes the establishment of such an environment extremely difficult through the suspension of large numbers of students in an inconsistent and often racially biased manner. Moreover, zero tolerance policies communicate to students that their voices and circumstances do not matter (Curwin & Mendler, 1997). In a 1994–1995 national survey of 7th through 12th graders, students reported feeling less connected to their school when it temporarily expelled students for minor infractions such as possession of alcohol and expelled students for their first major rule infraction (McNeeley, Nonnemaker, & Blum, 2002).

Recent research indicates that as schools become more militarized they become less safe, in large part because the first casualty is the central, critical relationship between teacher and student, a relationship that is now being damaged or broken in favor of tough-sounding, impersonal, and uniform procedures. (Ayers, Ayers, & Dohrn, 2001, p. xii)

Unfortunately, very little research has directly assessed the effectiveness of zero tolerance in terms of making schools safer overall. The effectiveness of zero tolerance policies is often evaluated by pointing to increases or decreases in school suspension and expulsion rates. Both are cited as indicators of improvements in school safety. Because suspension and expulsion rates are influenced by a variety of factors other than school violence, the effectiveness of zero tolerance policies rests on their ability to decrease victimization rates among students inside as well as outside of school (Skiba, 2000). According to a National Center for Education Statistics study of school violence, schools that reported no crime were less likely to have zero tolerance policies (Heaviside et al., 1998). This study, however, did not control for possible confounding variables. For instance, the findings may reflect the tendency of schools with zero tolerance policies to report more offenses to the police. Also, schools with more discipline problems may be more likely to adopt zero tolerance strategies. More comprehensive research is needed to systematically assess the effects of zero tolerance policies.

At the policy level and district level, zero tolerance policies are extremely popular because they demonstrate a concrete reaction to and disapproval of school violence (Noguera, 1995). Also, zero tolerance policies were designed to prevent and respond swiftly to grave incidents involving students bringing a weapon to school to hurt another student or a teacher (Skiba, 2000). Zero tolerance, however, has become a discipline philosophy that suspends increasing numbers of students, especially minority students, for nonviolent infractions or scuffles. Growing research documents the negative effects of out-of-school suspensions and challenges the assumption that zero tolerance policies are effective.

It is not the goal of zero tolerance, however, but more often the methods of its implementation that create controversy in schools and communities. There are few newspaper editorials condemning schools and school boards for expelling a student who carried a knife to school for the sole purpose of attacking another student. But the classic zero tolerance strategy of punishing minor or even trivial events severely, or dramatically extending the length of school suspension or expulsion, has led to cries of injustice across the country. (Skiba, 2000, p. 15)

School security. Zero tolerance policies are increasingly supported by enhanced school security embodied in electronic surveillance, security staff, and adult supervision of public spaces. In 2000, 82% of high schools reported having staff or volunteers monitor hallways, and 45% reported routinely checking bags, desks, and lockers. Also, sizable percentages of high schools reported having uniformed police officers (30%), using surveillance cameras (24%), and using metal detectors (10%) (Centers for Disease Control and Prevention, 2002; Small et al., 2001). As is the case with airports and courts, high schools are increasingly using security personnel and equipment to prevent violence.

The effectiveness of the school security approach has not been thoroughly evaluated (Gottfredson et al., 2000; Skiba, 2000; Skiba & Peterson, 2000). Two cross-sectional national studies found that schools using these strategies reported higher levels of violence and lower levels of safety (Heaviside et al., 1998; Mayer & Leone, 1999). Although these results may simply reflect the fact that unsafe schools use security measures, the positive relationship between security use and violence suggests that security measures are insufficient to make schools safe.

Field research has shown that many students and teachers have negative perceptions of security guards as ineffective and sometimes harassing. This sharply contrasts with the view of administrators, who tend to have an extremely positive perception of security guards (Astor et al., 1999; Devine, 1996). Similar to zero tolerance, school security strategies have been criticized for alienating students from school and undermining relationships inside schools (Mayer & Leone, 1999; Noguera, 1995; Skiba, 2000). More extensive research on school security programs needs to be conducted to assess the negative effects identified in field and survey research and identify if, when, and how security procedures can be used effectively. For instance, in a school struggling with weapon violence, can the use of metal detectors or police be productive as a temporary solution?

Criticisms of Prevention and Discipline Strategies

Prevention programs and disciplinary strategies both assume that violence is caused by students' violent impulses or negative experiences outside of school. Violent behavior, however, emerges from an interaction between people's personality and their environment (Astor, Pitner, & Duncan, 1998; Devine, 1996; Laub & Sampson, 1993; Loeber & Stouthamer-Loeber, 1998; Tolan, Guerra, & Kendall, 1995). By focusing only on students, schools neglect how the school environment inhibits or exacerbates the chance of violence (Devine, 1996; Haynes, 1996). This is deeply problematic, because the school environment is related to the occurrence and severity of school violence (see later section focusing on environmental strategies).

Insufficient attention has been paid by educational researchers to the quality of human interactions that occur between children and adults at schools. A healthy school climate supports children's healthy development and facilitates their acquisition of the effective social and intellectual skills they need to survive and thrive. An unhealthy one leads to conflict among children, parents, and school personal and makes children's social and intellectual development difficult if at all possible. (Haynes, 1996, p. 309)

Also, the omission of environmental causes of violence can foster negative stereotypes that large number of students are violent and will be violent in any context (see Office of the Surgeon General, 2001). "Much of America is convinced that young people—particularly African American youth and children of color—are a menace; that these children, violent and without remorse, must be contained and feared" (Obidah, 2000, p. 57). Although the portrayal of youth as more violent and callous is prevalent in the media:

There is no evidence that young people involved in violence during the peak years of the early 1990s were more frequent or more vicious offenders than youths in earlier years. The increased lethality resulted from gun use, which has since decreased dramatically. There is no scientific evidence to document the claim of increased seriousness or callousness. (Office of the Surgeon General, 2001, p. 5)

A second myth is that abused and neglected children or aggressive children with behavioral problems will inevitably become violent; "most young people exposed to multiple risks will not become violent" (Office of the Surgeon General, 2001, p. 77). Although a relationship between child abuse and violent behavior exists (Office of the Surgeon General, 2001), less than 20% of youth who are abused or neglected display delinquent behavior (Lawrence, 1998). While recognizing that students' experiences outside of school affect their chance of becoming violent at school, researchers have to counter misconceptions about "violent" youth and stress the fact that experience and environment can facilitate prosocial behavior.

Environmental Strategies

A growing body of research documents that school context influences the occurrence and severity of school violence. Specifically, schools that possess an engaging curriculum and operate as communities characterized by respectful and supportive relationships tend to be safer (Bryk & Driscoll, 1988; Casella, 2001; Gottfredson, 2001; Learning First Alliance, 2001; Sandler et al., 2000; Sebring et al., 1996). Strong relationships among and between students and teachers are hypothesized to increase students' connection to school and, consequently, their tendency to value and respect its rules. Students' connection and attachment to school predict decreased involvement in violence (Jenkins, 1995; Resnick et al., 1997). Quasi-experimental research has shown that efforts to improve relationships among and between teachers and students can reduce the occurrence of school violence (Gottfredson, 2001). In fact, efforts to improve the climate of schools may have a larger impact on school violence than student-focused efforts such as prevention programs (Gottfredson, 2001; Office of the Surgeon General, 2001).

Other initiatives attempt to increase students' attachment to school by modifying a school's curriculum. A variety of approaches, such as pushing students to solve problems, connecting schoolwork with real-world experiences, and integrating students' culture into lessons, have been proposed as ways to increase students' engagement (Erickson, 1987; Newmann & Wehlage, 1995; Wasley, Hampel, & Clark, 1997). Also, academic support for failing students may disrupt the cycle of misbehavior and academic failure (McEnvoy & Welker, 2000). The vast range of instructional efforts and their possible effects on students' engagement is a topic deserving its own review, and these issues are not explored in depth here. Generally, supporters of environmental strategies argue that making schools relevant, valuable, and personable will make them safe.

The urban schools that I know that feel safe . . . don't have metal detectors or armed security guards, and their principals don't carry baseball bats. What these schools do have is a strong sense of community and collective responsibility. Such schools are seen by students as sacred territory, too special to be spoiled by crime and violence, and too important to risk one being excluded. (Noguera, 1995, p. 207)

Less quasi-experimental research has been conducted on school change strategies, because quasi-experimental designs are especially difficult to implement at the school level (Gottfredson, 2001; Office of the Surgeon General, 2001). As a result, most findings on school climate rely on survey and field research. This makes the direction of causality between positive school climate and low levels of school violence ambiguous. Also, the cross-sectional nature of most studies means that they describe the characteristics of safe schools but provide little information on how to transform the environment of schools struggling with violence. This is problematic, because

consistent effects on attachment and commitment to school and on achievement do not often translate into reductions in problem behavior. . . . Future research should attempt to further understand these apparent disconnects between cognitive and affective risk factors and problem behavior. (Gottfredson, 2001, p. 157)

A THEORY OF PREVENTION

Social-cognitive prevention programs, fair and consistent rules, strong relationships among and between teachers and students, and a strong academic program can work to make schools safer. Each of these strategies, however, has weaknesses. Schools have had trouble implementing effective prevention and discipline programs, and efforts to increase students' commitment to school and academic achievement do not always reduce student misbehavior. The interweaving of promise and problems suggests the need to synthesize these disparate theories of violence prevention, understand how these strategies can be effectively implemented in schools, and identify the mechanisms through which each of the strategies improves student behavior.

Although recent reviews insightfully document and critique contemporary initiatives to reduce school violence (Learning First Alliance, 2001; Office of the Surgeon General, 2001), discussions of student-centered approaches often occur in parallel with discussions about school organization. This is problematic, because violent behavior emerges from interactions between students' environment and personality (Laub & Sampson, 1993; Loeber & Stouthamer-Loeber, 1998; Pepler & Slaby, 1994; Tolan et al., 1995). Responding to this finding, the most successful approaches combine social-cognitive programs with efforts to improve students' school or home environment (Office of the Surgeon General, 2001). More generally, alternative juvenile justice programs that address problems through supervision and counseling while helping students reshape their environment by providing academic assistance and access to jobs or community service have produced significantly lower recidivism rates than imprisonment (Mendel, 2001). Combining individual and environmental change strategies can produce substantial improvements in youth behavior.

Building on such work, this review argues that four elements interact to make schools safe: quality relationships among and between staff and students, a schoolwide commitment to teaching nonviolent behavior, responsiveness to students' culture and community, and a strong academic program. These four factors are briefly reviewed in the sections to follow. It is not enough to profile safe schools; the mechanisms through which these factors interact to reduce violence are examined in order to support and spur discussion about contemporary and future violence prevention strategies.

Social Capital

Positive relationships between people and membership in groups such as families, churches, and civic organizations can produce positive benefits for both individuals and groups (Coleman, 1988; Putnam, 1993; Sullivan & Transue, 1999). Just as financial resources help people and communities accomplish goals, strong social relationships among people constitute a type of "social capital" that has visible benefits for a community.

If physical capital is wholly tangible, being embodied in observed material form, and human capital is less tangible, being embodied in the skills and knowledge acquired by an individual, social capital is less tangible yet, for it exists in the relations among persons. Just as physical capital and human capital facilitate productive activity, social capital does as well. For example, a group within which there is extensive trustworthiness . . . is able to accomplish much more than a comparable group without the trustworthiness. (Coleman, 1988, p. S100)

High levels of social capital are associated with lower levels of crime and violence. A cross-sectional study of crime in Chicago showed that crime was less prevalent in communities where adults trusted one another and were willing to intervene in problems (Sampson, Raudenbush, & Earls, 1997). Similarly, a variety of cross-sectional studies have revealed that schools with strong professional relationships among adults are safer (Bryk & Driscoll, 1988; Gottfredson, 2001; Noguera, 2001; Sebring et al., 1996). Quasi-experimental research and fieldwork suggest that improving professional relationships among educators does causally reduce school violence (Gottfredson, 2001; Office of the Surgeon General, 2001; Zane, 1994).

The mechanisms through which high levels of trust and cooperation among adults translate into lower levels of school violence, however, are not well understood and need to be delineated (Baker, 1998). As is the case with any resource, social capital is domain specific and needs to be mobilized and targeted toward the issue of violence in order to make schools safer.

Teaching Nonviolence

In the past, the mission of public schools was conceptualized broadly as educating students to become citizens who value critical thought, tolerance, and freedom (Dewey, 1916/1970; Newmann, 1981; Tyack & Duban, 1995). Over the last decade, raising student achievement is increasingly seen as the sole mission of schools, while poor attendance, disruptive behavior, and school violence are viewed as problems residing in students that specialists such as deans, psychologists, or security personnel handle (Aronson, 2000; Devine, 1996; Frymier & Gansneder, 1989). Consequently, schools have responded to school violence by adding programs, staff, and rules. Ironically, the growth of security and prevention programs may unintentionally be diminishing teachers' involvement in student discipline, because managing students' behavior is considered another person's job or dictated by policy (Casella, 2001; Devine, 1996).

Safe schools are more likely to emerge when teachers and all adults in schools view teaching respectful behavior as part of their job. For instance, differences between Catholic and public schools in classroom orderliness and cutting are partially explained by the tendency of Catholic schools to operate as a community. A sense of community grows from a diffuse teacher role in which teachers view guiding students ethically as part of their job (Bryk, Lee, & Holland, 1993). Disciplinary incidents are seen as an opportunity to provide guidance and reaffirm students' membership in the community. In fact, an "ethic of caring" and diffuse teacher roles is associated with students being more committed to school and less likely to become involved in violence (Astor et al., 1999; Bryk & Driscoll, 1988; Learning First Alliance, 2001;

Noddings, 1988; Zane, 1994). In a study of eight safe urban public schools, Sander et al. (2001) found that school discipline policy was driven by and part of the school mission.

Effective Instruction

Boredom and lack of academic challenge increase the likelihood of disruptive behavior. Administrators agreed that if students are academically challenged in class, they are less likely to misbehave. (Browne, 2001, p. 190)

Effective discipline consists of not simply trying to prevent negative behavior but actively engaging students academically. If youth value their work at school and feel connected to school, they are less likely to act violently than if they feel alienated (Resnick et al., 1997). Discipline policy and efforts to reduce school violence must be closely intertwined with efforts to improve academic achievement and engagement. The strong links between academic failure and discipline problems were discussed earlier.

Also, a strong academic focus prevents behavior and discipline from becoming the primary focus of schools. In some schools, discipline problems and discussions of such problems overshadow the academic mission (Zane, 1994). The focus becomes controlling instead of educating students. For instance, Browne's (2001) study of four similar schools in Dade County revealed low out-of-school suspension rates in schools that viewed their mission as educating all students and high suspension rates in schools that were primarily focused on demonstrating an intolerance of misbehavior.

Conversely, schools may sacrifice academic rigor in order to create a caring environment. A national study showed that the achievement of students was lower in schools serving low-income students when the students reported a caring environment but low academic expectations (Shouse, 1996). Only when a caring environment was coupled with high academic expectations was students' learning higher than average. A study of Chicago middle schools also showed that schools with high academic expectations and strong relationships between students and teachers achieved the largest academic gains for their students (Lee, Smith, Perry, & Smylie, 1999). Phillips (1997) raises the concern that a focus on caring relationships can lead to liberal patronizing and low expectations, especially for minority and low-income students. Although it is important for schools to actively work to foster prosocial behavior, the mission of the school cannot be allowed to become primarily about behavior at the expense of academic rigor.

Responsiveness to Students' Culture and Community

One major problem associated with contemporary discipline policies is that minority students, especially African American students, are disproportionately suspended (Skiba et al., 2000). A wide body of research documents how different cultural expectations, communication styles, and stereotypes collide to diminish academic opportunities of minority students and increase confrontations and punishment (Anyon,

1995; Cummins, 1986; McDermott, 1977; Reston, Sheets, & Gay, 1996; Schwartz, 2001; Townsend, 2000). This research suggests a variety of approaches such as monitoring discipline practices for bias, including students' culture in the curriculum, fostering better communication strategies for teachers and students, and establishing high academic expectations to minimize cultural conflicts. The establishment of fair discipline policies and the ability of schools to prevent discipline problems rely on adults in the school being respectful and responsive to students' culture.

ADULT RELATIONSHIPS

The remainder of this chapter shifts to an attempt to understand how the four elements just described interact to make schools safer. The present section focuses on relationships among adults, and the subsequent section addresses relationships between teachers and students. The organization and climate of schools is largely shaped by the structure and quality of relationships that exist among adults in schools. Specifically, quality of adult relationships is hypothesized to influence school safety through its effect on the quality and scope of prevention and discipline initiatives.

Implementation Quality

Prevention Programs

Although research on the "technology" of prevention has advanced in the past decade, we know little about the conditions necessary to apply these advances under real-world conditions. (Gottfredson, 2001, p. 256)

A national survey conducted in 1998 assessed the extent to which high school prevention programs (a) integrated scientifically validated best practices and (b) involved a large percentage of students for enough time to induce behavioral change. Only approximately 20% of prevention programs were shown to be well implemented (Gottfredson et al., 2000). Poor implementation has been found to diminish or undermine the effectiveness of similar public health prevention programs: "A number of quite theoretically correct programs have been only marginally effective because environmental influences and implementation concerns have not been addressed fully" (Winett, 1995, p. 341). Little direct research has explored organizational factors that influence implementation quality.

Social capital theory argues that "dense networks of interactions . . . probably broaden the participants' sense of self, developing the 'I' in the 'we' or (in the language of rational choice theorists) enhancing the participants' 'taste' for collective benefits" (Putnam, 1995, p. 67). In support of this hypothesis, strong professional relationships among and between school staff and parents enable greater organization improvements during periods of school reform (Bryk, Sebring, Kerbow, Rollow, & Easton, 1998; Sebring et al., 1995):

The social fabric woven among members of a school community is foundational for school improvement. Sustaining organizational change is highly unlikely in schools marred by distrust and disrespect, both within the staff and between staff and parents. (Sebring et al., 1995, p. 63)

Strong professional relationships provide schools social capital that enables them to implement higher quality prevention programs. The strength of professional relationships among faculty predicts the proportion of students who are involved in a prevention program and their extent of involvement (Gottfredson et al., 2000). Also, the processes through which a school identifies the need for violence prevention, implements a program, and operates the program can build social capital and influence teachers' perceptions, support, and involvement. Prevention programs that involve teachers from program inception and that are initiated by the school tend to be more broadly implemented and to include more effective instructional techniques (Gottfredson et al., 2000; Thorton et al., 2000). Involving teachers from the beginning builds teachers' trust and connection with the program.

Moreover, teacher involvement needs to be continual. Well-implemented programs provide incentives for staff to stay involved in the project and maintain its integrity (Office of the Surgeon General, 2001). Consistent involvement also enhances the quality of programs by adapting them to the local context (Gottfredson, 2001) and incrementally improving them over time (Stringfield & Herman, 1994). If prevention programs are to be effective, teachers need to have positive and evolving relationships with the programs.

The success of prevention programs is also tied to their responsiveness to the local school context and culture of students.

Skillfully developed interventions will carefully study the culture (norms, values, themes, symbols, and language) of their target groups through ethnographic and elicitation research methods involving collaboration. . . . More than just intuitively appealing and politically correct, culturally sensitive interventions . . . seem more acceptable and effective than generic and potentially culturally insensitive programs. (Winett, 1995, p. 348)

Students and teachers bring a diverse set of values and cultural experiences to prevention curriculums that influence how they learn and interpret the curriculums (Daiute, Stern, & Lelutiu-Weinberger, in press). Thus, the success of prevention programs relies on discussing, identifying, and negotiating the meaning of different values and assumptions instead of simply teaching a determined set of "correct" values.

School Discipline

Although nearly all high schools have written discipline policies, a national survey revealed that only half are consistent in how they enforce these policies (Gottfredson et al., 2000). Substantial organizational effort is required to translate rules into consistent practice. As suggested by the theory of social capital, strong relationships among teachers, administrators, and parents predict greater consistency in schools' discipline policies (Gottfredson et al., 2000; Verdugo & Schneider, 1999). For instance, an organizational intervention involving seven high schools increased the clarity and consistency of rules by increasing teachers' and students' involvement in school improvement efforts while simultaneously working with the school district to clarify its discipline policy. These efforts reduced school violence and fostered a stronger professional community (Gottfredson, 1986). A strong professional community may support more consistent discipline policies by increasing teachers' investment in the policies, facilitating teachers' communication about the meaning and application of the policies, and providing mutual support and a sense of accountability among teachers. Empirical research is needed to better explore, delineate, and test these proposed mechanisms.

Involving teachers in planning disciplinary policies is a critical component of successful school policies (Dwyer & Osher, 2000; Gottfredson et al., 2000; National Education Association, 1996). Conversely, weak administrative support for establishing consistent policies, turnover of school or program officials, or resistance among teachers diminishes the ability of schools to establish consistent policies (Gottfredson et al., 1993). Discipline policies are more consistent when organizational space is created for teachers to communicate, respond to, and revise the policies.

An important task for future research is identifying the process through which a school moves from inconsistent discipline policies to more consistent policies. Schools facing violence problems tend to be schools struggling with poor relationships among staff and poorly implemented discipline codes (Bryk & Driscoll, 1988; Gottfredson, 2001; Mayer & Leone, 1999). If social relationships among school staff are ignored, discipline reforms and violence prevention programs are biased toward working better in schools with less serious safety problems.

Scope of Programs

Instead of perceiving prevention and discipline initiatives as programs, very safe schools tend to integrate values such as respect into their school mission and align their school practices with these values (Curwin & Mendler, 1997; Noguera, 1995; Sandler et al., 2000). The belief that teaching nonviolent behavior is the responsibility of all school staff helps reduce violence by increasing staff members' commitment to model prosocial behavior, increasing the ability of staff to intervene effectively, and heightening adults' ownership of public spaces.

Prevention Programs

The shared belief among school staff that teaching students to behave nonviolently is a school goal enhances the effectiveness of social-cognitive interventions by encouraging adults to model social-cognitive skills throughout the school. In schools, social problems are often addressed through techniques used to teach other academic subjects (Gottfredson et al., 2000; Tyack & Duban, 1995). Although classroom prevention programs are easy to integrate into a school day, classroom programs implicitly view behavioral change as an intellectual process. This approach is incomplete, because adolescents tend to learn social skills and behavior by seeing them modeled in school and elsewhere in their lives (Aronson, 2000; Bandura, 1986; Thorton et al., 2000). For instance, a meta-analysis of drug prevention programs showed that programs modeling desired behavior through interactive instruction, role-playing, and rehearsal reduced substance abuse more than programs relying on lectures (Tobler & Stratton, 1997). Gottfredson (2001) observed the same pattern in her review of violence prevention programs.

At a school level, students are more likely to internalize nonviolent behavior if educators model effective conflict-resolution techniques and act in ways consistent with nonviolent policies (Dryfoos, 1998; Learning First Alliance, 2001; Sandler et al., 2000).

> The W. T. Grant Consortium on the School-Based Promotion of Social Competence researchers note, however, that not only do young people need to learn these skills, they also need to see them modeled and need to practice them in a setting where they are provided with feedback and with reinforcements for choosing to use these skills and for using them well. (Lantieri & Patti, 1998, p. 360)

Consistently modeling social-cognitive skills throughout the school can substantially reduce school violence. An evaluation of a program called Peacemakers that works with teachers and students to resolve conflict peacefully revealed a 41% reduction in aggression-related disciplinary incidents and a 67% decrease in suspensions for violent behavior (Brooks et al., 2000). Moreover, a recent Centers for Disease Control and Prevention report concluded that "the effectiveness of social-cognitive interventions depends largely on a whole-school approach. In other words, all members of the school community—from administrators to teachers to students and other school personnel—should have a role" (Thorton et al., 2000, p. 121).

These results suggest that an important step in creating a school violence prevention strategy is to determine a core set of values that all staff approve, model, and are held accountable for (Curwin & Mendler, 1997). Delineation of a few clear organizational values enhances the quality of school change efforts by creating a framework in which to coordinate efforts (Bryk et al., 1998). For instance, a greater proportion of students are exposed to prevention programs in high schools with clear and focused goals. Unfortunately, concern over school violence has pushed many high schools to implement a wide array of prevention programs that are uncoordinated (Gottfredson et al., 2000).

A growing number of researchers argue that multilayered prevention programs are the most effective and inexpensive strategy to prevent violence (Dryfoos, 1998; Dwyer & Osher, 2000; Skiba et al., 2001). For instance, Dwyer and Osher (2000) propose a three-level system composed of a schoolwide prevention plan, early intervention for misbehaving students, and intensive intervention for students with chronic behavioral problems. An effective schoolwide prevention plan consisting of coordinated anger-management and conflict-resolution training may prevent as much as 80% of problematic student behavior (Dwyer & Osher, 2000). Some students will exhibit chronic disciplinary problems that require intensive interventions. Strong relationships and a commitment to teaching nonviolent behavior throughout the school have an impact on the effectiveness of this type of schoolwide approach. Teachers have to trust that students referred for more intensive intervention will be helped but at the same time limit referrals by creating a positive classroom environment and resolving most problems in their classrooms. Reciprocally, successful resolution of referrals provides teachers needed support in addressing chronic misbehavior. A coordinated schoolwide prevention and intervention system requires strong relationships among faculty, a strong organizational focus, and a broad commitment to teaching nonviolent behavior.

School Discipline

Strong relationships among adults in schools, coupled with a belief that teaching nonviolence is a school's responsibility, enhance the ability of teachers to effectively prevent and intervene in violent incidents. Sociological research on social capital suggests a strong link between quality of relationships in a community and violence. For example, in Chicago, neighborhoods characterized by strong relationships among neighbors (i.e., social cohesion) were more likely to confront a truant youth or a person disturbing a public space (i.e., social control); in turn, neighborhoods where residents exerted high levels of informal social control experienced lower levels of violence (Sampson, 1997). Sampson et al. (1997) argued that these two concepts, social cohesion and control, measured a single underlying concept called collective efficacy.

The willingness of local residents to intervene for the common good depends in large part on conditions of mutual trust and solidarity among neighbors. Indeed, one is unlikely to intervene in a neighborhood context in which the rules are unclear and people mistrust or fear one another. It follows that socially cohesive neighborhoods will prove the most fertile contexts for the realization of informal social control. (p. 919)

Similarly, strong professional relationships may increase the ability of teachers to effectively and consistently address student disobedience. This provides one possible explanation of the documented relationship between the strength of a school's professional community and school violence (Bryk & Driscoll, 1988; Learning First Alliance, 2001). The likelihood of behavioral norms being adapted partially depends on the quality of relationships among actors and the degree to which they take mutual responsibility for enforcing the norms (Coleman, 1988, 1990). For instance, dropout rates may be lower in Catholic schools even after control for student characteristics, because parents and teachers transmit a consistent set of values (Coleman, 1988). "In a community where there is an extensive set of expectations and obligations connecting the adults, each adult can use his drawing account with other adults to help supervise and control his children" (Coleman, 1990, p. 318).

Similarly, the strength of relationships among faculty may facilitate consistent use and enforcement of discipline policies. Social capital, however, is domain specific (Sampson, Morenoff, & Earls, 1999), and therefore it is unlikely that positive professional relationships will translate into a consistent discipline policy unless teaching nonviolent behavior is part of the school mission. Unlike Catholic schools, public schools are pluralistic, and creating an agreed upon set of values is more difficult (Noguera, 2001). The broad concern over school violence, however, suggests a widespread consensus against violence. The fostering of positive parent and school relationships is important because it will make the discipline policy more responsive to community values and increase social closure.

Organizational factors can influence the closeness of relationships (i.e., social closure) in schools. In contemporary high schools, social closure is low, because most such schools are large and students pass through a variety of classrooms where teachers do not know each other (Gladden, 1998; Johnson et al., 2002; Klonsky, 2002; Noguera, 2001). Interventions have tried to address this problem by having teams of teachers work with the same set of students. For instance, a team of six teachers may teach English, math, social studies, and science to a group of 150 students. Creating teams of teachers creates high levels of social closure; teachers work with the same set of students, work collectively to solve student problems, and transmit consistent values, rewards, and punishments to students. In one such intervention, teachers reported decreases in students' disciplinary problems and commented that "if we think about our work as a team, no one of us had accomplished alone what we are now doing together" (Zane, 1994, p. 127). Other field research on this type of approach, called schools-within-schools, suggests that schools-within-schools operate to reduce violence by enhancing relationships among and between staff and students (Fine, 1994; Wasley et al., 1997). Quasi-experimental research has shown that creating teacher teams can reduce school violence (Felner, Ginter, & Primavera, 1982). High levels of social closure make it easier to mobilize social capital in addressing discipline.

More research needs to be conducted to understand how social control and closure operate in schools and to identify organizational characteristics that inhibit or encourage their development. For instance, how do teachers informally and successfully maintain order in their classroom? How can the ability of one teacher to maintain order in a classroom be used to help another teacher who is struggling to maintain order with the same group of students?

TEACHER-STUDENT RELATIONSHIPS

High levels of student alienation make school violence more likely (Learning First Alliance, 2001; National Institute of Education, 1978; Newmann, 1981; Sebring et al., 1996). By strengthening relationships between adults and students, schools can directly address students' sense of alienation and lower the likelihood of violence. In addition, strong relationships between students and teachers combine with high academic expectations, a commitment to nonviolent behavior, and cultural responsiveness to reduce violence by making discipline practices more effective and increasing the ownership of public spaces.

Student Alienation

The best-documented fact in the extensive United States literature on youth is the importance of social bonding between a young person and an adult. (Dryfoos, 1998, p. 39)

The large size of high schools (more than 25% of high schools serve 1,000 or more students), coupled with the division of the school day into multiple periods, results in teachers seeing 100 to 200 students a day for 45 to 50 minutes. High teacher-to-student ratios make the establishment of teacher-student relationships difficult and are associated with higher levels of school violence (Franklin & Crone, 1992; Gladden, 1998; Klonsky, 2002; Learning First Alliance, 2001; National Institute of Education, 1978). More generally, attachment to an adult in school reduces the chances of students becoming involved in violence (Blum & Rinehart, 1997; Thorton et al., 2000). Although the power of single relationships should not be over-estimated, strong relationships between students and teachers can powerfully influence students. One of the most widely reported predictors of resilience, a student functioning "healthfully" in the face of many stressors, is a relationship with a caring prosocial adult (Hill, Soriano, Chen, & LaFromboise, 1994).

Effective Discipline

The use and effect of punishment in schools is partially determined by the quality of relationships between students and teachers, the responsiveness of teachers to students' culture, and high academic expectations. These factors influence teachers' use of stereotypes, their tendency to discipline students for interpersonal or cultural misunderstandings, their capacity to align punishments to students' misbehavior, and their ability to influence students' behavior through punishment. People are most likely to use stereotypes when they have little information about a situation or person (Fiske & Taylor, 1991). The organization of high schools often restricts teachers' individualized knowledge of students and increases the odds that stereotypes will influence disciplinary decisions (Noguera, 1995; Powell, 2000). Improving relationships between students and teachers, however, does not guarantee more equitable discipline practices.

"Initially, most disciplinary problems are relatively minor disruptions, originate in classrooms, and are interpersonal in nature" (Reston et al., 1996, p. 84). Some perceived discipline problems emerge from different cultural styles of communication, such as the tendency of African American students to use call and response more than White students, and can be defused through effective communication (Reston et al., 1996; Sheets, 1996; Townsend, 2000). Fostering trust and cultural understanding between students and teachers can resolve inevitable misunderstandings without a need to resort to disciplinary actions. Disciplinary incidents and problems have been shown to be less frequent when students report liking their teacher (Reston et al., 1996).

Punishments that address the reasons fueling student misbehavior are more likely to resolve behavioral problems (Curwin & Mendler, 1997; Mayer, 1999). For instance, student misbehavior can be caused by students' desire to avoid a task or get attention. If students are misbehaving to avoid a task, sending them from the room may reinforce their negative behavior. Similarly, suspending a student for truancy is likely to worsen the problem (Noguera, 2001). In these instances, more effective approaches may involve providing additional academic support and requiring in-school suspensions. In contrast, a student who is misbehaving to get attention should not receive additional help or attention. Instead, positive rather than disruptive behaviors should be reinforced (Mayer, 1999). Effective responses to misbehavior require that teachers and students honestly identify, talk about, and address the reasons behind misbehavior.

The effectiveness of sanctions in reducing violent behavior depends on the sanction being delivered fairly, people's attachment to the institution or person delivering the punishment, and the reintegration of people back into their community (Sherman, 1993; Short, 1997).

1. Sanctions provoke future defiance of the law (persistence [*sic*], more frequent, or more serious violation) to the extent that offenders have weak bonds to the sanctioning agent and community, and that offenders deny their shame and become proud of their isolation from the sanctioning community.
2. Sanctions produce future deterrence of law-breaking (desistance, less serious violations) to the extent that offenders experience sanctioning conduct as legitimate, that offenders have strong bonds to the sanctioning agent and community, and that offenders accept their shame and remain proud of solidarity with community. (Sherman, 1993, as cited in Short, 1997, p. 191)

A similar theory of reintegrative shaming argues that punishment is most effective when it displays disapproval for people's behavior while sustaining a respectful relationship, involves ceremonies forgiving as well as punishing people, and focuses on the harmfulness of the act without labeling the person as harmful (Braithwaite, 1995). This work suggests that school discipline will be more effective when students value their participation in school and perceive punishments as fair. If a student perceives a punishment as unfair and views her or his school negatively, punishments may fuel feelings of disrespect and increase the likelihood that the student will reject school values (Braithwaite, 1995; Sherman, 1993). Teenagers are especially sensitive to being disrespected and develop notions of fairness in their teenage years (Advancement Project and Civil Rights Project, 2000; Casella, 2001). Finally, punishment needs to focus on resolving students' negative behaviors and reintegrating them back into class.

In support of this argument, ethnographic research has shown that punishment is more effective and classrooms are safer when teachers integrate three factors, as follows. "When I have asked students in interviews what makes a particular teacher special' and worthy of respect, the students consistently cite three characteristics: firmness, compassion, and an interesting, engaging, and challenging teaching style" (Noguera, 1995, p. 305). Social links between teachers and students help students struggling with violence or poor academic performance stay committed to school. More generally, schools tend to be safer when they actively work to build trust with students, address causes of violence, and set high academic standards (Sandler et al., 2000). For instance, a team of high school teachers attributed reductions in school violence to their ability to forge trusting relationships with their students and be fair.

Students know we will sit and listen. They can get angry and disagree, and we'll help them work through it. If teachers ask them a question, students know that teachers legitimately care about their response. . . . Students now trust talking rather than fighting. (Zane, 1994, p. 129)

Contemporary trends in school discipline, however, tend not to address the causes of violent behavior and exclude students instead of reintegrating them. For instance, high schools tend to use a limited range of punishments and often do not use positive reinforcements (Gottfredson et al., 2000). Because high school classes are often short, teachers are under pressure to keep classes focused on instruction, and this may bias teachers toward excluding students for minor misbehavior. More research needs to be conducted exploring the organizational factors that encourage use of a wide range of disciplinary practices or reliance on exclusionary practices. Some studies suggest that principals play a critical role in determining the tone of school discipline (Browne, 2001).

Violence in Public Spaces

Violent incidents and fear in high schools tend to cluster in public spaces such as hallways, lunchrooms, and bathrooms (Astor et al., 1999; Kenney & Watson, 1996; National Institute of Education, 1978; Sebring et al., 1996). A national study and a study of five midwestern high schools revealed that approximately 60% of serious violent incidents occurred during passing periods or at lunchtime, even though students spent less than 10% of their day in these situations. Conversely, classrooms were havens from serious violence, and the presence of an adult greatly reduced the chance of violence (Astor et al., 1999; National Institute of Education, 1978). While the frequency of violent events varied across school contexts, violent incidents consistently took place in public spaces (Astor et al., 1999).

Shifting from student to environmental explanations of school violence, researchers have identified overcrowding and weak ownership of public spaces as important issues (Astor et al., 1999; Devine, 1996). Crowded public spaces in schools are vulnerable to violence because they are hard to supervise, diminish students' sense of control, and decrease the chance students or adults will intervene. Crowded environments have been found to produce emotional strain and diminish people's feeling of control. This in turn can reduce people's tolerance for frustration (Darley & Gilbert, 1985) and make conflicts more likely. For instance, according to one high school student, "I think you should [be able to] go basically anywhere during lunch . . . because keeping a lot of people together kind of generates a fight" (Astor et al., 1999, p. 33). Also, people's tendency to intervene in a dispute or problem is inversely related to the number of bystanders witnessing the event. In crowded situations, people are less likely to recognize an emergency situation and take responsibility for intervening (Latane & Darley, 1970). Crowded public spaces such as hallways increase frustration and decrease the chance that students or adults will intervene.

A second factor contributing to the insecurity of public spaces is the increasingly narrow definition of high school teachers' professional role as teaching a curriculum and keeping their classroom safe. The responsibility for generally keeping students safe rests with administrators, security staffs, and students' families (Devine, 1996).

Teachers accepted responsibility for helping students learn in the areas of reading, writing, mathematics, and higher-order thinking skills. But they thought that parents and students were responsible for students' daily attendance, listening, attitude toward school, completion of homework, general behavior in school and attention in class. (Frymier & Gansneder, 1989, p. 145)

In this type of environment, security guards and specialists are viewed as dealing with behavioral "distractions." Increasing school safety becomes synonymous with increasing the size, extent, and effectiveness of the security force (Devine, 1996). As shown earlier, enhanced security technology and personnel cannot fully substitute for adults who know students (Astor et al., 1999; Devine, 1996; Mayer & Leone, 1999; Noguera, 1995). For instance, security staff in five midwestern high schools felt they could not effectively monitor the hundreds to thousands of students moving though public spaces and therefore denied responsibility for preventing violence in their schools' public spaces. In the same high schools, administrative policies on student conflicts in public spaces were unclear and contradictory. Consequently, no adults felt responsibility for monitoring approximately a third of the physical space in the schools (Astor et al., 1999). In one urban high school especially troubled by high rates of violence, a teacher stated that teachers controlled the classrooms and students controlled the hallways (Devine, 1996). Surveys and fieldwork suggest that the ownership of public spaces is weak in many high schools.

The presence of an adult who knows students is viewed as one of the most effective ways to prevent violence (Astor et al., 1999; Noguera, 1995; Thorton et al., 2000). Indeed, classrooms are consistently safer than public spaces in schools (Astor et al., 1999; National Institute of Education, 1978; Sebring et al., 1996). Astor et al. (1999) cautioned that improving connections and respect among teachers and students in classrooms may not improve school safety if these relationships remain isolated in classrooms and fail to extend to the public spaces where most school violence occurs. A commitment by adults to supervise students throughout the school as well as in their own classroom is required. Research on Catholic schools suggests that they experience lower levels of violence because students and teachers have strong relationships outside the classroom and adults feel responsible for supervising the full school (Bryk et al., 1993).

More generally, residents' ownership of public spaces such as parks, streets, and hallways in buildings is related to occurrence of violence (Astor et al., 1999; Sampson et al., 1997). Also, the size of high schools ensures that most students will be unknown by teachers supervising the hallways. Smaller schools might possess safer public areas because teachers and students will tend to know each other. Whether strong relationships among professionals in schools coupled with an expanded sense of responsibility can reduce violence in public spaces is an empirical question that needs to be tested.

A major challenge for establishing a stronger sense of ownership in public spaces will be overcoming fear. Incidents of violence in public spaces evoke fear that erodes teachers' willingness to intervene or monitor public spaces (Astor et al., 1999; Gottfredson et al., 2000). Astor et al. (1999) found that high school teachers often felt isolated when they intervened in fights because they felt the choice to intervene was an individual one and believed that the administration provided weak support. Exceptional teachers did intervene in fights, but school safety should not require teachers to act exceptionally. Teachers alone cannot be expected to simply take ownership of public spaces. Clear policies and administrative support are needed.

Problem-solving teams may offer an effective approach because they simultaneously address the insecurity of public spaces and teachers' feelings of isolation. For instance, one school created problem-solving teams in its 11th-grade classrooms that identified, assessed, and implemented solutions to crime-, order-, and fear-related problems. These teams were composed of classroom students, a police officer, and a number of classroom teachers. The teams created and implemented plans to address problems with orderliness in the hallways, lunchroom, and restrooms. Students in the school (relative to those in a control school) reported significant reductions in fear and violent incidents in the public spaces targeted by the project (Kenney & Watson, 1996). Beyond clarifying strategies to intervene in public spaces, research and interventions need to explore strategies (e.g., problem-solving groups) that will generate higher levels of ownership.

Relationships Among Students

The quality of relationships among students is also related to school safety. High school students reporting a strong sense of community are less likely to cut classes, drop out of school (Royal & Rossi, 1996), and engage in violent behavior (Battistich & Hom, 1997; Learning First Alliance, 2001). Also, students' involvement in violence is related to whether the dominant peer culture in a school values academic achievement and approves the use of violence (Office of the Surgeon General, 2001). A strong sense of community among students may reduce violence by increasing students' tendency to identify with other students. If people identify with a group, they tend to have more favorable and personable views of the members of that group (Aronson, 2000). This alone reduces aggressive behavior, because individuals are less likely to behave cruelly toward others when they are humanized or even personalized somewhat (Aronson, 2000; Bandura, Underwood, & Fromson 1975). Relationships among students in schools can be shaped by the structure of schools. Next, I explore how group strategies influence student behavior.

A popular approach for working with high-risk youth is peer counseling. In peer counseling programs, an adult typically leads a group of high-risk youth in discussions that encourage the students to voice and confront their behavioral or academic problems. These sessions are designed to generate peer pressure to conform to prosocial norms (Gottfredson, 2001). Evaluations have shown that peer counseling is ineffective in modifying students' behavior and is sometimes associated with increases in delinquent behavior (Gottfredson, 2001; Office of the Surgeon General, 2001). For instance, at-risk students participating in a 4-day psychological workshop demonstrated more negative interactions with teachers after the intervention. In this instance, group counseling created a negative peer group that shared antisocial norms (Caterall, 1987). Many of the students in the intervention had few institutional or group affiliations at school, and their desire for social connection took precedence over the content of the sessions.

Schools, however, can establish group dynamics that foster prosocial behavior. Aggression among youth can be reduced if students are given a common goal that requires the efforts of all students to accomplish (Aronson, 2000). This type of situation, however, rarely occurs in high school classrooms that tend to focus on individual performance and teacher-directed instruction; "it would be hard to find a high school or middle school that goes out of its way to demonstrate a high value on inclusion and cooperation among all of its students" (Aronson, 2000, p. 134). Addressing this problem, Aronson and Gonzalez (1988) developed a cooperative learning strategy called the jigsaw classroom. In the jigsaw classroom, students are divided into groups, and each student in the group is given a "piece" of an assignment that he or she must teach to other students in the group. In order to succeed on the assignment, students must not only learn the information given to them but help other students in the group effectively communicate their knowledge. With proper teacher guidance, students realize that their grade is reliant on helping instead of ridiculing low-achieving students in their group.

This program has been successful in decreasing tensions among students, increasing positive views of students across racial lines, and teaching the same amount of material to all students in the classroom (Aronson, 2000; Aronson & Gonzalez, 1988). Cooperative learning practices have generally shown promise in reducing violent behavior (Office of the Surgeon General, 2001) and were a key element of a successful anti-bullying program in Norway that reduced reported bullying rates in half over the course of 20 months (Olweus & Alsaker, 1991). However, cooperative learning strategies and strong relationships among students alone may not reduce violence (Gottfredson, 2001; Solomon et al., 1992). Cooperative practices are effective to the extent they teach students social-cognitive skills (Gottfredson, 2001). Successful use of cooperative learning strategies requires simultaneous instruction in academic and social skills.

Extracurricular activities also have been proposed as a method to address school violence. Extracurricular activities provide students opportunities to interact collectively and are often conducted between 3 and 6 p.m., when most adolescent violence occurs (Ayers, Ayers, & Dohrn, 2001). Studies have confirmed that students involved in extracurricular activities are more committed to school (McNeeley et al., 2002). Higher levels of commitment are in turn related to a decreased likelihood of violent behavior (Resnick et al., 1997). The need for extracurricular activities is more acute in economically impoverished areas (Hart, Atkins, & Ford, 1998).

The largest difference between affluent and impoverished communities has been shown to be access to prosocial activities (Furstenberg, Cook, Eccles, Elder, & Sameroff, 1999). Recent work suggests that involving students in community service programs can reduce their involvement in violence (Billig, 2000). Other reviews, however, have shown that extracurricular participation does not reduce violence, even though it does have other positive benefits for students (Gottfredson, 2001).

More research is needed to provide an understanding of whether and how extracurricular activities reduce school violence. As a result of the diverse nature of extracurricular activities, research needs to explore whether different types of extracurricular activities differentially influence students' propensity to behave violently.

CONCLUSION

As public concern has grown over school violence, the vast majority of schools have implemented a range of violence prevention programs (Gottfredson et al., 2000). Experience and assessment of initiatives have revealed both promise and problems. The mixed results of contemporary approaches highlight the need for a broader theoretical framework. This review argues that four elements interact to make schools safe: strong relationships between teachers and students, a broad commitment to teaching nonviolent behavior, a strong academic program, and responsiveness to students' community and culture. Each element has the potential to reduce school violence, but large reductions will be more likely when multiple elements are coordinated in schools. At present, many high schools have a large number of violence prevention initiatives that are often uncoordinated (Gottfredson et al., 2001). Empirical and theoretical work is needed to explore and test the interactions and relationships posited in this review.

Future violence prevention research and programs face three major challenges: reducing the strong relationship between community and school violence (National Education Association, 1996; Sebring et al., 1996), understanding the processes schools undergo to make themselves safer, and building a better understanding of how school organization influences school violence. Issues of school safety are acute in areas with high crime rates, and resources and research need to work to reduce this relationship. Also, longitudinal research is needed to understand how schools change and improve their level of safety. Most research on the relationship between school organization and violence is cross sectional and therefore provides limited insight into the process of change.

A better understanding of the links between school organization and violence is needed. For instance, high school teachers often assess school climate as poor; in a recent survey of small and large high schools, only approximately 19% of teachers reported high teacher morale in their schools (Johnson et al., 2002). Differences between elementary and high school climates are striking. For instance, in Chicago, the school climates of the best high schools approximate the school climates of the worst elementary schools (Sebring et al., 1995). The general tendency of high schools to be more alienating indicates organizational problems.

What is there about the structure and culture of the institution that propagates and reproduces the destructive interpersonal dynamics evident in so many schools? The vast majority of teachers that I meet seem genuinely concerned about their students, and sincerely desire to be effective at what they do. (Noguera, 1995, p. 205)

"Personalization is a matter of organization design rather than of individual teachers' values and practices" (McLaughlin & Talbert, 1990, p. 230). Size and anonymity, leadership, and teacher involvement are organizational factors that influence the safety of schools. General anonymity and weak professional relationships in high schools diminish the ability to reduce violence. Research on community crime (Sampson et al., 1999) and social closure (Coleman, 1990) highlights the fact that strengthening ties among and between teachers and parents can result in more consistent behavioral norms that are respected by students. A range of reforms such as smaller schools, smaller classes, team teaching, expert teachers, extensive extracurricular activities, more outreach to parents, and advisory periods have been proposed as ways to increase connections among teachers, parents, and students (Klonsky, 2002; Learning First Alliance, 2001).

School leadership also critically determines how discipline is expressed in a school. In schools where leadership is focused on providing educational opportunities to all students, discipline tends to take place inside the school, and suspensions are reserved for violent incidents. In contrast, schools focused on demonstrating intolerance for misbehavior tend to have higher out-of-school suspension rates and to suspend students for minor or first offenses (Browne, 2001).

Even in schools struggling with high levels of disorder and violence, some classrooms are orderly and engaging. Efforts to reduce violence need to better incorporate the experience and insights of successful teachers. On a broader level, involving teachers in discipline and prevention initiatives improves the quality of such initiatives. Instead of viewing violence prevention programs as elements to be added on top of schools in the form of additional interventions, serious reflection on how the structure of schools can be geared to reduce violence is needed.

NOTES

[1] Violent crimes include rape, robbery, aggravated assault, and simple assault.

[2] Emotional distress was measured as follows: "In the past week or past year, how often have you felt depressed (lonely, sad, fearful, crying, moody, had a poor appetite)?"

[3] Weapons were defined as objects such as guns, knives, and clubs.

[4] A number of comprehensive reviews of school violence prevention initiatives have recently been published and were instrumental in guiding this review (Gottfredson, 2001; Learning First Alliance, 2001; Office of the Surgeon General, 2001).

[5] The law was amended and now covers any weapon that can be used to cause harm, instead of just firearms.

REFERENCES

Advancement Project and Civil Rights Project. (2000). *Opportunities suspended: The devastating consequences of zero tolerance and school discipline policies.* Boston: Civil Rights Project.

Anyon, J. (1995). Race, social class, and educational reform in an inner-city school. *Teachers College Record, 97,* 69–94.

Aronson, E. (2000). *Nobody left to hate: Teaching compassion after Columbine.* New York: Worth.

Aronson, E., & Gonzalez, A. (1988). Desegregation, jigsaw, and the Mexican-American experience. In P. Katz & D. Taylor (Eds.), *Eliminating racism: Profiles in controversy.* New York: Plenum.

Astor, R., Behre, W., Fravil, K., & Wallace, J. (1997). Perceptions of school violence as a problem and reports of violent events: A national survey of school social workers. *Social Work, 42,* 55–68.

Astor, R., Meyer, H., & Behre, W. (1999). Unowned places and times: Maps and interviews about violence in high schools. *American Educational Research Journal, 36,* 3–42.

Astor, R., Pitner, R., & Duncan, B. (1998). Ecological approaches to mental health consultation with teachers on issues related to youth and school violence. *Journal of Negro Education, 65,* 336–355.

Ayers, W., Ayers, R., & Dohrn, B. (2001). Introduction: Resisting zero tolerance. In W. Ayers, B. Dohrn, & R. Ayers (Eds.), *Zero tolerance: Resisting the drive for punishment in our schools.* New York: New Press.

Ayers, W., Dohrn, B., & Ayers, R. (Eds.). (2001). *Zero tolerance: Resisting the drive for punishment in our schools.* New York: New Press.

Baker, J. (1998). Are we missing the forest for the trees? Considering the social context of school violence. *Journal of School Psychology, 36,* 29–44.

Bandura, A. (1986). *Social foundations of thought and action: A social cognitive theory.* Englewood Cliffs, NJ: Prentice Hall.

Bandura, A., Underwood, B., & Fromson, M. (1975). Disinhibition of aggression through diffusion of responsibility and dehumanization of victims. *Journal of Research in Personality, 9,* 253–269.

Battistich, V., & Hom, A. (1997). The relationship between students' sense of their school as a community and their involvement in problem behaviors. *American Journal of Public Health, 87,* 1997–2001.

Billig, S. (2000). Research on K–12 school-based service learning: The evidence builds. *Phi Delta Kappan, 81,* 658–664.

Blum, R., & Rinehart, P. (1997). *Reducing the risk: Connections that make a difference in the lives of youth.* Bethesda, MD: Add Health.

Braithwaite, J. (1995). Reintegrative shaming, republicanism, and policy. In H. Barlow (Ed.), *Crime and public policy: Putting theory to work.* New York: Westview Press.

Brooks, K., Schiraldi, V., & Ziedenberg, J. (2000). *School house hype: Two years later.* Washington, DC: Justice Policy Institute/Children's Law Center.

Browne, J. (2001). The ABCs of school discipline: Lessons from Miami-Dade County. In W. Ayers, B. Dohrn, & R. Ayers (Eds.), *Zero tolerance: Resisting the drive for punishment in our schools.* New York: New Press.

Bryk, A., & Driscoll, M. (1988). *The high school as community: The contextual influences and consequences for students and teachers.* Madison, WI: National Center on Effective Secondary Schools.

Bryk, A., Lee, V., & Holland, P. (1993). *Catholic schools and the common good.* Cambridge, MA: Harvard University Press.

Bryk, A., Sebring, P., Kerbow, D., Rollow, S., & Easton, J. (1998). *Chartering Chicago school reform: Democratic localism as a lever for change.* Boulder, CO: Westview Press.

Casella, R. (2001). *At zero tolerance: Punishment, prevention, and school violence.* New York: Peter Lang.

Caterall, J. (1987). An intensive group counseling dropout prevention intervention: Some cautions on isolating at-risk adolescents within high schools. *American Educational Research Journal, 24,* 521–540.

Centers for Disease Control and Prevention. (2002). *Injury fact book 2001–2002.* Atlanta, GA: Author.

CNN.com. (2001, March 8). An epidemic of violence: Incidents in schools rise sharply since Santee shooting. Available: http://www.cnn.com/2001/US/03/08/alarming.incidents/index.html

Coleman, J. (1988). Social capital in the creation of human capital. *American Journal of Sociology, 94,* S95–S120.

Coleman, J. (1990). *Foundations of social theory.* Cambridge, MA: Belknap Press of Harvard University Press.

Cummins, J. (1986). Empowering minority students: A framework for intervention. *Harvard Educational Review, 56,* 18–36.

Curwin, R., & Mendler, A. (1997). *As tough as necessary: Countering violence, aggression, and hostility in our schools.* Alexandria, VA: Association for Supervision and Curriculum Development.

Daiute, C., Stern, R., & Lelutiu-Weinberger, C. (in press). Negotiating violence prevention. *Journal of Social Issues.*

Darley, J., & Gilbert, D. (1985). Social psychological aspects of environmental psychology. In G. Lindzey & E. Aronson (Eds.), *Handbook of social psychology* (Vol. 2). New York: Random House.

Devine, J. (1996). *Maximum security: The culture of violence in inner-city schools.* Chicago: University of Chicago Press.

Dewey, J. (1970). Democracy and education. In S. M. Cahn (Ed.), *The philosophical foundations of education.* New York: Harper & Row. (Original work published 1916)

Dryfoos, J. (1998). *Safe passage: Making it through adolescence in a risky society.* New York: Oxford University Press.

Dwyer, K., & Osher, D. (2000). *Safeguarding our children: An action guide.* Washington, DC: U.S. Departments of Education and Justice.

Erickson, F. (1987). Transformation and school success: The politics and culture of educational achievement. *Anthropology and Education Quarterly, 18,* 335–356.

Felner, R., Ginter, M., & Primavera, J. (1982). Primary prevention during school transitions: Social support and environmental structure. *American Journal of Community Psychology, 10,* 277–290.

Fine, M. (1994). Chartering urban school reform. In M. Fine (Ed.), *Chartering urban school reform.* New York: Teachers College Press.

Fine, M., & Smith, K. (2001). Zero tolerance: Reflections on a failed policy that won't die. In W. Ayers, B. Dohrn, & R. Ayers (Eds.), *Zero tolerance: Resisting the drive for punishment in our schools.* New York: New Press.

Fiske, S., & Taylor, S. (1991). *Social cognition* (2nd ed.). New York: McGraw-Hill.

Franklin, B., & Crone, L. (1992, November). *School accountability: Predictors and indicators of Louisiana school effectiveness.* Paper presented at the meeting of the Mid-South Educational Research Association, Knoxville, TN.

Frymier, J., & Gansneder, B. (1989, October). The Phi Delta Kappa study of students at risk. *Phi Delta Kappan,* pp. 142–146.

Furstenberg, F., Cook, T., Eccles, J., Elder, G., & Sameroff, A. (1999). *Managing to make it: Urban families and adolescent success.* Chicago: University of Chicago Press.

Gladden, R. (1998). The small schools movement: A review of the literature. In M. Fine & J. Somerville (Eds.), *Small schools, big imaginations: A creative look at urban public schools.* Chicago: Cross City Campaign for Urban School Reform.

Gordon, R., Piana, L. D., & Keleher, T. (2000). *Facing the consequences: An examination of racial discrimination in U.S. public schools.* Oakland, CA: Applied Research Center.

Gordon, R., Piana, L. D., & Keleher, T. (2001). Zero tolerance: A basic racial report card. In W. Ayers, B. Dohrn, & R. Ayers (Eds.), *Zero tolerance: Resisting the drive for punishment in our schools.* New York: New Press.

Gottfredson, D. C. (1986). An empirical test of school-based environmental and individual interventions to reduce the risk of delinquent behavior. *Criminology, 24,* 705–731.

Gottfredson, D. C. (2001). *Schools and delinquency.* New York: Cambridge University Press.

Gottfredson, G. D., Gottfredson, D. C., & Czeh, E. R. (2000). *National Study of Delinquency Prevention in Schools*. Ellicott City, MD: Gottfredson Associates.

Gottfredson, D. C., Gottfredson, G. D., & Hybl, L. G. (1993). Managing adolescent behavior: A multiyear, multischool study. *American Educational Research Journal, 30*, 179–215.

Grogger, J. (1997). *Local violence, educational attainment, and teacher pay*. Cambridge, MA: National Bureau of Economic Research.

Hart, D., Atkins, R., & Ford, D. (1998). Urban America as a context for the development of moral identity in adolescence. *Journal of Social Issues, 54*, 513–530.

Haynes, N. (1996). Creating safe and caring school communities: Comer School Development Program schools. *Journal of Negro Education, 65*, 308–314.

Heaviside, S., Rowand, C., Williams, C., Farris, E., Burns, S., & McArthur, E. (1998). *Violence and discipline problems in U.S. public schools: 1996–97*. Washington, DC: National Center for Education Statistics.

Hill, H., Soriano, F., Chen, S., & LaFromboise, T. (1994). Sociocultural factors in the etiology and prevention of violence among ethnic minority youth. In J. Gentry & P. Schlegel (Eds.), *Reason to hope: A psychosocial perspective on violence and youth*. Washington, DC: American Psychological Association.

Jenkins, P. (1995). School delinquency and school commitment. *Sociology of Education, 68*, 221–239.

Johnson, J., Duffett, A., Farkas, S., & Collins, K. (2002). *Sizing things up: What parents, teachers and students think about large and small high schools*. New York: Public Agenda.

Kaplan, H., & Johnson, R. (1991). Negative social sanctions and juvenile delinquency: Effects of labeling in a model of deviant behavior. *Social Science Quarterly, 72*, 98–122.

Kaufman, P., Chen, X., Choy, S., Peter, K., Ruddy, S., Miller, A., Fleury, J., Chandler, K., Planty, M., & Rand, M. (2001). *Indicators of school crime and safety, 2001*. Washington, DC: U.S. Departments of Education and Justice.

Kenney, D., & Watson, T. (1996). Reducing fear in the schools: Managing conflict through students' problem solving. *Education and Urban Society, 28*, 436–455.

Klonsky, M. (2002, February). How smaller schools prevent school violence. *Educational Leadership*, pp. 65–69.

Lantieri, L., & Patti, J. (1998). Waging peace in our schools. *Journal of Negro Education, 65*, 356–368.

Latane, B., & Darley, J. (1970). Social determinants of bystander intervention in emergencies. In J. Macaulay & L. Berkowitz (Eds.), *Altruism and helping behavior*. New York: Academic Press.

Laub, J., & Sampson, R. (1993). Turning points in the life course: Why change matters to the study of crime. *Criminology, 31*, 301–325.

Lawrence, R. (1998). *School crime and juvenile justice*. New York: Oxford University Press.

Learning First Alliance. (2001). *Every child learning: Safe and supportive schools*. Washington, DC: Author.

Lee, V., Smith, J., Perry, T., & Smylie, M. (1999). *Social support, academic press, and student achievement: A view from the middle grades in Chicago*. Chicago: Consortium on Chicago School Research.

Leone, P., Mayer, M., Malmgren, K., & Meisel, S. (2000). School violence and disruption: Rhetoric, reality, and reasonable balance. *Exceptional Children, 33*, 1–20.

Loeber, R., & Stouthamer-Loeber, M. (1998, February). Development of juvenile aggression and violence: Some common misconceptions and controversies. *American Psychologist*, pp. 242–258.

Losen, D., & Edley, C. (2001). The role of law in policing abusive disciplinary practices: Why school discipline is a civil rights issue. In W. Ayers, B. Dohrn, & R. Ayers (Eds.), *Zero tolerance: Resisting the drive for punishment in our schools*. New York: New Press.

Mayer, M. (1999). Constructive discipline for school personnel. *Education and Treatment of Children, 22,* 36–54.

Mayer, M., & Leone, P. (1999). A structural analysis of school violence and disruption: Implications for creating safer schools. *Education and Treatment of Children, 22,* 333–356.

McDermott, R. (1977). Social relations as contexts for learning in school. *Havard Educational Review, 47,* 198–213.

McEnvoy, A., & Welker, R. (2000). Antisocial behavior, academic failure, and school climate: A critical review. *Journal of Emotional and Behavioral Disorders, 8,* 130–140.

McLaughlin, M., & Talbert, J. (1990, November). Constructing a personalized school environment. *Phi Delta Kappan, 72,* 230–235.

McNeeley, C., Nonnemaker, J., & Blum, R. (2002). Promoting school connectedness: Evidence from the National Longitudinal Study of Adolescent Health. *Journal of School Health, 72,* 138–146.

Mendel, R. (2001). *Less cost, more safety: Guiding lights for reform in juvenile justice.* Washington, DC: American Youth Policy Forum.

National Center for Education Statistics. (1998). *Student victimization at school: Indicator of the month.* Washington, DC: Author. (ERIC Document Reproduction Service No. ED 424 699)

National Education Association. (1996). *Safe schools manual: A resource on making schools, communities, and families safe for children.* Washington, DC: Author.

National Institute of Education. (1978). *Violent schools–safe schools: The safe school study report to Congress.* Washington, DC: U.S. Government Printing Office.

Newmann, F. (1981). Reducing student alienation in high schools: Implications of theory. *Harvard Educational Review, 51,* 546–564.

Newmann, F., Wehlage, G. (1995). *Successful school restructuring: A report to the public and educators by the Center on Organization and Restructuring of Schools.* Madison, WI: Center on Organization and Restructuring of Schools.

Noddings, N. (1988). An ethic of caring and its implications for instructional arrangements. *American Journal of Education, 96,* 215–230.

Noguera, P. (1995). Preventing and producing violence: A critical analysis of responses to school violence. *Harvard Educational Review, 65,* 189–213.

Noguera, P. (2001). Finding safety where we least expect it: The role of social capital in preventing school violence. In W. Ayers, B. Dohrn, & R. Ayers (Eds.), *Zero tolerance: Resisting the drive for punishment in our schools.* New York: New Press.

Obidah, J. (2000). On living (and dying) with violence: Entering youth voices in the discourse. In S. Spina (Ed.), *Smoke and mirrors: The hidden context of violence in schools and society.* Lanham, MD: Rowman & Littlefield.

Office of the Surgeon General. (2001). *Youth violence: A report of the surgeon general.* Washington, DC: Author.

Olweus, D., & Alsaker, F. (1991). Assessing change in a cohort-longitudinal study with hierarchical data. In D. Magnusson, L. Bergman, G. Rudinger, & B. Torestad (Eds.), *Problems and methods in longitudinal research: Stability and change.* Cambridge, England: Cambridge University Press.

Park, J. (1998). *State of our nation's youth 1998–1999.* Alexandria, VA: Horatio Alger Association.

Pepler, D., & Slaby, R. (1994). Theoretical and developmental perspectives on youth and violence. In L. Eron, J. Gentry, & P. Schlegel (Eds.), *Reason to hope: A psychosocial perspective on violence and youth.* Washington, DC: American Psychological Association.

Phillips, M. (1997). What makes schools effective? A comparison of the relationships of communitarian climate and academic climate to mathematics achievement and attendance during middle school. *American Educational Research Journal, 34,* 633–662.

Powell, L. (2000). *Small schools and the issue of race.* New York: Bank Street College of Education.

Putnam, R. (1993). *Making democracy work: Civic traditions in modern Italy.* Princeton, NJ: Princeton University Press.

Putnam, R. (1995). Bowling alone: America's declining social capital. *Journal of Democracy, 6,* 65–79.

Resnick, M., Bearman, P., Blum, R., Bauman, K., Harris, K., Jones, J., Tabor, J., Beuhring, T., Sieving, R., Shew, M., Ireland, M., Bearinger, L., & Udry, R. (1997). Protecting adolescents from harm: Findings from the National Longitudinal Study on Adolescent Health. *Journal of the American Medical Association, 278,* 823–832.

Reston, M., Sheets, R., & Gay, G. (1996, May). Student perceptions of disciplinary conflict in ethnically diverse classrooms. *NASSP Bulletin,* p. 84.

Royal, M., Rossi, R. (1996). Individual-level correlates of sense of community: Findings from workplace and school. *Journal of Community Psychology, 24,* 395–416.

Sampson, R. (1997). Collective regulation of adolescent misbehavior: Validation results from eighty Chicago neighborhoods. *Journal of Adolescent Research, 97,* 227–246.

Sampson, R., Morenoff, J., & Earls, F. (1999). Beyond social capital: Spatial dynamics of collective efficacy for children. *American Sociological Review, 64,* 633–660.

Sampson, R., Raudenbush, S., & Earls, F. (1997). Neighborhoods and violent crime: A multilevel study of collective efficacy. *Science, 277,* 918–924.

Sandler, S., Wong, F., Morales, E., & Patel, V. (2000). *Turning to each other not on each other: How school communities prevent racial bias in school discipline.* San Francisco: Justice Matters Institute.

Schiraldi, V., & Ziedenberg, J. (2001). How distorted coverage of juvenile crime affects public policy. In W. Ayers, B. Dohrn, & R. Ayers (Eds.), *Zero tolerance: Resisting the drive for punishment in our schools.* New York: New Press.

Schwartz, W. (2001). School practices for equitable discipline of African American Students. *ERIC Digest, Number 166* (ED455343).

Sebring, P., Bryk, A., Easton, J., Luppescu, S., Thum, Y., Lopez, W., & Smith, B. (1995). *Chartering reform in Chicago: Chicago teachers take stock.* Chicago: Consortium on Chicago School Research.

Sebring P., Bryk, A., Roderick, M., & Camburn, E. (1996). *Chartering reform in Chicago: The students speak.* Chicago: Consortium on Chicago School Research.

Sheets, R. H. (1996). Urban classroom conflict: Student-teacher perception: Ethnic integrity, solidarity, and resistance. *Urban Review, 28,* 165–183.

Sheley, J., & Wright, J. (1998). *High school youths, weapons, and violence: A national survey.* Washington, DC: Office of Justice Programs, National Institute of Justice.

Sherman, L. (1993). Defiance, deterrence, and irrelevance: A theory of the criminal sanction. *Journal of Research in Crime and Delinquency, 30,* 445–473.

Short, J. (1997). *Poverty, ethnicity, and violent crime.* Boulder, CO: Westview Press.

Shouse, R. (1996). Academic press and sense of community: Conflict, congruence, and implications for student achievement. *Social Psychology of Education, 1,* 47–68.

Skiba, R. (2000). *Zero tolerance, zero evidence: An analysis of school disciplinary practice.* Bloomington: Indiana Education Policy Center.

Skiba, R. (2001). When is disproportionality discrimination? The overrepresentation of Black students in school suspension. In W. Ayers, B. Dohrn, & R. Ayers (Eds.), *Zero tolerance: Resisting the drive for punishment in our schools.* New York: New Press.

Skiba, R., Michael, R., Nardo, A., & Peterson, R. (2000). *The color of discipline: Sources of racial and gender disproportionality in school punishment.* Bloomington: Indiana Education Policy Center.

Skiba, R., & Peterson, R. (2000). School discipline at a crossroads: From zero tolerance to early response. *Exceptional Children, 66,* 335–347.

Small, M., Everett, S., Crossett, L., Dahlberg, L., Albuquerque, M., Sleet, D., Greene, B., & Schmidt, E. (2001). School policy and environment: Results from the school health policies and programs study 2000. *Journal of School Health, 71,* 325–334.

Spina, S. (Ed.). (2000). *Smoke and mirrors: The hidden context of violence in schools and society.* Lanham, MD: Rowman & Littlefield.

Stringfield, S., & Herman, B. (1994). *Observations of partial implementations of the Coalition of Essential Schools: The need for higher reliability organizational methods.* Baltimore: Center for Research on Effective Schooling for Disadvantaged Students.

Sullivan, J., & Transue, J. (1999). The psychological underpinnings of democracy: A selective review of research on political tolerance, interpersonal trust, and social capital. *Annual Review of Psychology, 50,* 625–650.

Thorton, T. N, Craft, C. A., Dahlberg, L. L., Lynch, B. S., & Baer, K. B. (2000). *Best practice of youth violence prevention: A sourcebook for community action.* Atlanta, GA: Centers for Disease Control and Prevention.

Tobler, N. S., & Stratton, H. H. (1997). Effectiveness of school-based drug prevention programs: A meta-analysis of the research. *Journal of Primary Prevention, 18,* 71–128.

Tolan, P., Guerra, N., & Kendall, P. (1995). A developmental-ecological perspective on antisocial behavior in children and adolescents: Toward a unified risk and intervention framework. *Journal of Consulting and Clinical Psychology, 63,* 579–584.

Townsend, B. (2000). The disproportionate discipline of African American learners: Reducing school suspensions and expulsions. *Exceptional Children, 66,* 381–391.

Tyack, D., & Duban, L. (1995). *Tinkering toward utopia: A century of public school reform.* Cambridge, MA: Harvard University Press.

Verdugo, R., & Schneider J. (1999). Quality schools, safe schools: A theoretical and empirical discussion. *Education and Urban Society, 31,* 286–308.

Vossekuil, B., Reddy, M., Fein, R., Borum, R., & Modzeleski, W. (2000). *An interim report on the prevention of targeted violence in schools.* Washington, DC: U.S. Secret Service National Threat Assessment Center.

Wasley, P., Hampel, R., & Clark, R. (1997). *Kids and school reform.* San Francisco: Jossey-Bass.

Wilson, W. J. (1996). *When work disappears: The world of the new urban poor.* New York: Vintage Books.

Winett, R. (1995). A framework for health promotion and disease prevention programs. *American Psychologist, 50,* 341–350.

Zane, N. (1994). When "discipline problems" recede: Democracy and intimacy in urban charters. In M. Fine (Ed.), *Chartering urban school reform: Reflections on public high schools in the midst of change.* New York: Teachers College Press.

AERA Standards for 21st-Century Education Questions

Ethical Standards of the American Educational Research Association: Cases and Commentary

by Kenneth A. Strike, Melissa S. Anderson, Randall Curren, Tyll van Geel, Ivor Pritchard, and Emily Robertson

March 2002, ISBN 0-935302-28-X

This indispensable 21st-century volume communicates and clarifies the central intentions of the Standards. It also explores and discusses any ambiguities in the Standards and in the broader role of code of ethics and ethical obligations.

Members who wish to order *Ethical Standards of the American Educational Research Association: Cases and Commentary* may do so at the price of $30. Individual non-members or institutions may order it for $35. Please add $3 per item for postage and handling and send your order to

AERA Publication Sales
1230 17th Street, NW
Washington, DC 20036-3078